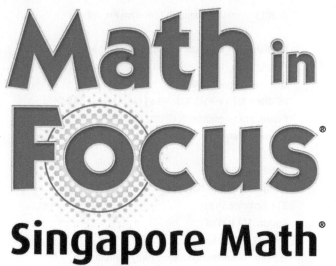

COURSE 2B

Student Book

Authors
Dr. Chee-Chong Lai
May-Kuen Leong
Wai-Cheng Low

U.S. Consultants
Dr. Richard Bisk
Andy Clark

Marshall Cavendish
Education

U.S. Distributor

Houghton
Mifflin
Harcourt

© 2018 Marshall Cavendish Education Pte Ltd

Published by Marshall Cavendish Education
Times Centre, 1 New Industrial Road, Singapore 536196
Customer Service Hotline: (65) 6213 9444
US Office Tel: (1-914) 332 8888 | Fax: (1-914) 332 8882
E-mail: tmesales@mceducation.com
Website: www.mceducation.com

Distributed by
Houghton Mifflin Harcourt
222 Berkeley Street
Boston, MA 02116
Tel: 617-351-5000
Website: www.hmheducation.com/mathinfocus

Cover: © Tim Laman/Getty Images

First published 2018

ISBN 978-1-328-88004-8

Printed in the United States of America

1 2 3 4 5 6 7 8   1401   23 22 21 20 19 18
4500673162   A B C D E

Course 2B Contents

CHAPTER

6

Angle Properties and Straight Lines

• Explore the Properties of Complementary Angles • Explore the Properties of Supplementary Angles • Explore the Properties of Adjacent Angles • Explore the Properties of Adjacent Angles on a Straight Line

Technology Activities • Explore the Relationship of Complementary Angles Using Geometry Software • Explore the Relationship of Supplementary Angles Using Geometry Software

In Student Book A and Student Book B, look for

Practice and Problem Solving	**Assessment Opportunities**
• **Practice** in every lesson • Real-world and mathematical problems in every chapter • Brain @ Work in every chapter • *Math Journal* exercises	• **Quick Check** at the beginning of every chapter to assess chapter readiness • **Guided Practice** after every Example to assess readiness to continue lesson • **Chapter Review/Test** in every chapter to review or test chapter material • Cumulative Reviews four times during the year

Volume and Surface Area of Solids

CHAPTER

9 Statistics

Big Idea Measures of central tendency and measures of variation are used to draw conclusions about populations.

       • Introduce the Concept of Measures of Variation • Understand Range
       • Understand Quartiles • Understand Interquartile Range

Technology Activity Use Spreadsheet Software to Find Quartiles, Interquartile Range, and Range

       • Represent Data in a Stem-and-Leaf Plot • Make Conclusions and Solve Problems Involving Stem-and-Leaf Plots

Welcome to

Math in Focus®

Singapore Math®
by Marshall Cavendish

What makes *Math in Focus®* different?

This world-class math program comes to you from the country of Singapore. We are sure that you will enjoy learning math with the interesting lessons you will find in these books.

▶ **Two books** The textbook is divided into 2 semesters. Chapters 1–5 are in Book A. Chapters 6–10 are in Book B.

▶ **Longer lessons** More concepts are presented in a lesson. Some lessons may last more than a day to give you time to understand the math.

▶ **Multiple representations** will help you make sense of new concepts and solve real-world and mathematical problems with ease.

About the book Here are the main features in this book.

Chapter Opener

Introduces chapter concepts and big ideas through a story or example. There is also a chapter table of contents.

Recall Prior Knowledge

Assesses previously learned concepts, definitions, vocabulary, and models relevant to the chapter.

Quick Check assesses readiness for the chapter.

Look for these features in each lesson.

 Instructions make use of multiple representations to help you become familiar with new ideas.

Use a Graph to Interpret Direct Proportion.

Each time the wheel on Mike's unicycle goes around, th
2 meters. The distance the unicycle moves forward is d
number of revolutions.

The table and the graph show the relationship betwee
and distance the wheel moves.

Revolutions (x)	1	2	3
Distance (y meters)	2	4	6

Example 1 **Tell whether quantities are in direc**

a) A pet store owner uses a table to decide how man
    put in an aquarium. Tell whether the number of fish
    the volume of the water, g gallons. If so, give the c
    tell what it represents in this situation. Then write

Volume of Water (g gallons)	4
Number of Fish (f)	6

Solution

For each pair of values, f and g:

Examples and **Guided Practice** provide step-by-step guidance through solutions.

Guided Practice

Copy and complete to determine whether y is directly proportional to x.

1 The table shows the distance traveled by a school bus, *y* miles, after *x* hours.

Time (x hours)	2	3	4
Distance Traveled (y miles)	100	150	200

Caution

Make sure that both ratios compare quantities in the same order when you write a proportion. In this case, each ratio compares dollars to T-shirts.

Cautions alert you to common mistakes and misconceptions related to the topics.

Math Notes are helpful hints and reminders.

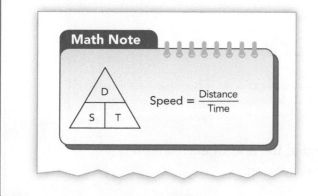

Think Math

In the equation $y = 2x$, x represents pounds of strawberries, and y represents the cost of strawberries. How can you use the equation to find the cost of buying 10 pounds of strawberries?

Think Math questions help you reason and explain mathematical situations.

Tell whether each graph represent a direct proportion. If so, find the constant of proportionality.

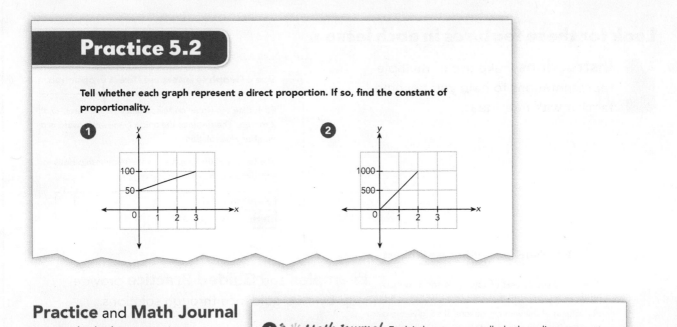

Practice and **Math Journal** are included in practice sets.

6 *Math Journal* Explain how you can tell whether a line represents a direct proportion.

Hands-On or **Technology Activities** provide opportunities for investigation, reinforcement, and extension.

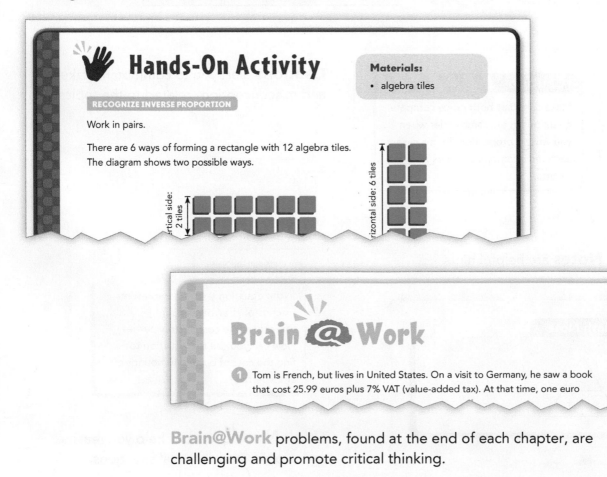

Hands-On Activity

Materials:
• algebra tiles

RECOGNIZE INVERSE PROPORTION

Work in pairs.

There are 6 ways of forming a rectangle with 12 algebra tiles. The diagram shows two possible ways.

vertical side: 2 tiles

horizontal side: 6 tiles

Brain @ Work

1 Tom is French, but lives in United States. On a visit to Germany, he saw a book that cost 25.99 euros plus 7% VAT (value-added tax). At that time, one euro

Brain@Work problems, found at the end of each chapter, are challenging and promote critical thinking.

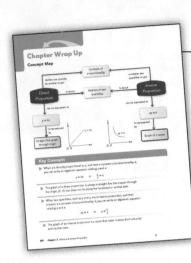

Chapter Wrap Up

Key concepts, definitions, and formulas are summarized for easy review.

The Chapter Wrap Up summaries contain concept maps like the one shown below.

The lines and arrows show how all the concepts in the chapter are related to one another and to the big ideas.

There may be more than one way to draw a concept map. With practice, you should be able to draw your own.

The red center boxes contain the big idea.

Other boxes represent key concepts of the chapter.

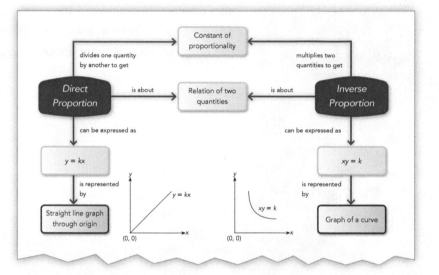

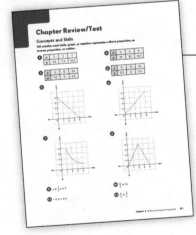

Chapter Review/Test

A practice test is found at the end of each chapter.

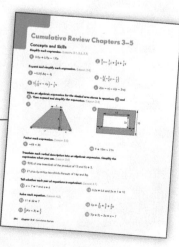

Cumulative Review

Cumulative review exercises can be found after Chapters 2, 5, 8, and 10.

BIG IDEA

▶ Angles formed on a straight line, or by parallel lines and a transversal, have special properties that are useful in solving problems.

Angle Properties and Straight Lines

Can you make that basket?

In basketball, the "launch angle" has a big effect on a player's chance of scoring. The launch angle is the acute angle the ball makes with the floor when the ball leaves the player's hands. The "release point," or the distance the player's hands are from the floor when the ball is released also affects the chances of scoring. Studies have shown that successful scorers tend to have a relatively high launch angle and release point. In this chapter, you will learn about various angle relationships.

Recall Prior Knowledge

Classifying angles

An angle is formed by two rays that share a common endpoint called a vertex. Angles can be named by letters or numbers. You can name this angle $\angle Q$, $\angle PQR$, or $\angle RQP$.

Angles are measured in degrees. The symbol for degrees is °. The statement m$\angle PQR = 30°$ means "the measure of angle PQR equals 30°."

There are 360° in a circle. If you place a pencil on a circle and move around the circle until you return to your starting point, the pencil will travel through an angle whose measure is 360°.

Angles are classified according to their measure.

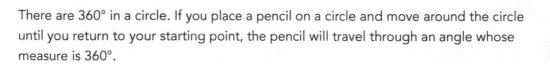

This is an acute angle. Its measure is less than 90°.

This is a right angle. Its measure is exactly 90°.

This is an obtuse angle. Its measure is greater than 90° but less than 180°.

This is a straight angle. Its measure is exactly 180°.

✓ Quick Check

Tell whether each angle is an acute, right, obtuse, or straight angle.

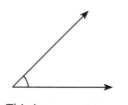

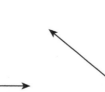

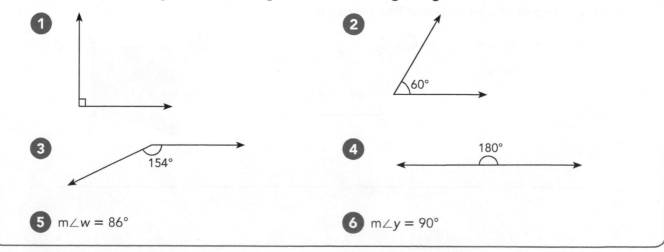

5 m$\angle w = 86°$

6 m$\angle y = 90°$

Identifying parallel lines and perpendicular lines

When two lines in the same plane do not intersect, they are parallel to each other. They are always the same distance apart. In the figure below, $\overleftrightarrow{AB}$ is parallel to $\overleftrightarrow{CD}$. So, you can write $\overleftrightarrow{AB} \parallel \overleftrightarrow{CD}$.

When two lines intersect to form a 90° angle, they are perpendicular to each other. In the figure below, $\overleftrightarrow{PQ}$ is perpendicular to $\overleftrightarrow{RS}$. So, you can write $\overleftrightarrow{PQ} \perp \overleftrightarrow{RS}$.

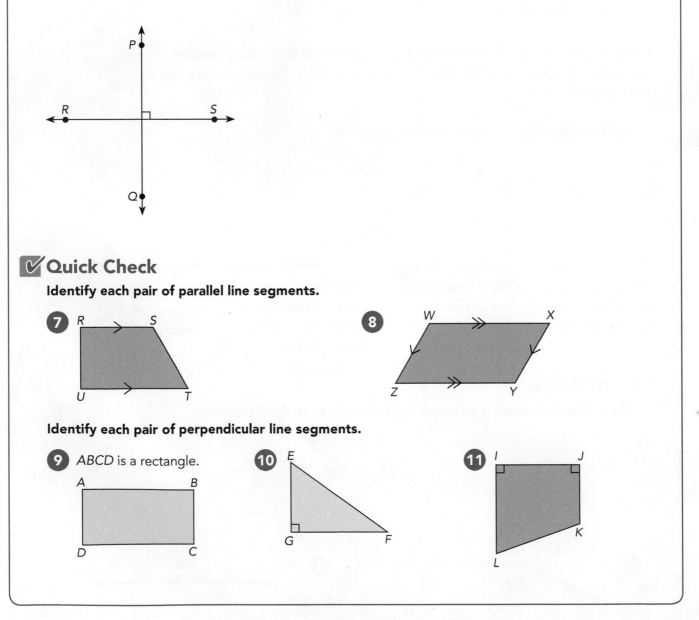

✔ Quick Check

Identify each pair of parallel line segments.

7

8

Identify each pair of perpendicular line segments.

9 ABCD is a rectangle.

10

11

6.1 Complementary, Supplementary, and Adjacent Angles

Lesson Objectives

- Explore the properties of complementary angles and supplementary angles.
- Explore the properties of adjacent angles.

Vocabulary

complementary angles

supplementary angles

adjacent angles

Explore the Properties of Complementary Angles.

In the diagrams below, m$\angle ABC$ = 30° and m$\angle DEF$ = 60°. The sum of the measures of these two angles is 90°. When the sum of the measures of two angles is 90°, the angles are called complementary angles.

$$m\angle ABC + m\angle DEF = 30° + 60°$$
$$= 90°$$

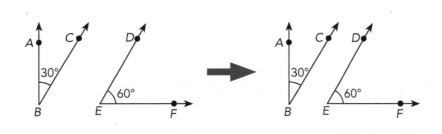

$\angle ABC$ and $\angle DEF$ are complementary angles.

$\angle ABC$ is called the complement of $\angle DEF$, and $\angle DEF$ is called the complement of $\angle ABC$.

Technology Activity

Materials:
• geometry software

EXPLORE THE RELATIONSHIP OF COMPLEMENTARY ANGLES USING GEOMETRY SOFTWARE

Work in pairs.

STEP 1 Construct $\overline{AB}$. Then construct a second line segment, $\overline{BC}$, that is perpendicular to $\overline{AB}$. Finally, construct line segment $\overline{BD}$.

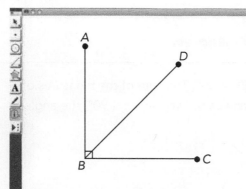

STEP 2 Select $\angle ABC$ and find its measure.

STEP 3 Select $\angle ABD$ and find its measure. Then select $\angle DBC$ and find its measure.

STEP 4 Use the calculate function of the program to find the sum of the measures of $\angle ABD$ and $\angle DBC$. What do you notice about the sum of their measures?

STEP 5 Select the point D and drag it so that you change the measures of $\angle ABD$ and $\angle DBC$. Record your results in a table as shown below.

m$\angle ABD$	m$\angle DBC$	m$\angle ABD$ + m$\angle DBC$
?	?	?
?	?	?

STEP 6 As the angle measures change, how does the sum of the angle measures change?

 Math Journal Describe what you notice about the sum of the measures of complementary angles.

Example 1 **Identify complementary angles.**

Name each pair of complementary angles.

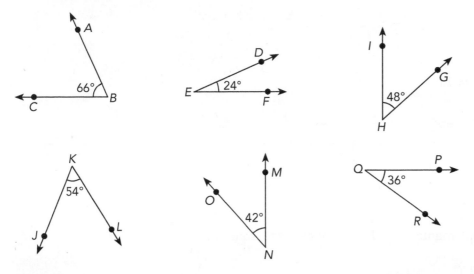

Solution

m∠ABC = 66° and m∠DEF = 24°.
Since 66° + 24° = 90°, ∠ABC and ∠DEF are complementary angles.

m∠GHI = 48° and m∠MNO = 42°.
Since 48° + 42° = 90°, ∠GHI and ∠MNO are complementary angles.

m∠JKL = 54° and m∠PQR = 36°.
Since 54° + 36° = 90°, ∠JKL and ∠PQR are complementary angles.

Guided Practice

Solve.

 Name three pairs of complementary angles.

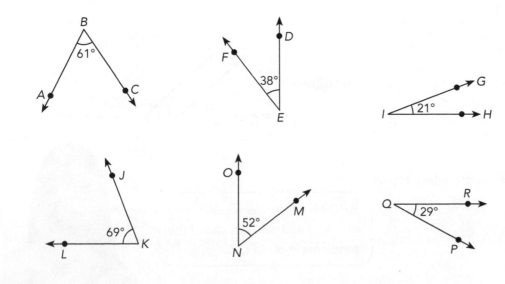

Example 2 **Find an angle measure involving complementary angles.**

Angles *K* and *P* are complementary. Find m∠*P* for each measure of ∠*K*.

a)   m∠*K* = 19°

b)   m∠*K* = 64°

Solution

a)   m∠*P* = 90° − 19° = 71°

b)   m∠*P* = 90° − 64° = 26°

Guided Practice

Copy and complete the table.

 Angles *A* and *B* are complementary. Find m∠*B* for each measure of ∠*A*.

m∠*A*	m∠*B*
28°	90° − 28° = __?__
73°	90° − 73° = __?__
36°	90° − __?__ = __?__
15°	__?__ − __?__ = __?__

Explore the Properties of Supplementary Angles.

In the diagrams below, m∠*PQR* = 42° and m∠*STU* = 138°. The sum of the measures of these two angles is 180°. When the sum of the measures of two angles is 180°, the angles are called supplementary angles.

m∠*PQR* + m∠*STU* = 42° + 138°
$$= 180°$$

∠*PQR* and ∠*STU* are supplementary angles.

> ∠*PQR* is called the supplement of ∠*STU* and ∠*STU* is called the supplement of ∠*PQR*.

Technology Activity

Materials:
- geometry software

EXPLORE THE RELATIONSHIP OF SUPPLEMENTARY ANGLES USING GEOMETRY SOFTWARE

Work in pairs.

STEP 1 Construct $\overline{PR}$. Then construct a second line segment, $\overline{SQ}$, as shown below.

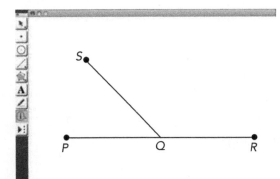

STEP 2 Select $\angle PQR$ and find its measure.

STEP 3 Select $\angle SQP$ and find its measure. Then select $\angle SQR$ and find its measure.

STEP 4 Use the calculate function of the program to find the sum of the measures of $\angle SQP$ and $\angle SQR$. What do you notice about the sum of their measures?

STEP 5 Select the point S and drag it so that you change the measures of $\angle SQP$ and $\angle SQR$. Record your results in a table as shown below.

m$\angle SQP$	m$\angle SQR$	m$\angle SQP$ + m$\angle SQR$
?	?	?
?	?	?

STEP 6 As the angle measures change, how does the sum of the angle measures change?

Math Journal Describe what you notice about the sum of the measures of supplementary angles.

Example 3 **Identify supplementary angles.**

Tell whether each pair of angles is supplementary.

a). $m\angle A = 96°$ and $m\angle B = 84°$

Solution

$m\angle A + m\angle B = 96° + 84°$
$= 180°$

So, $\angle A$ and $\angle B$ are a pair of supplementary angles.

b) $m\angle C = 16°$ and $m\angle D = 74°$

Solution

$m\angle C + m\angle D = 16° + 74°$
$= 90°$

So, $\angle C$ and $\angle D$ are not a pair of supplementary angles.

$\angle C$ and $\angle D$ are a pair of complementary angles.

c) $m\angle I = 36°$ and $m\angle J = 164°$

Solution

$m\angle I + m\angle J = 36° + 164°$
$= 200°$

So, $\angle I$ and $\angle J$ are not a pair of supplementary angles.

Guided Practice

Solve.

3 Tell whether each pair of angles is supplementary.

a) $m\angle X = 32°$ and $m\angle Y = 108°$

b) $m\angle A = 45°$ and $m\angle B = 45°$

c) $m\angle D = 12°$ and $m\angle E = 168°$

d) $m\angle V = 85°$ and $m\angle W = 95°$

Example 4 **Find an angle measure involving supplementary angles.**

Angles *K* and *P* are supplementary. Find m∠*P* for each measure of ∠*K*.

a)   m∠*K* = 22°

Solution

m∠*P* = 180° − 22° = 158°

b)   m∠*K* = 114°

Solution

m∠*P* = 180° − 114° = 66°

Guided Practice

Copy and complete the table.

4 Angles *A* and *B* are supplementary. Find m∠*B* for each measure of ∠*A*.

m∠A	m∠B
82°	180° − 82° = __?__
26°	180° − 26° = __?__
136°	180° − __?__ = __?__
105°	__?__ − __?__ = __?__

Explore the Properties of Adjacent Angles.

When two angles share a common vertex and side, but have no common interior points, they are called adjacent angles. Adjacent angles are next to and do not overlap each other. Some examples of adjacent angles are shown below.

∠*AOB* and ∠*BOC* are adjacent angles that share the common side $\overrightarrow{OB}$.

∠*DOE* and ∠*EOF* are adjacent angles that share the common side $\overrightarrow{OE}$.

∠*XOY* and ∠*YOZ* are adjacent angles that share the common side $\overrightarrow{OY}$.

This diagram may not be drawn to scale.
In the diagram, $\overrightarrow{QP}$ is perpendicular to $\overrightarrow{QR}$. Find the measure of $\angle SQR$.

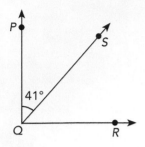

Think Math

$\angle PQR$ and $\angle SQR$ share the common side $\overrightarrow{QR}$. Explain why they are not adjacent angles.

Solution

$m\angle PQS + m\angle SQR = 90°$	Comp. $\angle$s
$41° + m\angle SQR = 90°$	Substitute.
$41° + m\angle SQR - 41° = 90° - 41°$	Subtract 41° from both sides.
$m\angle SQR = 49°$	Simplify.

"Comp. $\angle$s" is used as an abbreviation for complementary angles.

Guided Practice

This diagram may not be drawn to scale. Find the unknown angle measure.

5 In the diagram, $m\angle ABC = 90°$. Find the value of x.

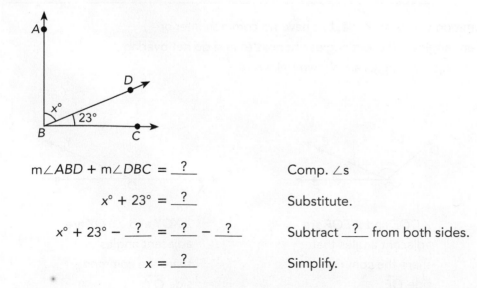

$m\angle ABD + m\angle DBC = \underline{\ ?\ }$	Comp. $\angle$s
$x° + 23° = \underline{\ ?\ }$	Substitute.
$x° + 23° - \underline{\ ?\ } = \underline{\ ?\ } - \underline{\ ?\ }$	Subtract $\underline{\ ?\ }$ from both sides.
$x = \underline{\ ?\ }$	Simplify.

Explore the Properties of Adjacent Angles on a Straight Line.

In the diagram below, ∠XOY and ∠YOZ are adjacent angles on a straight line, $\overleftrightarrow{XZ}$.
Notice that ∠XOZ is a straight angle. So, m∠XOY + m∠YOZ = 180°.

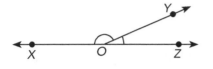

In the diagram below, ∠POR, ∠ROS, and ∠SOQ are also angles on a straight line, $\overleftrightarrow{PQ}$.
Notice that ∠POQ is a straight angle. So, m∠POR + m∠ROS + m∠SOQ = 180°.

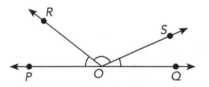

The sum of the measures of angles on one side of a straight line always equals 180°.

Caution ///////////

∠POR, ∠ROS, and ∠SOQ are not supplementary angles, because supplementary angles are a pair of angles whose measures total 180°.

Example 6 **Find measures of angles on a straight line.**

These diagrams may not be drawn to scale. Find the value of x.

a)   Given that $\overleftrightarrow{PR}$ is a straight line, find the value of x.

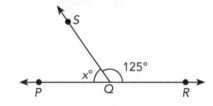

Solution

m∠PQS + m∠SQR = 180°	Adj. ∠s on a st. line
x° + 125° = 180°	Substitute.
x° + 125° − **125°** = 180° − **125°**	Subtract 125° from both sides.
x = 55	Simplify.

"Adj. ∠s on a st. line" is used as an abbreviation for adjacent angles on one side of a straight line.

Continue on next page ▶

b) In the diagram, $\angle AOC$, $\angle COD$, and $\angle DOB$ are angles on a straight line. Find the value of x.

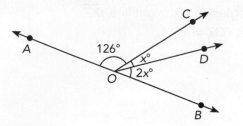

Solution

$m\angle AOC + m\angle COD + m\angle DOB = 180°$	Adj. $\angle$s on a st. line
$126° + x° + 2x° = 180°$	Substitute.
$126° + 3x° = 180°$	Simplify.
$3x° + 126° - 126° = 180° - 126°$	Subtract 126° from both sides.
$3x = 54$	Simplify.
$\dfrac{3x}{3} = \dfrac{54}{3}$	Divide both sides by 3.
$x = 18$	Simplify.

> The measure of $\angle COD$ is $x°$.
> The measure of $\angle DOB$ is twice as great, so its measure is $2x°$.

Guided Practice

These diagrams may not be drawn to scale. Given that $\overleftrightarrow{PQ}$ is a straight line, find the value of y.

6

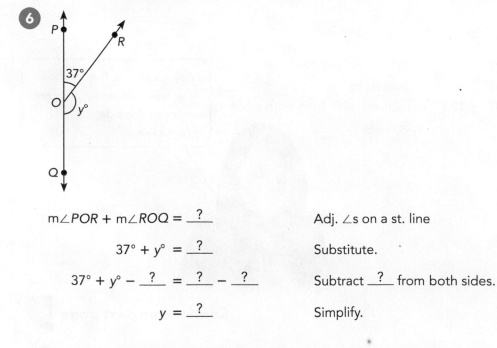

$m\angle POR + m\angle ROQ = \underline{\ ?\ }$	Adj. $\angle$s on a st. line
$37° + y° = \underline{\ ?\ }$	Substitute.
$37° + y° - \underline{\ ?\ } = \underline{\ ?\ } - \underline{\ ?\ }$	Subtract $\underline{\ ?\ }$ from both sides.
$y = \underline{\ ?\ }$	Simplify.

7

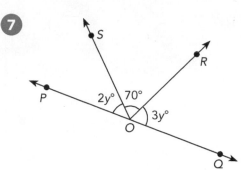

$$m\angle POS + m\angle SOR + m\angle ROQ = \underline{\quad?\quad}$$ 　　　　Adj. ∠s on a st. line

$$2y° + 70° + 3y° = \underline{\quad?\quad}$$ 　　　　Substitute.

$$\underline{\quad?\quad}y° + 70° = \underline{\quad?\quad}$$ 　　　　Simplify.

$$\underline{\quad?\quad}y° + 70° - \underline{\quad?\quad} = \underline{\quad?\quad} - \underline{\quad?\quad}$$ 　　Subtract _?_ from both sides.

$$\underline{\quad?\quad}y = \underline{\quad?\quad}$$ 　　　　Simplify.

$$\frac{?\,y}{?} = \frac{?}{?}$$ 　　　　Divide both sides by _?_.

$$y = \underline{\quad?\quad}$$ 　　　　Simplify.

Example 7　**Use ratios to find unknown angle measures.**

**This diagram may not be drawn to scale. In the diagram,
m∠PQR = 90° and the ratio a : b = 1 : 2.
Find the values of a and b.**

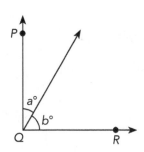

Solution

Method 1

Use bar models.

$$a° + b° = 90°$$ 　　　Comp. ∠s

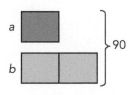

Since $a : b = 1 : 2$, in the bar model, if you represent a by 1 unit, then b is represented by 2 units and the total number of units in the bar model is $1 + 2 = 3$ units.

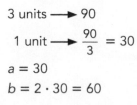

3 units ⟶ 90

1 unit ⟶ $\dfrac{90}{3} = 30$

$a = 30$

$b = 2 \cdot 30 = 60$

Continue on next page

Method 2

Use a variable to represent the measure of the angle.

The ratio $a : b = 1 : 2$. So, $b = 2 \cdot a = 2a$.

$$a° + b° = 90° \qquad \text{Comp. } \angle s$$
$$a + 2a = 90 \qquad \text{Substitute.}$$
$$3a = 90 \qquad \text{Simplify.}$$
$$\frac{3a}{3} = \frac{90}{3} \qquad \text{Divide both sides by 3.}$$
$$a = 30 \qquad \text{Simplify.}$$

$$b = 2 \cdot a$$
$$= 2 \cdot 30 \qquad \text{Substitute.}$$
$$= 60 \qquad \text{Simplify.}$$

Guided Practice

Complete.

8 This diagram may not be drawn to scale. In the diagram, $m\angle PQR = 90°$ and the ratio $x : y = 1 : 4$.
Find the values of x and y.

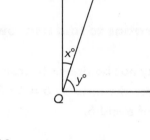

Method 1

Use bar models.

$x° + y° = 90°$ \qquad Comp. $\angle s$

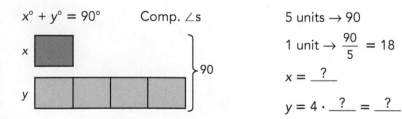

5 units → 90

1 unit → $\dfrac{90}{5} = 18$

$x = \underline{\;?\;}$

$y = 4 \cdot \underline{\;?\;} = \underline{\;?\;}$

Method 2

Use a variable to represent the measure of the angle.

The ratio $x : y = 1 : 4$. So, $y = \underline{\;?\;} \cdot x = \underline{\;?\;}$.

$$x° + y° = 90° \qquad \text{Comp. } \angle s$$
$$x + \underline{\;?\;} = 90 \qquad \text{Substitute.}$$
$$\underline{\;?\;}\, x = 90 \qquad \text{Simplify.}$$
$$\frac{?\,x}{?} = \frac{90}{?} \qquad \text{Divide both sides by } \underline{\;?\;}.$$
$$x = \underline{\;?\;} \qquad \text{Simplify.}$$

$$y = 4 \cdot x$$
$$= 4 \cdot \underline{\;?\;} \qquad \text{Substitute.}$$
$$= \underline{\;?\;} \qquad \text{Simplify.}$$

Practice 6.1

Tell whether each pair of angles is complementary.

1 m∠A = 25° and m∠B = 65°

2 m∠C = 105° and m∠D = 7°

3 m∠E =112° and m∠F = 68°

4 m∠G = 45° and m∠H = 45°

Tell whether each pair of angles is supplementary.

5 m∠A = 130° and m∠B = 50°

6 m∠C = 90° and m∠D = 80°

7 m∠E = 120° and m∠F = 60°

8 m∠G = 60° and m∠H = 30°

Find the measure of the complement of the angle with the given measure.

9 19°

10 64°

11 7°

12 35°

Find the measure of the supplement of the angle with the given measure.

13 78°

14 4°

15 153°

16 101°

These diagrams may not be drawn to scale. ∠ABD and ∠DBC are complementary angles. Find the value of x.

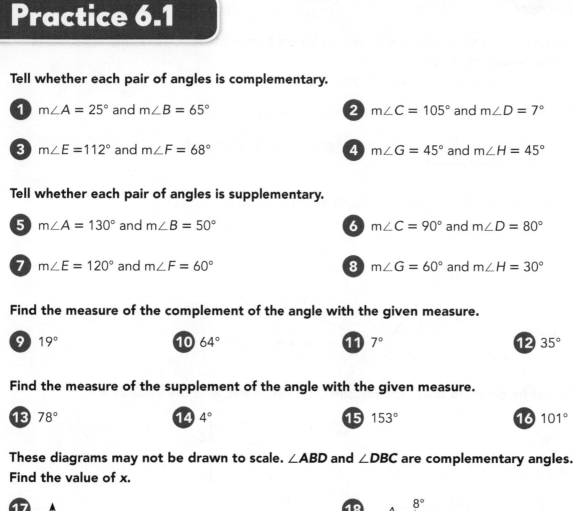

17

18

These diagrams may not be drawn to scale. ∠PQS and ∠SQR are supplementary angles. Find the value of m.

19

20

Answer each of the following.

21 The measure of an angle is 7°. Find the measure of its complement.

22 The measure of an angle is 84°. Find the measure of its supplement.

23 📓 *Math Journal*

  a) Find the measures of the complement and the supplement of each of the
  following angles, where possible.

  $m\angle W = 2°$ $m\angle X = 40°$ $m\angle Y = 32°$ $m\angle Z = 115°$

  b) Which angle in **a)** does not have both a complement and a supplement?

  c) In general, what must be true about the measure of an angle that has both
  a complement and a supplement?

24 📓 *Math Journal* Identify all the angles in each diagram. Tell which angles
  are adjacent. Explain your reasoning.

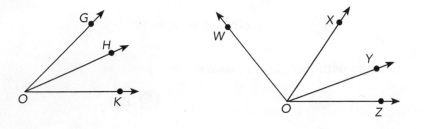

These diagrams may not be drawn to scale. The measure of $\angle ABC = 90°$. Find the value of x.

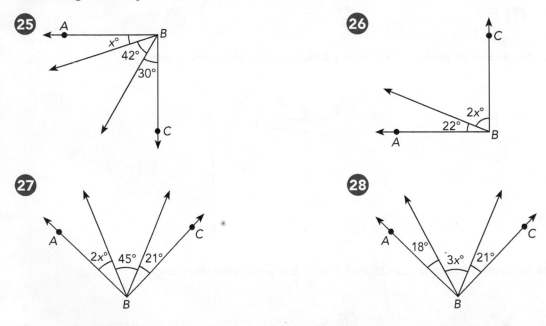

25

26

27

28

These diagrams may not be drawn to scale. $\overleftrightarrow{PR}$ is a straight line. Find the value of *m*.

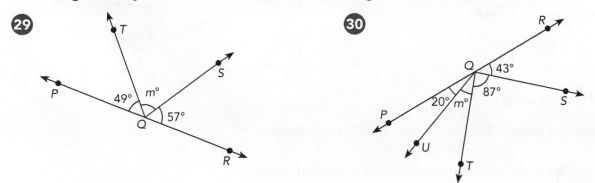

29

30

These diagrams may not be drawn to scale. In the diagram, the ratio $a : b = 2 : 3$. Find the values of a and b.

31

32 $\overrightarrow{PR}$ is a straight line.

Solve.

33 The diagram shows the pattern on a stained glass window. $\overleftrightarrow{AC}$ is a straight line. $\angle EBD$ and $\angle DBA$ are complementary angles and m$\angle DBA = 30°$. Find the measures of $\angle EBD$ and $\angle CBD$.

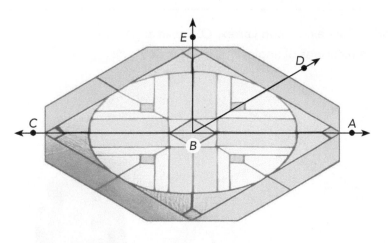

34 The diagram shows a kite. The two diagonals $\overline{MP}$ and $\overline{QT}$ are perpendicular to each other. Identify all pairs of complementary angles and all pairs of supplementary angles that are not pairs of right angles.

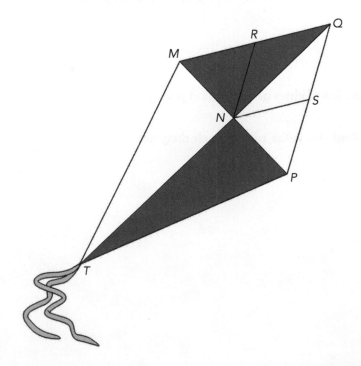

6.2 Angles that Share a Vertex

Lesson Objectives

- Explore and apply the properties of angles at a point.
- Explore and apply the properties of vertical angles.

Vocabulary

vertical angles

congruent angles

Explore and Apply the Properties of Angles at a Point.

In the diagram below, angles 1, 2, 3, and 4 share a common vertex, O. These angles are called angles at a point. The sum of the measures of angles at a point is 360°.

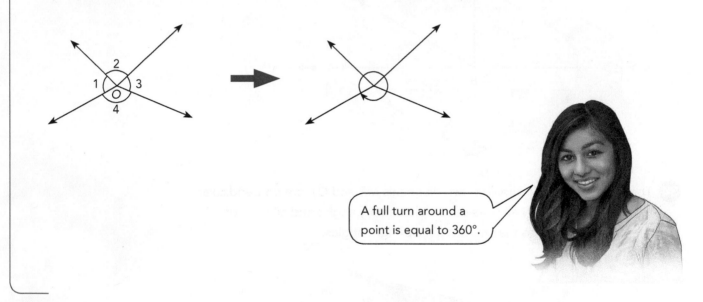

A full turn around a point is equal to 360°.

Example 8 Use algebra to solve problems involving angles at a point.

These diagrams may not be drawn to scale. Find the value of x in each diagram.

a)

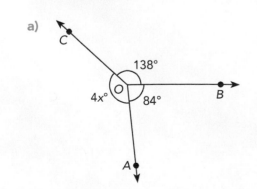

Solution

$$m\angle AOC + m\angle AOB + m\angle BOC = 360°$$ $\angle$s at a point

$$4x° + 84° + 138° = 360°$$ Substitute.

$$4x° + 222° = 360°$$ Simplify.

$$4x° + 222° - \mathbf{222°} = 360° - \mathbf{222°}$$ Subtract 222° from both sides.

$$4x = 138$$ Simplify.

$$\frac{4x}{4} = \frac{138}{4}$$ Divide both sides by 4.

$$x = 34.5$$ Simplify.

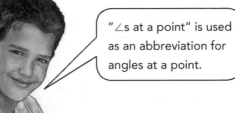

"$\angle$s at a point" is used as an abbreviation for angles at a point.

b)

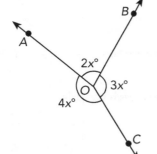

Solution

$$m\angle AOC + m\angle AOB + m\angle BOC = 360°$$ $\angle$s at a point

$$4x° + 2x° + 3x° = 360°$$ Substitute.

$$9x = 360$$ Simplify.

$$\frac{9x}{9} = \frac{360}{9}$$ Divide both sides by 9.

$$x = 40$$ Simplify.

Caution ///////

Remember that the value $x = 40$ is not the measure of any of the angles in the diagram in **b)**. The angle measures are as follows:

$m\angle AOB = 2 \cdot x° = 2 \cdot 40° = 80°$

$m\angle BOC = 3 \cdot x° = 3 \cdot 40° = 120°$

$m\angle AOC = 4 \cdot x° = 4 \cdot 40° = 160°$

Guided Practice

This diagram is not drawn to scale. Find the unknown angle measure.

 Find the value of p in the diagram.

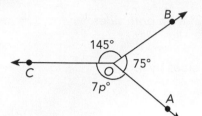

$m\angle AOC + m\angle AOB + m\angle BOC = 360°$ $\angle$s at a point

$\underline{\;?\;} + \underline{\;?\;} + \underline{\;?\;} = \underline{\;?\;}$ Substitute.

$\underline{\;?\;} + \underline{\;?\;} = \underline{\;?\;}$ Simplify.

$\underline{\;?\;} + \underline{\;?\;} - \underline{\;?\;} = \underline{\;?\;} - \underline{\;?\;}$ Subtract $\underline{\;?\;}$ from both sides.

$\underline{\;?\;} = \underline{\;?\;}$ Simplify.

$\dfrac{?}{?} = \dfrac{?}{?}$ Divide both sides by $\underline{\;?\;}$.

$\underline{\;?\;} = \underline{\;?\;}$ Simplify.

Example 9   **Use algebra to solve problems involving angle measures.**

This diagram may not be drawn to scale. $\overleftrightarrow{AB}$ is a straight line. Find the value of each variable.

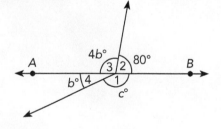

Solution

$m\angle 2 + m\angle 3 = 180°$	Adj. $\angle$s on a st. line
$4b° + 80° = 180°$	Substitute.
$4b° + 80° - 80° = 180° - 80°$	Subtract 80° from both sides.
$4b = 100$	Simplify.
$\dfrac{4b}{4} = \dfrac{100}{4}$	Divide both sides by 4.
$b = 25$	Simplify.
$m\angle 1 + m\angle 4 = 180°$	Adj. $\angle$s on a st. line
$c° + b° = 180°$	Substitute.
$c° + 25° = 180°$	Substitute $b = 25$.
$c° + 25° - 25° = 180° - 25°$	Subtract 25° from both sides.
$c = 155$	Simplify.

Guided Practice

Solve.

2 This diagram may not be drawn to scale. $\overleftrightarrow{BE}$ and $\overleftrightarrow{CA}$ are straight lines. Find the value of each variable.

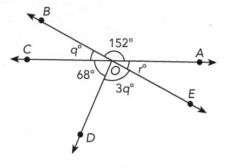

m∠AOB + m∠AOE = 180°	Adj. ∠s on a st. line
$\underline{\ ?\ } + \underline{\ ?\ } = \underline{\ ?\ }$	Substitute.
$\underline{\ ?\ } + \underline{\ ?\ } - \underline{\ ?\ } = \underline{\ ?\ } - \underline{\ ?\ }$	Subtract 152° from both sides.
$\underline{\ ?\ } = \underline{\ ?\ }$	Simplify.
m∠BOC + m∠COD + m∠DOE = 180°	Adj. ∠s on a st. line
$\underline{\ ?\ } + \underline{\ ?\ } + \underline{\ ?\ } = \underline{\ ?\ }$	Substitute.
$\underline{\ ?\ } + \underline{\ ?\ } = \underline{\ ?\ }$	Simplify.
$\underline{\ ?\ } + \underline{\ ?\ } - \underline{\ ?\ } = \underline{\ ?\ } - \underline{\ ?\ }$	Subtract 68° from both sides.
$\underline{\ ?\ } = \underline{\ ?\ }$	Simplify.
$\dfrac{?}{?} = \dfrac{?}{?}$	Divide both sides by $\underline{\ ?\ }$.
$\underline{\ ?\ } = \underline{\ ?\ }$	Simplify.

3 This diagram may not be drawn to scale. $\overleftrightarrow{PQ}$ is a straight line. Find the value of each variable.

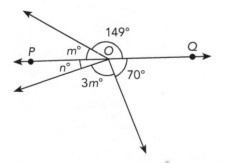

Example 10 Use ratios to find angle measures in a diagram.

This diagram may not be drawn to scale. In the diagram, the ratio $a : b : c = 1 : 2 : 2$. Find the values of a, b, and c.

Solution

Method 1

Use bar models.

$a° + b° + c° = 360°$ ∠s at a point

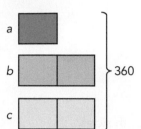

360

Since $a : b : c = 1 : 2 : 2$, if you represent a by 1 unit, then b and c are 2 units each in the bar model. The total number of units in the bar model is $1 + 2 + 2 = 5$ units.

5 units → 360

1 unit → $\dfrac{360}{5} = 72$

$a = 72$

$b = 2 \cdot 72 = 144$

$c = 2 \cdot 72 = 144$

Method 2

Use a variable to represent the measure of the angle.

The ratio $a : b : c = 1 : 2 : 2$. So, $b = 2 \cdot a$ and $c = 2 \cdot a$.

$$
\begin{aligned}
a° + b° + c° &= 360° && \text{∠s at a point} \\
a + 2a + 2a &= 360 && \text{Substitute.} \\
5a &= 360 && \text{Simplify.} \\
\frac{5a}{5} &= \frac{360}{5} && \text{Divide both sides by 5.} \\
a &= 72 && \text{Simplify.}
\end{aligned}
$$

$$
\begin{aligned}
b &= 2 \cdot a \\
&= 2 \cdot 72 && \text{Substitute } a = 72. \\
&= 144 && \text{Simplify.}
\end{aligned}
$$

$$
\begin{aligned}
c &= 2 \cdot a \\
&= 2 \cdot 72 && \text{Substitute } a = 72. \\
&= 144 && \text{Simplify.}
\end{aligned}
$$

Guided Practice

Complete.

4 This diagram may not be drawn to scale. In the diagram at the right, the ratio $a : b : c = 1 : 3 : 5$. Find the values of a, b, and c.

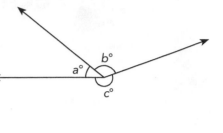

The ratio $a : b : c = 1 : 3 : 5$. So, $b = 3 \cdot a$ and $c = 5 \cdot a$.

$a° + b° + c° = 360°$	$\angle$s at a point
$\underline{\ ?\ } + \underline{\ ?\ } + \underline{\ ?\ } = \underline{\ ?\ }$	Substitute.
$\underline{\ ?\ } = \underline{\ ?\ }$	Simplify.
$\dfrac{?}{?} = \dfrac{?}{?}$	Divide both sides by $\underline{\ ?\ }$.
$\underline{\ ?\ } = \underline{\ ?\ }$	Simplify.

$b = 3 \cdot a$

$= \underline{\ ?\ } \cdot \underline{\ ?\ }$	Substitute $a = \underline{\ ?\ }$.
$= \underline{\ ?\ }$	Simplify.

$c = 5 \cdot a$

$= \underline{\ ?\ } \cdot \underline{\ ?\ }$	Substitute $a = \underline{\ ?\ }$.
$= \underline{\ ?\ }$	Simplify.

Explore and Apply the Properties of Vertical Angles.

When two lines intersect each other at a point, they form four angles. The nonadjacent angles are called vertical angles.

In the diagram below, $\angle 1$ and $\angle 3$ are vertical angles, and $\angle 2$ and $\angle 4$ are vertical angles.

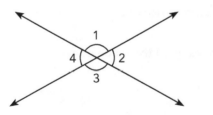

Caution ///////

Vertical angles are formed by intersecting lines. The angles in the diagram below are not vertical angles.

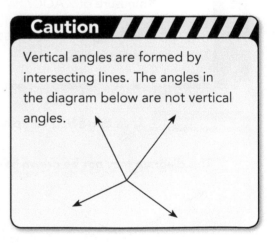

Because $\angle 1$ and $\angle 2$ are adjacent angles that form a straight line, they are supplementary. $\angle 2$ and $\angle 3$ are also adjacent angles that form a straight line. So, they are also supplementary.

You can deduce that $\qquad m\angle 1 + m\angle 2 = 180°$ and $m\angle 2 + m\angle 3 = 180°$.

From the equations, you can see that $\angle 1$ and $\angle 3$ are equal in measure. When two angles have the same angle measure, they are called **congruent angles**. So, vertical angles are congruent.

Technology Activity

Materials:
- geometry software

EXPLORE THE RELATIONSHIP AMONG VERTICAL ANGLES USING GEOMETRY SOFTWARE

Work in pairs.

STEP 1 Construct intersecting line segments, $\overline{AB}$ and $\overline{CD}$, as shown.

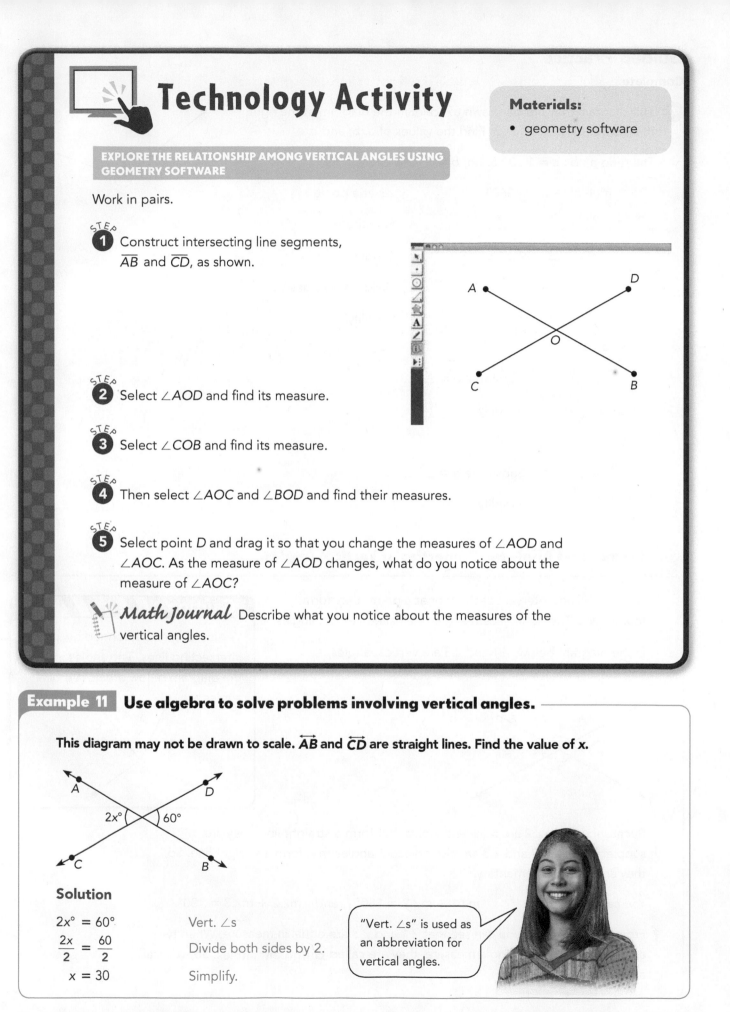

STEP 2 Select $\angle AOD$ and find its measure.

STEP 3 Select $\angle COB$ and find its measure.

STEP 4 Then select $\angle AOC$ and $\angle BOD$ and find their measures.

STEP 5 Select point D and drag it so that you change the measures of $\angle AOD$ and $\angle AOC$. As the measure of $\angle AOD$ changes, what do you notice about the measure of $\angle AOC$?

Math Journal Describe what you notice about the measures of the vertical angles.

Example 11 **Use algebra to solve problems involving vertical angles.**

This diagram may not be drawn to scale. $\overleftrightarrow{AB}$ and $\overleftrightarrow{CD}$ are straight lines. Find the value of x.

Solution

$2x° = 60°$ Vert. ∠s

$\dfrac{2x}{2} = \dfrac{60}{2}$ Divide both sides by 2.

$x = 30$ Simplify.

"Vert. ∠s" is used as an abbreviation for vertical angles.

Guided Practice

This diagram may not be drawn to scale. Find the unknown angle measure.

5 $\overleftrightarrow{AB}$ and $\overleftrightarrow{CD}$ are straight lines. Find the value of y.

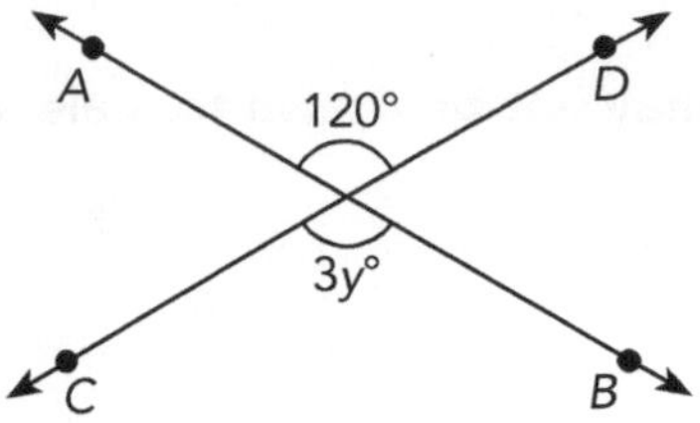

$\underline{\quad?\quad} = \underline{\quad?\quad}$ Vert. ∠s

$\dfrac{?}{?} = \dfrac{?}{?}$ Divide both sides by __?__ .

$\underline{\quad?\quad} = \underline{\quad?\quad}$ Simplify.

Example 12 **Apply reasoning to find measures of angles formed by intersecting lines.**

This diagram may not be drawn to scale. In the diagram, two straight lines intersect to form angles 1, 2, 3, and 4. Find the value of each variable if m∠1 = 76°.

Solution

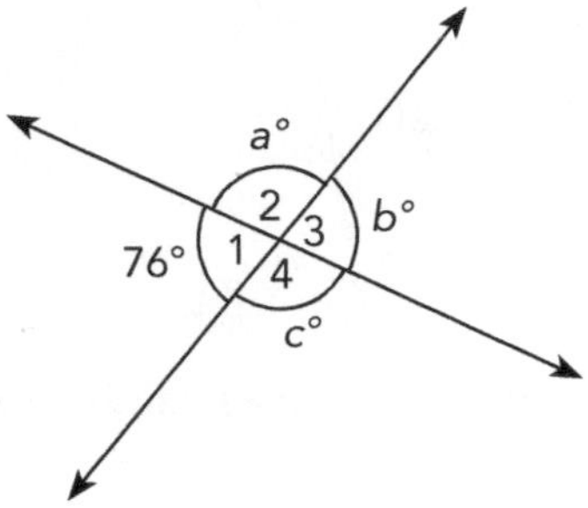

$m\angle 1 + m\angle 2 = 180°$ Supp. ∠s

$76° + a° = 180°$ Substitute.

$76° + a° - 76° = 180° - 76°$ Subtract 76° from both sides.

$a = 104$ Simplify.

$m\angle 3 = m\angle 1$ Vert. ∠s

$b° = 76°$ Substitute.

$b = 76$

$m\angle 4 = m\angle 2$ Vert. ∠s.

$c° = 104°$ Substitute.

$c = 104$

Guided Practice

This diagram may not be drawn to scale. Find the unknown angle measure.

6 In the diagram, two straight lines intersect to form angles 1, 2, 3, and 4. Find the value of each variable if m∠1 = 114°.

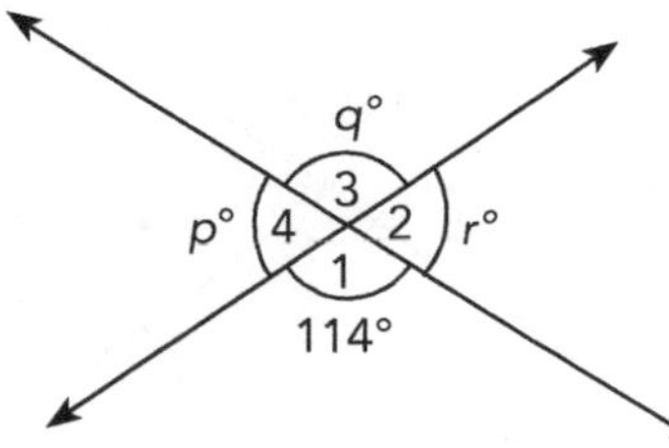

$m\angle 1 + m\angle 2 = 180°$ Supp. ∠s

$\underline{\quad?\quad} + \underline{\quad?\quad} = \underline{\quad?\quad}$ Substitute.

$\underline{\quad?\quad} + \underline{\quad?\quad} - \underline{\quad?\quad} = \underline{\quad?\quad} - \underline{\quad?\quad}$ Subtract __?__ from both sides.

$\underline{\quad?\quad} = \underline{\quad?\quad}$ Simplify.

$m\angle 3 = m\angle 1$ Vert. ∠s

$q° = 114°$ Substitute.

$\underline{\quad?\quad} = \underline{\quad?\quad}$

$m\angle 4 = m\angle 2$ Vert. ∠s

$\underline{\quad?\quad} = \underline{\quad?\quad}$ Substitute.

$\underline{\quad?\quad} = \underline{\quad?\quad}$

Practice 6.2

These diagrams may not be drawn to scale. Find the value of each variable.

1

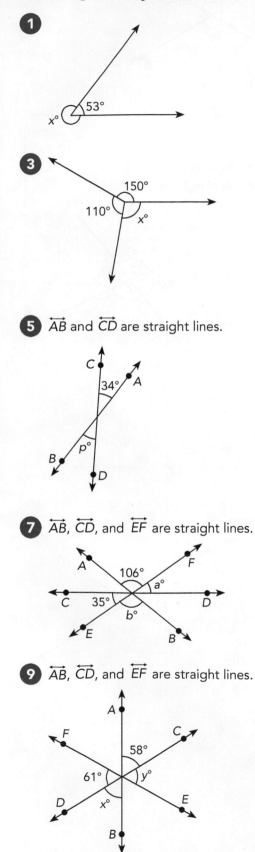

$x°$ $53°$

2

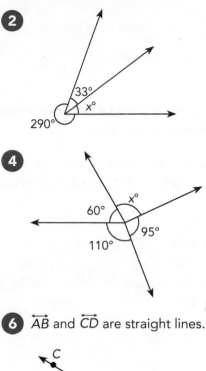

$33°$ $x°$ $290°$

3

$150°$ $110°$ $x°$

4

$60°$ $x°$ $95°$ $110°$

5 $\overleftrightarrow{AB}$ and $\overleftrightarrow{CD}$ are straight lines.

C $34°$ A $p°$ B D

6 $\overleftrightarrow{AB}$ and $\overleftrightarrow{CD}$ are straight lines.

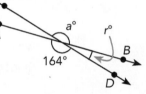

C A $a°$ $r°$ B $164°$ D

7 $\overleftrightarrow{AB}$, $\overleftrightarrow{CD}$, and $\overleftrightarrow{EF}$ are straight lines.

A $106°$ F $a°$ C $35°$ D $b°$ E B

8 $\overleftrightarrow{AB}$, $\overleftrightarrow{CD}$, and $\overleftrightarrow{EF}$ are straight lines.

A $b°$ F $31°$ C D $a°$ E $126°$ B

9 $\overleftrightarrow{AB}$, $\overleftrightarrow{CD}$, and $\overleftrightarrow{EF}$ are straight lines.

A F C $58°$ $61°$ $y°$ D $x°$ E B

10 $\overleftrightarrow{AB}$ and $\overleftrightarrow{CD}$ are straight lines.

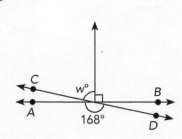

C $w°$ B A $168°$ D

These diagrams may not be drawn to scale. Find the value of _k_.

11 The ratio $\angle 1 : \angle 2 : \angle 3 : \angle 4 = 3 : 2 : 1 : 3$.

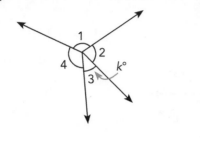

12 $\overleftrightarrow{AB}$ and $\overleftrightarrow{CD}$ are straight lines.

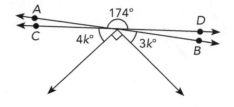

13

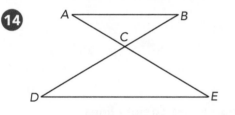

Name the pairs of vertical angles.

14

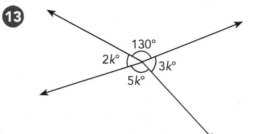

15

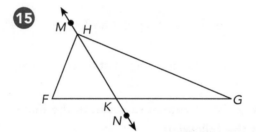

16 $\overleftrightarrow{PS}$ and $\overleftrightarrow{RN}$ are straight lines.

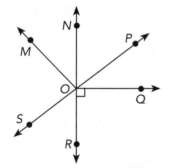

These diagrams may not be drawn to scale. Find the value of each variable.

17

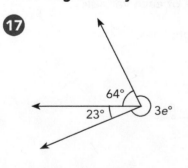

18 $\overleftrightarrow{AB}$ and $\overleftrightarrow{CD}$ are straight lines.

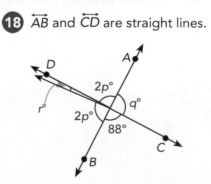

These diagrams may not be drawn to scale. Find the value of each variable.

19 $\overleftrightarrow{AB}$, $\overleftrightarrow{CD}$, and $\overleftrightarrow{EF}$ are straight lines.
The ratio $a : b : c = 1 : 2 : 2$.

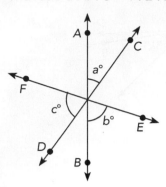

20 $\overleftrightarrow{AB}$ and $\overleftrightarrow{CD}$ are straight lines.

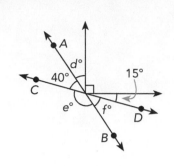

Answer each of the following.

21 This diagram may not be drawn to scale. In the diagram, the ratio $p : q : r = 1 : 2 : 3$. Find the values of p, q, and r.

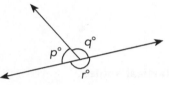

22 If $\angle P$ and $\angle N$ are angles at a point and m$\angle P = 149°$, what is the m$\angle N$?

23 If $67°$, $102°$, $15°$, and $x°$ are angles at a point, what is the value of x?

This diagram may not be drawn to scale. In the diagram below, $\overleftrightarrow{MP}$ and $\overleftrightarrow{QR}$ are straight lines. Answer each of the following.

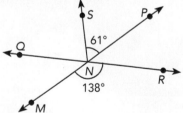

24 Name the angle that is vertical to $\angle MNR$.

25 What kind of angles are $\angle RNP$ and $\angle PNS$?

26 Find the measure of $\angle QNS$.

27 Find the measure of $\angle PNR$.

These diagrams may not be drawn to scale. Use an equation to find the value of each variable.

28 $\overleftrightarrow{AB}$ is a straight line.

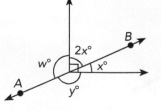

29 $\overleftrightarrow{AB}$ and $\overleftrightarrow{CD}$ are straight lines.

These diagrams may not be drawn to scale. $\overleftrightarrow{AB}$ and $\overleftrightarrow{CD}$ are two intersecting lines. Find the values of p and q.

30 The ratio $\angle 1 : \angle 2 = 3 : 1$.

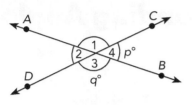

31

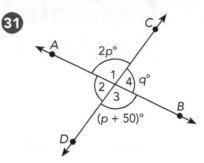

Solve.

32 The diagram below shows the flag of the Philippines. $m\angle ADB = 60°$ and $m\angle ADC = m\angle BDC$. Find the measures of $\angle ADC$ and $\angle BDC$.

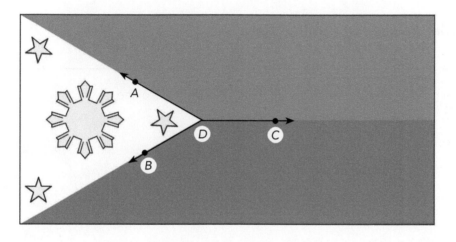

33 *Math Journal* The diagram shows a pattern on a carpet.

a) Are $\angle 4$ and $\angle 6$ vertical angles? Explain why or why not.

b) Suppose $m\angle 4 = m\angle 6$. Are $\angle 4$ and $\angle 5$ supplementary angles? Explain your answer.

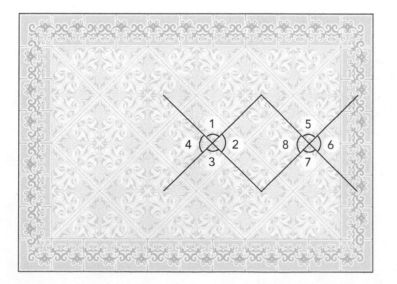

Alternate Interior, Alternate Exterior, and Corresponding Angles

Lesson Objectives

- Identify the types of angles formed by parallel lines and a transversal.
- Write and solve equations to find unknown angle measures in figures.

Vocabulary

transversal

alternate interior angles

alternate exterior angles

corresponding angles

Identify the Types of Angles Formed by Parallel Lines and a Transversal.

The symbol || is used to denote parallel lines. In the diagram, line *AB* is parallel to line *CD*. So, you can write $\overleftrightarrow{AB} \parallel \overleftrightarrow{CD}$.

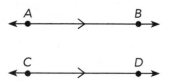

In the diagram below, line $\overleftrightarrow{PQ}$ intersects $\overleftrightarrow{AB}$ and $\overleftrightarrow{CD}$. $\overleftrightarrow{PQ}$ is called a transversal. Notice that a transversal forms many angles. Some of the angle pairs have special names. These names tell how the angle pairs are related to the two parallel lines.

The interior angles (∠3, ∠4, ∠5, and ∠6) are between the parallel lines.

The exterior angles (∠1, ∠2, ∠7, and ∠8) are outside the parallel lines.

Alternate interior or **alternate exterior angles** are on opposite sides of the transversal.

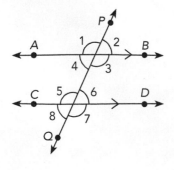

You can see that there are 8 angles formed when $\overleftrightarrow{PQ}$ intersects $\overleftrightarrow{AB}$ and $\overleftrightarrow{CD}$.

Alternate interior angles

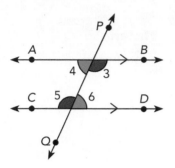

∠3 and ∠5 are alternate interior angles. ∠4 and ∠6 are also alternate interior angles.

Alternate exterior angles

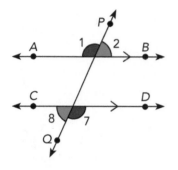

∠1 and ∠7 are alternate exterior angles. ∠2 and ∠8 are also alternate exterior angles.

Corresponding angles

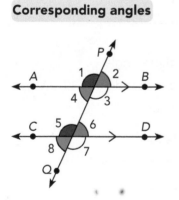

∠1 and ∠5 are corresponding angles. ∠4 and ∠8 are also corresponding angles. There are 4 pairs of corresponding angles altogether in the diagram.

Think Math

In addition to ∠1 and ∠5, and ∠4 and ∠8, what are the other two pairs of corresponding angles in the diagram?

Hands-On Activity

Materials:

- protractor

Work in pairs.

STEP 1 On a piece of paper, draw a pair of parallel lines, $\overleftrightarrow{AB}$ and $\overleftrightarrow{CD}$, as shown. Draw a transversal $\overleftrightarrow{PQ}$ that intersects the pair of parallel lines. Use a protractor to measure the angles in the diagram.

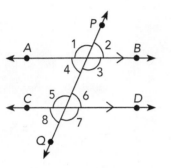

STEP 2 Record your results in a table like the one shown.

Angle	1	2	3	4	5	6	7	8
Measure	?	?	?	?	?	?	?	?

 Math Journal What do you notice about the measures of these angle pairs: Alternate interior angles, alternate exterior angles, and corresponding angles? Make a conjecture about the angle measures for each pair.

Math Journal Compare the conjecture that you have made for corresponding angles, alternate interior angles, and alternate exterior angles with the conjectures made by other students. What do you observe?

When two parallel lines are cut by a transversal,

- the alternate interior angles are always congruent (alt. int. ∠s, || lines).
- the alternate exterior angles are always congruent (alt. ext. ∠s, || lines).
- the corresponding angles are always congruent (corr. ∠s, || lines).

Example 13 **Identify alternate interior, alternate exterior, and corresponding angles.**

Use the diagram to answer the following.

$\overleftrightarrow{EF}$, $\overleftrightarrow{CD}$, and $\overleftrightarrow{GH}$ are straight lines. $\overleftrightarrow{EF}$ is parallel to $\overleftrightarrow{CD}$.

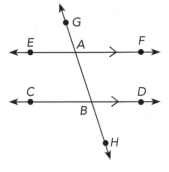

a) Identify two pairs of alternate interior angles.

Solution

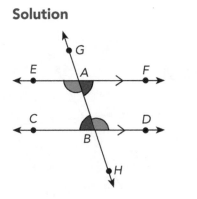

Alternate interior angles are a pair of angles that lie inside the pair of parallel lines and on the opposite sides of the transversal.

$\angle EAB$ and $\angle ABD$, $\angle FAB$ and $\angle ABC$ are the two pairs of alternate interior angles.

b) Identify two pairs of alternate exterior angles.

Solution

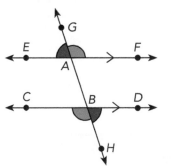

Alternate exterior angles are a pair of angles that lie outside the pair of parallel lines and on the opposite sides of the transversal.

$\angle GAE$ and $\angle DBH$, $\angle GAF$ and $\angle CBH$ are the two pairs of alternate exterior angles.

Continue on next page

c) Identify two pairs of corresponding angles.

Solution

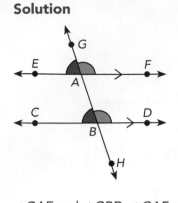

∠GAF and ∠GBD, ∠GAE and ∠GBC are corresponding angles.

Guided Practice

Use the diagram at the right to complete the following questions.

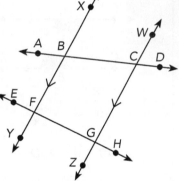

1 $\overleftrightarrow{AD}$, $\overleftrightarrow{EH}$, $\overleftrightarrow{XY}$, and $\overleftrightarrow{WZ}$ are straight lines and $\overleftrightarrow{XY}$ is parallel to $\overleftrightarrow{WZ}$. Identify all the pairs of angles formed by the intersection of $\overleftrightarrow{AD}$ with $\overleftrightarrow{XY}$ and $\overleftrightarrow{WZ}$.

a) Corresponding angles: ∠ABX and ∠BCW; __?__ ; __?__ ; __?__

b) Alternate interior angles: ∠XBC and ∠BCG; __?__

2 Name another transversal of the parallel lines in the diagram.

3 Identify one pair of each of the following angles formed by the intersection of $\overleftrightarrow{EH}$ with $\overleftrightarrow{XY}$ and $\overleftrightarrow{WZ}$.

a) Corresponding angles

b) Alternate interior angles

c) Alternate exterior angles

Write and Solve Equations to Find Unknown Angle Measures.

You can write equations to solve for unknown angles or variables using the properties below.

- Complementary angles
- Supplementary angles
- Angles at a point
- Vertical angles
- Alternate interior angles
- Alternate exterior angles
- Corresponding angles

Example 14 **Use properties of parallel lines and transversals to find angle measures.**

This diagram may not be drawn to scale. In the diagram, $\overleftrightarrow{MN}$ is parallel to $\overleftrightarrow{PQ}$. Find each of the following angle measures.

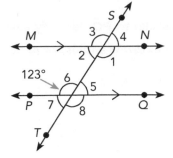

a) $m\angle 3$

Solution

$\overleftrightarrow{MN}$ is parallel to $\overleftrightarrow{PQ}$ and $\overleftrightarrow{ST}$ is the transversal.

$m\angle 3 = m\angle 6 = 123°$ Corr. $\angle$s

b) $m\angle 1$

Solution

$m\angle 1 = m\angle 6 = 123°$ Alt. int. $\angle$s

c) $m\angle 2$

Solution

$\angle 2$ and $\angle 3$ are supplementary angles.

$m\angle 2 + m\angle 3 = 180°$ Supp. $\angle$s
$m\angle 2 + 123° = 180°$ Substitute.
$m\angle 2 + 123° - \mathbf{123°} = 180° - \mathbf{123°}$ Subtract 123° from both sides.
$m\angle 2 = 57°$ Simplify.

"Corr. $\angle$s" is used as an abbreviation for corresponding angles and "alt. int. $\angle$s" is used as an abbreviation for alternate interior angles.

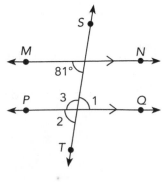

Guided Practice

Complete.

 4 This diagram may not be drawn to scale. In the diagram, $\overleftrightarrow{MN}$ is parallel to $\overleftrightarrow{PQ}$.
Find the measures of $\angle 1$, $\angle 2$, and $\angle 3$.

$m\angle 1 = \underline{\ ?\ }$ Alt. int. $\angle$s

$m\angle 2 = \underline{\ ?\ }$ Corr. $\angle$s

$m\angle 3 + \underline{\ ?\ } = 180°$ Supp. $\angle$s

$m\angle 3 + \underline{\ ?\ } = 180°$ Substitute $m\angle 2 = \underline{\ ?\ }$.

$m\angle 3 + \underline{\ ?\ } - \underline{\ ?\ } = 180° - \underline{\ ?\ }$ Subtract $\underline{\ ?\ }$ from both sides.

$m\angle 3 = \underline{\ ?\ }$ Simplify.

Practice 6.3

$\overleftrightarrow{MN}$ is parallel to $\overleftrightarrow{PQ}$. Identify each pair of angles as corresponding, alternate interior, alternate exterior angles, or none of the above.

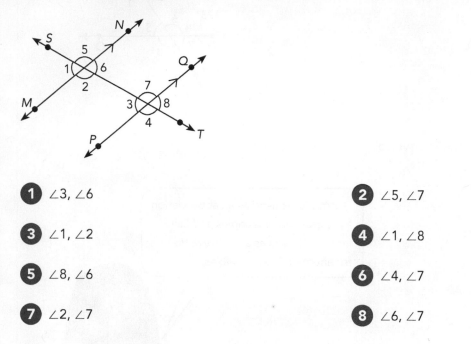

1 ∠3, ∠6

2 ∠5, ∠7

3 ∠1, ∠2

4 ∠1, ∠8

5 ∠8, ∠6

6 ∠4, ∠7

7 ∠2, ∠7

8 ∠6, ∠7

$\overleftrightarrow{AB}$ is parallel to $\overleftrightarrow{CD}$. Use the diagram to answer the following.

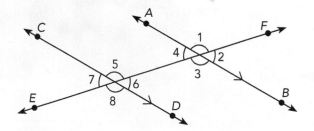

9 Name two angles that have the same measure as ∠2.

10 Name an angle that is supplementary to ∠6.

11 If m∠4 = 46°, find m∠5.

12 If m∠1 = 131°, find m∠7.

These diagrams may not be drawn to scale. Find the measure of each numbered angle.

13 $\overrightarrow{MN}$ is parallel to $\overrightarrow{PQ}$.

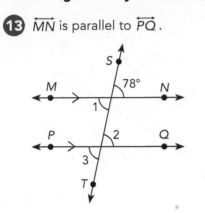

14 $\overrightarrow{MN}$ is parallel to $\overrightarrow{PQ}$.

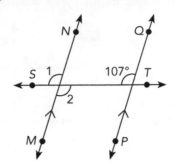

15 $\overrightarrow{PQ}$ is parallel to $\overrightarrow{RS}$.

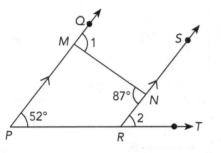

16 $\overrightarrow{PQ}$ is parallel to $\overrightarrow{RS}$.

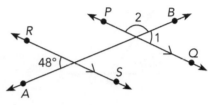

17 $\overleftrightarrow{AB}$ is parallel to $\overleftrightarrow{CD}$ and $\overleftrightarrow{MN}$ is parallel to $\overleftrightarrow{PQ}$.

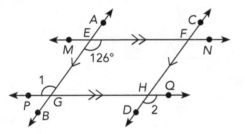

18 $\overleftrightarrow{AB}$ is parallel to $\overleftrightarrow{CD}$ and $\overleftrightarrow{MN}$ is parallel to $\overleftrightarrow{PQ}$.

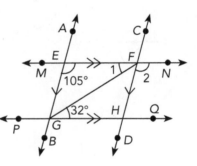

These diagrams may not be drawn to scale. Find the value of each variable.

19 $\overrightarrow{PQ}$ is parallel to $\overrightarrow{RS}$.

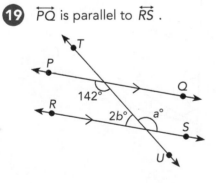

20 $\overrightarrow{PQ}$ is parallel to $\overrightarrow{RS}$.

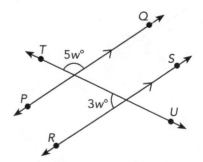

Math Journal Determine whether $\overleftrightarrow{AB}$ is parallel to $\overleftrightarrow{CD}$. Use the fact that two lines are parallel if a pair of corresponding angles formed by a transversal are congruent. Explain your answer.

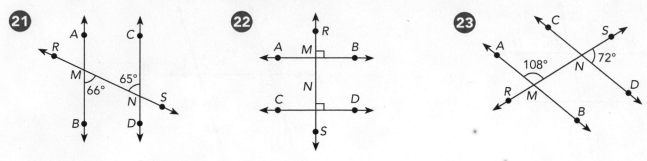

21 **22** **23**

These diagrams may not be drawn to scale. $\overline{MN}$ is parallel to $\overline{PQ}$. Find each unknown angle measure.

24

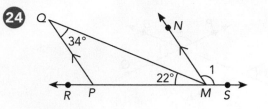

25

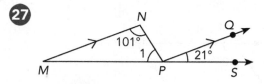

26

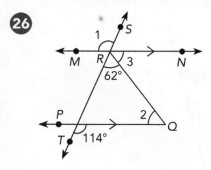

27

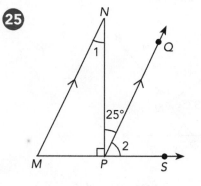

28

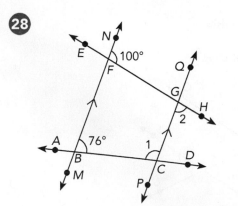

29

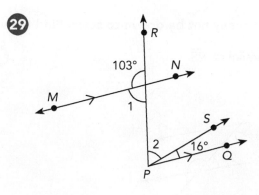

These diagrams may not be drawn to scale. $\overline{AB}$ **is parallel to** $\overline{CD}$. **Find the value of x.**

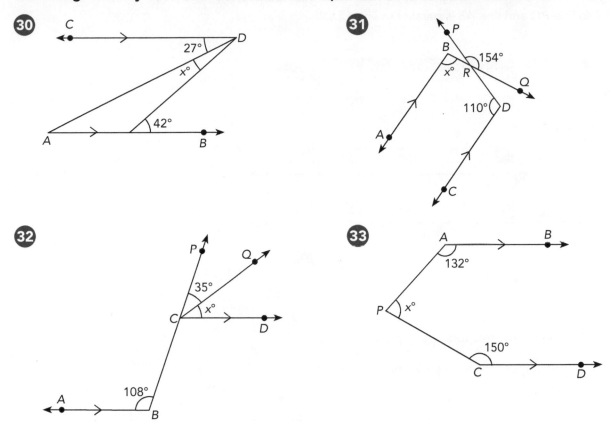

30

31

32

33

Solve. Show your work.

34 In the diagram below, $\overleftrightarrow{MN}$ is parallel to $\overleftrightarrow{PQ}$. $m\angle 1 = (x + 28)°$ and $m\angle 2 = (3x + 14)°$.
Write and solve an equation to find the measures of $\angle 1$ and $\angle 2$.

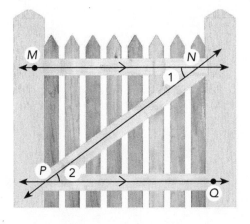

35 *Math Journal* In a plane, if a line is perpendicular to one of two parallel
lines, is it also perpendicular to the other? Explain your reasoning.

36 The diagram below contains examples of parallel lines cut by transversals. Line *MN* is parallel to line *PQ* and line *AB* is parallel to line *CD*.

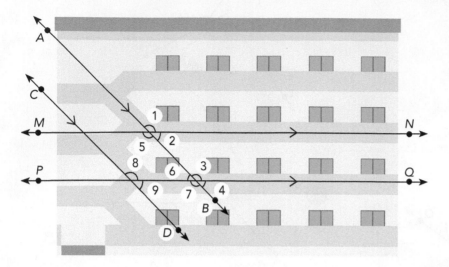

a)   Name two pairs of corresponding angles.

b)   Name all the angles that have the same measure as ∠1.

37 The two mirrors used in a periscope are parallel to each other as shown.
m∠1 = 3x°, m∠2 = (60 − x)°, and m∠3 = 90°. Write and solve an equation to find the value of x. Then find the measure of ∠4.

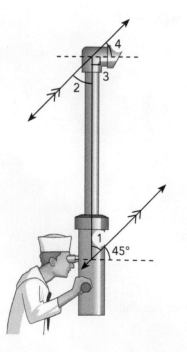

38 *Math Journal* Use a diagram to illustrate each of the following:
transversal, corresponding angles, alternate exterior angles, and
alternate interior angles. Label your diagram and explain which angles are
congruent.

6.4 Interior and Exterior Angles

Lesson Objectives

- Explore and apply the properties of the interior angles of a triangle.
- Explore and apply the properties of the exterior angles of a triangle.

Vocabulary

interior angles

exterior angles

Explore and Apply the Properties of the Interior Angles of a Triangle.

In triangle *ABC*, ∠1, ∠2, and ∠3 are its interior angles.
These angles lie inside the triangle.

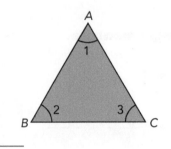

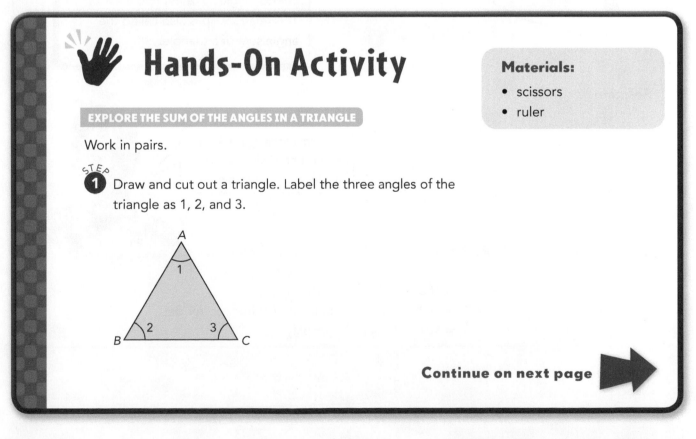

Hands-On Activity

Materials:
- scissors
- ruler

EXPLORE THE SUM OF THE ANGLES IN A TRIANGLE

Work in pairs.

STEP 1 Draw and cut out a triangle. Label the three angles of the triangle as 1, 2, and 3.

Continue on next page

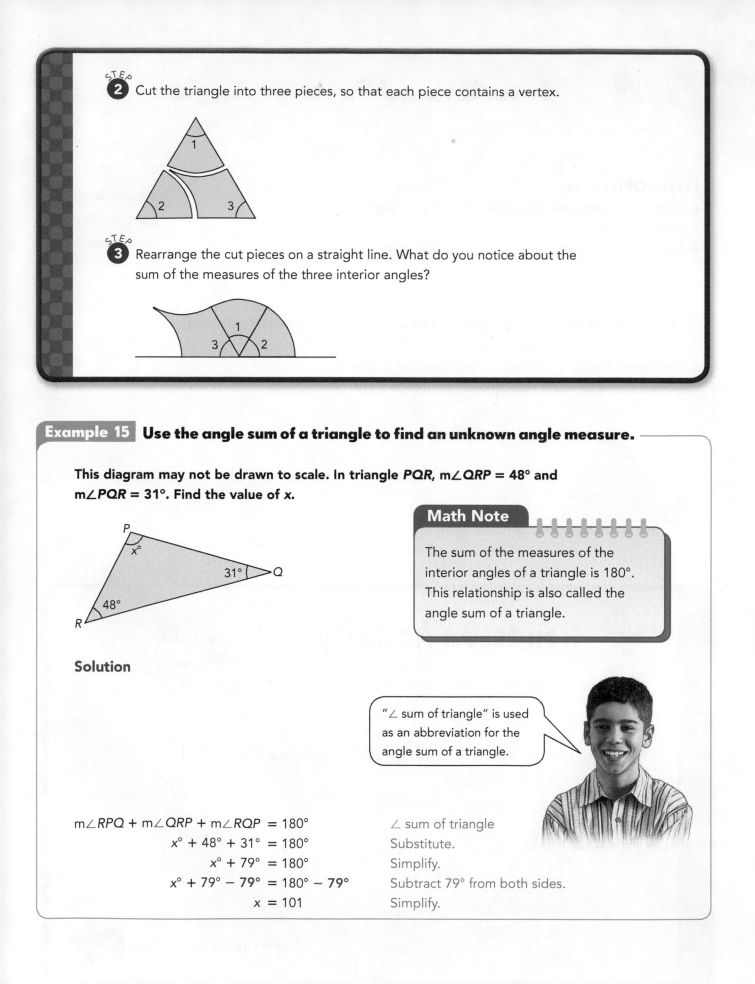

STEP 2 Cut the triangle into three pieces, so that each piece contains a vertex.

STEP 3 Rearrange the cut pieces on a straight line. What do you notice about the sum of the measures of the three interior angles?

Example 15 **Use the angle sum of a triangle to find an unknown angle measure.**

This diagram may not be drawn to scale. In triangle *PQR*, m∠*QRP* = 48° and m∠*PQR* = 31°. Find the value of *x*.

Math Note

The sum of the measures of the interior angles of a triangle is 180°. This relationship is also called the angle sum of a triangle.

Solution

"∠ sum of triangle" is used as an abbreviation for the angle sum of a triangle.

m∠*RPQ* + m∠*QRP* + m∠*RQP* = 180°	∠ sum of triangle
$x° + 48° + 31° = 180°$	Substitute.
$x° + 79° = 180°$	Simplify.
$x° + 79° - 79° = 180° - 79°$	Subtract 79° from both sides.
$x = 101$	Simplify.

Guided Practice

This diagram may not be drawn to scale. Find the unknown angle measure.

1 Find the value of p.

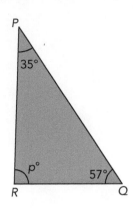

$$m\angle RPQ + m\angle QRP + m\angle PQR = 180°$$ $\angle$ sum of triangle

$\underline{\quad?\quad} + \underline{\quad?\quad} + \underline{\quad?\quad} = \underline{\quad?\quad}$ Substitute.

$\underline{\quad?\quad} + \underline{\quad?\quad} = \underline{\quad?\quad}$ Simplify.

$\underline{\quad?\quad} + \underline{\quad?\quad} - \underline{\quad?\quad} = \underline{\quad?\quad} - \underline{\quad?\quad}$ Subtract $\underline{\quad?\quad}$ from both sides.

$\underline{\quad?\quad} = \underline{\quad?\quad}$ Simplify.

Example 16 **Use the angle sum of a triangle to find an unknown angle measure in an isosceles triangle.**

This diagram may not be drawn to scale. Triangle *PQR* is an isosceles triangle where $m\angle QPR = 40°$. Find the value of *x*.

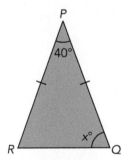

In an isosceles triangle, the angles opposite the congruent sides are congruent.

Solution

$m\angle PRQ = m\angle PQR = x°$ Isosceles triangle

$m\angle QPR + m\angle PQR + m\angle PRQ = 180°$ $\angle$ sum of triangle

$40° + x° + x° = 180°$ Substitute.

$40° + 2x° = 180°$ Simplify.

$40° + 2x° - 40° = 180° - 40°$ Subtract 40° from both sides.

$2x = 140$ Simplify.

$\dfrac{2x}{2} = \dfrac{140}{2}$ Divide both sides by 2.

$x = 70$ Simplify.

Guided Practice

This diagram may not be drawn to scale. Find the unknown angle measures.

2 Triangle XYZ is an isosceles triangle and m∠XYZ = 55°. Find the value of x.

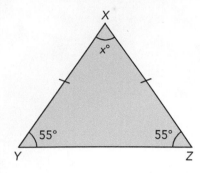

m∠XYZ + m∠XZY + m∠YXZ = 180°   ∠ sum of triangle

___?___ + ___?___ + ___?___ = ___?___   Substitute.

___?___ + ___?___ = ___?___   Simplify.

___?___ + ___?___ − ___?___ = ___?___ − ___?___   Subtract ___?___ from both sides.

___?___ = ___?___   Simplify.

Explore and Apply the Properties of the Exterior Angles of a Triangle.

In the diagram below, the sides of triangle ABC have been extended to form angles 4, 5, and 6. Because these angles lie outside the triangle, they are called exterior angles of triangle ABC. Angles 7, 8, and 9 are also exterior angles of a triangle.

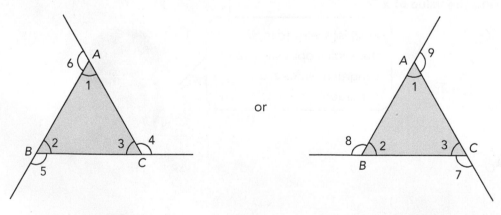

or

The interior angle 3 and the exterior angle 4 are adjacent angles on a straight line. The sum of adjacent angles on a straight line is 180°.
So, m∠3 + m∠4 = 180°.

You also know that the sum of the measures of the interior angles of a triangle is 180°.
So, m∠1 + m∠2 + m∠3 = 180°.

> **Math Note**
>
> A triangle has 6 exterior angles, 2 at each vertex.

You can use these two equations to demonstrate a property about the exterior angles of a triangle.

$$
\left.
\begin{aligned}
m\angle 3 + m\angle 4 &= 180° \\
m\angle 3 + m\angle 7 &= 180° \\
m\angle 3 + m\angle 1 + m\angle 2 &= 180°
\end{aligned}
\right\}
\quad
\begin{aligned}
m\angle 1 + m\angle 2 &= m\angle 4 \\
\text{or}& \\
m\angle 1 + m\angle 2 &= m\angle 7
\end{aligned}
$$

The exterior angle of a triangle is always supplementary to the interior angle it is adjacent to, and is always equal to the sum of the other two interior angles of the triangle.

So, $m\angle 1 + m\angle 2 = m\angle 4$ or $m\angle 7$

$\quad m\angle 1 + m\angle 3 = m\angle 5$ or $m\angle 8$

$\quad m\angle 2 + m\angle 3 = m\angle 6$ or $m\angle 9$

> Adding $m\angle 4$ or $m\angle 7$ to $m\angle 3$ is equivalent to adding $m\angle 1$ and $m\angle 2$ to $m\angle 3$. You can conclude that $m\angle 4 = m\angle 1 + m\angle 2$ or $m\angle 7 = m\angle 1 + m\angle 2$.

Example 17 **Use exterior angle relationships to find angle measures.**

These diagrams may not be drawn to scale. Find the value of the variable.

a)

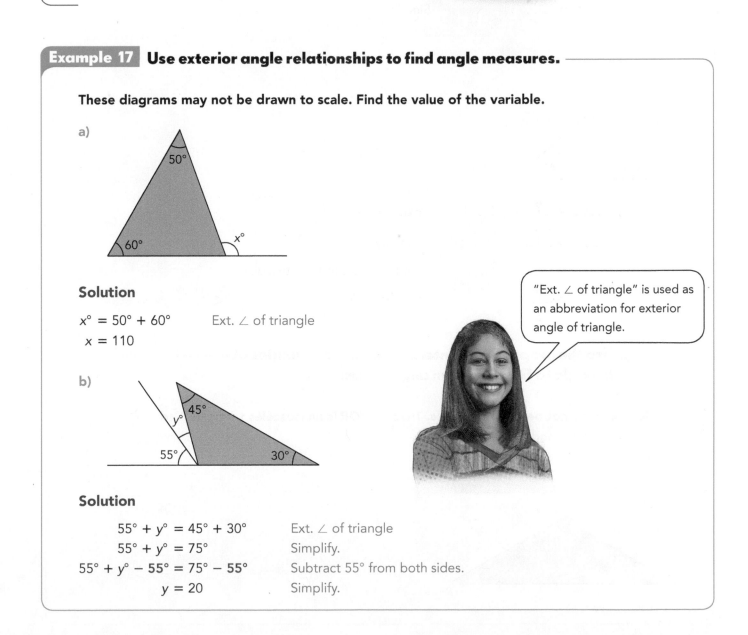

Solution

$x° = 50° + 60°$ Ext. $\angle$ of triangle

$\ x = 110$

> "Ext. $\angle$ of triangle" is used as an abbreviation for exterior angle of triangle.

b)

Solution

$\qquad 55° + y° = 45° + 30°$ Ext. $\angle$ of triangle

$\qquad 55° + y° = 75°$ Simplify.

$55° + y° - 55° = 75° - 55°$ Subtract 55° from both sides.

$\qquad\qquad\ y = 20$ Simplify.

Guided Practice

These diagrams may not be drawn to scale. Find the value of each variable.

3

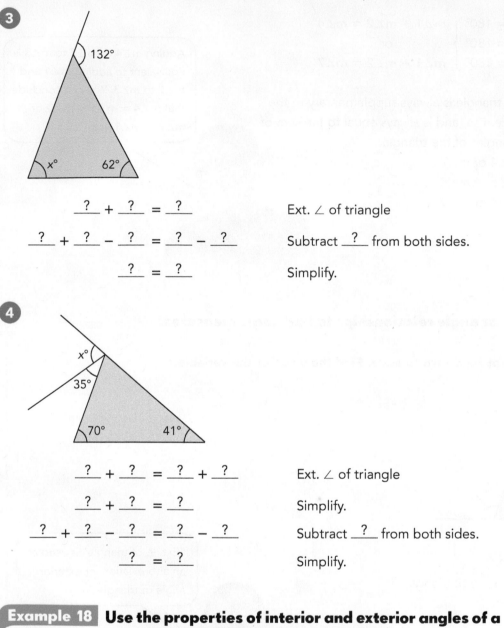

$$\underline{} + \underline{} = \underline{} \qquad \text{Ext. } \angle \text{ of triangle}$$

$$\underline{} + \underline{} - \underline{} = \underline{} - \underline{} \qquad \text{Subtract } \underline{} \text{ from both sides.}$$

$$\underline{} = \underline{} \qquad \text{Simplify.}$$

4

$$\underline{} + \underline{} = \underline{} + \underline{} \qquad \text{Ext. } \angle \text{ of triangle}$$

$$\underline{} + \underline{} = \underline{} \qquad \text{Simplify.}$$

$$\underline{} + \underline{} - \underline{} = \underline{} - \underline{} \qquad \text{Subtract } \underline{} \text{ from both sides.}$$

$$\underline{} = \underline{} \qquad \text{Simplify.}$$

Example 18 **Use the properties of interior and exterior angles of a triangle to find unknown angle measures.**

This diagram may not be drawn to scale. Triangle *PQR* is an isosceles triangle. Find the measures of ∠1 and ∠2.

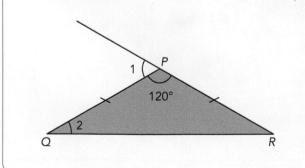

Solution

Method 1

Use the isosceles triangle PQR to express $m\angle PRQ$ in terms of $m\angle 2$.

$\overline{PQ} = \overline{PR}$

$m\angle PRQ = m\angle PQR$
$\qquad\quad = m\angle 2$

In an isosceles triangle, the angles opposite the congruent sides are congruent.

Then find $m\angle 2$. Use the angle sum of a triangle to write and solve an equation.

$m\angle 2 + m\angle PRQ + 120° = 180°$	$\angle$ sum of triangle
$m\angle 2 + m\angle 2 + 120° = 180°$	Substitute $m\angle PRQ = m\angle 2$.
$2 \cdot m\angle 2 + 120° = 180°$	Simplify.
$2 \cdot m\angle 2 + 120° - \mathbf{120°} = 180° - \mathbf{120°}$	Subtract 120° from both sides.
$2m\angle 2 = 60°$	Simplify.
$\dfrac{2m\angle 2}{2} = \dfrac{60°}{2}$	Divide both sides by 2.
$m\angle 2 = 30°$	Simplify.

Finally, use the property of the exterior angles of a triangle to find $m\angle 1$.

$m\angle 1 = m\angle 2 + m\angle PRQ$	Ext. $\angle$ of triangle
$\quad = m\angle 2 + m\angle 2$	Substitute $m\angle PRQ = m\angle 2$.
$\quad = 30° + 30°$	Substitute $m\angle 2 = 30°$.
$\quad = 60°$	Simplify.

Method 2

Use the property of adjacent angles on a straight line to find $m\angle 1$.

$m\angle 1 + 120° = 180°$	Adj. $\angle$s on a st. line
$m\angle 1 + 120° - \mathbf{120°} = 180° - \mathbf{120°}$	Subtract 120° from both sides.
$m\angle 1 = 60°$	Simplify.

Use the property of exterior angles of a triangle to find $m\angle 2$.

$m\angle 2 + m\angle PRQ = m\angle 1$	Ext. $\angle$ of triangle
$m\angle 2 + m\angle 2 = m\angle 1$	Substitute $m\angle PRQ = m\angle 2$.
$2m\angle 2 = 60°$	Simplify and substitute $m\angle 1 = 60°$.
$\dfrac{2m\angle 2}{2} = \dfrac{60°}{2}$	Divide both sides by 2.
$m\angle 2 = 30°$	Simplify.

Guided Practice

Complete.

5 This diagram may not drawn to scale. Triangle *ABC* is an isosceles triangle. Find the measures of ∠1 and ∠2.

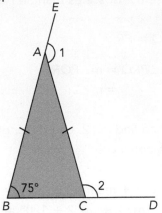

$AB = AC$

$m\angle ACB = m\angle ABC$

$= \underline{\ ?\ }$

$m\angle 1 = \underline{\ ?\ } + \underline{\ ?\ }$ Ext. ∠ of triangle

$= \underline{\ ?\ }$ Simplify.

$m\angle 2 = 180° - \underline{\ ?\ }$ Adj. ∠s on a st. line

$= \underline{\ ?\ }$ Simplify.

6 This diagram may not be drawn to scale. Triangle *EFG* is an isosceles triangle and $\overleftrightarrow{EF}$ is parallel to $\overleftrightarrow{HI}$. Find the value of x.

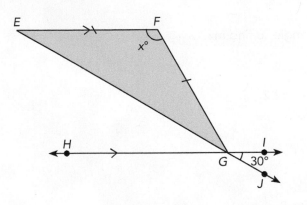

$m\angle FEG = m\angle IGJ$ Corr. ∠s

$= \underline{\ ?\ }$

$m\angle FGE = m\angle FEG$ Isosceles triangle

$= \underline{\ ?\ }$

$\underline{\ ?\ } + \underline{\ ?\ } + \underline{\ ?\ } = \underline{\ ?\ }$ ∠ sum of triangle

$\underline{\ ?\ } + \underline{\ ?\ } = \underline{\ ?\ }$ Simplify.

$\underline{\ ?\ } + \underline{\ ?\ } - \underline{\ ?\ } = \underline{\ ?\ } - \underline{\ ?\ }$ Subtract $\underline{\ ?\ }$ from both sides.

$\underline{\ ?\ } = \underline{\ ?\ }$ Simplify.

Practice 6.4

These diagrams may not be drawn to scale. Find the value of y.

1

67°

y   52°

2

18°

y   26°

3

y

20°

42°

4

27°

y

51°

5

y

28°   30°

6

56°   y

123°

These diagrams may not be drawn to scale. Find m∠1 and m∠2 in each diagram.

7

62°

2   1

8

28°   38°

76°

1

2

9

70°

1

50°   2

10

70°

1

43°   2

These diagrams may not be drawn to scale. Use an equation to find the value of y.

11

$3y°$

$y°$ $80°$

12

$2y°$

$3y°$

These diagrams may not be drawn to scale. Find the value of x and name the type of triangle that is shown.

13

$60°$

$x°$ $x°$

14

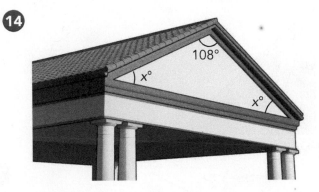

$108°$

$x°$

$x°$

15

$x°$

$62°$

These diagrams may not be drawn to scale. Find the measure of each numbered angle.

16

$148°$

1

$63°$ 2

3

17

$140°$

1

2     $15°$

These diagrams may not be drawn to scale. Find the measure of each numbered angle.

18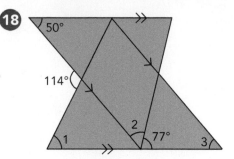

19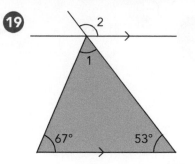

Solve.

20 $\overleftrightarrow{BE}$ is parallel to $\overleftrightarrow{FH}$. Find the measure of $\angle CAD$ in terms of $\angle 1$ and $\angle 2$.

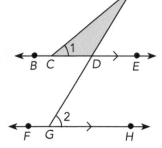

21 📝 *Math Journal* Explain why each of the following statement is true.

a) A triangle cannot have two right angles.

b) The interior angle measures of an isosceles triangle cannot be 96°, 43°, and 43°.

22 $m\angle 1 = 2x°$, $m\angle 2 = (x - 5)°$, and $m\angle 3 = 100°$. Use an equation to find the value of x and then find the measures of $\angle 1$ and $\angle 2$.

These diagrams may not be drawn to scale. Use an equation to find the value of x.

23

24

Use an equation to find the value of x.

25

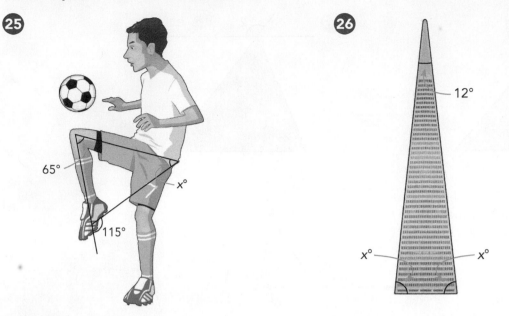

65°

x°

115°

26

12°

x°   x°

Brain @ Work

ABCD is a rhombus, and the measure of ∠*BCD* is 68°. *BDE* is a triangle where the measure of ∠*BED* is 36° and the measure of ∠*BDE* is 73°.
Find m∠*EBC*. Show how you obtain your answer.

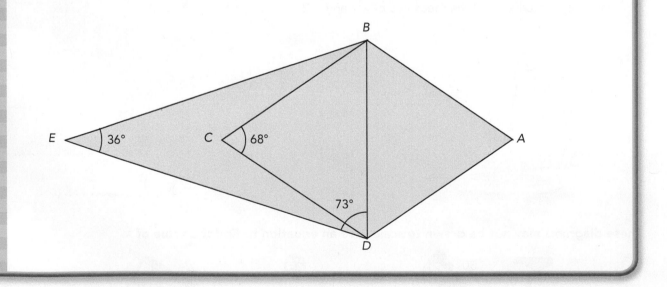

Chapter Wrap Up

Concept Map

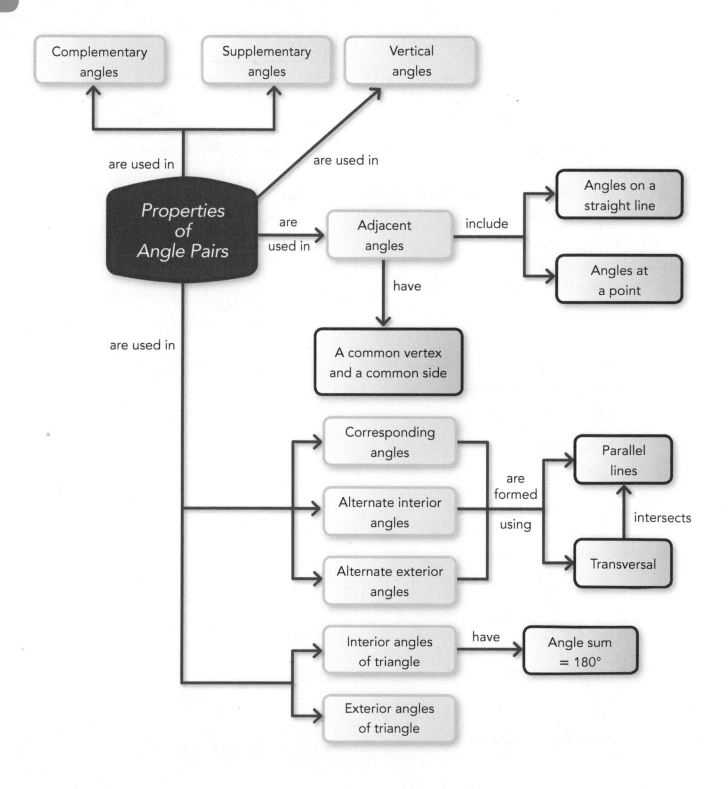

▶ Two angles with measures that add up to 90°
are called complementary angles.

$m\angle 1 + m\angle 2 = 90°$

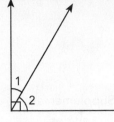

▶ Two angles with measures that add up to 180°
are called supplementary angles.

$m\angle 1 + m\angle 2 = 180°$

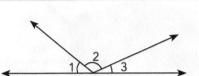

▶ The measures of adjacent angles on one side of a
straight line add up to 180°.

$m\angle 1 + m\angle 2 + m\angle 3 = 180°$

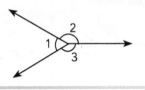

▶ The sum of the measures of all angles at a
point is 360°.

$m\angle 1 + m\angle 2 + m\angle 3 = 360°$

▶ Vertical angles are congruent.

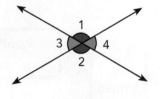

$m\angle 1 = m\angle 2$ and $m\angle 3 = m\angle 4$

▶ Alternate interior angles are congruent.

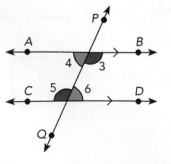

$m\angle 4 = m\angle 6$ and $m\angle 3 = m\angle 5$

▶ Alternate exterior angles are congruent.

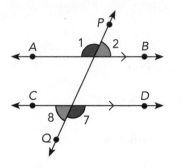

$m\angle 1 = m\angle 7$ and $m\angle 2 = m\angle 8$

▶ Corresponding angles are congruent.

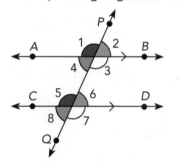

$m\angle 1 = m\angle 5$, $m\angle 2 = m\angle 6$, $m\angle 3 = m\angle 7$, and $m\angle 4 = m\angle 8$

▶ The sum of the measures of the interior angles of a triangle is always 180°.

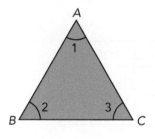

$m\angle 1 + m\angle 2 + m\angle 3 = 180°$

▶ The measure of an exterior angle of a triangle is equal to the sum of the measures of the interior angles that are not adjacent to the exterior angle.

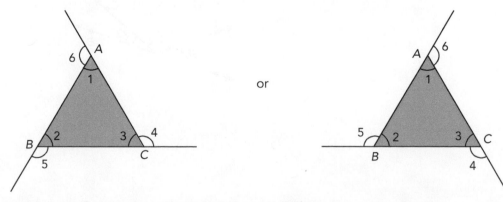

or

$m\angle 1 + m\angle 2 = m\angle 4$, $m\angle 1 + m\angle 3 = m\angle 5$, and $m\angle 2 + m\angle 3 = m\angle 6$

Chapter Review/Test

Concepts and Skills

Tell whether each pair of angles are supplementary, complementary or neither.

1 m∠1 = 23° and m∠2 =157°

2 m∠3 = 65° and m∠4 = 25°

3 m∠5 = 43° and m∠6 = 57°

4 m∠7 = 82° and m∠8 = 8°

5 m∠9 = 110° and m∠10 = 80°

6 m∠11 = 18° and m∠12 = 62°

Tell whether the following list of angle measures are complementary or supplementary.

m∠A = 67°, m∠B = 80°, m∠C = 131°, m∠D = 21°,
m∠E = 51°, m∠F = 46°, m∠G = 10°, m∠H = 120°,
m∠J = 69°, m∠K = 60°, m∠P = 49°, m∠Q = 113°,
m∠R = 44°, m∠S = 41°

7 Name two pairs of complementary angles.

8 Name two pairs of supplementary angles.

Copy and complete.

9 Name two pairs of angles for each type of angle pair.

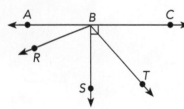

Type of Angles	1st Pair	2nd Pair
Complementary angles	?	?
Supplementary angles	?	?

These diagrams may not be drawn to scale. Find the measure of each numbered angle.

10 $\overleftrightarrow{AB}$ is a straight line.

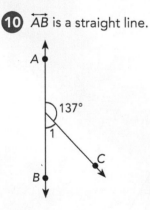

11 $\overrightarrow{AB}$ is a straight line.

These diagrams may not be drawn to scale. Find the measure of each numbered angle.

12

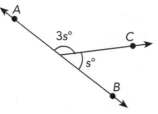

13 $\overleftrightarrow{AB}$ is a straight line.

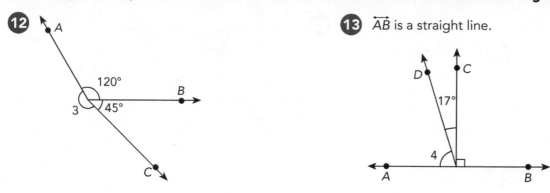

These diagrams may not be drawn to scale. Use an equation to find the value of each variable.

14 $\overleftrightarrow{AB}$ is a straight line.

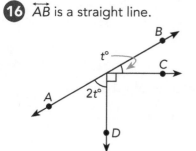

15 $\overleftrightarrow{AB}$ is a straight line.

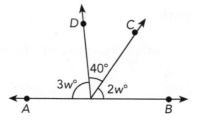

16 $\overleftrightarrow{AB}$ is a straight line.

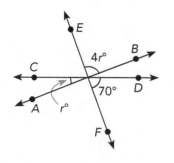

17

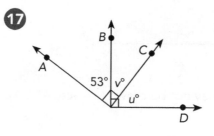

18 $\overleftrightarrow{AB}$, $\overleftrightarrow{CD}$, and $\overleftrightarrow{EF}$ are straight lines.

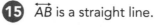

19

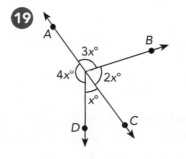

These diagrams may not be drawn to scale. $\overline{MN}$ is parallel to $\overline{PQ}$. Find the measure of each numbered angle.

20

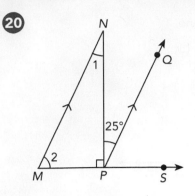

21

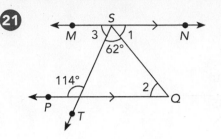

Problem Solving

Solve. Show your work.

22 This diagram may not be drawn to scale. Find the value of *x*.

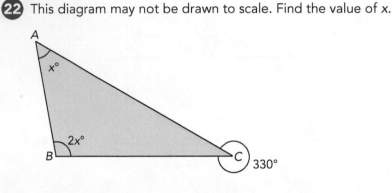

23 This diagram may not be drawn to scale. *ABCD* is a rhombus. Find the measures of ∠1 and ∠2.

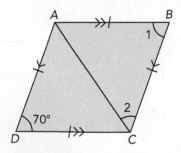

24 This diagram may not be drawn to scale. *ABCD* is a rectangle. $\overline{AE}$ and $\overline{DC}$ are straight lines. ∠*FBG* is a right angle, m∠*ABF* = 74°, and m∠*BEG* = 42°. Find the measures of ∠*EBG* and ∠*BGC*.

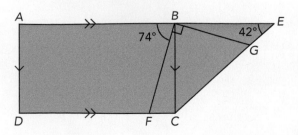

25 The diagram shows the flag of the United Kingdom. m∠*MNR* = 90°. Name two pairs of complementary and supplementary angles.

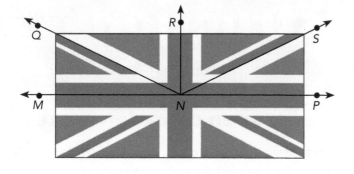

26 m∠1 = 15° and m∠2 = 131°. $\overrightarrow{AB}$ is a straight line. Find the measure of ∠3.

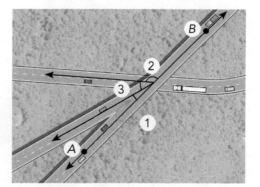

27 The diagram shows ∠1 and ∠2, which are formed by $\overleftrightarrow{MN}$ intersecting $\overrightarrow{PQ}$ and $\overrightarrow{RS}$. In the diagram, m∠1 = (12x + 7)°, m∠2 = (10x + 15)°, and x = 4. Explain how you know that $\overrightarrow{PQ}$ is parallel to $\overrightarrow{RS}$.

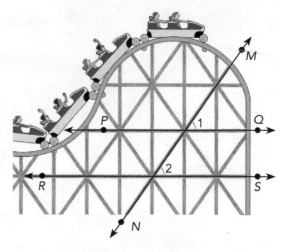

28 In the diagram, m∠1 = (5x − 20)°, m∠2 = (2x + 14)°, and m∠3 = 18°. Use an equation to find the measures of ∠1 and ∠2.

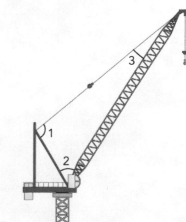

Geometric Construction

▶ Triangles and quadrilaterals can be constructed using a compass, a protractor, and a straightedge.

Have you ever seen a garden maze?

Landscape architects design gardens, parks, and other outdoor spaces. A landscape architect can use patterns and geometric shapes to design a garden maze. To create a scale drawing of the maze, the architect needs to understand how these geometric shapes fit together, and how lines and angles are related to each other. In this chapter, you will learn about geometric constructions and scale drawings.

EXIT

Recall Prior Knowledge

Classifying triangles

Triangles can be classified by either their angle measures or the lengths of their sides.

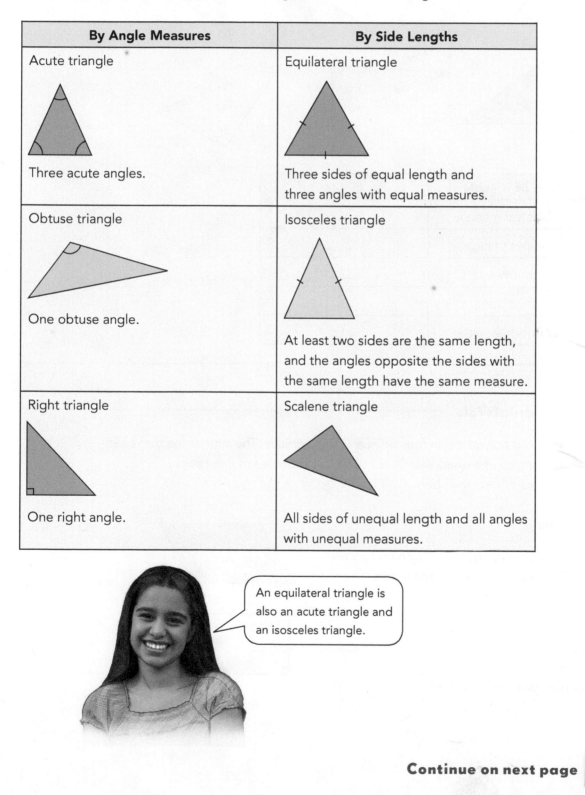

By Angle Measures	By Side Lengths
Acute triangle Three acute angles.	Equilateral triangle Three sides of equal length and three angles with equal measures.
Obtuse triangle One obtuse angle.	Isosceles triangle At least two sides are the same length, and the angles opposite the sides with the same length have the same measure.
Right triangle One right angle.	Scalene triangle All sides of unequal length and all angles with unequal measures.

An equilateral triangle is also an acute triangle and an isosceles triangle.

Continue on next page

✓ Quick Check

Copy and complete the table by classifying the triangles.

1

Type of Triangle	Figure
Equilateral triangle	?
Isosceles triangle	?
Right triangle	?
Acute triangle	?
Obtuse triangle	?

Naming quadrilaterals

A quadrilateral is a polygon with four sides and four vertices. The sum of the measures of the interior angles of a quadrilateral is 360°. The properties of five special quadrilaterals are summarized below.

Parallelogram

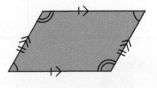

- Opposite sides are equal in length and parallel.
- Opposite angles have equal measures.

Rectangle

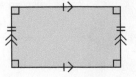

- Opposite sides are equal in length and parallel.
- All interior angles are right angles.
- Diagonals have equal lengths.

Rhombus

- All sides have equal lengths.
- Opposite sides are parallel.
- Opposite angles have equal measures.
- Diagonals intersect at right angles.

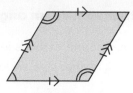

Square

- All sides have equal lengths.
- Opposite sides are parallel.
- All interior angles are right angles.
- Diagonals have equal lengths.

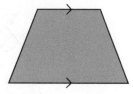

Trapezoid

- Only one pair of opposite sides is parallel.

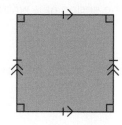

✓ Quick Check

Copy and complete the table.

2

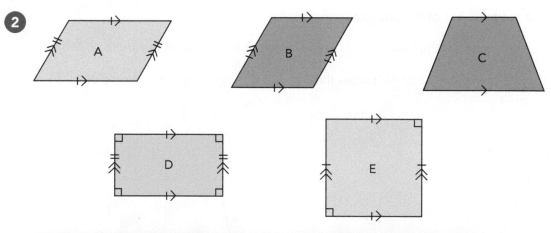

Common Property	Type(s) of Quadrilateral
All sides have equal lengths.	?
The measure of every interior angle is 90°.	?
Both pairs of opposite sides are parallel.	?
Only one pair of opposite sides is parallel.	?
The diagonals are perpendicular to each other.	?
The diagonals have equal lengths.	?

A ray starts from one endpoint and extends infinitely in one direction. It is specified by a point and a direction. A ray has one endpoint that marks the position from where it begins.

A ray starting from point A and passing through B is called $\overrightarrow{AB}$, which is read as "ray AB." The endpoint is written and read first.

An angle's measure is between 0° and 180°. Use the following steps to find the measure of an angle.

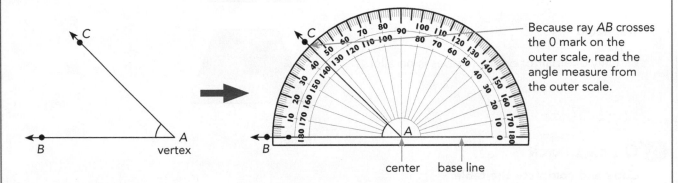

Because ray AB crosses the 0 mark on the outer scale, read the angle measure from the outer scale.

center   base line

STEP 1   Place the base line of the protractor on ray AB.

STEP 2   Place the center of the base line of the protractor at the vertex of the angle.

STEP 3   Read the outer scale. Ray AC passes through the 45° mark. So, the measure of the angle is 45°.

☑ Quick Check

Measure ∠ABC.

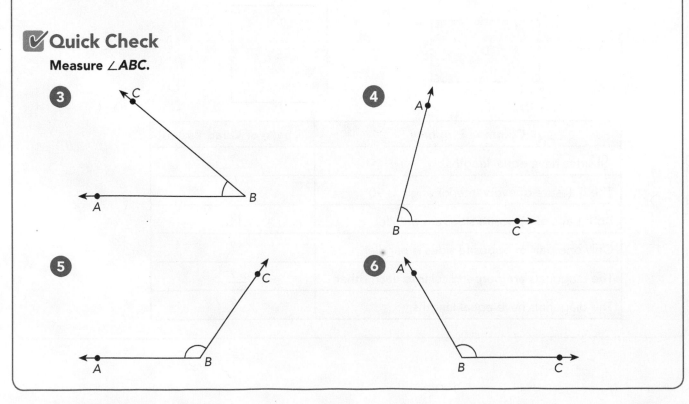

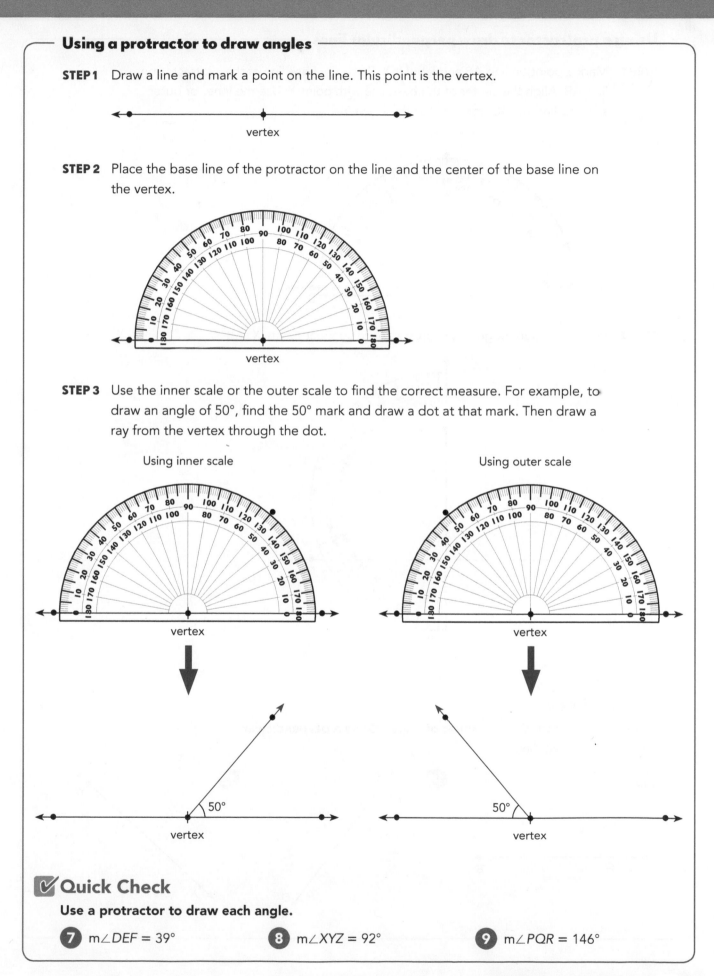

Using a protractor to draw angles

STEP 1 Draw a line and mark a point on the line. This point is the vertex.

vertex

STEP 2 Place the base line of the protractor on the line and the center of the base line on the vertex.

vertex

STEP 3 Use the inner scale or the outer scale to find the correct measure. For example, to draw an angle of 50°, find the 50° mark and draw a dot at that mark. Then draw a ray from the vertex through the dot.

Using inner scale

vertex

Using outer scale

vertex

50°

vertex

50°

vertex

✓ Quick Check

Use a protractor to draw each angle.

7 m∠DEF = 39°　　　**8** m∠XYZ = 92°　　　**9** m∠PQR = 146°

Using a protractor to draw perpendicular lines

STEP 1 Mark a point on line *AB* and label it *X*. Place the base line of the protractor on line *AB*. Align the center of the base line with point *X*. Use the inner or outer scale to find the 90° mark. Label this point *Y*.

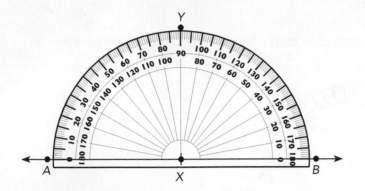

STEP 2 Use the straight edge of the protractor to connect points *X* and *Y*.

✓ Quick Check

Copy $\overleftrightarrow{AB}$, $\overrightarrow{CD}$, and $\overrightarrow{XY}$ on a sheet of paper. Draw a perpendicular line to each given line.

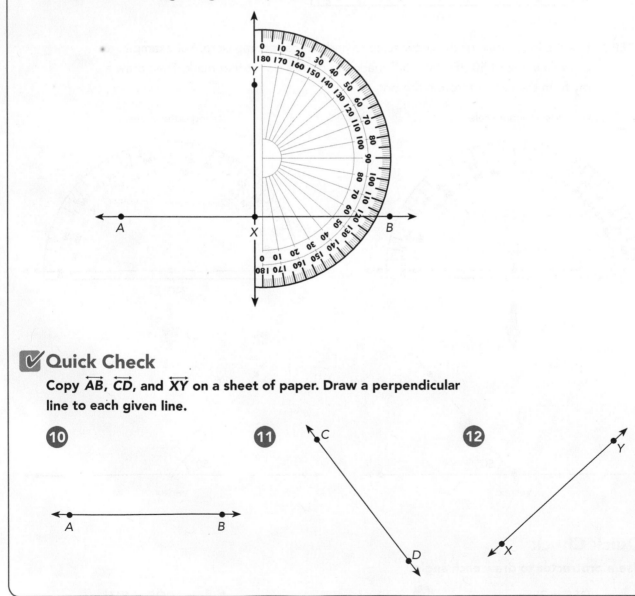

10

11

12

7.1 Constructing Angle Bisectors

Lesson Objectives

- Understand the meaning of an angle bisector.
- Construct an angle bisector.

Vocabulary

bisector   bisect

equidistant   straightedge

Understand the Meaning of an Angle Bisector.

For any angle, you can draw a ray that divides the angle into two angles with equal measures. This ray is called the angle bisector.

Ray *BD* is the angle bisector of $\angle ABC$.

So, $m\angle ABD = m\angle DBC = \frac{1}{2} m\angle ABC$.

You can also say that $\overrightarrow{BD}$ **bisects** $\angle ABC$.

> **Math Note**
>
> "To bisect" something means to cut it into two equal parts.

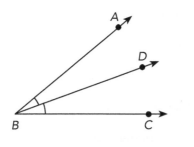

> An angle has only one bisector because if $m\angle ABC$ is $x°$, only one ray divides it into two angles of measure $\frac{x°}{2}$.

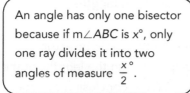

The bisector of an acute angle forms two acute angles.
The bisectors of both right and obtuse angles also form two acute angles.

Hands-On Activity

Materials:

• ruler

EXPLORE THE DISTANCE BETWEEN POINTS ON THE SIDES OF AN ANGLE AND POINTS ON THE ANGLE BISECTOR

Work in pairs.

$\overrightarrow{QS}$ is the angle bisector of $\angle YQX$. Points X and Y are **equidistant** from point Q.

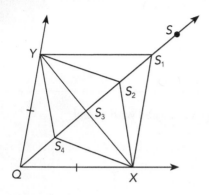

Points S_1, S_2, S_3, and S_4 lie on $\overrightarrow{QS}$, the angle bisector of $\angle YQX$.

STEP 1 Measure and record each length to the nearest tenth of a centimeter.

$S_1X = \underline{\ ?\ }$ cm $S_1Y = \underline{\ ?\ }$ cm

$S_2X = \underline{\ ?\ }$ cm $S_2Y = \underline{\ ?\ }$ cm

$S_3X = \underline{\ ?\ }$ cm $S_3Y = \underline{\ ?\ }$ cm

$S_4X = \underline{\ ?\ }$ cm $S_4Y = \underline{\ ?\ }$ cm

STEP 2 Compare the lengths of $\overline{S_1X}$ and $\overline{S_1Y}$. Then compare the lengths of the two segments in each of the following pairs: $\overline{S_2X}$ and $\overline{S_2Y}$, $\overline{S_3X}$ and $\overline{S_3Y}$, and $\overline{S_4X}$ and $\overline{S_4Y}$. What do you observe about each pair of segment lengths?

Math Journal Suppose you choose any point on the angle bisector. Do you think you will observe the same relationship between the lengths of the segments that connect the point to points X and Y? What conclusion can you make?

> From the activity, any two points on the sides of an angle that are the same distance from the vertex are also the same distance from any point on the angle bisector.

Introduce Geometric Constructions.

When you carry out a geometric construction, you draw lengths, shapes, angles, or lines accurately using only a compass, a **straightedge**, and a pencil. There are no measurements that involve units such as inches or degrees.

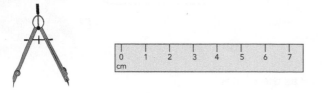

A compass is a V-shaped tool that can be used to construct circles or arcs of circles.

A straightedge is a geometric tool that is used to draw a line segment between two points or to extend an existing line. It has no markings on it.

Math Note

When making geometric constructions, only the unmarked edge of the ruler is used.

In a geometric construction, you use a compass to draw arcs and to transfer distances. You use a straightedge to draw lines and segments between two points, but not of a specific length.

A compass also allows you to check whether distances are equal, and a straightedge can be also used to check whether points lie on the same line.

Construct an Angle Bisector.

You can use a compass, a straightedge, and a pencil to construct an angle bisector. Based on what you saw in the activity, you need to first locate two points on the sides of the angle that are the same distance from the vertex. Then find a point N inside the angle that is the same distance from each of these points. Then $\overrightarrow{BN}$ is the angle bisector.

The following steps show how you can construct the angle bisector for $\angle ABC$.

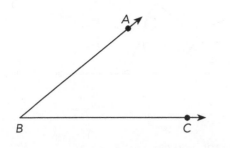

Because there is only one angle bisector of the angle, you know that $\overrightarrow{BN}$ is the angle bisector.

Continue on next page

STEP 1 With the compass point at *B*, draw an arc that intersects the two rays *AB* and *BC*. Label the points of intersection as *P* and *Q*.

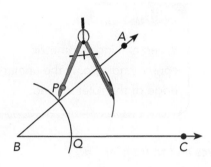

You know that *P* and *Q* are equidistant from *B*, because both points lie on an arc with *B* as its center.

STEP 2 Using the same radius, draw an arc with *P* as the center.

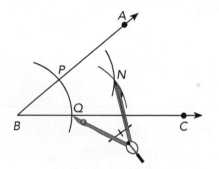

STEP 3 Using *Q* as the center, draw another arc with the same radius. Label the point where the two arcs intersect as *N*.

You know *N* is equidistant from *P* and *Q*, because you used the same setting on your compass.

STEP 4 Use a straightedge to draw $\overrightarrow{BN}$.

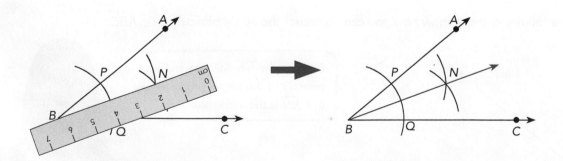

$\overrightarrow{BN}$ is the angle bisector of ∠*ABC*. After drawing the angle bisector, you can use a protractor to check that it divides the angle into two angles with equal measures.

Example 1 **Construct the angle bisector of a given angle.**

Bisect ∠*ABC*.

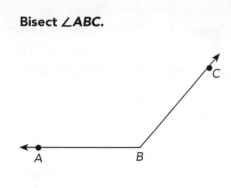

Solution

With the compass point at the vertex, draw an arc that intersects $\vec{BA}$ and $\vec{BC}$. Label the intersection points as *P* and *Q*.

Using the same radius, draw an arc with *P* as the center.

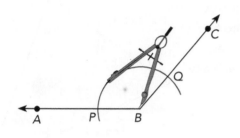

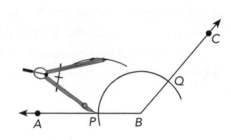

Using *Q* as the center, draw another arc with the same radius. Label the point where the two arcs intersect as *N*.

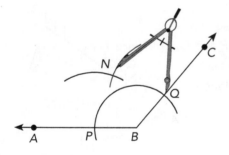

You only need to find one point that is equidistant from *P* and *Q*, because there is only one angle bisector. All other points equidistant from *P* and *Q* are on $\vec{BN}$.

Use a straightedge to draw $\vec{BN}$.

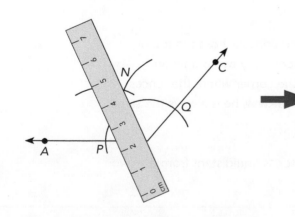

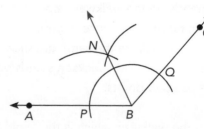

Guided Practice

Trace or copy ∠PQR. Then draw the angle bisector of ∠PQR.

1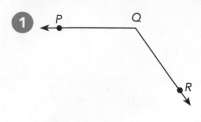

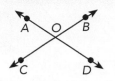

Think Math

Two lines intersect to form four angles. Bisect the angles, using the least number of arcs and lines. How many arcs and lines did you use?

Example 2 | **Apply angle bisectors in real-world problems.**

The diagram shows a triangular plot of land in Mr. Jackson's backyard. The plot is fenced on two sides as shown. Mr. Jackson wants to grow flowers and vegetables. So, he decides to divide the garden into two parts by creating a walkway that is equidistant from the two fences. Explain how a geometric construction can be used to add the walkway to the diagram.

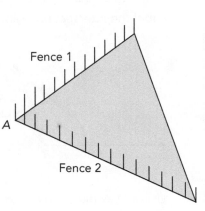

Solution

The walkway is to be equidistant from the two fences. So, choose two points that are the same distance from *A* such as the fifth post, *P* and *Q*, on each side. Find all the points that are equidistant from these two points. This is the angle bisector of the angle made by the two fences.

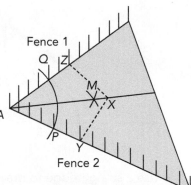

If Mr. Jackson stands on the walkway at point *X*, he is equidistant from point *Z* on Fence 1 and from point *Y* on Fence 2. Suppose you choose any two points on Fence 1 and Fence 2 that are the same distance from the corner where the fences intersect. No matter where Mr. Jackson stands on the walkway, he is always the same distance from those two points.

So, any point on the walkway, which is the angle bisector, is equidistant from the two sides of the angle formed by Fence 1 and Fence 2.

Guided Practice

Complete.

2 Two walls intersect to form a right angle. In gym class, the students use the two walls to play a game in which the players line up so that each player is equidistant from the two walls.

  a) Copy the diagram and draw a line to show where students should line up.

  b) What is the measure of the angle formed by the students and Wall 1? How do you know?

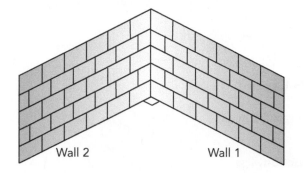

Wall 2   Wall 1

Example 3 **Use an angle bisector to construct an angle of another measure.**

Construct a 45° angle whose vertex is point A.

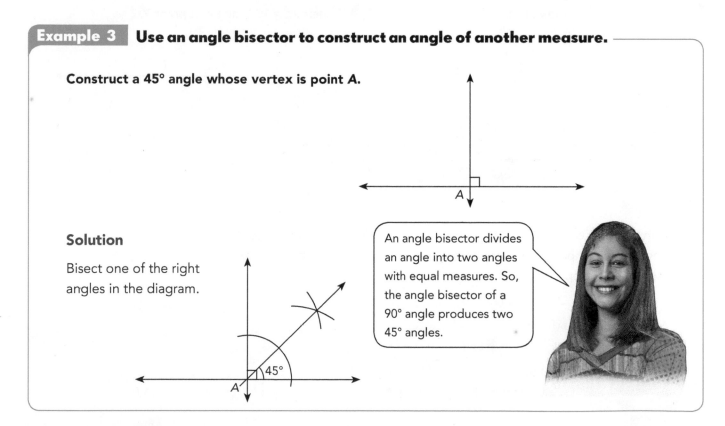

Solution

Bisect one of the right angles in the diagram.

An angle bisector divides an angle into two angles with equal measures. So, the angle bisector of a 90° angle produces two 45° angles.

45°

A

Guided Practice

Trace or copy the diagram. Then complete.

3 Use ∠X to construct a 15° angle whose vertex is point X.

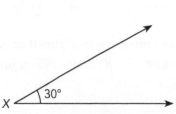

X   30°

Construct the angle bisector of ∠ABC on a copy of each figure.

1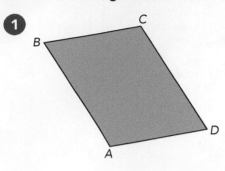

2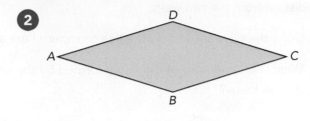

Draw each angle with a protractor. Then construct its angle bisector.

3 m∠POR = 75°

4 m∠ADE = 122°

Copy the angle shown. Then perform the indicated construction.

5 Construct a 25° angle at point X.

6 Construct a 108° angle at point Y.

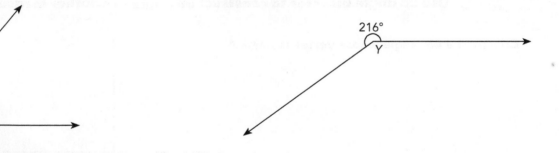

Solve.

7 Justin wants to construct the angle bisector of ∠XYZ. Trace or copy the diagram. Using only a compass and a straightedge, construct the angle bisector and describe each step clearly.

8 Draw two straight lines intersecting at an angle of 108°. Find the points that are equidistant from the two sides of each 108° angle formed by the intersecting lines.

9 Draw an obtuse angle of any measure and label it as ∠XYZ. Construct an angle that is one-fourth the measure of ∠XYZ, describing briefly the steps involved.

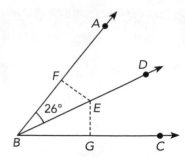

10 The diagram shows ∠ABC with $\overrightarrow{BD}$ being its angle bisector and BF = BG. E is a point on $\overrightarrow{BD}$ and m∠ABD = 26°. Copy and complete.

m∠DBC = ___?___

Length of $\overline{EG}$ = Length of ___?___

11 Officials are planning to build a new airport to serve three major cities in one region. The cities are located at W, X, and Y, which are represented by the vertices of the triangle shown. The officials want to place the airport at the intersection of the angle bisectors of ∠XWY and ∠XYW. Copy or trace the triangle. Find the possible location of the airport and label it point Q.

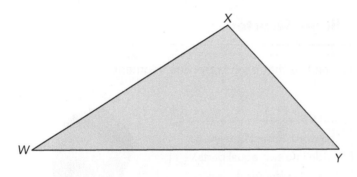

12 Joshua used a square piece of paper to make a paper airplane. As a first step, he made several folds in the paper, as shown in the diagram. First he folded along diagonal $\overline{QS}$, then he unfolded the paper. Next he folded along $\overline{QT}$ so that $\overline{PQ}$ lined up with $\overline{QS}$. Then he unfolded the paper again. In the diagram, what is the measure of ∠PQT? Give a brief explanation for your answer.

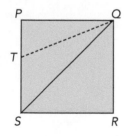

13 Kimberly wants to bisect the straight angle shown, and then bisect one of the resulting angles. She then wants to continue this process until she obtains an angle of measure 11.25°. How many times does she need to construct an angle bisector to produce an angle with this measure? Explain.

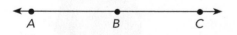

14 Max designed a support for a bridge. In his design, five spokes are attached to a metal beam. The angles formed by the spokes all have the same measure. Explain how Max can use geometric construction to accurately draw his design.

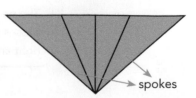

spokes

Constructing Perpendicular Bisectors

Lesson Objectives
- Understand the meaning of a perpendicular bisector.
- Construct a perpendicular bisector.

Vocabulary

perpendicular bisector

midpoint

Understand the Meaning of a **Perpendicular Bisector.**

The perpendicular bisector of a line segment is the line that bisects the line segment and is perpendicular to it.

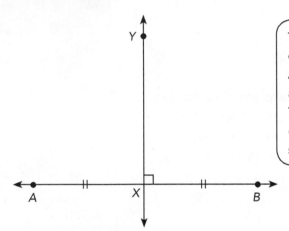

The word "bisect" means to divide into two equal parts. An angle bisector divides an angle into two equal parts. The perpendicular bisector of a segment divides the segment into two equal parts.

$\overleftrightarrow{XY}$ is the perpendicular bisector of line segment AB.

So, $AX = XB = \frac{1}{2} AB$

and $m\angle AXY = m\angle BXY = 90°$.

You can also say that the line XY bisects the line segment AB.

Since $AX = XB$, you can also say that $\overline{XY}$ passes through the **midpoint** of the line segment AB. The midpoint of a line segment is its middle point. It is equidistant from both endpoints.

The perpendicular bisector of a line segment always passes through the midpoint of the segment at a right angle.

Hands-On Activity

Materials:
• ruler

EXPLORE THE DISTANCE BETWEEN POINTS ON THE PERPENDICULAR BISECTOR OF A SEGMENT AND THE ENDPOINTS OF THE SEGMENT

Work in pairs.

Line XY is the perpendicular bisector of line segment AB. Points W, X, Y, and Z are four points on the perpendicular bisector of $\overline{AB}$.

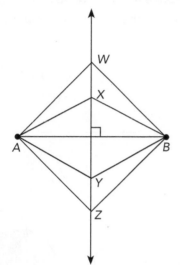

STEP 1 Measure and record each length to the nearest tenth of a centimeter.

AW = _?_ cm	BW = _?_ cm
AX = _?_ cm	BX = _?_ cm
AY = _?_ cm	BY = _?_ cm
AZ = _?_ cm	BZ = _?_ cm

STEP 2 Compare the lengths of $\overline{AW}$ and $\overline{BW}$. Then compare the lengths of each of the following pairs of segments: $\overline{AX}$ and $\overline{BX}$, $\overline{AY}$ and $\overline{BY}$, and $\overline{AZ}$ and $\overline{BZ}$. What do you notice about each pair of line segment lengths?

✎ *Math Journal* Suppose you choose any point on the perpendicular bisector and measure the distances from that point to points A and B. What do you predict about the distances? What conclusion can you make?

> From the activity, any point on the perpendicular bisector of a line segment is equidistant from the two endpoints of the line segment.

Construct a Perpendicular Bisector.

A compass, a straightedge, and a pencil can be used to construct the perpendicular bisector of a line segment. From the activity, you know you can do this by finding points that are equidistant from the endpoints.

A ————————————— B

STEP 1 With the compass point at *A*, draw arcs with the same radius above and below $\overline{AB}$. The arcs should have a radius greater than half the length of $\overline{AB}$.

STEP 2 Using the same radius, place the compass point at *B* and draw arcs above and below $\overline{AB}$. Label the points where the arcs intersect as *E* and *F*.

Math Note

Geometers say: "Two points determine a line." This means that given any two points, you can draw only one line through them.

You know that all four lengths, *AE*, *BE*, *AF*, and *BF* are the same, because the same compass setting was used. So *E* is equidistant from *A* and *B*, and so is *F*.

STEP 3 Use a straightedge to draw a line through *E* and *F*.

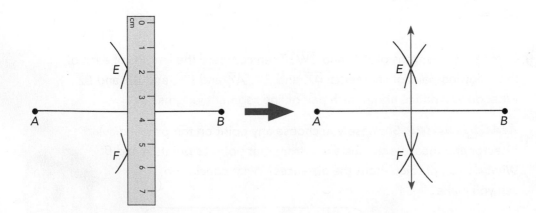

The $\overleftrightarrow{EF}$ is the perpendicular bisector of $\overline{AB}$. You can use a ruler and protractor to check that $\overleftrightarrow{EF}$ divides the line segment into two line segments of equal length and that $\overleftrightarrow{EF}$ is perpendicular to $\overline{AB}$.

Bisect line segment AB.

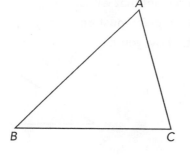

Solution

Place the compass point at A. Then draw an arc on each side of $\overline{AB}$. The radius of the arcs should be greater than half the length of $\overline{AB}$.

Using the same radius, set the compass point at B. Draw two more arcs on each side of $\overline{AB}$. Label the points where the arcs intersect as E and F.

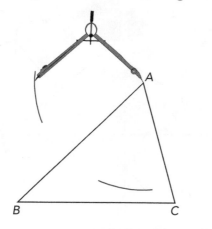

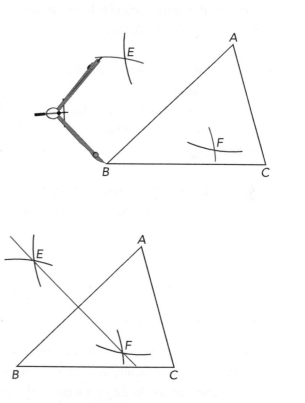

Use a straightedge to draw a line through E and F.

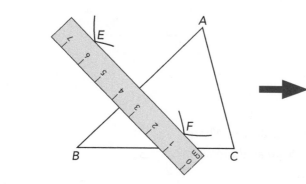

Guided Practice

Complete.

1 Copy or trace triangle XYZ. Then draw the perpendicular bisector of line segment XY.

Think Math

Construct the perpendicular bisector of line segment PQ, using only a compass and a straightedge. You are not allowed to draw any arcs below $\overline{PQ}$.

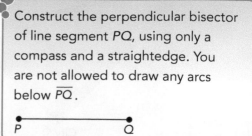

Example 5 **Apply perpendicular bisectors in real-world problems.**

Officials want to build a water purification plant that will be used by three towns. The water purification plant must be equidistant from all three towns. Describe how you find the location of the purification plant.

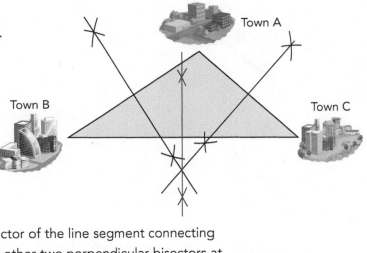

Solution

First draw the perpendicular bisector of the segment connecting Towns A and B. You know that all points on the perpendicular bisector are equidistant from Towns A and B.

Then draw the perpendicular bisector of the line segment connecting Towns A and C. All points on this perpendicular bisector are equidistant from Towns A and C.

Notice that the perpendicular bisectors intersect at a point. This point is equidistant from all three towns. So, this point marks the location of the water purification plant.

Check: You can draw the perpendicular bisector of the line segment connecting Towns B and C to show that it intersects the other two perpendicular bisectors at the same point.

Guided Practice

Copy the triangle and complete.

2 A trucking company has most of its business in Cities P, Q, and R. Where should it locate its new facility so that it is equidistant from all three cities? Mark the location of the facility on a copy of the map.

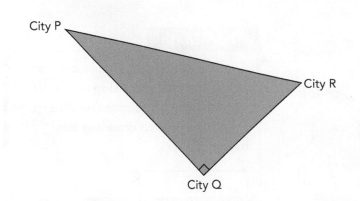

Practice 7.2

Draw each line segment and construct its perpendicular bisector.

1 $XY = 5$ cm

2 $PQ = 6.8$ cm

3 $AB = 8.8$ cm

4 $MN = 11$ cm

5 Draw a line segment between 4 inches and 5 inches and label the endpoints M and N. Construct the perpendicular bisector of $\overline{MN}$. Explain briefly if you could construct a different perpendicular bisector of $\overline{MN}$.

6 ✏️ *Math Journal* In the diagram below, point M is the midpoint of $\overline{AB}$. Ben drew line segment XY through point M. He labeled it as the perpendicular bisector of $\overline{AB}$. Do you agree with Ben? Give a reason for your answer.

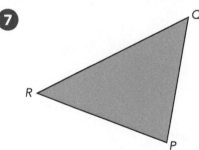

Draw the perpendicular bisectors of $\overline{PQ}$ and $\overline{PR}$ on a copy of each polygon. Label the point where the two perpendicular bisectors meet as W.

7

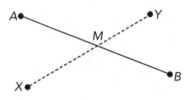

8

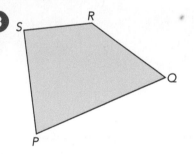

On a copy of WXYZ, mark the points that are described, if possible. Otherwise, explain why you cannot.

9 The point that is equidistant from points W, X, and Y.

10 The point that is equidistant from $\overline{WX}$, $\overline{WZ}$, and $\overline{XY}$.

11 The point that is equidistant from $\overline{WX}$ and $\overline{WZ}$, and also from points X and Y.

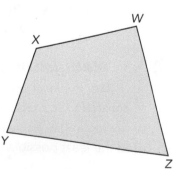

Solve.

12 Mark the point on $\overline{QR}$ that is equidistant from points Q and R on a copy of triangle PQR.

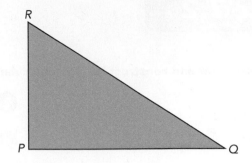

13 Mr. Smith wants to put a circular water sprinkler in his triangular-shaped garden. His garden has a tree at each vertex. The water sprinkler is to be equidistant from the trees. Copy or trace the given triangle. Mark point W to show where Mr. Smith should put the water sprinkler.

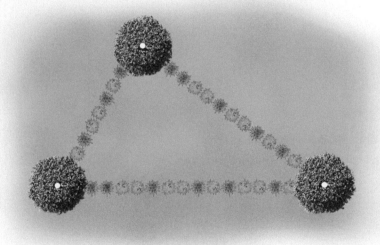

14 *Math Journal* Melissa was asked to bisect a very long line segment using a compass and a straightedge. Melissa opened the compass to the widest possible setting. She found that it was not wide enough to do the standard construction that she had learned in math class. Is it possible for Melissa to bisect the very long line segment with only her compass and a straightedge? Explain and give a suggestion.

15 *Math Journal* Copy the rectangle shown. Use the least possible number of arcs and lines to construct the perpendicular bisectors of each side of the rectangle. Explain how you know you have used the least possible number.

7.3 Constructing Triangles

Lesson Objectives

- Construct a triangle with given measures.
- Determine whether a unique triangle, more than one triangle, or no triangle can be drawn from given side lengths.

Vocabulary

included side

included angle

Construct a Triangle with Given Measures.

In earlier lessons you learned to construct figures using only a compass and straightedge. Now you will use a compass, a protractor, and a ruler to construct triangles from given information about the triangles.

> In this lesson, you will learn construction techniques that involve measurement tools such as a ruler and a protractor.

Making and labeling a quick sketch of the triangle first can help you decide how to begin your construction. The sketch can also help you check your completed drawing.

Some of the ways that you can construct a unique triangle involve knowing any of the measures of the following.

a) Two angles and an **included side**

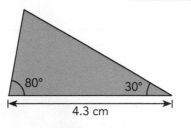

80° 30°

4.3 cm

b) Two sides and the **included angle**

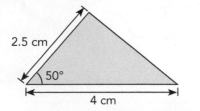

2.5 cm

50°

4 cm

Math Note

An "included side" in a triangle is the side that is common to two angles in the triangle.

An "included angle" in a triangle is the angle formed by two sides of the triangle.

> Depending on the measures you are given for a triangle, you may be able to construct one unique triangle, more than one triangle, or no triangle.

Example 6 **Construct a triangle given the lengths of all three sides.**

In triangle *ABC*, *AB* = 7 cm, *BC* = 2 cm, and *AC* = 6 cm. Use a compass and a ruler to construct triangle *ABC*.

Solution

STEP 1 Sketch the triangle.

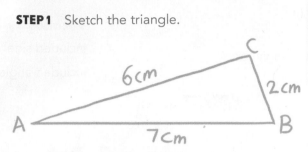

> Choose one side of the triangle to sketch first. Be sure to label the endpoints so you know where to draw the other two sides.

STEP 2 Use a ruler to draw a segment that is 7 centimeters long. Label the endpoints *A* and *B* to form $\overline{AB}$.

A ————————— B
     7 cm

STEP 3 Because *AC* = 6 centimeters, use the ruler to set the compass to a radius of 6 centimeters. Then using *A* as the center, draw an arc of radius 6 centimeters above $\overline{AB}$.

A ————————— B
     7 cm

STEP 4 Because *BC* = 2 centimeters, use the ruler to set the compass to a radius of 2 centimeters. Then using *B* as the center, draw an arc of radius 2 centimeters that intersects the first arc. Label the point of intersection as *C*.

A ————————— B
     7 cm

STEP 5 Use the ruler to draw $\overline{AC}$ and $\overline{BC}$.

6 cm   2 cm

A ————————— B
     7 cm

> The intersection of the two arcs is 6 centimeters from *A* and 2 centimeters from *B*. So, *AC* = 6 cm and *BC* = 2 cm.

Guided Practice

Construct the triangle from the given information. Use a compass and ruler.

1 Triangle *PQR*: *PQ* = 5.6 cm, *QR* = 4.5 cm, and *PR* = 8.2 cm.

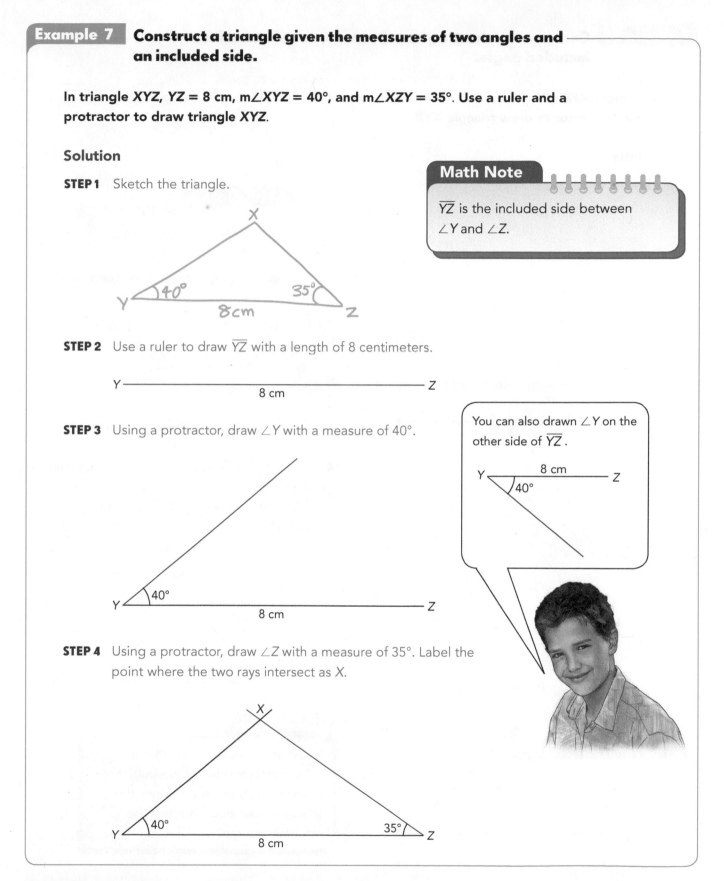

Example 7 **Construct a triangle given the measures of two angles and an included side.**

In triangle *XYZ*, *YZ* = 8 cm, m∠*XYZ* = 40°, and m∠*XZY* = 35°. Use a ruler and a protractor to draw triangle *XYZ*.

Solution

STEP 1 Sketch the triangle.

Math Note

$\overline{YZ}$ is the included side between ∠*Y* and ∠*Z*.

STEP 2 Use a ruler to draw $\overline{YZ}$ with a length of 8 centimeters.

Y —————————————— Z
8 cm

STEP 3 Using a protractor, draw ∠*Y* with a measure of 40°.

You can also drawn ∠*Y* on the other side of $\overline{YZ}$.

STEP 4 Using a protractor, draw ∠*Z* with a measure of 35°. Label the point where the two rays intersect as *X*.

Guided Practice

Construct the triangle from the given information. Use a ruler and compass.

2 Triangle *ABC*: *BC* = 4 cm, m∠*ABC* = 25°, and m∠*ACB* = 120°.

Example 8 **Construct a triangle given the measures of two sides and an included angle.**

In triangle *XYZ*, *XY* = 5 cm, *XZ* = 3.5 cm, and m∠*YXZ* = 50°. Use a compass, a ruler, and a protractor to draw triangle *XYZ*.

Solution

STEP 1 Sketch the triangle.

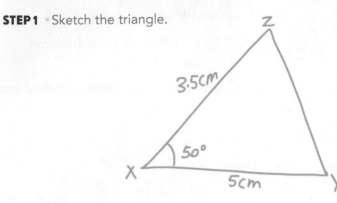

Math Note

∠*YXZ* is the included angle between sides $\overline{XZ}$ and $\overline{XY}$.

STEP 2 Use a ruler to draw $\overline{XY}$ with a length of 5 centimeters.

X ———————————— Y
5 cm

STEP 3 Using a protractor, draw ∠*X* with a measure of 50°.

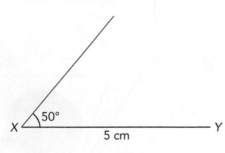

STEP 4 Because *XZ* = 3.5 centimeters, set the compass to a radius of 3.5 centimeters. Then using *X* as the center, draw an arc intersecting the ray drawn in Step 3. Label this point of intersection as *Z*.

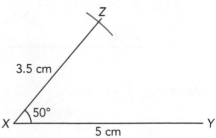

STEP 5 Draw $\overline{YZ}$.

Z
3.5 cm
50°
X   5 cm   Y

Think Math

Could you have started with the 3.5 centimeter side? How would this change the steps used to draw the triangle? How would it affect the resulting triangle?

Guided Practice

Construct the triangle from the given information. Use a compass, ruler, and protractor.

3 Triangle *KLM*: *KL* = 8.2 cm, *KM* = 6.9 cm, and m∠*LKM* = 75°.

Example 9

Construct a triangle given the measures of two sides and a nonincluded angle.

In triangle WXY, WY = 4.5 cm, WX = 2.5 cm, and m∠XYW = 25°. Use a compass, a ruler, and a protractor to draw an obtuse triangle WXY.

Solution

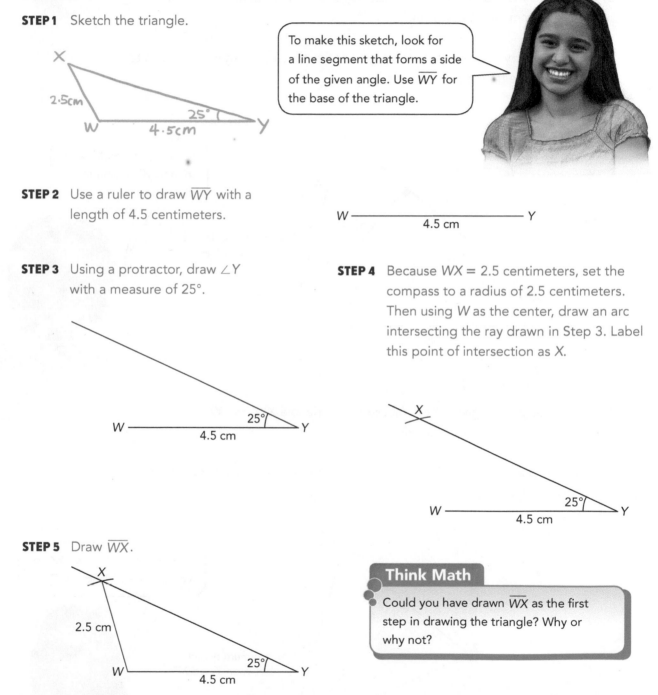

STEP 1 Sketch the triangle.

To make this sketch, look for a line segment that forms a side of the given angle. Use $\overline{WY}$ for the base of the triangle.

STEP 2 Use a ruler to draw $\overline{WY}$ with a length of 4.5 centimeters.

W ———————— Y
4.5 cm

STEP 3 Using a protractor, draw ∠Y with a measure of 25°.

STEP 4 Because WX = 2.5 centimeters, set the compass to a radius of 2.5 centimeters. Then using W as the center, draw an arc intersecting the ray drawn in Step 3. Label this point of intersection as X.

STEP 5 Draw $\overline{WX}$.

Think Math

Could you have drawn $\overline{WX}$ as the first step in drawing the triangle? Why or why not?

Guided Practice

Construct the triangle from the given information. Use a compass, ruler, and protractor.

4 Triangle KLM: KL = 7 cm, KM = 9 cm, and m∠KLM = 125°.

Identify the Conditions that Determine a Unique Triangle.

Is it always possible to draw a triangle given information about some of its measures? Do the measures you are given always produce only one triangle? Think about these examples.

a) Suppose you are given these measures for triangle XYZ: $m\angle YXZ = 40°$, $XY = 7.4$ cm, and $YZ = 3$ cm.

When you try to draw the triangle, you notice that $\overline{YZ}$ is not long enough to intersect the third side of the triangle.

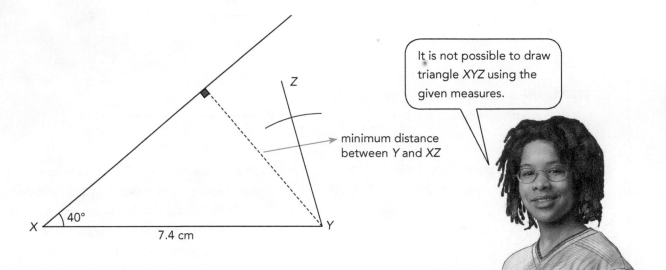

minimum distance between Y and XZ

It is not possible to draw triangle XYZ using the given measures.

b) Suppose you are given these measures for triangle XYZ: $m\angle YXZ = 40°$, $XY = 7.4$ cm, and $YZ = 5.2$ cm.

You draw $\overline{XY}$ and $\angle X$. Then, when you try to draw $\overline{YZ}$, you discover that you can draw two different triangles.

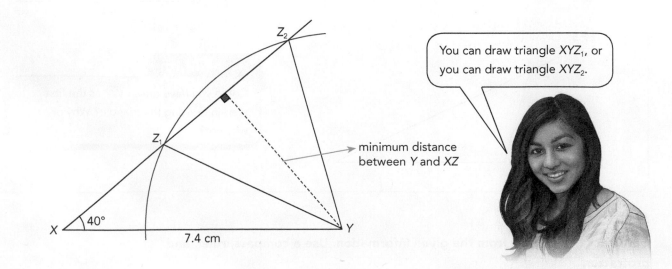

minimum distance between Y and XZ

You can draw triangle XYZ_1, or you can draw triangle XYZ_2.

Hands-On Activity

Materials:
- protactor
- compass
- ruler

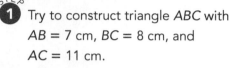
DECIDE WHETHER GIVEN MEASURES CAN BE USED TO CONSTRUCT ONE TRIANGLE, MORE THAN ONE TRIANGLE, OR NO TRIANGLES

Work in pairs.

STEP 1 Try to construct triangle ABC with $AB = 7$ cm, $BC = 8$ cm, and $AC = 11$ cm.

STEP 2 Try to construct triangle DEF with $DE = 4.6$ cm, $EF = 6$ cm, and $DF = 12$ cm.

STEP 3 Try to construct triangle GHI with $GH = 6$ cm, $HI = 5$ cm, and $m\angle GHI = 50°$.

STEP 4 Try to construct triangle JKL with $JK = 6$ cm, $JL = 4.7$ cm, and $m\angle JKL = 50°$.

STEP 5 Try to construct triangle MNP with $MN = 7$ cm, $m\angle MNP = 60°$, and $m\angle PMN = 40°$.

STEP 6 Were there any triangles you could not construct? Were there any triangles that you could construct in more than one way? Explain.

Math Journal Use your results to decide whether you can always construct exactly one triangle from the given information. Justify your answer.

a) Given three side lengths

b) Given two side lengths and an angle measure

Example 10 **Decide whether a triangle can be drawn from given information about its measures.**

Construct a triangle from the given information. Then determine the number of triangles that can be formed.

a) $AB = 8$ cm, $BC = 6.5$ cm, and $AC = 3.8$ cm.

Solution

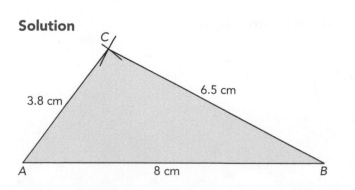

There is one unique triangle ABC.

Continue on next page

b) $XY = 7$ cm, $YZ = 5.5$ cm, and $m\angle YXZ = 50°$.

Solution

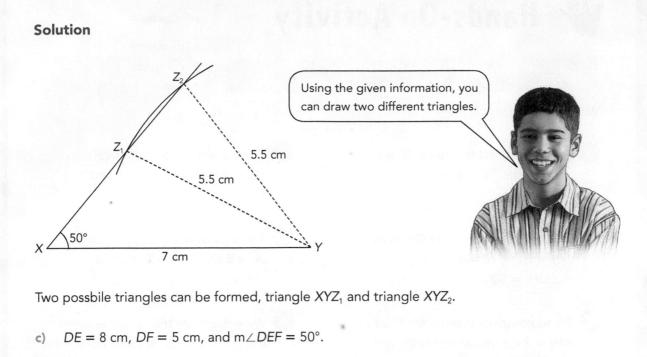

Using the given information, you can draw two different triangles.

Two possbile triangles can be formed, triangle XYZ_1 and triangle XYZ_2.

c) $DE = 8$ cm, $DF = 5$ cm, and $m\angle DEF = 50°$.

Solution

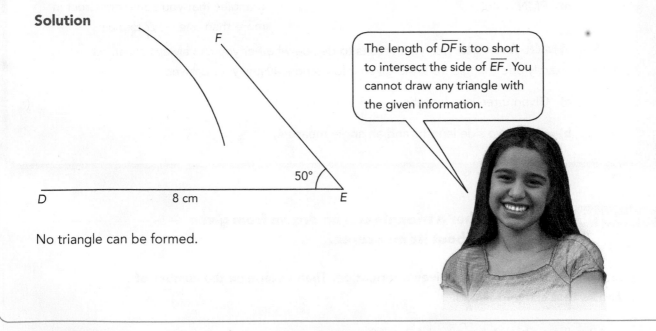

The length of $\overline{DF}$ is too short to intersect the side of $\overline{EF}$. You cannot draw any triangle with the given information.

No triangle can be formed.

Guided Practice

Find the number of triangles that can be constructed. Try constructing the triangles to make your decision.

5 $PQ = 4.8$ cm, $QR = 5.4$ cm, and $m\angle PQR = 100°$.

6 $AB = 6.2$ cm, $BC = 4.8$ cm, and $m\angle BAC = 75°$.

7 $ST = 7.7$ cm, $SU = 5.2$ cm, and $m\angle STU = 40°$.

Practice 7.3

Use the given information to construct each triangle.

1 In triangle *CDE*, *CD* = 7 cm, *DE* = 4 cm, and *CE* = 6.5 cm.

2 In triangle *ABC*, *BC* = 6 cm, m∠*ABC* = 30°, and m∠*ACB* = 60°. Find m∠*BAC* and *AC*.

3 In an equilateral triangle, each side length is 6.5 centimeters long.

4 In triangle *ABC*, *AB* = 4 cm, *AC* = 5 cm, and m∠*ABC* = 40°.

5 In triangle *ABC*, *AB* = 6 cm, *BC* = 8 cm, and *AC* = 10 cm. What kind of triangle is triangle *ABC*? Classify it by both sides and angles.

6 In triangle *XYZ*, *XY* = *XZ* = 4 cm and *YZ* = 5 cm. Find m∠*XZY*.

Solve. Show your work.

7 Triangle *PQR* has the dimensions shown in the diagram.

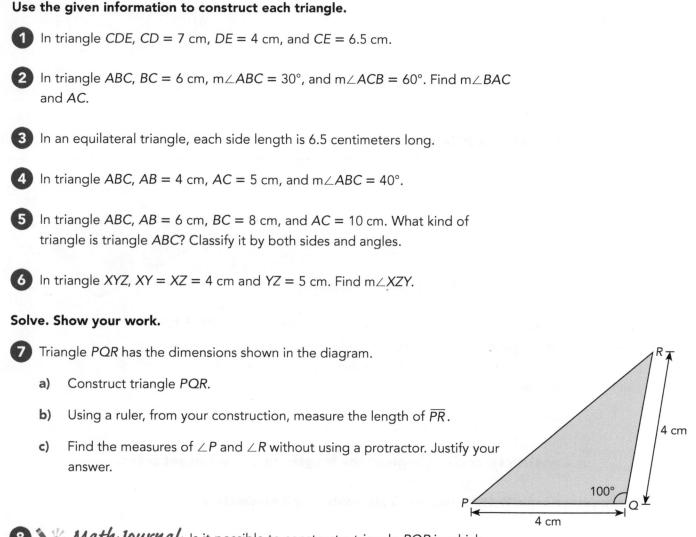

   a) Construct triangle *PQR*.

   b) Using a ruler, from your construction, measure the length of $\overline{PR}$.

   c) Find the measures of ∠*P* and ∠*R* without using a protractor. Justify your answer.

8 *Math Journal* Is it possible to construct a triangle *PQR* in which *PQ* = 12 cm, *PR* = 5 cm, and *QR* = 4 cm? Explain.

9 Three triangles have angle measures of 50° and 60°. In one triangle, the side included between these angles is 2 centimeters. In the second triangle, the included side length is 3 centimeters, and in the third triangle, the included side length is 4 centimeters.

   a) Construct the three triangles.

   b) In each triangle, what is the measure of the third angle?

   c) Using the triangles constructed to help you, what can you deduce about the number of triangles that can be constructed if you are given three angle measures of a triangle but not the measure of any side length?

10 *Math Journal* Suppose you are given three angle measures whose sum is 180°. Can you form a triangle given this information? Are there other different triangles you can form? Explain.

7.4 Constructing Quadrilaterals

Lesson Objective

- Construct a rectangle, square, rhombus, or parallelogram.

Use Properties of Quadrilaterals.

There are many types of quadrilaterals. All quadrilaterals have the following common properties:

- Four sides
- Four angles
- Two diagonals
- The sum of the measures of the four interior angles is 360°

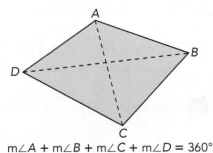

$$m\angle A + m\angle B + m\angle C + m\angle D = 360°$$

You can use a compass, a protractor, and a ruler to construct a quadrilateral. Making and labeling a quick sketch first can help you decide how to use these tools. The sketch can also help you check your completed drawing.

Example 11 Construct a rectangle given the lengths of two adjacent sides.

Construct rectangle **WXYZ** measuring 5 centimeters by 3 centimeters.

Solution

STEP 1 Sketch the rectangle.

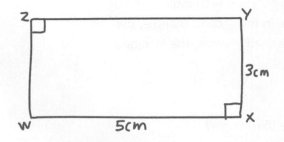

STEP 2 Use a ruler to draw $\overline{WX}$ so that it is 5 centimeters long.

W ————————— X
     5 cm

STEP 3   Using a protractor, draw ∠W with a measure of 90°.

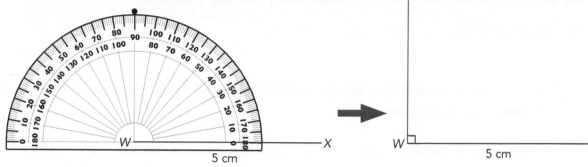

STEP 4   Because WZ = 3 centimeters, set the compass to a radius of 3 centimeters. Then using W as the center, draw an arc intersecting the ray drawn in Step 3. Label this point of intersection as Z. Because XY = 3 centimeters, use the same compass setting. Using X as the center, draw an arc as shown.

STEP 5   Because YZ = 5 centimeters, set the compass to a radius of 5 centimeters. Then using Z as the center, draw an arc to intersect the arc drawn in Step 4. Label this point of intersection as Y.

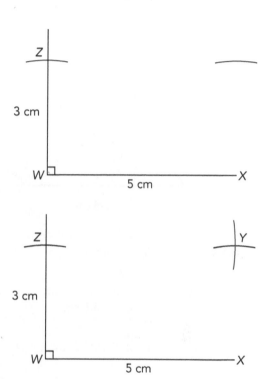

STEP 6   Draw $\overline{YZ}$ and $\overline{XY}$.

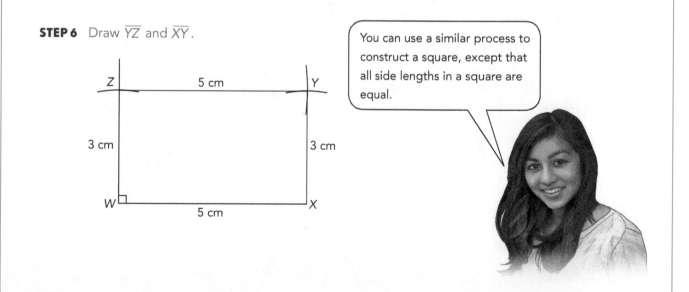

You can use a similar process to construct a square, except that all side lengths in a square are equal.

Guided Practice

Construct the quadrilateral from the given dimension. Use a ruler and protractor.

1 Rectangle *ABCD* measuring 7 centimeters by 5 centimeters.

Example 12 **Construct a parallelogram given the lengths of the adjacent sides and an included angle.**

Construct parallelogram *WXYZ* with *WX* = 5.5 cm, *XY* = 4 cm, and m∠*WXY* = 120°.

Solution

STEP 1 Sketch the parallelogram.

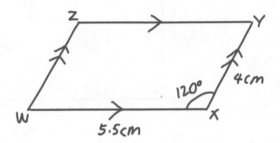

STEP 2 Use a ruler to draw $\overline{WX}$ so that it is 5.5 centimeters long.

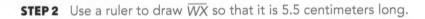

W ——————————————— X
5.5 cm

STEP 3 Using a protractor, draw ∠*X* with a measure of 120°.

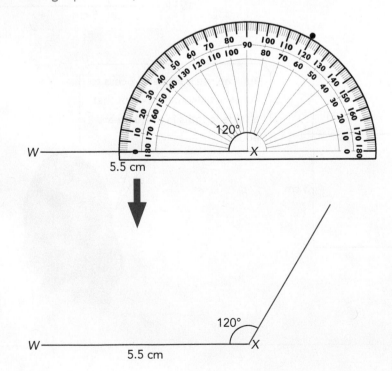

STEP 4 Because $XY = 4$ centimeters, set the compass to a radius of 4 centimeters. Then using X as the center, draw an arc intersecting the ray drawn in Step 3. Label this point of intersection as Y. Because $WZ = 4$ centimeters, use the same compass setting. Using W as the center, draw an arc as shown.

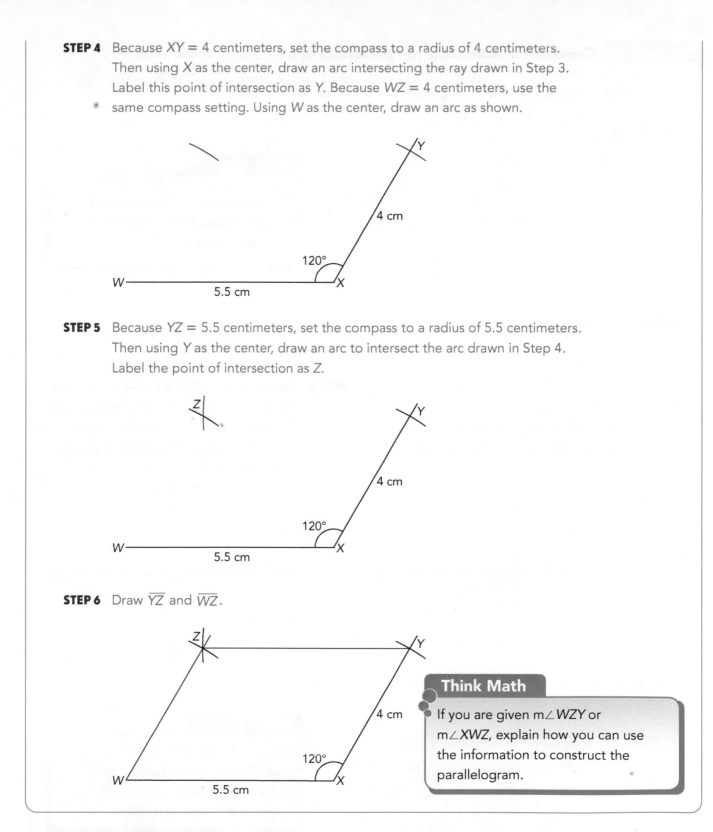

STEP 5 Because $YZ = 5.5$ centimeters, set the compass to a radius of 5.5 centimeters. Then using Y as the center, draw an arc to intersect the arc drawn in Step 4. Label the point of intersection as Z.

STEP 6 Draw $\overline{YZ}$ and $\overline{WZ}$.

Think Math

If you are given m∠*WZY* or m∠*XWZ*, explain how you can use the information to construct the parallelogram.

Guided Practice

Construct the quadrilateral from the given information. Use a compass, ruler, and protractor.

2 Parallelogram *KLMN*: $KL = 6.4$ cm, $LM = 4.8$ cm, and m∠*KLM* = 60°.

Construct rhombus *ABCD* with diagonal *AC* = 6 cm and *AB* = 3.5 cm.

Solution

STEP 1 Sketch the rhombus.

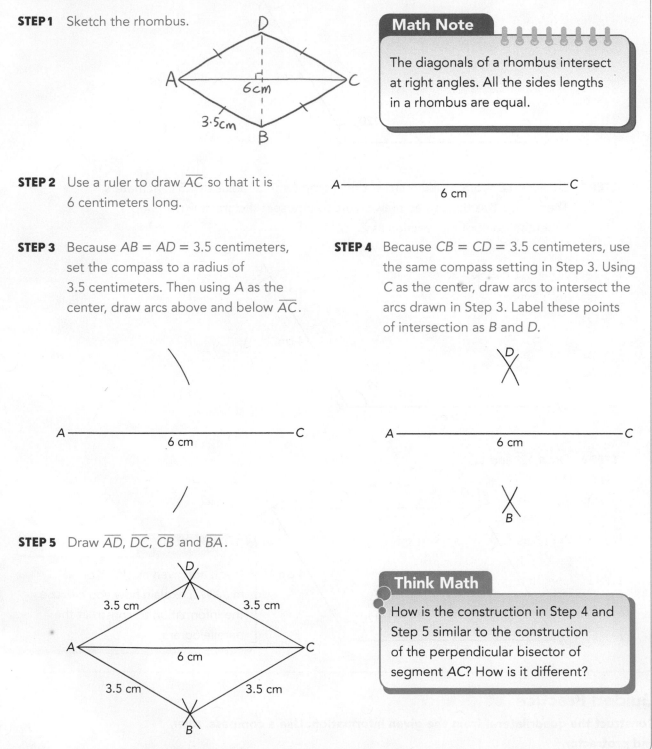

Math Note

The diagonals of a rhombus intersect at right angles. All the sides lengths in a rhombus are equal.

STEP 2 Use a ruler to draw $\overline{AC}$ so that it is 6 centimeters long.

A ———————————— C
6 cm

STEP 3 Because *AB* = *AD* = 3.5 centimeters, set the compass to a radius of 3.5 centimeters. Then using *A* as the center, draw arcs above and below $\overline{AC}$.

A ———————————— C
6 cm

STEP 4 Because *CB* = *CD* = 3.5 centimeters, use the same compass setting in Step 3. Using *C* as the center, draw arcs to intersect the arcs drawn in Step 3. Label these points of intersection as *B* and *D*.

A ———————————— C
6 cm

STEP 5 Draw $\overline{AD}, \overline{DC}, \overline{CB}$ and $\overline{BA}$.

Think Math

How is the construction in Step 4 and Step 5 similar to the construction of the perpendicular bisector of segment *AC*? How is it different?

Guided Practice

Construct the quadrilateral from the given information. Use a ruler, compass, and protractor.

3 Rhombus *PQRS* with diagonal *PR* = 6.2 cm and *PQ* = 4.5 cm.

Practice 7.4

Construct each quadrilateral from the given information.

1 Rectangle *KLMN* measuring 5.3 centimeters by 4.7 centimeters.

2 Square with side lengths of 7 centimeters.

3 Rhombus *DEFG* with diagonal *DF* = 6 cm and *DE* = 4.5 cm.

4 Parallelogram *PQRS* with *PQ* = 3.8 cm, *QR* = 5 cm, and m∠*QPS* = 70°.

5 Quadrilateral *ABCD* with *AB* = 6.7 cm, *BC* = 7.2 cm, *AD* = 4.9 cm, *CD* = 6.2 cm, and m∠*ABC* = 55°.

Solve. Show your work.

6 Construct quadrilateral *ABCD* with diagonal *AC* = 5 cm, *AB* = *CD* = 4 cm, *BC* = 6 cm, and *AD* = 6 cm.

    a) What type of quadrilateral is *ABCD*? Explain your reasoning.

    b) Draw $\overline{BD}$ to intersect $\overline{AC}$ at point *E*. Find the lengths of $\overline{AE}$, $\overline{CE}$, $\overline{BE}$, and $\overline{DE}$.

    c) Do the diagonals $\overline{AC}$ and $\overline{BD}$ bisect each other? Justify your answer.

7 Construct a quadrilateral *STUV* by following Steps 1 to 5.

    STEP 1 Draw $\overline{ST}$ so that *ST* = 5 cm.
    STEP 2 With *T* as the center, draw $\overline{TU}$ perpendicular to $\overline{ST}$, with *TU* = 4 cm.
    STEP 3 With *U* as the center, draw an arc of radius 5 centimeters.
    STEP 4 With *S* as the center, draw an arc of radius 4 centimeters to intersect the arc drawn in Step 3. Label this point of intersection as *V*.
    STEP 5 Complete the construction of quadrilateral *STUV*.

    a) Find each of the angles in quadrilateral *STUV*.

    b) Name the quadrilateral.

    c) Find the lengths of the diagonals. What do you notice?

8 Construct a quadrilateral *ABCD* with all sides of length 3 centimeters and diagonal *BD* = 5.2 cm.

    a) What type of quadrilateral is *ABCD*? Explain your reasoning.

    b) Find the measure of each of the angles formed by the intersection of the diagonals.

9 Construct quadrilateral ABCD with diagonal AC = 6 cm, AB = 3 cm, BC = 4 cm, CD = 4.5 cm, and AD = 9 cm. What type of quadrilateral does ABCD seem to be? Explain your reasoning.

10 Construct the figure below using the given dimensions.

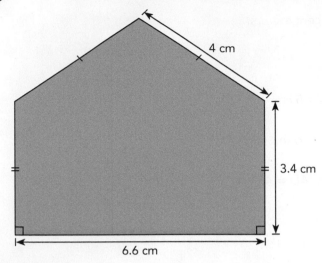

11 **a)** Construct quadrilateral ABCD with AB = 6 cm, BC = 3 cm, AD = 4 cm, m∠BAD = 120°, and m∠ABC = 100°.

b) Find the length of $\overline{CD}$.

c) Label the midpoints of the four sides of this quadrilateral as W, X, Y, and Z. Join them to form quadrilateral WXYZ.

d) Compare the lengths of $\overline{WX}$ and $\overline{YZ}$. Compare the lengths of $\overline{XY}$ and $\overline{WZ}$. What do you notice?

12 Construct parallelogram PQRS with PQ = 6 cm, a height of 4.5 centimeters and interior angles 45° and 135°.

13 Draw rhombus ABCD with AC = 5 cm and AB = 6.5 cm. Also draw diagonal $\overline{BD}$. How are the two diagonals related to each other? Explain.

14 Jenny plans to make a trapezoidal bookmark for each of her teachers. The top will be 5 centimeters long and have right angles at either end. The right side will be 12 centimeters long, and the bottom of the bookmark will make a 50° angle with this side. Construct a template for Jenny's bookmark. How long is the left side of Jenny's template to the nearest centimeter?

15 Martha plans to cut squares of paper from a roll of wrapping paper. She will package the squares to sell as origami papers to raise funds for a charity. If the area of the square paper is 64 square centimeters, construct the square Martha can use as a template.

16 Jessie plans to make a patchwork pattern from colored paper by repeating a rhombus whose diagonals measure 4 centimeters and 5 centimeters. Use the given dimensions to construct a template for the rhombus.

7.5 Understanding Scale Drawings

Lesson Objectives
- Identify the scale factor in diagrams.
- Solve problems involving scale drawings of geometric figures.

Vocabulary

scale

scale factor

Recognize Scale Drawings.

Geometric constructions and scale drawings are closely related to each other in real life. For example, engineers and designers use geometric principles and constructions to make actual-sized drawings of objects like machine components or pieces for do-it-yourself assembly kits.

However, it is not always possible to draw an object at its actual size. You may need to use a scale drawing that shows the object at a larger or a smaller size. Floor plans and maps are examples of scale drawings. You might also find a scale drawing in the instructions for sewing a dress from a pattern.

In this lesson, you will learn about scale so that you can read and interpret scale drawings.

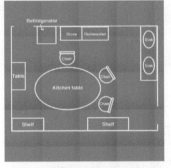

Blueprints

Dress patterns

Maps

Understand Scale and Scale Factor.

The scale of a scale drawing is a comparison of a length in the drawing to the corresponding length in the actual object. In the scale drawing of a deck shown at the right, the scale is 1 inch = 10 feet. The same scale can be written as 1 inch : 10 feet, or 1 inch to 10 feet.

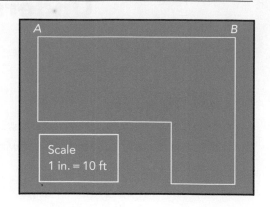

The scale factor of a scale drawing is the ratio of a length in the drawing to the corresponding length in the actual figure. The two lengths are expressed in the same units. You can find the scale factor for the drawing shown by remembering that 1 foot = 12 inches, and rewriting 10 feet as 120 inches.

$$\text{Scale factor} = \frac{1}{120}$$

The scale factor is sometimes called the constant of proportionality.

Example 14 **Calculate a scale factor.**

Using a photocopier, you want to reduce this poster to the smaller size shown. What percent reduction should you choose?

Solution

The 30-inch length of the poster is to be 6 inches in the reduction. The 20-inch height is to be 4 inches in the reduction. Find the scale factor of the reduction. Then write the scale factor as a percent.

$$\text{Scale factor} = \frac{6 \text{ in.}}{30 \text{ in.}} \longrightarrow \begin{array}{l} \text{Reduced length} \\ \text{Actual length} \end{array}$$

$$= \frac{1}{5}$$

$$= 20\%$$

Caution ///////

Remember that the first length in a scale or scale factor is the length in the scale drawing. The second length is the length in the original figure.

You need to reduce it to 20% of its original size.

> You can check your answer by multiplying the scale factor by the height of the original poster. You should get the height of the reduced copy.
>
> $20 \cdot \dfrac{1}{5} = 4$ in.

Guided Practice

Calculate the scale factor.

1. In the diagram, trapezoid B has been enlarged to produce trapezoid A. Find the scale factor.

   Length of A = <u>?</u> cm

   Length of B = <u>?</u> cm

   Scale factor = $\dfrac{\text{Scaled length}}{\text{Original length}}$

   $= \dfrac{?}{?}$

   $= ?$

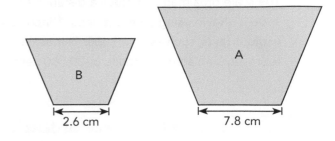

B
2.6 cm

A
7.8 cm

✋ # Hands-On Activity

Materials:
- different sizes of grid paper
- ruler

REDRAW A GIVEN FIGURE ON GRID PAPER AT A DIFFERENT SCALE

Work in pairs.

The drawing shows a figure formed by nine squares and a triangle enclosed in a polygon. You can use different-sized grids to produce the same drawing at different scales.

^{STEP}
1 Use two different-sized grids. Redraw the figure on one grid. Have your partner redraw the figure on another grid.

^{STEP}
2 Use a ruler to measure a length in the original drawing. Measure the corresponding length in your scale drawings. Then find the scale factor for each drawing. You can use the following to calculate the scale factor:

$$\frac{\text{Length in reduced or enlarged drawing}}{\text{Length in original drawing}}$$

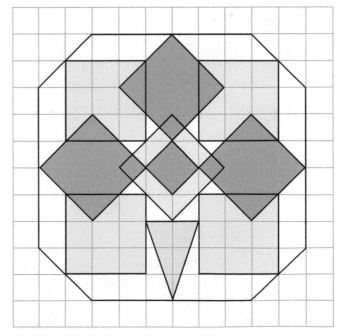

Use Map Scales.

The scale on a map compares a distance on the map to an actual distance. Often the scale is shown using different units: 1 inch : 24 meters. Sometimes a map scale is written without units, such as 1 : 20,000. This scale factor means that 1 centimeter on a map represents an actual distance of 20,000 centimeters.

Example 15 | **Calculate an actual distance from the scale of a map.**

The scale of a map 1 inch : 25 miles. If the length of Whitley Road on the map is 4.4 inches, find the actual length of Whitley Road, in miles.

Solution

1 inch : 25 miles means 1 inch on the map represents 25 miles on the ground.
Map scale = Map length : Actual length

Let x miles be the actual length of Whitley Road.
1 inch : 25 miles = 4.4 inches : x miles

$$\frac{1 \text{ in.}}{25 \text{ mi}} = \frac{4.4 \text{ in.}}{x \text{ mi}} \qquad \text{Write ratios in fraction form.}$$

$$\frac{1}{25} = \frac{4.4}{x} \qquad \text{Write without units.}$$

$$1 \cdot x = 25 \cdot (4.4) \qquad \text{Write cross products.}$$

$$x = 110 \qquad \text{Simplify.}$$

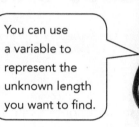
You can use a variable to represent the unknown length you want to find.

The actual length of Whitley Road is 110 miles.

Guided Practice

Complete.

2 The scale of a map is 1 inch : 15 miles. If the distance on the map between John's home and his school is 0.6 inch, find the actual distance in miles.

____?__ : __?__ means __?__.

Let x miles be the actual distance.
1 inch : 15 miles = 0.6 inch : x miles

$$\frac{1 \text{ in.}}{15 \text{ mi}} = \frac{0.6 \text{ in.}}{x \text{ mi}} \qquad \text{Write ratios in fraction form.}$$

$$\frac{1}{15} = \frac{0.6}{x} \qquad \text{Write without units.}$$

$$1 \cdot x = \underline{} \cdot \underline{} \qquad \text{Write cross products.}$$

$$x = \underline{} \qquad \text{Simplify.}$$

The actual distance is __?__ miles.

Example 16 **Calculate the distance on a map from the original distance.**

The actual distance between Mr. Herd's office and his home is 120 miles. A map that shows his office and his home uses the scale 1 inch : 50 miles. How far apart on the map are Mr. Herd's office and his home?

Solution

1 inch : 50 miles means 1 inch on the map represents 50 miles on the ground.
Map scale = Map length: Actual length

Let y inches be the length on the map.
1 inch : 50 miles = y inches : 120 miles

$$\frac{1 \text{ in.}}{50 \text{ mi}} = \frac{y \text{ in.}}{120 \text{ mi}}$$ Write ratios in fraction form.

$$\frac{1}{50} = \frac{y}{120}$$ Write without units.

$$50y = 120$$ Write cross products.

$$\frac{50y}{50} = \frac{120}{50}$$ Divide both sides by 50.

$$y = 2.4$$ Simplify.

On the map, Mr. Herd's office and his home are 2.4 inches apart.

Guided Practice

Complete.

3 The actual distance between Boston and New York is 220 miles. The scale on a particular map is 1 inch : 25 miles. How far apart on the map are the two cities?

1 inch : 25 miles means 1 inch on the map represents 25 miles on the ground.

Let x inches be the length on the map.
1 inch : 25 miles = x inches : 220 miles

$$\frac{1 \text{ in.}}{25 \text{ mi}} = \frac{x \text{ in.}}{220 \text{ mi}}$$ Write ratios in fraction form.

$$\frac{1}{25} = \frac{x}{220}$$ Write without units.

$$\underline{\quad?\quad} x = \underline{\quad?\quad}$$ Write cross products.

$$\frac{?}{?} x = \frac{?}{?}$$ Divide both sides by $\underline{\ ?\ }$.

$$x = \underline{\quad?\quad}$$ Simplify.

On the map, the two cities are $\underline{\ ?\ }$ apart.

Example 17 **Calculate the actual length from a scale drawing.**

An S scale (or S gauge) model train is a scaled model of an actual train. All the cars are built on a scale of 1 : 64. The length of an S scale locomotive is 8 inches long. The length of an S scale coal tender is 5 inches. Find the actual lengths of the locomotive and the coal tender in feet. Round your answer to the nearest tenth.

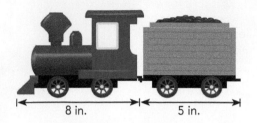

8 in.   5 in.

Solution

Let x be the actual length of the locomotive, and y be the actual length of the coal tender.

1 : 64 = Scaled length of the locomotive : Actual length of the locomotive

$1 : 64 = 8 : x$	Substitute values.
$\dfrac{1}{64} = \dfrac{8}{x}$	Write ratios in fraction form.
$x = 8 \cdot 64$	Write cross products.
$x = 512$	Simplify.

$12 \text{ in.} = 1 \text{ ft}$

$512 \text{ in.} = \dfrac{1}{12} \cdot 512$

$\approx 42.7 \text{ ft}$

The actual length of the locomotive is about 42.7 feet.

1 : 64 = Scaled length of coal tender : Actual length of coal tender

$1 : 64 = 5 : y$	Substitute values.
$\dfrac{1}{64} = \dfrac{5}{y}$	Write ratios in fraction form.
$y = 5 \cdot 64$	Write cross products.
$y = 320$	Simplify.

$12 \text{ in.} = 1 \text{ ft}$

$320 \text{ in.} = \dfrac{1}{12} \cdot 320$

$\approx 26.7 \text{ ft}$

Remember to write the ratios in the same order when you set up your proportion.

The actual length of the coal tender is about 26.7 feet.

Guided Practice

Calculate.

4 A model car is built using a scale of 1 : 18. The length of the model car is 12 inches. Find the actual length of the car in feet.

Hands-On Activity

Work individually.

A square that has a side length of 1 centimeter has an area of 1 square centimeter. In this activity, you will explore how enlarging such a square by a scale factor affects its area.

STEP 1 Suppose you enlarge the square by a factor of 2. Find the side length and the area of the resulting square.

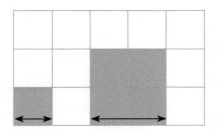

Length of square = __?__ cm
(twice the original length)

Area of square = __?__ cm²
(increased by a factor of 4)

STEP 2 Suppose you enlarge the square by a factor of 3. Find the side length and the area of the resulting square.

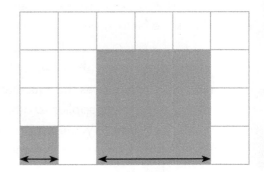

Length of square = __?__ cm
(three times the original length)

Area of square = __?__ cm²
(increased by a factor of 9)

STEP 3 Suppose you enlarge the square by a factor of 4. Find the side length and the area of the resulting square.

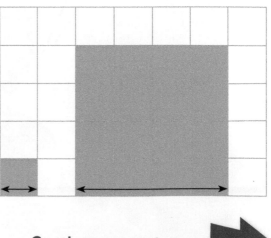

Length of square = __?__ cm
(four times the original length)

Area of square = __?__ cm²
(increased by a factor of __?__)

Continue on next page →

STEP

4 Copy and complete the table.

Scale Factor	Length	Area
1	1 cm	$1 \cdot 1 = 1 \text{ cm}^2$
2	2 cm	$2 \cdot 2 = 2^2 = 4 \text{ cm}^2$
3	3 cm	$\underline{\ ?\ } \cdot \underline{\ ?\ } = \underline{\ ?\ } \text{ cm}^2$
4	$\underline{\ ?\ }$ cm	$\underline{\ ?\ } \cdot \underline{\ ?\ } = \underline{\ ?\ } \text{ cm}^2$
5	$\underline{\ ?\ }$ cm	$\underline{\ ?\ } \cdot \underline{\ ?\ } = \underline{\ ?\ } \text{ cm}^2$
k	$\underline{\ ?\ }$ cm	$\underline{\ ?\ } \cdot \underline{\ ?\ } = \underline{\ ?\ } \text{ cm}^2$

Copy and complete.

a) Increasing the length of a square by a factor of 5 increases the area by a factor of $\underline{\ ?\ }$.

b) Increasing the length of a square by scale factor k increases the area by a factor of $\underline{\ ?\ }$.

Math Journal Compare the side lengths and the areas for the various scale factors. What pattern do you observe?

From the above activity, the area of a square increases as the square of the scale factor. This property applies to other two-dimensional figures. If you enlarge a figure by a scale factor of 3, its area will be enlarged by a scale of $3^2 = 9$.

Interpret Areas in Scale Drawings.

You have seen that a map scale of 1 : 10 means that a length of 1 centimeter on the map corresponds to an actual length of 10 centimeters. On such a map, an area of 1 square centimeter corresponds to an actual area of $10 \cdot 10 = 100$ square centimeters.

A scale of 1 inch : 9 feet on a map means that 1 inch on the map corresponds to an actual length of 9 feet. On such a map, an area of 1 square inch corresponds to an actual area of $9 \cdot 9 = 81$ square feet.

Example 18 **Calculate the actual area from a scale drawing.**

The scale on a map is 1 inch : 4 feet. The map shows a garden, and on the map the area of the garden is 8 square inches. Find the actual area of the garden.

Solution

Map length : Actual length = 1 in. : 4 ft
Map area : Actual area = $1\ \text{in}^2 : 4^2\ \text{ft}^2$

Let x represent the actual area of the garden in square feet.

$$\frac{\text{Area of garden on map}}{\text{Actual area of garden}} = \frac{1}{16} \qquad \text{Write a proportion.}$$

$$\frac{8}{x} = \frac{1}{16} \qquad \text{Substitute.}$$

$$x = 8 \cdot 16 \qquad \text{Write the cross products.}$$

$$x = 128 \qquad \text{Simplify.}$$

You can write a proportion using the ratio of the areas to find the value of x.

The actual area of the garden is 128 square feet.

Guided Practice

Complete.

5 Sylvia makes a map of her yard. On a map, 1 inch represents 8 feet. On the map, the area of a patch of grass is 12 square inches. Find the actual area of the patch of grass.

Map length : Actual length = _?_ : _?_

Map area : Actual area = _?_ : _?_

Let y represent the actual area of the patch of grass in square feet.

$$\frac{\text{Area of patch of grass on map}}{\text{Actual area of patch of grass}} = \frac{1}{64} \qquad \text{Write a proportion.}$$

$$\frac{?}{?} = \frac{?}{?} \qquad \text{Substitute.}$$

$$y = \underline{\ ?\ } \cdot \underline{\ ?\ } \qquad \text{Write the cross products.}$$

$$y = \underline{\ ?\ } \qquad \text{Simplify.}$$

The actual area of the grass patch is _?_ square feet.

Example 19 **Calculate an area given the actual area and a scale.**

The actual floor area of an auditorium is 4,500 square feet. Jim needs to make a scale drawing of the auditorium to calculate the cost of carpeting the floor. He uses a scale of 1 inch : 25 feet. Find the area of the floor in Jim's scale drawing.

Solution

Drawing length : Actual length = 1 in. : 25 ft

Drawing area : Actual area = $1 \text{ in}^2 : 25^2 \text{ ft}^2$

Let x represent the area of the floor in the scale drawing in square inches.

$$\frac{\text{Area of floor on scale drawing}}{\text{Actual area of floor}} = \frac{1}{625} \qquad \text{Write a proportion.}$$

$$\frac{x}{4,500} = \frac{1}{625} \qquad \text{Substitute.}$$

$$625 \cdot x = 4,500 \qquad \text{Write cross products.}$$

$$\frac{625x}{625} = \frac{4,500}{625} \qquad \text{Divide both sides by 625.}$$

$$x = 7.2 \qquad \text{Simplify.}$$

The floor area in the scale drawing is 7.2 square inches.

Guided Practice

Copy and complete.

 A blueprint is a type of scale drawing used by architects. An architect is making a blueprint for a conference room that will have a floor area of 196 square feet. If the scale on the blueprint is 1 inch : 7 feet, find the area of the conference room floor on the blueprint.

Blueprint length : Actual length = __?__ : __?__

Blueprint area : Actual area = __?__ : __?__

Let y represent the area of the conference room on the blueprint in square inches.

$$\frac{\text{Area of room on blueprint}}{\text{Actual area of room}} = \frac{?}{?} \qquad \text{Write a proportion.}$$

$$\frac{?}{?} = \frac{?}{?} \qquad \text{Substitute.}$$

$$\underline{\quad?\quad} = \underline{\quad?\quad} \qquad \text{Write cross products.}$$

$$\frac{?}{?} = \frac{?}{?} \qquad \text{Divide both sides by } \underline{\ ?\ }.$$

$$\underline{\quad?\quad} = \underline{\quad?\quad} \qquad \text{Simplify.}$$

The floor area of the conference room on the blueprint is __?__ square inches.

Practice 7.5

Solve. Show your work.

1 A model of a ship is 6 inches long.
The actual ship is 550 feet (6,600 inches).
Find the scale factor used for the model.

6 in.

2 On a blueprint, the length of a wall is 5 inches. The actual length of the wall is 85 feet. What scale is used for the blueprint?

3 An artist made a painting of a water pitcher.
Then the artist reduced the size of the painting.
Find the scale factor of the reduction.

12 in.

8 in.

4 The height of a building in a drawing is 15 inches. If the actual height of the building is 165 feet, find the scale factor of the drawing.

5 In a scale drawing, a sofa is 3 inches long. If the actual length of the sofa is 5 feet long, find the scale factor.

6 Daniel is making a scale drawing of his classroom for a project. The length of his classroom is 30 feet long. In his drawing, the length of the classroom is 6 inches. Find the scale factor of Daniel's drawing.

7 Two cities are 7 inches apart on a map. If the scale of the map is 0.5 inch : 3 miles, what is the actual distance between the two cities?

8 A road map of New Orleans uses a scale of 1 inch : 3 miles. If Carlton Avenue is 1.3 inches long on the map, what is the actual length of the street?

9 The scale of a map is 1 inch : 85 miles.

a) On the map, the river is 14 inches long. Find the actual length of the river in miles.

b) The actual distance between two towns is 765 miles. Find the distance on the map between these towns.

10 Goodhope River is 48 miles long. What is the length of the river on a map with a scale of 1 inch : 15 miles?

11 A map is drawn using a scale of 1 inch : 165 miles. The length of a road on the map is 12 inches. Find the actual length of the road.

12 On a particular map, 2 inches represents an actual distance of 64 miles. Towns A and B are 608 miles apart. Find the distance between the two towns, in inches, on the map.

13 On a particular map, 1 inch represents an actual distance of 2.5 miles. The actual area of a lake is 12 square miles. Find the area of the lake on the map.

14 On the map, the area of a nature preserve is 54.2 square inches. If the scale of the map is 1 inch : 8 miles, find the actual area of the nature preserve.

15 The map shows two roads labeled A and B.

a) Using a ruler, measure, in centimeters, the lengths of roads A and B.

b) Using the scale given, find, in kilometers, the actual lengths of roads A and B.

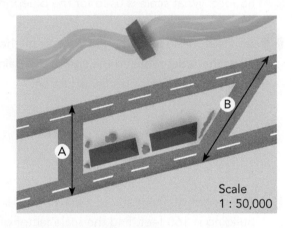

Scale
1 : 50,000

16 The map shows seven cities in Florida. Using the scale on the map, use a ruler to measure the distance between the following pairs of cities. Then find the actual distance between them in miles.

a) Orlando and West Palm Beach

b) Fort Myers and Miami Beach

17 Use the scale on the floor plan of a house to find each of the following.

a) The actual length and width of room 1.

b) The width of the door on the floor plan if its actual width is 0.8 meter.

c) The actual area of the floor of the house to the nearest square meter.

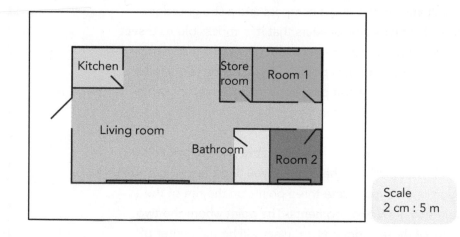

Scale
2 cm : 5 m

18 A tower is drawn using a scale of 1 inch : 3 feet. The height of the tower in the drawing is 1 foot 5 inches. Then, an architect decides to make a new scale drawing of the tower. In the new scale, the scale is 1 inch : 5 feet. Find the height of the tower in the new drawing.

19 Each student walked in a straight line from one point to another. Use a centimeter ruler to measure distances on the map shown. Use the scale on the map to find the distance each student walked in meters.

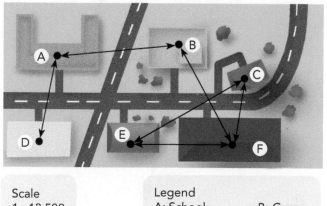

Scale
1 : 12,500

Legend
A: School   B: Gym
C: Restaurant   D: Library
E: Movie theater F: Motel

a) Ethan walked from the library to the school, and then to the gym.

b) Joshua walked from the motel to the restaurant, and then to the movie theater.

c) Chloe walked from the gym to the motel, and then to the movie theater.

Brain @ Work

1. You know you can bisect any angle using a compass and a straightedge. Geometers have known for thousands of years that it is impossible to trisect any given angle using a compass and straightedge. (The word *trisect* means to divide into three equal parts.) But it is possible to trisect certain angles, including a right angle. Using only a compass and straightedge, show how you can draw a right angle that is trisected.

2. You accidentally broke your mother's favorite plate. You want to ask an artist to reproduce it. You ask your math teacher to help you find the original size of the plate. She suggests that you locate three points on the rim of the plate and use the points to draw two segments. The point where the two perpendicular bisectors of these segments intersect will be the center of the plate. From that you can measure the radius. Copy and complete the diagram below. Then measure to find the diameter of the plate.

Chapter Wrap Up

Concept Map

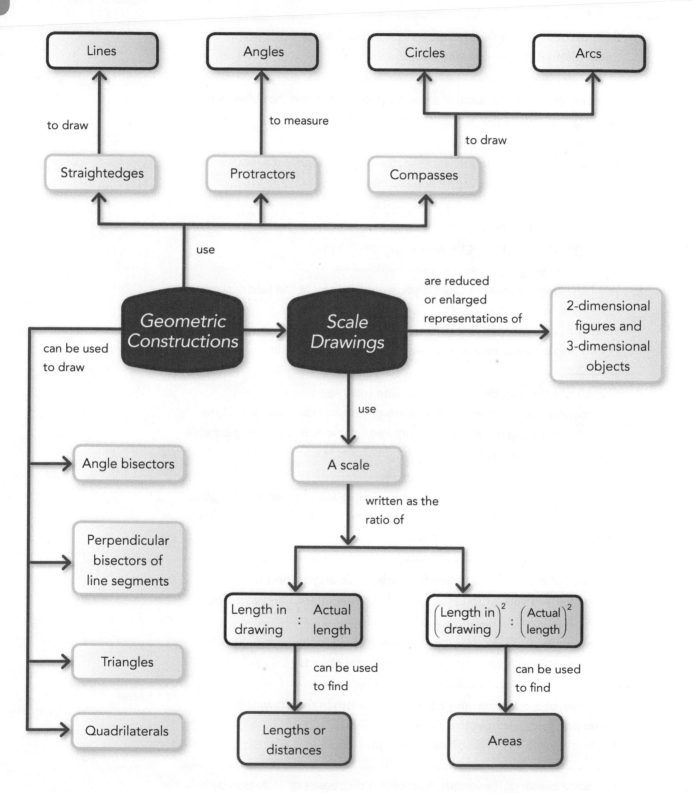

Key Concepts

▶ An angle bisector is a ray that divides the angle into two angles with equal measures.

▶ Each point on an angle bisector is equidistant from any two points on the angle that are equidistant from the vertex.

▶ The perpendicular bisector of a line segment is the line that bisects the line segment and is perpendicular to it.

▶ Any point on the perpendicular bisector of a line segment is equidistant from the two endpoints of the line segment.

▶ You can draw a triangle given the lengths of three sides or certain combinations of side lengths and angle measures.

▶ You can draw a unique triangle if you are given any of the following:
  • lengths of the three sides
  • lengths of two sides and the measure of the included angle
  • two angle measures and the length of the included side.

▶ Sometimes you can draw more than one triangle using the given information about a triangle. If you are given two side lengths and the measure of an angle not included between those sides, you may be able to draw two triangles.

▶ Sometimes you cannot draw a triangle given a set of three side lengths. You can only draw a triangle if the sum of the lengths of any two sides is less than the length of the third side.

▶ All types of quadrilaterals have four sides, four angles, and two diagonals. The sum of the measures of the four interior angles is 360°.

▶ Scale drawings are used to represent reductions or enlargements of two-dimensional figures or three-dimensional objects.

▶ The scale of a scale drawing compares a length in the drawing to the corresponding length in the object.
Scale = Length in drawing : Actual length

▶ In a scale drawing, if a length in an object decreases or increases by a factor of k, then the area of the object decreases or increases by a factor of k^2.

Chapter Review/Test

Concepts and Skills

Construct the angle bisector of ∠ABC on a copy of each figure using a compass and straightedge.

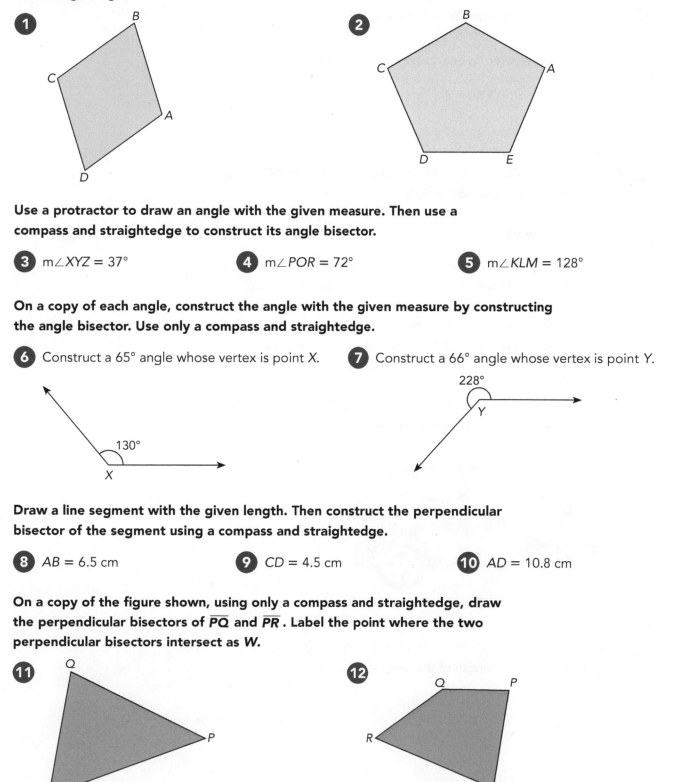

1 B, C, A, D

2 B, C, A, D, E

Use a protractor to draw an angle with the given measure. Then use a compass and straightedge to construct its angle bisector.

3 m∠XYZ = 37°

4 m∠POR = 72°

5 m∠KLM = 128°

On a copy of each angle, construct the angle with the given measure by constructing the angle bisector. Use only a compass and straightedge.

6 Construct a 65° angle whose vertex is point X.

7 Construct a 66° angle whose vertex is point Y.

228°
Y

130°
X

Draw a line segment with the given length. Then construct the perpendicular bisector of the segment using a compass and straightedge.

8 AB = 6.5 cm

9 CD = 4.5 cm

10 AD = 10.8 cm

On a copy of the figure shown, using only a compass and straightedge, draw the perpendicular bisectors of $\overline{PQ}$ and $\overline{PR}$. Label the point where the two perpendicular bisectors intersect as W.

11 Q, P, R

12 Q, P, R, S

Use the given information to find the number of triangles that can be constructed. Try constructing the triangles to make your decision.

13. Triangle *WXY*: *WX* = 4.5 cm, m∠*XWY* = 60°, and m∠*WXY* = 40°.

14. Triangle *ABC*: *AB* = 5 cm, *AC* = 4.5 cm, and m∠*CAB* = 60°.

15. Triangle *DEF*: *DE* = 4 cm, *EF* = 3 cm, and *DF* = 8 cm.

Use the given information to construct each quadrilateral.

16. Rhombus *DEFG* with diagonal *DF* = 4.2 cm and *DE* = 5 cm.

17. Parallelogram *ABCD* with *AB* = 7 cm, *DA* = 4.5 cm, and m∠*ABC* = 50°.

18. Quadrilateral *ABCD* such that *AB* = 5 cm, *AD* = 3.5 cm, *BC* = 4 cm, m∠*BAD* = 60°, and m∠*ABC* = 90°.

Solve. Show your work.

19. A rectangular garden is 15 meters long and 9 meters wide. Use a scale of 1 centimeter to 3 meters, make a scale drawing of the garden.

20. The scale of the floor plan of a room is 1 inch : 6.5 feet. On the floor plan, the room is 8 inches long and 6 inches wide. What are the actual dimensions of the room?

21. A model of a car is made using the scale 1 : 25. The actual length of the car is 4.8 meters. Calculate the length of the model of the car in centimeters.

22. The scale on a map is 1 inch : 120 miles. On the map, a highway is 5 inches long. Find the actual length of the highway in miles.

Problem Solving

Solve.

23 Joe constructed an isosceles triangle *WXY* such that *WX* = *WY* = 5 cm and *XY* = 4 cm. Construct another isosceles triangle *ABC* such that *AB* = *AC* = 10 cm and *BC* = 8 cm. Is triangle *ABC* an enlargement or a reduction of triangle *WXY*? Explain your answer and give the scale factor. Justify your answer.

24 James was asked to design a square decorative tile with a side length of 90 millimeters. Construct the square on which James will draw his design.

25 Harry is designing a theater platform in the shape of a rhombus using a blueprint. The lengths of the diagonals on his blueprint are 4 centimeters and 9 centimeters. Construct the rhombus. Then measure a side length. If the scale of the drawing is 1 centimeter : 2 meters, about what length of skirting does Harry need to go around all four edges of the platform?

26 Michael wants to make some kites out of a plastic sheet for a family picnic. Before making the kites he wants to make a $\frac{1}{4}$ scale model to find the lengths and angles needed for each kite. The diagram shows the measurements of the actual kite. He knows that $\overline{AC}$ is the perpendicular bisector of $\overline{BD}$, and that $\overline{AN}$ should be 6 inches long. Construct the model he will use and find the measures of $\angle ABC$ and the lengths *AB* and *BC* in the actual kite.

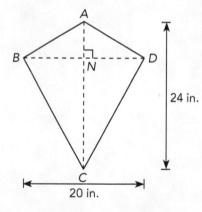

27 The scale of a map is 1 inch to 5 feet. Find the area of a rectangular region on the map if the area of the actual region is 95 square feet.

28 The floor plan of a building has a scale of $\frac{1}{4}$ inch to 1 foot. A room has an area of 40 square inches on the floor plan. What is the actual room area in square feet?

29 The scale of a map is 1: 2,400. If a rectangular piece of property measures 2 inches by 3 inches on the map, what is the actual area of this piece of property to the nearest tenth of an acre? (1 acre = 43,560 ft²)

Volume and Surface Area of Solids

BIG IDEA

▶ Solids such as pyramids, cylinders, cones, and spheres are all around you. You can find their surface areas and volumes to solve real-world problems.

How large is the aquarium?

Have you ever been to an aquarium? Fish, sea turtles, stingrays, and other aquatic animals are often kept in a giant cylindrical tank that visitors can walk around. To find the amount of glass used to make the tank, you can find the surface area of the tank. To find the amount of water the tank holds, you can find the volume of the tank.

In this chapter, you will learn how to find the volume and surface area of various three-dimensional objects, including many that you see in everyday life.

Recall Prior Knowledge

Applying surface area and volume formulas for prisms

A square prism has a height of 11 inches and a volume of 275 cubic inches. Find the length of each side of the square base.

In the formula $V = Bh$, B represents the area of the base and h represents the height.

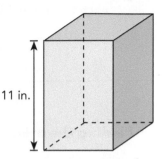

11 in.

Volume = 275 in³

$$V = Bh$$ Write the formula for the volume of a prism.

$$275 = B \cdot 11$$ Substitute.

$$\frac{275}{11} = B \cdot \frac{11}{11}$$ Divide both sides by 11.

$$25 = B$$ Simplify.

The area of the square base is 25 square inches.

$$\sqrt{25} = 5 \text{ in.}$$ Find the length of a side of the base.

The length of each side of the square base is 5 inches.

✓ Quick Check

Solve.

1 A cube has edges measuring 6 centimeters each.

    a) Find its volume.   **b)** Find its surface area.

2 The volume of a cube is 512 cubic centimeters. Find the length of each edge of the cube.

Finding the surface area of a square pyramid

A square pyramid has four faces that are congruent isosceles triangles. Find the surface area of the square pyramid if the area of its base is 256 square centimeters and the height of each triangular face is 10 centimeters.

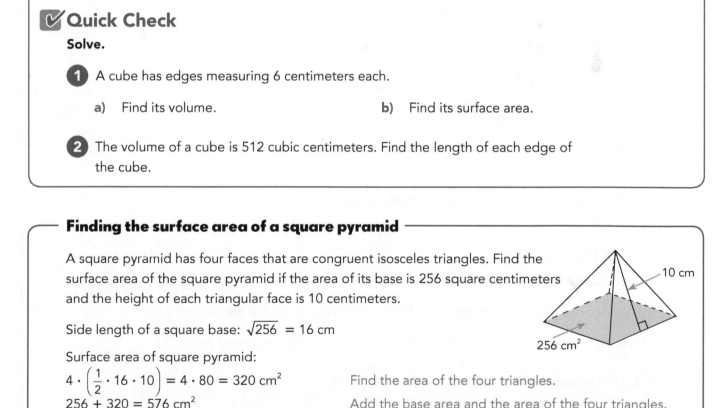

10 cm

256 cm²

Side length of a square base: $\sqrt{256} = 16$ cm

Surface area of square pyramid:

$$4 \cdot \left(\frac{1}{2} \cdot 16 \cdot 10 \right) = 4 \cdot 80 = 320 \text{ cm}^2$$ Find the area of the four triangles.

$$256 + 320 = 576 \text{ cm}^2$$ Add the base area and the area of the four triangles.

The surface area of the square pyramid is 576 square centimeters.

Continue on next page

Solve.

3 A pyramid has a square base measuring 10 inches on each side.
It has four faces that are congruent isoceles triangles. The height of
each triangle is 13 inches. Find the surface area of the pyramid.

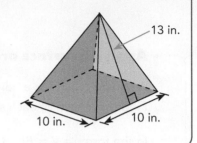

Finding the area and circumference of a circle

A paper plate has a diameter of 9 inches. Use 3.14 as an approximation for π.

a) Find the area of the paper plate.

$9 \div 2 = 4.5$ in.   Use Radius = Diameter ÷ 2.

Area of paper plate:

$\pi r^2 \approx 3.14 \cdot 4.5^2$ Use the formula for area and substitute the radius.
$= 3.14 \cdot 20.25$ Evaluate 4.5^2.
$= 63.585$ in^2 Multiply.

The area of the paper plate is 63.585 square inches.

b) Find the circumference of the paper plate.

Circumference of paper plate:

$\pi d \approx 3.14 \cdot 9$ Use the formula for circumference and substitute the diameter.
$= 28.26$ in.   Multiply.

The circumference of the paper is 28.26 inches.

✓ **Quick Check**

Solve. Use 3.14 as an approximation for π.

4 Shawn makes waffles for breakfast. Each waffle is a circle with a diameter of 6 inches.

    a) Find the circumference of a waffle.   **b)** Find the area of the waffle.

5 The circumference of a wheel is 320.28 centimeters.

    a) Find the radius of the wheel.   **b)** Find the area of the wheel.

Identifying nets of prisms and pyramids

Name the solid that each net forms.

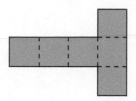

This is a net of a cube.

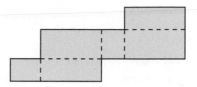

This is a net of a rectangular prism.

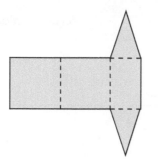

This is a net of a triangular prism.

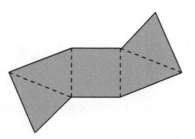

This is a net of a square pyramid.

✓ Quick Check

Match each solid to its net.

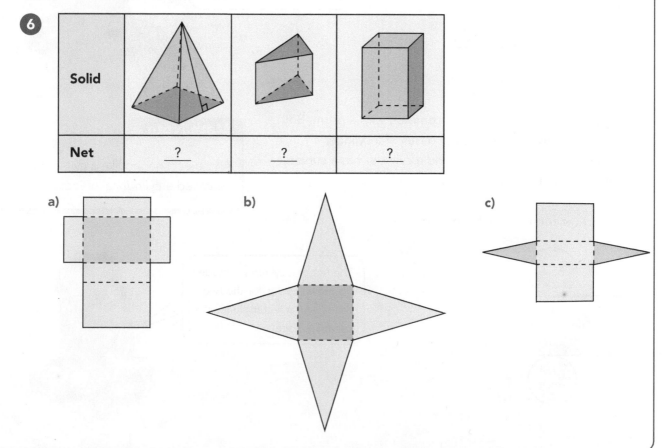

8.1 Recognizing Cylinders, Cones, Spheres, and Pyramids

Lesson Objectives

- Recognize cylinders, cones, and spheres.
- Identify cross sections of solids.

Recognize Cylinders.

A solid cylinder has a curved surface and two parallel bases that are congruent circles.

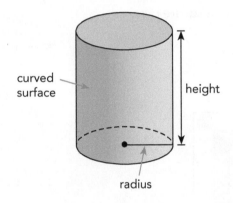

curved surface

height

radius

The radius of a cylinder is the radius of one of its bases. The height is the perpendicular distance between the parallel bases.

A cylinder has some things in common with a prism. Both solids have two bases. But the bases of a cylinder are circles instead of a polygon, and a cylinder has a curved surface instead of flat faces.

Math Note

An object shaped like a cylinder can be called a *cylindrical* object.

The cylinder has the net shown below.

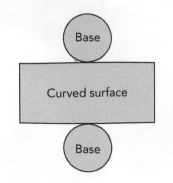

Base

Curved surface

Base

The net of a cylinder is made up of two circles for the two bases, and a rectangle for the curved surface.

Recognize Cones.

A cone has a circular base, a curved surface, and one vertex. The curved surface of the cone is also called its **lateral surface**.

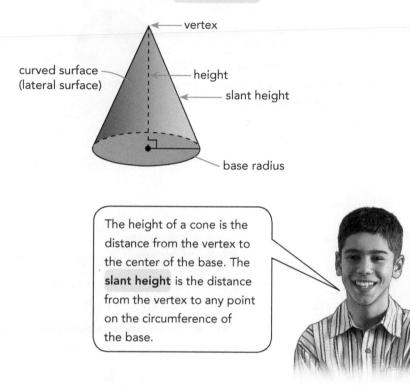

The height of a cone is the distance from the vertex to the center of the base. The **slant height** is the distance from the vertex to any point on the circumference of the base.

A cone has some things in common with a pyramid. Both solids have only one base with a vertex above the center of the base (when the base is horizontal). But the base of a cone is a circle instead of a polygon.

The cone has the net shown below.

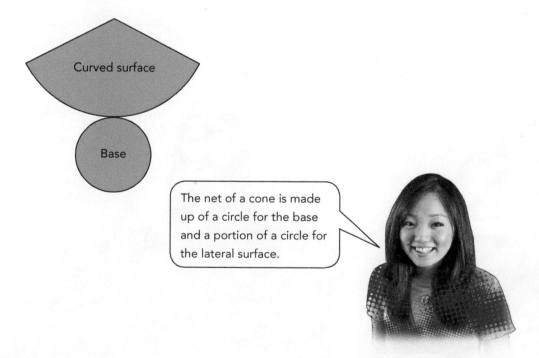

The net of a cone is made up of a circle for the base and a portion of a circle for the lateral surface.

Recognize Spheres.

A sphere has a curved surface. Every point on the surface is an equal distance from the center of the sphere.

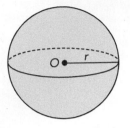

The distance from the center of a sphere to any point on its surface is called the radius of the sphere. Each segment joining the center to a point on the sphere is also called a radius.

If you slice a sphere in half you will get two **hemispheres**, as shown below.

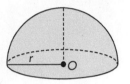

Math Note

An object shaped like a sphere can be called a *spherical* object.

Identify Cross Sections of Solids.

A **plane** is a flat surface that extends infinitely in two dimensions. When a flat plane slices through a solid, the result is a **cross section**. The shape of the cross section depends on how the plane slices the solid.

Suppose a plane could slice through Earth at the equator. The plane would divide Earth into a northern hemisphere and a southern hemisphere. The cross section you would see is the circle formed by the equator.

The intersection of a solid and a plane is a cross section.

Northern hemisphere

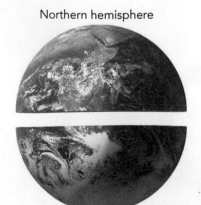

Southern hemisphere

 **Hands-On Activity**

Materials:
- clay
- string

FIND THE SHAPE OF CROSS SECTIONS OF SOLIDS

Work in pairs.

 STEP 1 Make three clay cubes. Use the string to slice a cube vertically so that the cross section is parallel to one face, as shown. Sketch the cross section and describe its shape.

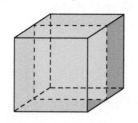

STEP 2 Use a string to slice another cube diagonally, as shown. Sketch the cross section and describe its shape.

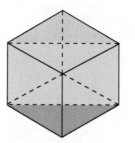

 STEP 3 Use a string to slice the last cube through the midpoints of each of three edges that share a common vertex, as shown. Sketch the cross section and describe its shape.

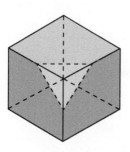

Math Journal Are you able to slice a cube in other ways to form the cross section in **STEP 1** to **STEP 3**?

Identify Cross Sections of a Square Pyramid.

You can slice a square pyramid through $\overline{AB}$ so that the cross section is parallel to its base. The cross section is a square.

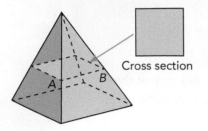

Cross section

You can also slice the square pyramid through its vertex and through $\overline{DE}$ so that the cross section is perpendicular to the base. The cross section formed is not a square. It is a triangle.

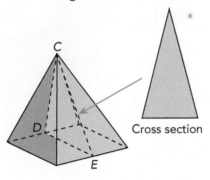

Cross section

> **Think Math**
>
> A rectangular pyramid and a rectangular prism have congruent bases. A plane slices each solid so that the cross section formed is parallel to the base. How are the two cross sections formed the same? How are they different?

In general, when you slice a pyramid parallel to its base, the cross section has the same shape as the base of the pyramid. When you slice a pyramid through its vertex and its base so that the cross section is perpendicular to the base, the cross section is a triangle.

Example 1 **Identify cross sections of solids.**

Tell what cross section is formed when a plane slices the solid as described.

a) A plane slices a rectangular prism parallel to its base.

Solution

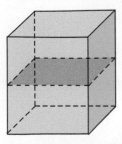

The cross section is a rectangle.

b) A plane slices a triangular prism parallel to its base.

Solution

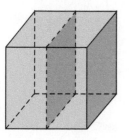

The cross section is a triangle.

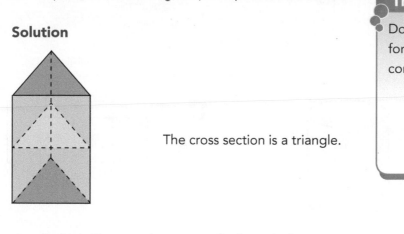
c) A plane slices a cube perpendicular to its base.

Solution

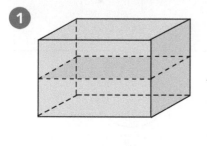

The cross section is a square.

Guided Practice

For each solid, name the shape of the cross section formed when the solid is sliced by the plane shown.

1
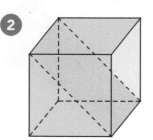

2

3
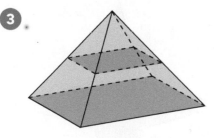

4
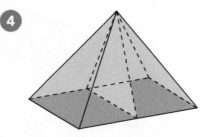

Practice 8.1

Match each solid to its net.

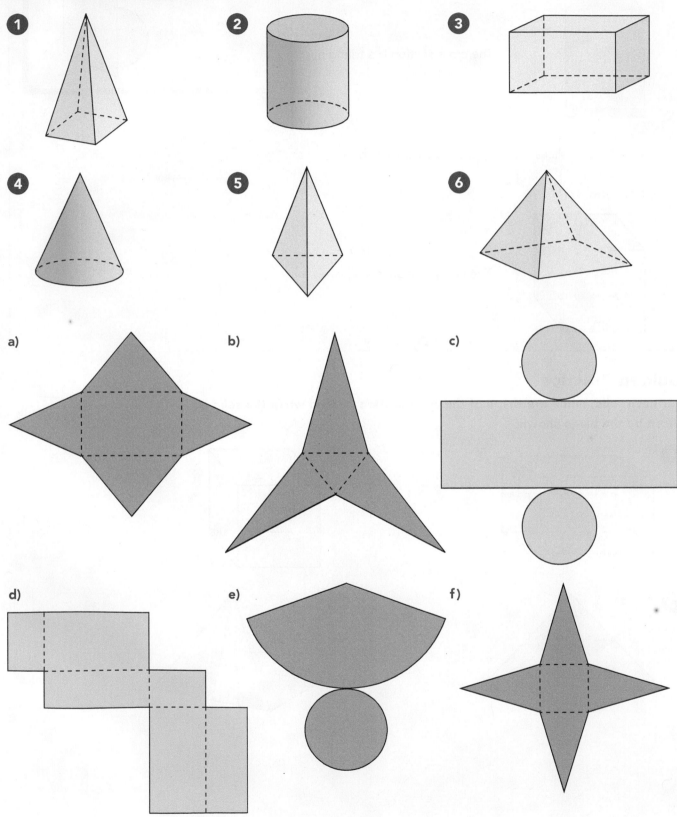

Name the solid that can be formed from each net.

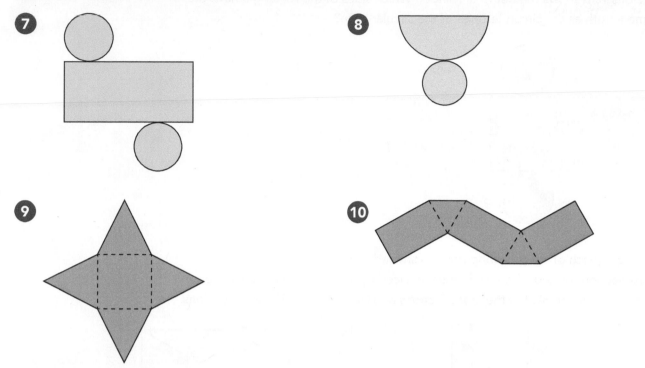

7

8

9

10

Solve. Show your work.

11 Tell what cross section is formed when a plane slices a square pyramid as described.

a) Perpendicular to its base and passes through its vertex.

b) Parallel to its base.

12 The diagram shows a cone and its net.

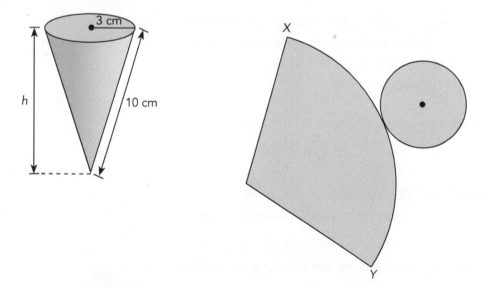

a) Copy the net of the cone and label these dimensions on the net.

b) How is the circumference of the base of the cone related to the curve XY?

13 The diagram shows the net of a cylinder. Which sides of the rectangle have the same length as the circumference of the circular base?

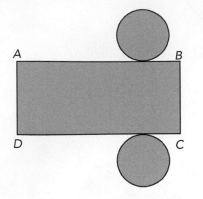

14 A base of each of the following prism is shaded. Name the shape of the cross section formed when each prism is sliced by a plane parallel to each base. Copy each prism. Sketch the cross sections and label them with the dimensions.

a)

b)

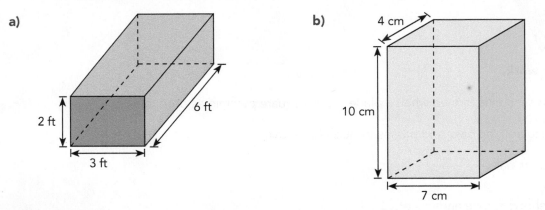

15 A cross section that is parallel to one of the bases of a rectangular prism is 3 inches wide and 6 inches long. A cross section that is perpendicular to its bases and parallel to two other faces is 4 inches wide and 6 inches long. What are the dimensions of the rectangular prism?

16 The area of the base of a square pyramid is 64 square centimeters. Several planes slice through the pyramid parallel to the base to form square cross sections.

a) Besides the cross section formed by a plane slicing the base, how many cross sections parallel to the base can be formed with areas that are perfect squares?

b) Find the sum of the area of the base and the areas of the cross sections found in a).

Lesson Objectives

- Find the volume and surface area of cylinders.
- Solve real-world problems involving cylinders.

Find the Volume of a Cylinder.

You have learned earlier that prisms have uniform cross sections when they are sliced parallel to the bases. From this property you found that the volume of a prism is given by the following formula:

Volume of a prism = Area of base · Height

$$\text{or } V = Bh$$

A cylinder also has uniform cross sections when sliced parallel to its bases. These cross sections are congruent to the circular bases. So, you can use the formula $V = Bh$ to find its volume, too.

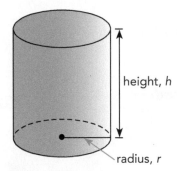

height, h

radius, r

Volume of a cylinder = Area of base · Height

$$= \pi r^2 \cdot h$$
$$= \pi r^2 h$$

The base of a cylinder is a circle. The base area of a cylinder is calculated using the formula for the area of a circle.

Solve. Show your work.

Find the volume of a cylinder with a diameter of 3 inches and a height of 5 inches. Use 3.14 as an approximation for π. Round your answer to the nearest tenth.

Solution

First find the radius of the cylinder.

Radius = Diameter ÷ 2
       = 3 ÷ 2 = 1.5 in.

$V = \pi r^2 h$	Use the formula for volume.
$\approx 3.14 \cdot 1.5 \cdot 1.5 \cdot 5$	Substitute for π, r, and h.
$= 35.325$	Multiply.
$\approx 35.3 \text{ in}^3$	Round to the nearest tenth.

The volume of the cylinder is about 35.3 cubic inches.

5 in.

diameter = 3 in.

Caution ///////

Check to see what dimensions are given in a problem before using any formula. In this example, you need to use the diameter to find the radius before you can use the formula.

Guided Practice

Use the given dimensions to find the volume of each cylinder. Use 3.14 as an approximation for π. Round your answer to the nearest tenth.

1 Radius = 5 cm, Height = 7.5 cm

2 Diameter = 7 in., Height = 5 in.

At a grocery store, a package of breadsticks is shaped like a cylinder. The volume of the cylindrical package is 36.9 cubic inches. The radius is 1.4 inches. What is the height of the cylindrical package? Round your answer to the nearest inch. Use 3.14 as an approximation for π.

Solution

Use the formula for volume to find the height, h, of the cylinder.

Volume of cylindrical can $= \pi r^2 h$	Use the formula.
$36.9 \approx 3.14 \cdot 1.4 \cdot 1.4 \cdot h$	Substitute for V, π, and r.
$36.9 = 6.1544h$	Multiply.
$\dfrac{36.9}{6.1544} = \dfrac{6.1544h}{6.1544}$	Divide both sides by 6.1544.
$5.996 \approx h$	Simplify.
$h \approx 6.0$	Round to the nearest tenth.

The height of the cylindrical package is about 6.0 inches.

1.4 in.

h in.

Bread Sticks

Yeast Free!   Gluten FREE!

Volume = 36.9 in³

Guided Practice

Complete. Use 3.14 as an approximation for π.

3 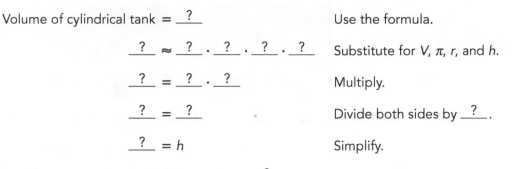 The volume of a cylindrical tank of water is 1,808.64 cubic meters. The radius is 12 meters. What is the height of the cylindrical tank?

Use the formula for volume to find the height, h, of the cylinder.

Volume of cylindrical tank = ___?___   Use the formula.

___?___ $\approx$ ___?___ · ___?___ · ___?___ · ___?___   Substitute for V, π, r, and h.

___?___ = ___?___ · ___?___   Multiply.

___?___ = ___?___   Divide both sides by ___?___.

___?___ = h Simplify.

The height of the cylindrical tank is about ___?___ meters.

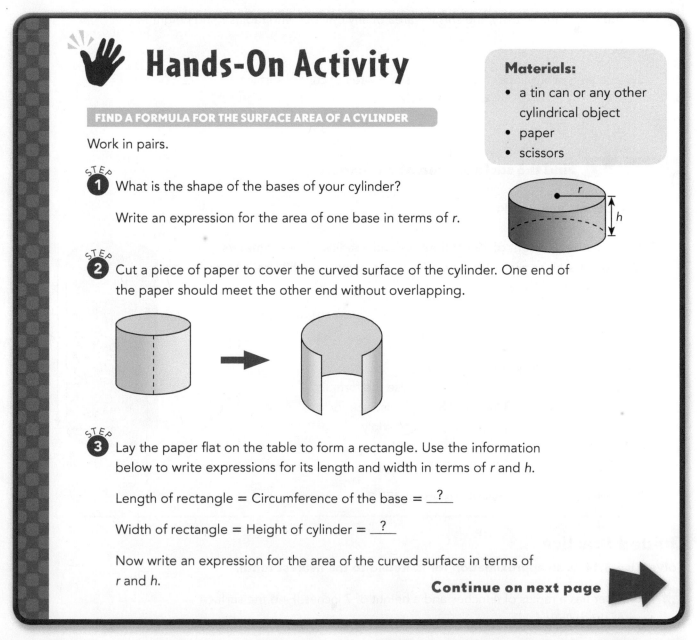

Hands-On Activity

Materials:
- a tin can or any other cylindrical object
- paper
- scissors

FIND A FORMULA FOR THE SURFACE AREA OF A CYLINDER

Work in pairs.

STEP 1 What is the shape of the bases of your cylinder?

Write an expression for the area of one base in terms of r.

STEP 2 Cut a piece of paper to cover the curved surface of the cylinder. One end of the paper should meet the other end without overlapping.

STEP 3 Lay the paper flat on the table to form a rectangle. Use the information below to write expressions for its length and width in terms of r and h.

Length of rectangle = Circumference of the base = ___?___

Width of rectangle = Height of cylinder = ___?___

Now write an expression for the area of the curved surface in terms of r and h.

Continue on next page

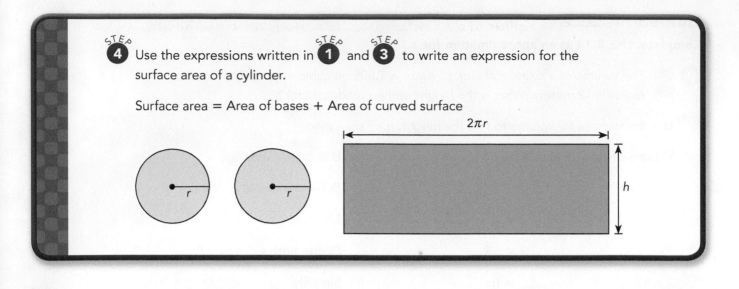

STEP **4** Use the expressions written in **1** and **3** to write an expression for the surface area of a cylinder.

Surface area = Area of bases + Area of curved surface

Find the Surface Area of a Cylinder.

As you saw in the Activity, the surface area of any cylinder with radius r and height h is given by:

Surface area of a cylinder = Area of bases + Area of curved surface
$$= 2\pi r^2 + 2\pi rh$$

Example 4 Find the surface area of a cylinder.

Solve. Show your work.

A cylinder has a height of 15 centimeters and a radius of 4 centimeters. What is the surface area of the cylinder to the nearest tenth? Use 3.14 as an approximation for π.

Solution

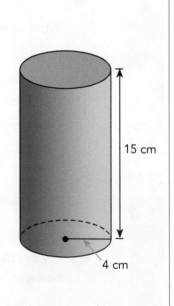

Surface area of the cylinder
$= 2\pi r^2 + 2\pi rh$ Use the formula.
$\approx 2 \cdot 3.14 \cdot 4 \cdot 4 + 2 \cdot 3.14 \cdot 4 \cdot 15$ Substitute for π, r, and h.
$= 100.48 + 376.8$ Multiply.
$= 477.28$ Add.
$\approx 477.3 \text{ cm}^2$ Round to the nearest tenth.

The surface area of the cylinder is about 477.3 square centimeters.

Guided Practice

Solve. Use 3.14 as an approximation for π. Round to the nearest tenth.

4 A cylinder has a radius of 4 inches and a height of 7 inches. Find the surface area of the cylinder.

Solve. Show your work.

Find the radius of a cylinder if the area of its curved surface is 12π square meters and its height is 2.5 meters.

2.5 m

Area of curved surface = 12π m²

radius = ?

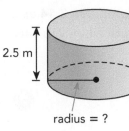

The area of the curved surface is given in terms of π. The area of 12π square meters is the exact surface area of the curved surface. If you substitute a value for π, such as 3.14, you would get an approximate value for the surface area: $12\pi \approx 12 \cdot 3.14 = 37.68$.

Leaving measures in terms of π can help simplify calculations. Because π is a number, you can add, subtract, multiply, or divide it.

Solution

Area of curved surface = $2\pi rh$ Use a formula for the area of the curved surface.

$12\pi = 2\pi r \cdot 2.5$ Substitute the surface area and height.

$12\pi = 2 \cdot 2.5 \cdot \pi r$ Multiply 2 by 2.5.

$12\pi = 5\pi r$ Simplify.

$\dfrac{12\pi}{5\pi} = \dfrac{5\pi r}{5\pi}$ Divide both sides by 5π.

$2.4 = r$ Simplify.

The radius of the cylinder is 2.4 meters.

Guided Practice

Solve.

5 The area of the curved surface of a cylindrical can is 162π square centimeters and its height is 9 centimeters. What is the diameter of the can?

Area of curved surface = $2\pi rh$ Use the formula for the area of the curved surface.

$\underline{\quad?\quad} = 2\pi r \cdot \underline{\quad?\quad}$ Substitute the surface area and height.

$\underline{\quad?\quad} = 2 \cdot \underline{\quad?\quad} \cdot \pi r$ Multiply 2 by $\underline{\quad?\quad}$.

$\underline{\quad?\quad} = \underline{\quad?\quad}$ Simplify.

$\dfrac{?}{?} = \dfrac{?}{?}$ Divide both sides by $\underline{\quad?\quad}$.

$\underline{\quad?\quad} = r$ Simplify.

The diameter of the can is $\underline{\quad?\quad}$ centimeters.

Practice 8.2

For this practice, you may use a calculator. Use 3.14 as an approximation for π.
Round your answers to the nearest tenth when you can.

Find the volume of each cylinder.

1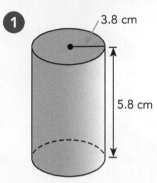

3.8 cm

5.8 cm

2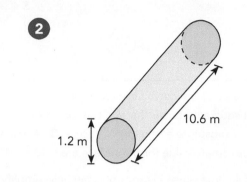

1.2 m

10.6 m

Solve.

3 A cylinder has a radius of 6 centimeters and a height of 28 centimeters. What is the volume?

4 A cylinder has a volume of 239 cubic centimeters and a height of 6 centimeters. What is the radius?

5 Jenny is making a cylindrical pencil holder in shop class. It will be 14 centimeters high and 8 centimeters across. The bottom and sides of the container will be made of metal.

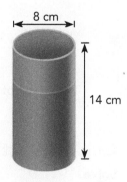

8 cm

14 cm

a) What is the area of the base?

b) What is the area of the curved surface of the pencil holder?

c) What is the total surface area of the pencil holder?

6 You want to make a tube with a height of 8 inches and a radius of 5 inches out of cardboard. The tube will be open at both ends. How much cardboard will you need to make the tube?

7 The volume of a soup can is 125.6 cubic inches. The diameter of the can is 8 inches. What is the height of the soup can?

8 in.

h

8 Mrs. Lavender bought a cylindrical lampshade with height 14 inches and diameter 10 inches. As shown in the diagram, the lampshade is open at the top and bottom. Find the surface area of the lampshade.

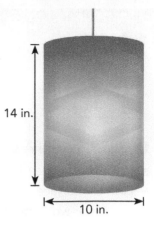
14 in.
10 in.

9 The volume of a cylinder is 121π cubic inches and its height is 4 inches.

a) What is the radius of the cylinder?

b) What is the surface area of the cylinder? Give your answer in terms of π.

10 The diagram shows a mallet made by attaching two solid cylinders together. What is the volume of the mallet?

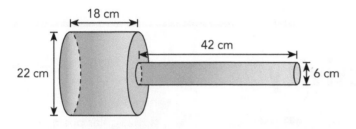
18 cm
42 cm
22 cm
6 cm

11 A company makes cylindrical cans for peaches. Each can has a radius of 4 centimeters and a height of 12 centimeters. The company plans to increase the volume of each can by 25%.

a) What will be the height of the new can if the radius remains the same?

b) What will be the radius of the new can if the height remains the same?

12 A cylindrical water tank has a radius of 5 feet and a height of 10 feet. The volume of water in the tank is 565.2 cubic feet.

a) What is the height of the water in the tank?

b) What percent of the tank's volume is filled with water?

13 Eric is painting 8 wooden cylinders. Each cylinder has a radius of 6.2 inches and a height of 12.4 inches. Eric can paint 50 square inches of wood using one pint of paint. How much paint will Eric need to paint all the wooden cylinders?

14 The area of the curved surface of a cylindrical jar is 1,584 square centimeters. The height of the jar is 28 centimeters.

a) What is the circumference of the jar?

b) What is the radius of the jar?

15 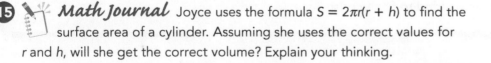 *Math Journal* Joyce uses the formula $S = 2\pi r(r + h)$ to find the surface area of a cylinder. Assuming she uses the correct values for r and h, will she get the correct volume? Explain your thinking.

8.3 Finding Volume and Surface Area of Pyramids and Cones

Lesson Objectives

- Find the volume of pyramids and cones.
- Find the surface area of cones.
- Solve real-world problems involving pyramids and cones.

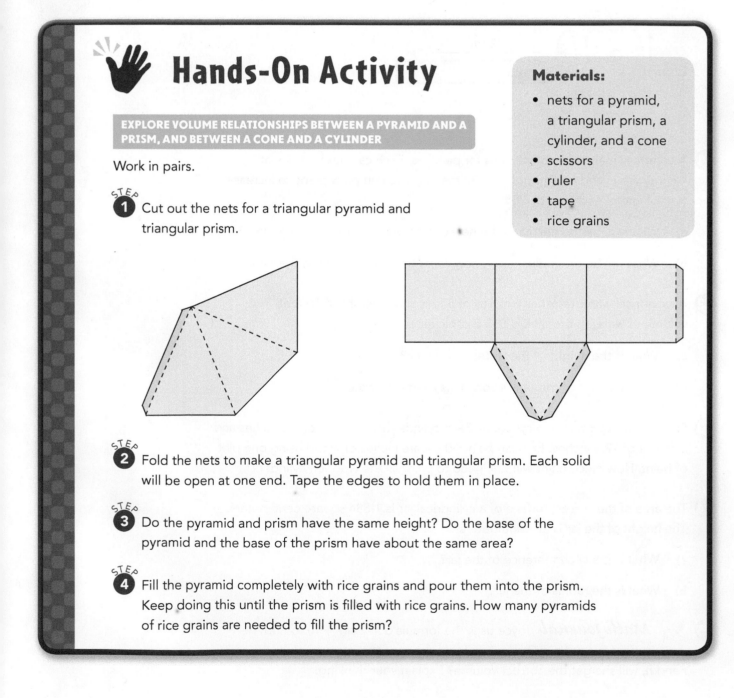

Hands-On Activity

Materials:

- nets for a pyramid, a triangular prism, a cylinder, and a cone
- scissors
- ruler
- tape
- rice grains

EXPLORE VOLUME RELATIONSHIPS BETWEEN A PYRAMID AND A PRISM, AND BETWEEN A CONE AND A CYLINDER

Work in pairs.

STEP 1 Cut out the nets for a triangular pyramid and triangular prism.

STEP 2 Fold the nets to make a triangular pyramid and triangular prism. Each solid will be open at one end. Tape the edges to hold them in place.

STEP 3 Do the pyramid and prism have the same height? Do the base of the pyramid and the base of the prism have about the same area?

STEP 4 Fill the pyramid completely with rice grains and pour them into the prism. Keep doing this until the prism is filled with rice grains. How many pyramids of rice grains are needed to fill the prism?

Math Journal What is the relationship between the volume of a triangular pyramid and the volume of a triangular prism with the same base and height? Suggest a formula for the volume of a pyramid.

STEP 5 Cut out the nets for a cylinder and cone.

STEP 6 Use the cutouts of the rectangle and circle to make a cylinder. Tape the edges to hold them in place. The cylinder will be open at one end.

STEP 7 Fold the cutout of the sector of the circle to make a cone. Tape the edges to hold them in place. The cone will be open at its wide end.

STEP 8 Are the cylinder and the cone about the same height? Do the base of the cylinder and the base of the cone have about the same area?

STEP 9 Fill the cone completely with rice grains and pour them into the cylinder. Keep doing this until the cylinder is filled with rice grains. How many cones of rice grains are needed to fill the cylinder?

Math Journal What is the relationship between the volume of a cone and the volume of a cylinder with the same base and height? Suggest a formula for the volume of a cone.

Find the Volume of a Pyramid and a Cone.

The diagrams show a square pyramid, a rectangular pyramid, and a triangular pyramid.

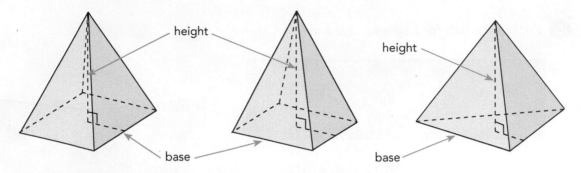

Before you find the volume of a pyramid, you have to find the area of the base. Then you can use the formula below. In the formula, *B* is the area of the base, and *h* is the height.

Volume of a pyramid $= \frac{1}{3} Bh$

The volume of a pyramid is one-third the volume of a prism with the same height and base area as the pyramid. Similarly, the volume of a cone is one-third the volume of a cylinder with the same height and base area as the cone.

Volume of a cone $= \frac{1}{3} Bh$

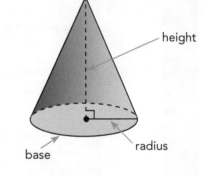

Example 6 **Find the volume of a pyramid.**

Solve. Show your work.

What is the volume of the rectangular pyramid?

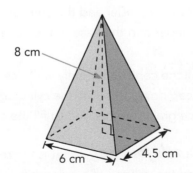

Solution

Volume of pyramid $= \frac{1}{3} Bh$ Use the formula.

$= \frac{1}{3} \cdot (6 \cdot 4.5) \cdot 8$ Substitute for *B* and *h*.

$= 72 \text{ cm}^3$ Multiply.

The volume of the rectangular pyramid is 72 cubic centimeters.

Guided Practice

Solve.

1 The base of a pyramid is a right triangle. The triangle has a base of
5 centimeters and a height of 3 centimeters. The pyramid has a height of
6 centimeters. What is the volume of the pyramid?

Use the formula for the volume of a pyramid.

Volume of pyramid

$= \frac{1}{3} Bh$ Use the formula.

$= \frac{1}{3} \cdot (\underline{\ ?\ } \cdot \underline{\ ?\ } \cdot \underline{\ ?\ }) \cdot \underline{\ ?\ }$ Substitute for B and h.

$= \underline{\ ?\ } \text{ cm}^3$ Multiply.

The volume of the pyramid is $\underline{\ ?\ }$ cubic centimeters.

2 A square pyramid has a height of 12 meters. If a side of the base measures
5.5 meters, what is the volume of the pyramid?

Example 7   **Find the height of a pyramid given its volume and the area of the base.**

Solve. Show your work.

The rectangular pyramid shown below has a volume of 260 cubic inches.
The base has a length of 15 inches and a width of 8 inches.
What is the height of the pyramid?

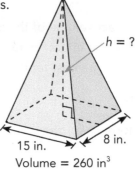

Solution

Let the height of the pyramid be h inches. Use the formula for the
volume of a pyramid.

Volume of pyramid $= \frac{1}{3} Bh$ Use the formula.

$260 = \frac{1}{3} \cdot (15 \cdot 8) \cdot h$ Substitute for the volume and dimensions of the base.

$260 = 40 \cdot h$ Multiply.

$\dfrac{260}{40} = \dfrac{40 \cdot h}{40}$ Divide both sides by 40.

$6\frac{1}{2} = h$ Simplify.

The height of the pyramid is $6\frac{1}{2}$ inches.

Guided Practice

Solve.

3 A square pyramid has a volume of 400 cubic centimeters. The length of the base is 10 centimeters. What is the height of the pyramid?

Let the height of the pyramid be h centimeters.

Volume of pyramid $= \dfrac{1}{3} Bh$	Use the formula.
$\underline{\ ?\ } = \dfrac{1}{3} \cdot (\underline{\ ?\ } \cdot \underline{\ ?\ }) \cdot h$	Substitute for the volume and dimensions of the base.
$\underline{\ ?\ } = \underline{\ ?\ } \cdot h$	Multiply both sides by $\underline{\ ?\ }$.
$\underline{\ ?\ } = \underline{\ ?\ }$	Divide both sides by $\underline{\ ?\ }$.
$\underline{\ ?\ } = h$	Simplify.

The height of the pyramid is $\underline{\ ?\ }$ centimeters.

4 A rectangular pyramid has a volume of 58 cubic meters. If the sides of the base measure 3 meters by 5 meters, what is the height of the pyramid?

Example 8   Find the volume of a cone.

Solve. Show your work.

Find the exact volume of the cone. Use 3.14 as an approximation for π to find the approximate volume of the cone. Round your answer to the nearest tenth.

Solution

Use the formula for the volume of a cone, $V = \dfrac{1}{3} Bh$.

height = 7 cm

radius = 3 cm

Volume of cone $= \dfrac{1}{3} \cdot \pi r^2 \cdot h$	Use the formula.
$= \dfrac{1}{3} \cdot (\pi \cdot 3 \cdot 3) \cdot 7$	Substitute for π, r, and h.
$= 21\pi$	Multiply.
$\approx 65.9 \text{ cm}^3$	Round to the nearest tenth.

The exact volume of the cone is 21π cubic centimeters.

An approximate volume is 65.9 cubic centimeters.

> Sometimes it is convenient to leave an answer in terms of π. This gives an exact answer. Exact answers are especially useful if you are combining the results of two or more calculations that involve π.

Guided Practice

Solve.

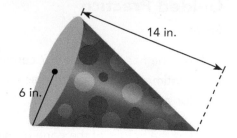

14 in.

6 in.

5 A party hat is in the shape of a cone. Find the exact volume of the party hat. Use 3.14 as an approximation for π to find the approximate volume of the cone. Round your answer to the nearest tenth.

Use the formula for the volume of a cone, $V = \frac{1}{3}Bh$.

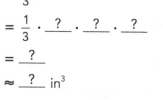

Volume of the party hat $= \frac{1}{3} \cdot \pi r^2 \cdot h$	Use the formula.
$= \frac{1}{3} \cdot \underline{\ ?\ } \cdot \underline{\ ?\ } \cdot \underline{\ ?\ }$	Substitute for π, r, and h.
$= \underline{\ ?\ }$	Multiply.
$\approx \underline{\ ?\ }$ in^3	Round to the nearest tenth.

The exact volume of the party hat is $\underline{\ ?\ }$ cubic inches.

An approximate volume is $\underline{\ ?\ }$ cubic inches.

6 The diagram shows a cone-shaped container. Find the exact volume of the container. Use 3.14 as an approximation for π to find the approximate volume of the container. Round your answer to the nearest tenth.

9 cm

14 cm

Example 9 **Find the radius of a cone given its volume and height.**

A safety cone has a height of 30 inches and a volume of 2,009.6 cubic inches. What is the radius of the safety cone (excluding its base)? Use 3.14 as an approximation for π.

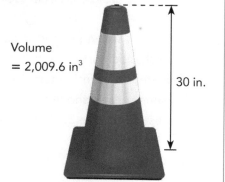

Volume = 2,009.6 in^3

30 in.

Solution

Let the radius of the safety cone be r inches.

Volume of cone $= \frac{1}{3}Bh$	Use the formula for the volume of a cone.
$2{,}009.6 \approx \frac{1}{3} \cdot (3.14 \cdot r^2) \cdot 30$	Substitute for the volume and dimensions.
$2{,}009.6 = 31.4 \cdot r^2$	Multiply.
$\dfrac{2{,}009.6}{31.4} = \dfrac{31.4 \cdot r^2}{31.4}$	Divide both sides by 31.4.
$64 = r^2$	Simplify.
$\sqrt{64} = r$	Find the square root of both sides.
$8 = r$	Simplify.

The radius of the safety cone is about 8 inches.

Guided Practice

Solve.

7 A cone has a height of 57 centimeters and a volume of 2,923.34 cubic centimeters. What is the radius of the cone? Use 3.14 as an approximation for π.

Let the height of the cone be h centimeters.

Volume of cone $= \frac{1}{3} \cdot \pi r^2 \cdot h$	Use the formula for the volume of a cone.
$\underline{\quad?\quad} \approx \frac{1}{3} \cdot \underline{\quad?\quad} \cdot r^2 \cdot \underline{\quad?\quad}$	Substitute for the volume, π, and h.
$\underline{\quad?\quad} = \underline{\quad?\quad} \cdot r^2$	Multiply.
$\underline{\quad?\quad} = \underline{\quad?\quad}$	Divide both sides by $\underline{\quad?\quad}$.
$\underline{\quad?\quad} = r^2$	Simplify.
$\underline{\quad?\quad} = r$	Find the square roots of both sides.
$\underline{\quad?\quad} = r$	Simplify.

The radius of the cone is about $\underline{\quad?\quad}$ centimeters.

8 A cone has a height of 7.2 inches and a volume of 188.4 cubic inches. What is the radius of the cone? Use 3.14 as an approximation for π.

Example 10 | **Solve a real-world problem involving a cone.**

Suzanne is serving yogurt in cone-shaped parfait glasses. The cone-shaped part of each glass has a height of 9 centimeters and a diameter of 7 centimeters. How many cubic centimeters of yogurt can Suzanne serve if she fills 3 parfait glasses? Round your answer to the nearest tenth. Use 3.14 as an approximation for π.

Solution

Radius of the cone:

$7 \div 2 = 3.5$ cm   The radius is half the diameter.

Volume of 3 cones:

$$3 \cdot \frac{1}{3} \cdot \pi r^2 \cdot h = 3 \cdot \frac{1}{3} \cdot (3.14 \cdot 3.5^2) \cdot 9 \qquad \text{Substitute for } \pi, r, \text{ and } h.$$
$$= 346.185 \qquad \text{Multiply.}$$
$$\approx 346.2 \text{ cm}^3 \qquad \text{Round to the nearest tenth.}$$

Suzanne can serve about 346.2 cubic centimeters of yogurt if she fills 3 parfait glasses.

Guided Practice

Solve.

9 Jean wants to sell lemonade in cone-shaped paper cups. Each cup has a diameter of 4 centimeters and a height of 8 centimeters. She wants to make enough lemonade for 50 cups. How much lemonade does Jean need to make? Round your answer to the nearest tenth. Use 3.14 as an approximation for π.

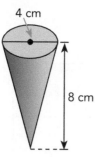

Find the Surface Area of a Cone.

The length from O to A on a right circular cone is called the slant height of the cone. The slant height is the distance between the vertex and a point on the circumference of base. When you cut the cone along $\overline{OA}$ and flatten it, you will get a portion of a circle with center O and radius ℓ units.

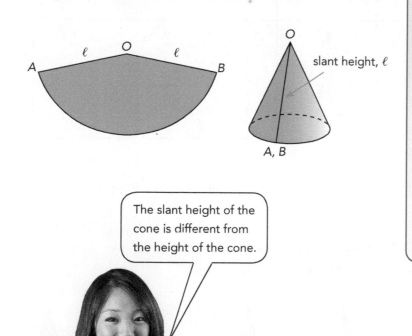

> The slant height of the cone is different from the height of the cone.

Math Note

A right circular cone is a cone that has its vertex directly above the center of its base. Other cones can have the vertex off to one side, as shown.

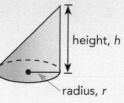

The volume formula applies to all cones with a circular base. The surface area formula applies only to right circular cones.

Hands-On Activity

Work in pairs.

STEP 1 Copy and complete the table. For each pyramid, the base has edges of length b. The slant height is h.

Type of Pyramid	Number of Lateral Faces	Diagram	Area of All Lateral Triangular Faces
Triangular	3	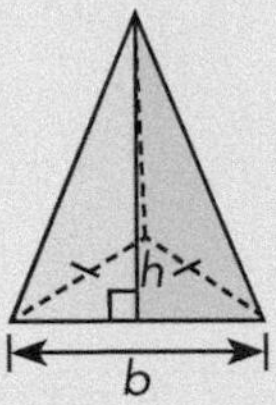	$\frac{1}{2}bh + \frac{1}{2}bh + \frac{1}{2}bh$ $= \frac{1}{2}(3b)h$ $= \frac{1}{2} \cdot$ Perimeter of base $\cdot$ Slant height
Square	4	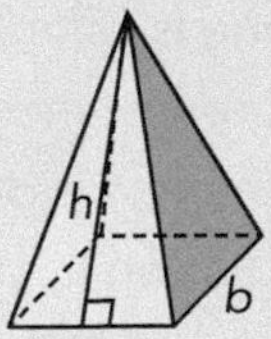	$\underline{\ ?\ } + \underline{\ ?\ } + \underline{\ ?\ } + \underline{\ ?\ }$ $= \frac{1}{2} \cdot \underline{\ ?\ } \cdot \underline{\ ?\ }$ $= \frac{1}{2} \cdot \underline{\ ?\ } \cdot \underline{\ ?\ }$
Pentagonal	5	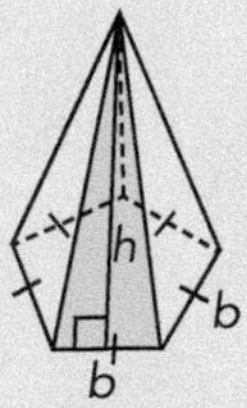	$\underline{\ ?\ } + \underline{\ ?\ } + \underline{\ ?\ } + \underline{\ ?\ } + \underline{\ ?\ }$ $= \frac{1}{2} \cdot \underline{\ ?\ } \cdot \underline{\ ?\ }$ $= \frac{1}{2} \cdot \underline{\ ?\ } \cdot \underline{\ ?\ }$

STEP 2 In general, what is the formula for the area of all the lateral triangular faces of a pyramid?

STEP 3 Suppose the number of sides of the base of the pyramid increases as shown below. Name the solid that is eventually formed.

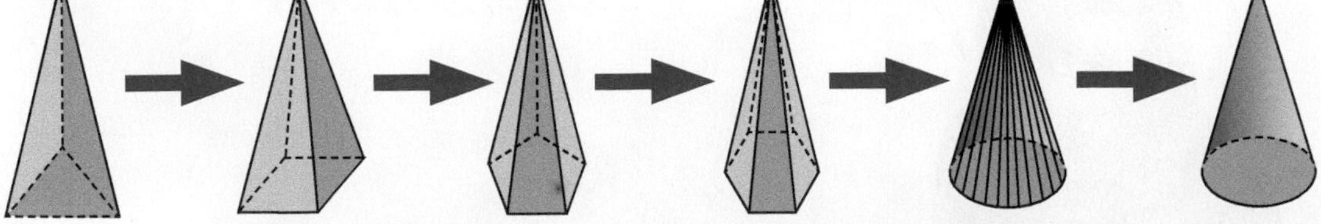

STEP 4 The formula for the curved surface area of a cone is related to the formula for the surface area of the triangular faces of a pyramid. Copy and complete the formula for the curved surface area of a cone. Let r represent the radius of the base of a cone. Let ℓ represent the slant height of the cone.

$\dfrac{1}{2} \cdot$ Perimeter of base $\cdot$ Slant height	Formula for the surface area of the triangular faces of a pyramid.
$= \dfrac{1}{2} \cdot$ Circumference of circle $\cdot$ Slant height	The perimeter of the base of a cone is the circumference of a circle.
$= \dfrac{1}{2} \cdot \underline{\ ?\ } \cdot \ell$	Substitute the formula for the circumference of a circle.
$= \underline{\ ?\ }$	Formula for the area of a curved surface of a cone.

Use the Formula for the Surface Area of a Cone.

To find the surface area, you find the sum of the area of its base and the area of its curved surface. The curved surface is called the lateral surface.

The area of the base of a cone is πr^2, where r is the radius of the cone.

The area of the lateral surface is $\pi r \ell$, where ℓ is the slant height of the cone.

Surface area of a cone = Area of the base + Area of the lateral surface
$$= \pi r^2 + \pi r \ell$$

Lateral means "side." Prisms, pyramids, cylinders, and cones all have lateral surfaces. The lateral surface area of a solid does not include the area of the base (or bases).

Example 11 **Find the area of the curved surface of a cone.**

Solve. Show your work.

The diagram shows a cone with a radius of 5 centimeters and a slant height of 15 centimeters.

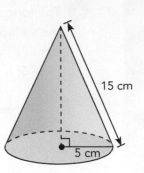

a) What is the exact area of the curved surface of the cone?

Solution

$\pi r \ell = \pi \cdot 5 \cdot 15$ Use the formula for the lateral surface area of a cone.

$= 75\pi \text{ cm}^2$ Multiply.

The exact area of the curved surface of the cone is 75π square centimeters.

b) What is the total surface area of the cone? Find both the exact value and an approximate value. Use 3.14 as an approximation for π.

Solution

Total surface area of the cone:

Area of base + Lateral surface area

$= \pi r^2 + 75\pi$ The lateral surface area is 75π.

$= \pi \cdot 5 \cdot 5 + 75\pi$ Substitute 5 for r.

$= 25\pi + 75\pi$ Multiply.

$= 100\pi$ Add.

$\approx 314 \text{ cm}^3$ Substitute 3.14 for π.

The total surface area of the cone is exactly 100π square centimeters and approximately 314 square centimeters.

Guided Practice

Solve.

10 A solid cone has a radius of 7 inches and a slant height of 14 inches.

a) What is the exact area of the cone's curved surface?

$\pi r \ell = \underline{\ ?\ } \cdot \underline{\ ?\ } \cdot \underline{\ ?\ }$ Use the formula for the lateral surface area of a cone.

$= \underline{\ ?\ } \text{ in}^2$ Multiply.

The exact area of the cone's curved surface is $\underline{\ ?\ }$ square inches.

b) What is the total surface area of the cone? Find both the exact value and an approximate value. Use $\frac{22}{7}$ as an approximation for π.

Total surface area of the cone:

Area of base + Area of curved surface = $\pi r^2 +$ _?_   The lateral surface area is _?_ .

$=$ _?_ · _?_ · _?_ + _?_   Substitute _?_ for r.

$=$ _?_ + _?_   Multiply.

$=$ _?_   Add.

$\approx$ _?_ in²   Substitute _?_ for π.

The total surface area of the cone is exactly _?_ square inches, and approximately _?_ square inches.

11 The radius of a cone is 3 inches, and the slant height is 12 inches.

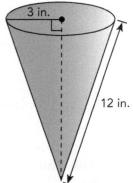

a) What is the exact area of the cone's curved surface?

b) What is the total surface area of the cone? Find both the exact value and an approximate value. Use 3.14 as an approximation for π.

Example 12 **Find the slant height of a cone given its radius and the area of its curved surface.**

The wrapper of a frozen yogurt cone has an area of 159 square centimeters. The radius of the cone is 4 centimeters. Find the slant height of the cone to the nearest tenth. Use 3.14 as an approximation for π.

Area of curved surface = 159 cm²

Solution

Let the slant height of the cone be ℓ centimeters. Notice that the wrapper covers only the curved surface of the cone.

Area of wrapper $= \pi r \ell$ Use the formula for the lateral surface area of a cone.

$159 \approx 3.14 \cdot 4 \cdot \ell$ Substitute for the area of wrapper, π, and the radius.

$159 = 12.56 \cdot \ell$ Multiply.

$\dfrac{159}{12.56} = \dfrac{12.56 \cdot \ell}{12.56}$ Divide both sides by 12.56.

$12.7 \approx \ell$ Simplify and round to the nearest tenth.

The slant height of the cone is about 12.7 centimeters.

Guided Practice

Solve.

12 A conical straw hat has a diameter of 16 inches and a lateral surface area of 251.2 square inches. Find the approximate slant height of the straw hat. Use 3.14 as an approximation for π.

16 in.

Let the lateral height of the hat be ℓ inches.

Area of lateral surface of hat = $\pi r \ell$	Use the formula for the lateral surface area of a cone.
$\underline{\quad?\quad} \approx \underline{\quad?\quad} \cdot \underline{\quad?\quad} \cdot \ell$	Substitute for the area of the lateral surface, π, and the radius.
$\underline{\quad?\quad} = \underline{\quad?\quad} \cdot \ell$	Multiply.
$\underline{\quad?\quad} = \underline{\quad?\quad}$	Divide both sides by $\underline{\quad?\quad}$.
$\underline{\quad?\quad} = \ell$	Simplify and round.

The slant height of the hat is about $\underline{\quad?\quad}$ inches.

Example 13 **Solve a real-world problem involving a cone.**

A cone-shaped roof has a radius of 14 feet and a slant height of 17 feet. The roof is covered completely with glass. The cost of glass is $40 per square foot. What is the cost of covering the roof with glass? Use 3.14 as an approximation for π.

Solution

First find the area of its curved surface.

$\pi r \ell \approx 3.14 \cdot 14 \cdot 17$ Use the formula for the area of the curved surface of a cone.
$\quad\quad = 747.32 \text{ ft}^2$ Find the area of the curved surface of the roof.

Cost of covering the roof with glass:

$40 \cdot 747.32 = 29{,}892.80$ Multiply the cost of glass per square foot by the area of the curved surface to find the total cost.

The cost of covering the roof is about $29,892.80.

Guided Practice

Solve.

13 Jessica makes a cone-shaped paper filter to line a cone-shaped funnel. The funnel has a radius of 5 inches and a slant height of 10 inches. Suppose Jessica wants to make cone-shaped filters for 25 such funnels. About how many square inches of filter paper will she need? Use 3.14 as an approximation for π.

For this practice, you may use a calculator and use 3.14 as an approximation for π. Round your answers to the nearest tenth when you can.

Find the volume of each pyramid.

1

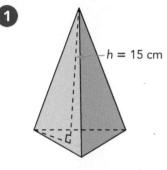

$h = 15$ cm

Base area $= 72$ cm^2

2

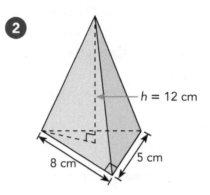

$h = 12$ cm

8 cm

5 cm

3 A rectangular pyramid with a height of 10 inches and a base that measures 9 inches by 7 inches.

4 A square pyramid with a height of 18 feet and a base that is 12 feet on each edge.

Find the exact and an approximate volume for each cone.

5

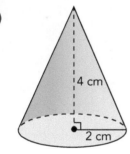

4 cm

2 cm

6

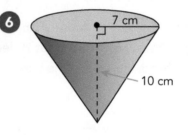

7 cm

10 cm

7 A solid cone with a diameter of 10 centimeters and a height of 8 centimeters.

8 A cone with a radius of 4.9 centimeters and a height of 6.9 centimeters.

Find the exact and an approximate surface area for each solid cone. Round your approximation to the nearest square unit.

9 A cone with a radius of 2.5 centimeters and a slant height of 5.6 centimeters.

10 A cone with a diameter of 72 centimeters and a slant height of 48 centimeters.

11 A cone with a diameter of 18 meters and a slant height of 22 meters.

Solve.

12 A square pyramid has a volume of 605 cubic centimeters and a height of 15 centimeters.

   a) What is the area of the base of the pyramid?

   b) What is the length of an edge of the base?

13 The volume of a square pyramid is 333 cubic centimeters. The length of an edge of the base of the pyramid is 10 centimeters. What is the height of the pyramid rounded to the nearest centimeter?

14 A candle in the shape of a cone has a radius of 5 centimeters. The slant height is 15 centimeters.

   a) What is the area of the base of the candle?

   b) What is the area of the curved surface of the candle?

   c) Suppose the candle is wrapped in plastic. If there is no overlap, how much plastic is needed?

15 A cone has a slant height of 8.5 centimeters. The height of the cone is 7.5 centimeters and the radius is 4 centimeters.

   a) What is the area of the lateral surface?

   b) What is the volume of the cone?

16 One of the entrances to the Louvre Museum in France is in the shape of a pyramid. The entrance has a height of about 70 feet and a volume of about 233,330 cubic feet. What is the area of the base of the pyramid to the nearest foot?

Volume = 233,330 ft^3

17 ✏️ *Math Journal* Cylinder P and cone Q have the same radius and height. The volume of cylinder P is 393 cubic centimeters. Joseph says that the volume of cone Q is 131 cubic centimeters. Explain how Joseph arrived at his answer.

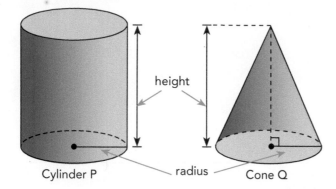

Cylinder P   radius   Cone Q
height

18 A circle has a radius of 61 milimeters. Three-quarters of the circle is used to form a net for the curved part of a cone. The net is taped together to form the cone without any overlap. The height of the finished cone is 40 millimeters.

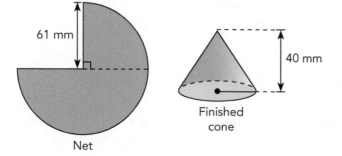

61 mm

Net

40 mm

Finished cone

a) What is the circumference of the base of the cone?

b) What is the radius of the cone?

c) What is the volume of the cone?

d) What is the area of the curved surface of the cone?

19 Martha used a filter in the shape of a cone to filter sand from a liquid. The volume of liquid that the filter can hold is 66 cubic centimeters. The height of the filter is 6 centimeters. What is the diameter of the filter? Round your answer to the nearest tenth.

Finding Volume and Surface Area of Spheres

Lesson Objectives

- Find the volume and surface area of spheres.
- Solve real-world problems involving spheres.

Find the Volume of a Sphere.

The volume of a sphere with a radius of r units is given by the formula below.

$$V = \frac{4}{3} \pi r^3$$

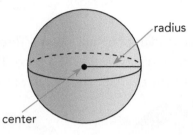
radius
center

Example 14 **Find the volume of a sphere given its radius.**

An iron ball has a diameter of 6 centimeters. Find the volume of the iron ball to the nearest cubic centimeter. Use 3.14 as an approximation for π.

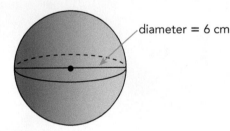
diameter = 6 cm

The diameter of the iron ball is a segment that passes through the center and has its endpoints on the surface of the iron ball. The diameter is twice the length of the radius.

Solution

Radius of the iron ball:

$6 \div 2 = 3$ cm   The radius is half the diameter.

Volume of the iron ball:

$\frac{4}{3} \pi r^3 \approx \frac{4}{3} \cdot 3.14 \cdot 3 \cdot 3 \cdot 3$ Use the formula for the volume of a sphere.

$= 113.04$ Multiply.

≈ 113 cm^3 Round to the nearest centimeter.

The volume of the iron ball is about 113 cubic centimeters.

Guided Practice

Solve.

1 The diameter of a sphere is 8.8 meters. What is the volume of the sphere? Round your answer to the nearest hundredth. Use 3.14 as an approximation for π.

8.8 m

Radius of the sphere:

$8.8 \div$ __?__ $=$ __?__ m   The radius is half the diameter.

Volume of the sphere:

$\frac{4}{3}\pi r^3 \approx \frac{4}{3} \cdot$ __?__ $\cdot$ __?__ $\cdot$ __?__ $\cdot$ __?__   Use the formula for the volume of a sphere.

$\phantom{\frac{4}{3}\pi r^3} = $ __?__   Multiply.

$\phantom{\frac{4}{3}\pi r^3} \approx$ __?__ m³   Round to the nearest hundredth.

The volume of the sphere is about __?__ cubic meters.

Example 15   **Find the radius of a sphere given its volume.**

While on vacation, Mike buys a sphere made of polished agate. The volume of the sphere is 65.42 cubic inches. What is the radius of the sphere to the nearest tenth? Use 3.14 as an approximation for π.

Solution

Volume of sphere $= \frac{4}{3}\pi r^3$ Use the formula for the volume of a sphere.

$65.42 \approx \frac{4}{3} \cdot 3.14 \cdot r^3$ Substitute for the volume and π.

$65.42 = \dfrac{12.56 \cdot r^3}{3}$ Multiply.

$3 \cdot 65.42 = \dfrac{12.56 \cdot r^3}{3} \cdot 3$ Multiply both sides by 3.

$196.26 = 12.56 \cdot r^3$ Multiply.

$\dfrac{196.26}{12.56} = \dfrac{12.56 \cdot r^3}{12.56}$ Divide both sides by 12.56.

$15.63 \approx r^3$ Evaluate.

$\sqrt[3]{15.63} = r$ Find the cube root of both sides.

$2.5 \approx r$ Round to the nearest tenth.

The radius of the sphere is about 2.5 inches.

You can use a calculator to find the cube root of 15.63.

Enter the following: 15.63 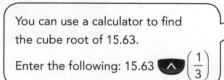 $\left(\frac{1}{3}\right)$

Guided Practice

Solve.

2 Diane bought a spherical ball made of quartz at a garage sale. The volume of the ball is 1,450 cubic centimeters. What is the radius of the ball to the nearest centimeter? Use 3.14 as an approximation for π.

Volume of the spherical ball $= \frac{4}{3}\pi r^3$ Use the formula for the volume of a sphere.

$\underline{\quad?\quad} \approx \frac{4}{3} \cdot \underline{\quad?\quad} \cdot r^3$ Substitute the volume and π.

$\underline{\quad?\quad} = \underline{\quad?\quad}$ Multiply.

$3 \cdot \underline{\quad?\quad} = \underline{\quad?\quad} \cdot 3$ Multiply both sides by 3.

$\underline{\quad?\quad} = \underline{\quad?\quad} \cdot r^3$ Multiply.

$\underline{\quad?\quad} = \underline{\quad?\quad}$ Divide both sides by $\underline{\quad?\quad}$.

$\underline{\quad?\quad} \approx r^3$ Evaluate.

$\underline{\quad?\quad} = r$ Find the cube root of both sides.

$\underline{\quad?\quad} \approx r$ Round to the nearest centimeter.

The radius of the spherical ball is about $\underline{\quad?\quad}$ centimeters.

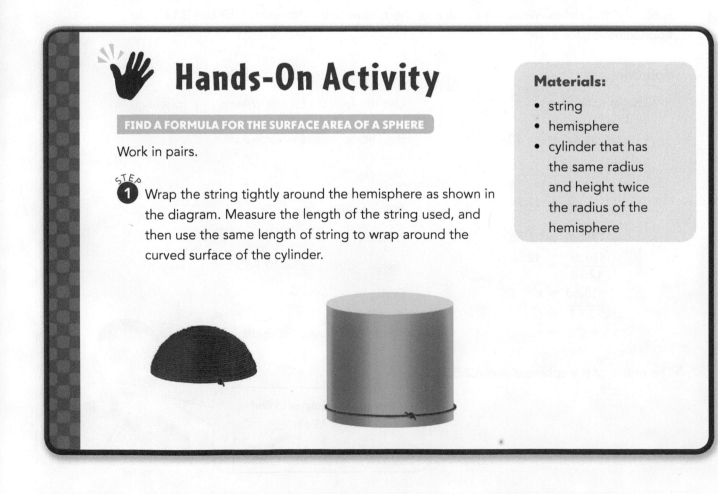

Hands-On Activity

FIND A FORMULA FOR THE SURFACE AREA OF A SPHERE

Work in pairs.

STEP 1 Wrap the string tightly around the hemisphere as shown in the diagram. Measure the length of the string used, and then use the same length of string to wrap around the curved surface of the cylinder.

Materials:
- string
- hemisphere
- cylinder that has the same radius and height twice the radius of the hemisphere

STEP 2 How much of the curved surface of the cylinder does the string cover? If you wrap the whole sphere with string, how much of the curved surface of the cylinder would the same string cover?

STEP 3 How is the surface area of the sphere related to the area of the curved surface of the cylinder?

STEP 4 Copy and complete the following to write a formula for the surface area of a sphere. (Hint: The height of a cylinder is twice the radius of a sphere.)

Surface area of a sphere = Area of cylinder's curved surface

$= 2\pi rh$ Use the formula for the surface area of a cylinder's curved surface.

$= 2\pi r(\underline{\ ?\ })$ Substitute. Use the fact that $h = 2r$.

$= \underline{\ ?\ }\ \pi r^2$ Simplify.

Find the Surface Area of a Sphere.

From the activity, it appears that the formula for the surface area of a sphere, S, is:

$$S = 4\pi r^2$$

This is a result that you will prove in a later course.

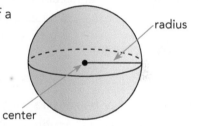

Example 16 | **Find the surface area of a sphere.**

A sphere has a radius of 3 centimeters. What is the surface area of the sphere? Use 3.14 as an approximation for π.

Solution
Surface area of a sphere

$= 4\pi r^2$ Use the formula for the surface area of a sphere.

$\approx 4 \cdot 3.14 \cdot 3 \cdot 3$ Substitute for π and r.

$= 113.04 \text{ cm}^2$ Evaluate.

The surface area of the sphere is about 113.04 square centimeters.

Guided Practice

Solve.

3 What is the surface area of a sphere with a radius of 6 centimeters? Use 3.14 as an approximation for π.

Example 17 **Find the radius of a sphere given its surface area.**

A tennis ball has a surface area of 14,095.46 square millimeters. What is the radius of the tennis ball? Use 3.14 as an approximation for π.

Solution

Surface area of tennis ball $= 4\pi r^2$	Use the formula for the surface area of a sphere.
$14{,}095.46 \approx 4 \cdot 3.14 \cdot r^2$	Substitute for the surface area and π.
$14{,}095.46 = 12.56 \cdot r^2$	Multiply.
$\dfrac{14{,}095.46}{12.56} = \dfrac{12.56 \cdot r^2}{12.56}$	Divide both sides by 12.56.
$1{,}122.25 = r^2$	Evaluate.
$\sqrt{1{,}122.25} = r$	Find the square root of both sides.
$33.5 = r$	Find r.

The radius of the tennis ball is about 33.5 millimeters.

Guided Practice

Solve.

4 A spherical rubber ball has a surface area of 3,215.36 square centimeters. What is the radius of the rubber ball to the nearest centimeter? Use 3.14 as an approximation for π.

Surface area of rubber ball $= 4\pi r^2$	Use the formula for the surface area of a sphere.
$\underline{?} \approx 4 \cdot \underline{?} \cdot r^2$	Substitute for the surface area and π.
$\underline{?} = \underline{?} \cdot r^2$	Multiply.
$\underline{?} = \underline{?}$	Divide both sides by $\underline{?}$.
$\underline{?} = r^2$	Evaluate.
$\underline{?} = r$	Find the square root of both sides.
$\underline{?} = r$	Find r.

The radius of the rubber ball is about $\underline{?}$ centimeters.

Practice 8.4

For this practice, you may use a calculator and use 3.14 as an approximation for π. Round your answers to the nearest tenth when you can.

Solve.

1 What is the volume of a sphere with a radius of 5 centimeters?

2 What is the surface area of a sphere with a radius of 4.4 centimeters?

3 A fully inflated beach ball has a radius of 10 inches.

    a)   What is the surface area of the beach ball?

    b)   What is the volume of air inside the beach ball?

4 What is the surface area of a sphere

    a)   with a diameter of 28.6 centimeters?

    b)   with a volume of 3,680 cubic centimeters?

5 A billiard ball has a surface area of 84 square centimeters. What is the radius of the billiard ball?

6 A bowl is in the shape of a hemisphere. The radius of the bowl is 10 centimeters. How many liters of water can the bowl hold? (1,000 cm³ = 1 liter)

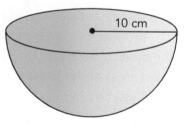

7 *Math Journal*

    a)   What dimension of a sphere do you need to find its surface area and volume?

    b)   Suppose a sphere has a radius greater than 1 unit. If you double the radius, which value will increase by a greater amount, the volume or the surface area of the sphere? Explain your thinking.

8 A basketball is shipped in a cube-shaped box. The basketball just touches the sides of the box, as shown.

    a)   What is the radius of the basketball?

    b)   What is the volume of the basketball?

    c)   About what percent of the space in the cube is occupied by the basketball?

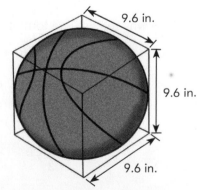

A solid metal ball with a radius of 10 inches is melted and made into smaller spherical metal balls with a radius of 2 inches each. How many smaller spherical balls can be made?

10 Nathan cuts a clay sphere in half to get two hemispheres. He measures the circumference of the hemispheres to be 175.84 centimeters.

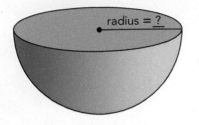

Circumference = 175.84 cm

a) What is the radius of each hemisphere?

b) What is the total surface area of each solid hemisphere?

11 The volume of a sphere is 3,052.08 cubic meters.

a) What is the radius of the sphere?

b) What is the surface area of the sphere?

12 Once you know how to find the surface area of a sphere, you can use the surface area formula to see why the volume formula works.

Think of a sphere as being divided up into hundreds of "pyramids" that have a common vertex at the center of the sphere. The surface of the sphere is made up of the bases of all these pyramids. The height of each pyramid is r, and you can call the areas of the bases B_1, B_2, B_3, and so on. To find the surface area of the sphere, you can find the sum of the areas of all the bases.

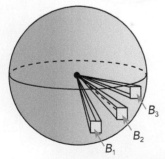

Show why the volume formula works by supplying a reason for each step below.

$$\text{Volume of sphere} = \frac{1}{3}r \cdot B_1 + \frac{1}{3}r \cdot B_2 + \frac{1}{3}r \cdot B_3 \ldots \qquad \underline{\quad ? \quad}$$

$$= \frac{1}{3}r(B_1 + B_2 + B_3 + \ldots) \qquad \underline{\quad ? \quad}$$

$$= \frac{1}{3}r(4\pi r^2) \qquad \underline{\quad ? \quad}$$

$$= \frac{4}{3}\pi r^3 \qquad \underline{\quad ? \quad}$$

8.5 Real-World Problems: Composite Solids

Lesson Objective

- Solve real-world problems involving composite solids.

Find the Volume and Surface Area of a Composite Solid.

To find the volume or surface area of a composite solid, you first identify the basic solids which make up the composite solid. Next find the volume or surface area of each solid, and then add or subtract the volumes or surface areas to find the volume or surface area of the composite solid.

Example 18 Find the volume of a composite solid.

Solve. Show your work.

A composite solid is made up of a cone and a cylinder. The height of the solid is 13 centimeters. The height of the cylinder is 7 centimeters and its radius is 8 centimeters. Find the volume of the composite solid to the nearest cubic centimeter. Use 3.14 as an approximation for π.

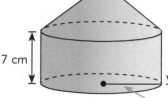

Solution

Volume of the cylinder:

$\pi r^2 h = \pi \cdot 8 \cdot 8 \cdot 7$ Use the formula for the volume of a cylinder.

$= 448\pi$ cm^3 Evaluate.

To find the volume of the cone, you need to know the height of the cone.

Height of cone = 13 − 7 = 6 cm

Volume of the cone:

$\frac{1}{3}\pi r^2 h = \frac{1}{3} \cdot \pi \cdot 8 \cdot 8 \cdot 6$ Use the formula for the volume of a sphere.

$= 128\pi$ cm^3 Multiply.

Volume of the composite solid:

$448\pi + 128\pi = 576\pi$ Add the volumes of the cylinder and the cone.

$\approx 1{,}809$ cm^3 Multiply and round.

The volume of the composite solid is about 1,809 cubic centimeters.

Guided Practice

Solve.

1 A composite solid is made up of a cone and a cylinder. The slant
height of the cone is 25 centimeters. The height of the cylinder is
15 centimeters and its radius is 12 centimeters. The height of
the solid is 37 centimeters. Use 3.14 as an approximation for π.

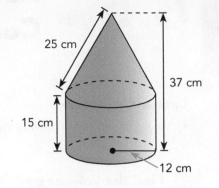

25 cm

37 cm

15 cm

12 cm

a) Find the volume of the composite solid to the nearest
cubic centimeter.

Volume of the cylinder:

$\pi r^2 h = \underline{\ ?\ } \cdot \underline{\ ?\ } \cdot \underline{\ ?\ } \cdot \underline{\ ?\ }$ Use the formula for volume of a cylinder.

$= \underline{\ ?\ }$ cm^3 Evaluate.

Volume of the cone:

Height of cone $= \underline{\ ?\ } - \underline{\ ?\ }$

$= \underline{\ ?\ }$ cm

$\frac{1}{3}\pi r^2 h = \frac{1}{3} \cdot \underline{\ ?\ } \cdot \underline{\ ?\ } \cdot \underline{\ ?\ } \cdot \underline{\ ?\ }$ Use the formula for the volume of a cone.

$= \underline{\ ?\ }$ cm^3 Multiply.

Volume of the composite solid:

$\underline{\ ?\ } + \underline{\ ?\ } = \underline{\ ?\ }$ Add the volumes of the cylinder and the cone.

$\approx \underline{\ ?\ }$ cm^3 Multiply and round.

The volume of the composite solid is about $\underline{\ ?\ }$ cubic centimeters.

b) Find the surface area of the composite solid to the nearest square centimeter.

> Surface area of composite solid
> = Area of lateral surface of cone
>   + Area of curved surface of cylinder
>   + Area of base of cylinder.

Surface area of composite solid
$= \pi r \ell + 2\pi r h + \pi r^2$ Use the formula.

$= \pi \cdot \underline{\ ?\ } \cdot \underline{\ ?\ } + 2 \cdot \pi \cdot \underline{\ ?\ } \cdot \underline{\ ?\ } + \pi \cdot \underline{\ ?\ } \cdot \underline{\ ?\ }$ Substitute for ℓ, r, and h.

$= \underline{\ ?\ } + \underline{\ ?\ } + \underline{\ ?\ }$ Evaluate each term.

$= \underline{\ ?\ }$ Add.

$\approx \underline{\ ?\ }$ cm^2 Multiply and round.

The surface area of the composite solid is about $\underline{\ ?\ }$ square centimeters.

Example 19 Solve a real-world problem involving a composite solid.

A wooden toy is made up of a cone attached to a hemisphere with a diameter of 10 centimeters. The slant height of the cone is 13 centimeters. What is the surface area of the toy? Use 3.14 as an approximation for π. Round your answer to the nearest tenth.

Solution

> Surface area of toy
> = Surface area of the hemisphere
> + Area of lateral surface of the cone

Radius of the hemisphere:

$10 \div 2 = 5$ cm

Surface area of the hemisphere:

$\frac{1}{2} \cdot 4\pi r^2 = \frac{1}{2} \cdot 4 \cdot \pi \cdot 5 \cdot 5$ Surface area of a hemisphere $= \frac{1}{2} \cdot$ surface area of a sphere.

$\qquad\qquad = 50\pi$ cm^2 Multiply.

Area of the lateral surface of the cone:

$\pi r \ell = \pi \cdot 5 \cdot 13$ Use the formula for the area of the lateral surface of a cone.

$\qquad = 65\pi$ cm^2 Multiply.

Surface area of the toy:

$50\pi + 65\pi = 115\pi$ Add the two areas.

$\qquad\qquad \approx 361.1$ cm^2 Multiply and round to the nearest tenth.

The surface area of the toy is about 361.1 square centimeters.

Guided Practice

Solve.

2 A birdhouse looks like a cube with a square pyramid on top. As shown, the birdhouse has a circular entrance with a diameter of 4 inches. Find the exterior surface area of the birdhouse.

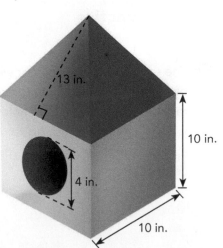

Example 20 **Solve a real-world problem involving a composite solid.**

A candle holder is in the shape of a cube with a cylindrical hole through the middle. The edge length of the cube is 15 centimeters. The height of the cylindrical hole is 9 centimeters. Its radius is 2.5 centimeters.

What is the volume of the candle holder? Use 3.14 as an approximation for π. Round your answer to the nearest cubic centimeter.

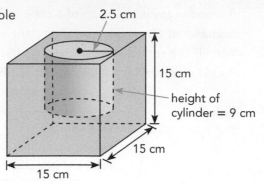

2.5 cm

15 cm

height of
cylinder = 9 cm

15 cm

15 cm

Solution

Volume of the cube:

$\ell^3 = 15 \cdot 15 \cdot 15$ Volume of a cube $= \ell^3$.

    $= 3{,}375$ cm^3 Multiply.

The height of the hole is 9 centimeters.

> The height of the cylindrical hole is less than the height of the candle holder.

Volume of the cylindrical hole:

$\pi r^2 h \approx 3.14 \cdot 2.5 \cdot 2.5 \cdot 9$ Use the formula for volume of a cylinder.

    $= 176.625$ cm^3 Multiply.

Volume of the candle holder:

Volume of candle holder = Volume cube − Volume of cylindrical hole

                  $= 3{,}375 - 176.625$

                  $= 3{,}198.375$

                  ≈ 3.198 cm^3

The volume of the candle holder is about 3,198 cubic centimeters.

Guided Practice

Solve.

3 The solid shown is a cylinder with a cone-shaped hole. The diameter of the cylinder is 22 centimeters. Its height is 15 centimeters. The radius of the cone-shaped hole is 7 centimeters and the height is 10 centimeters. Find the volume of the solid. Use 3.14 as an approximation for π. Round your answer to the nearest cubic centimeter.

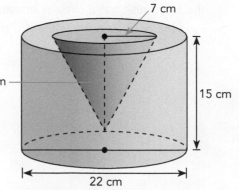

7 cm

10 cm

15 cm

22 cm

For this practice, you may use a calculator and use 3.14 as an approximation for π. Round your answers to the nearest tenth when you can.

Solve.

1 Jack has a cylindrical block that has a radius of 0.6 cm and is 22 centimeters long. He puts together 8 such blocks to form the composite solid shown. What is the volume of the composite solid?

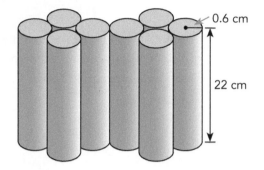

0.6 cm

22 cm

2 The trophy for a basketball tournament is made up of a miniature basketball attached to a rectangular prism. The radius of the basketball is 5 centimeters. The prism measures 8 centimeters by 5 centimeters by 15 centimeters. What is the volume of the trophy to the nearest cubic centimeter?

5 cm

15 cm

Inter School Basketball Tournament

CHAMPION

5 cm

8 cm

3 A necklace is made up of 50 spherical beads. Each bead has a radius of 8 millimeters.

a) What is the volume of the necklace?

b) What is the surface area of the necklace?

4 A crystal trophy is made up of a rectangular pyramid whose base is attached to the top of a rectangular prism. The base of the pyramid and the top of the prism are each 4 inches long and 3 inches wide. The height of the pyramid is 2.5 inches and the height of the prism is 9.5 inches. What is the volume of the crystal trophy?

5 At a food stand, you can buy a paper cone filled with slush made of frozen juice. The slush forms a hemisphere on top of the cone, as shown. What is the volume of the cone of slush?

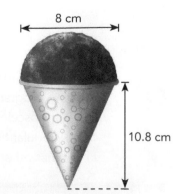

8 cm

10.8 cm

6 A wooden paper towel holder is composed of two cylinders. The diameter of the base is 12 centimeters and its height is 2 centimeters. The combined height of the two cylinders is 30 centimeters. What is the volume of the paper towel holder?

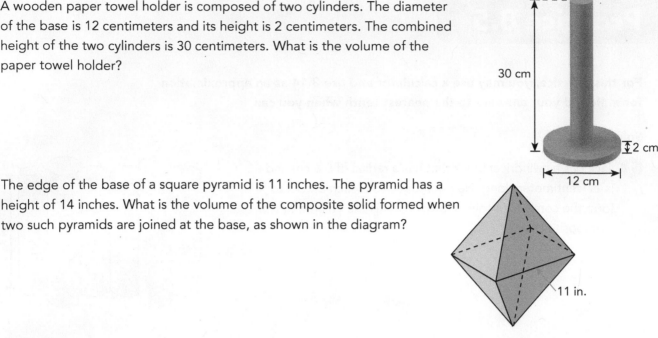

7 The edge of the base of a square pyramid is 11 inches. The pyramid has a height of 14 inches. What is the volume of the composite solid formed when two such pyramids are joined at the base, as shown in the diagram?

8 A clock in the shape of an hour glass is made up of two identical cones connected at their vertices. The radius of each cone is 7 centimeters. The combined height of the two cones is 11.8 centimeters. What is the volume of the clock?

9 Jason made a long pole by joining three different lengths of cylindrical poles together. Each pole has the same diameter of 18 cm. The diagram below is not drawn to scale.

a) What is the volume of the long pole?

b) What is the surface area of the long pole?

Brain @ Work

How can you make the following cross sections by slicing a cube? Use a computer drawing program or pencil and paper to show your answers for a) and b).
a) An isosceles triangle
b) A regular hexagon
c) What other polygons can be cross sections of a cube?

Chapter Wrap Up

Concept Map

Solid	Diagram	Volume	Surface Area, S
Cylinder	radius, r; height, h	$V = Bh$, where B is the area of the base. or $V = \pi r^2 h$	$S = 2\pi rh + 2\pi r^2$ or $S = Ch + 2B$, where C is the circumference of the base.
Cone	height, h; slant height, ℓ; radius, r	$V = \dfrac{1}{3}Bh$, where B is the area of the base. or $V = \dfrac{1}{3}\pi r^2 h$	$S = \pi r^2 + \pi r\ell$
Pyramid	height, h; slant height, s	$V = \dfrac{1}{3}Bh$, where B is the area of the base.	$S = B + \dfrac{1}{2}Ps$, where B is the area of the base and P is the perimeter of the base.
Sphere	radius, r	$V = \dfrac{4}{3}\pi r^3$	$S = 4\pi r^2$

Chapter Review/Test

Concepts and Skills

For this review, *r* represents radius and *h* represents height. You may use a calculator and use 3.14 as an approximation for π. Round your answers to the nearest tenth unless otherwise stated.

1 Find the volume of each cylinder to the nearest unit. Use the given dimensions.

a) *r* = 4.2 inches; *h* = 14 inches

b) *r* = 7 centimeters; *h* = 12 centimeters

2 Find the volume of each cone to the nearest unit. Use the given dimensions.

a) *r* = 3 centimeters; *h* = 8 centimeters

b) *r* = 8 inches; *h* = 15 inches

3 Find the volume of each pyramid. Use the given dimensions.

a) A square base with edge length of 6 centimeters; *h* = 4 centimeters.

b) A rectangular base with length of 6 inches and width = 3.3 inches; *h* = 7 inches.

4 Find the volume of each sphere to the nearest unit. Use the given dimensions.

a) *r* = 9.6 centimeters

b) *d* = 26 centimeters

5 Find the exact surface area of each solid.

a)   3 ft

6 ft

b)   28 m

c)   10 in.

6 in.

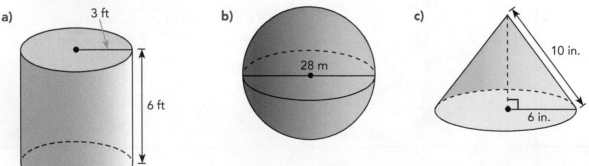

6 Find the volume and surface area of each solid. Round to the nearest tenth.

a) A solid cone with a diameter of 5 feet, a slant height of 7 feet, and a height of 6.5 feet.

b) A sphere with a radius of 28 millimeters.

c) A solid cylinder with a radius of 1.4 inches and a height of 4.2 inches.

Problem Solving

Solve. Show your work.

7 The volume of a cone is 450 cubic centimeters and the radius of the base is 5 centimeters. What is the height of the cone to the nearest tenth?

8 The surface area of a sphere is 498.96 square centimeters. What is the radius of the sphere to the nearest tenth?

9 A cone with a height of 6 inches and a slant height of 7.5 inches has a lateral surface with an area of approximately 106 square inches.

a) What is the radius? Round to the nearest tenth.

b) What is the volume of the cone? Round to the nearest tenth.

10 A cylinder, a cone, and a sphere are shown below. Each solid has a radius of 1 inch and a height of 2 inches. Which of them has the greatest volume? Justify your answer.

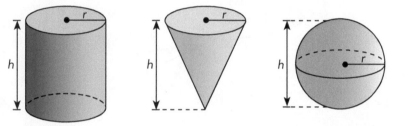

11 Two metal cubes each have an edge length of 4 centimeters. They are melted and recast into a square pyramid with a height of 5 centimeters. Find the area of the base of the pyramid.

12 A conical party hat has a diameter of 7 centimeters and a slant height of 14.5 centimeters. Paul wants to wrap the lateral surface of the party hat with plastic wrap. How much plastic wrap will he use? Round to the nearest square centimeter.

13 The composite solid shown is made up of a hemisphere attached to the top of a cube. The diameter of the hemisphere is the same as the edge length of the cube. Find the volume of the composite solid. Round to the nearest tenth.

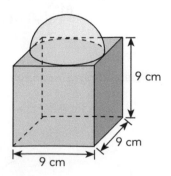

9 cm

9 cm

9 cm

14 The circumference of a fully inflated beach ball is 12π, or about 37.68 inches. What is the radius of the beach ball? What is the volume of the beach ball? Round to the nearest tenth if necessary.

15 A pyramid made of clay has a square base of length 8 inches and a height of 12 inches. The pyramid is reshaped into a cylinder with a radius of 8 inches. What is the height of the cylinder? Round to the nearest inch.

Cumulative Review Chapters 6–8

Concepts and Skills

Tell whether each pair of angles is supplementary, complementary, or neither. (Lesson 6.1)

1 m∠1 = 18° and m∠2 = 82°

2 m∠3 = 103° and m∠4 = 77°

3 m∠5 = 95° and m∠6 = 85°

4 m∠7 = 21° and m∠8 = 69°

These diagrams may not be drawn to scale. Find the measure of each numbered angle. (Lessons 6.1, 6.2)

5 $\overleftrightarrow{PR}$ is a straight line.

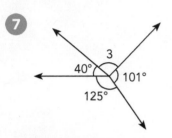

6 $\overleftrightarrow{PR}$ is a straight line.

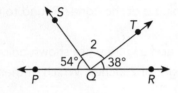
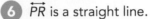

7

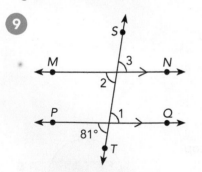

8

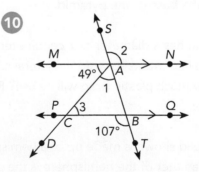

These diagrams may not be drawn to scale. $\overleftrightarrow{MN}$ is parallel to $\overleftrightarrow{PQ}$. Find the measure of each numbered angle. (Lesson 6.3)

9

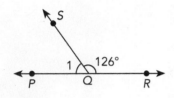

10

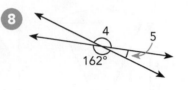

These diagrams may not be drawn to scale. Find the measures of ∠1 and ∠2 in each diagram. (Lesson 6.4)

11 Triangle ABC is an isosceles triangle.

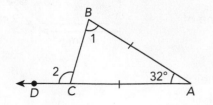

12 $\overleftrightarrow{PR}$ is a straight line.

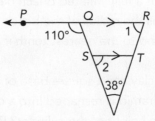
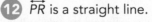

Use the given information to construct each polygon.

13 Construct triangle ABC with sides AB = 5.8 cm, BC = 6.6 cm, and AC = 4.5 cm.
(Lessons 7.1, 7.2, 7.3)

    a) Measure the angles of the triangle.

    b) Use a compass and straightedge to bisect angle B.

    c) Use a compass and straightedge to construct the perpendicular bisector of AB.

    d) The two bisectors intersect at a point D, label D in your construction.

    e) Measure the distances BD and CD.

14 Construct quadrilateral PQRS with PQ = PR = 7.8 cm, PQ ∥ SR, m∠PQR = 73°,
and RS = 4 cm. (Lessons 7.1, 7.2, 7.4)

    a) Measure the length of PS.

    b) Use a compass and straightedge to construct the angle bisector of ∠S.

    c) Use a compass and straightedge to construct the perpendicular bisector of $\overline{PQ}$.

    d) Label the point where the angle bisector and perpendicular bisector intersect
as W.

Solve. Show your work. (Lesson 7.5)

15 Jacob builds a model plane that is 800 millimeters long. If the actual plane
is 40 meters, what is the scale of the model? (10 mm = 1 cm)

16 The scale of a map is 1 : 1,500. If a square piece of land measures 4 inches
on each side on the map, find the actual area of this piece of land to the
nearest tenth of an acre. (1 acre = 43,560 ft²)

Match each solid with its net. (Lesson 8.1)

17

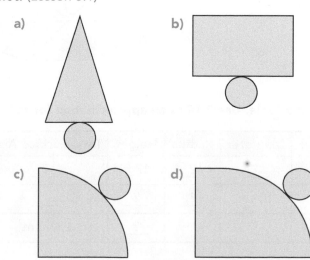

18

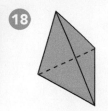

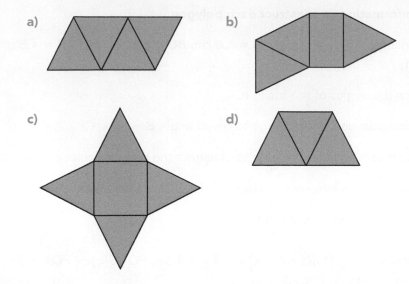

a)

b)

c)

d)

For each solid, sketch and describe the shape of the cross section formed when a plane slices the solid in the direction indicated. (Lesson 8.1)

19 A cube of length 6 centimeters perpendicular to a base and parallel to two opposite faces.

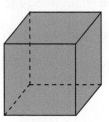

20 A cylinder of radius 3 centimeters parallel to its bases.

21 A right triangle base prism parallel to its bases.

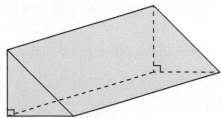

22 **Copy and complete the table. Use 3.14 as an approximation for π.** (Lesson 8.2)

Volume of Solid Cylinder	Diameter	Radius	Height	Total Surface Area
942 ft³	?	?	12 ft	?
879.2 cm³	10 cm	?	?	?
?	?	4 m	?	251.2 m²

Find the exact surface area of each solid cone. (Lesson 8.3)

23 A cone with radius of 8.7 meters and a slant height of 12.8 meters.

24 A cone of diameter 16.8 centimeters and slant height 20.6 centimeters.

Find the volume of each solid. Use 3.14 as an approximation for π. Round your answers to the nearest tenth when you can. (Lessons 8.3, 8.4)

25 A square pyramid with a height of 13 centimeters and a base that is 8 centimeters on each edge.

26 An octagonal pyramid with a height of 8.2 inches and a base area of 34.5 square inches.

27 A cone with a radius of 6.5 centimeters and a height of 14 centimeters.

28 A cone with a diameter of 24.6 feet and a height of 18.5 feet.

29 A sphere with a radius of 9.6 feet.

30 A sphere with a diameter of 39.8 centimeters.

Problem Solving

These diagrams may not be drawn to scale. Find the value of each variable. (Chapter 6)

31
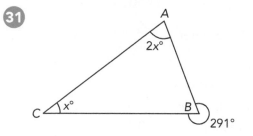

32
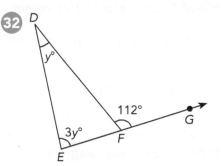

33
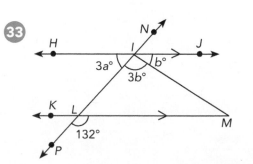

34
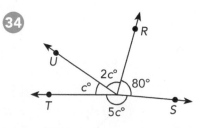

Solve. Show your work.

35 Segment *AB* is parallel to segments *CD* and *EF*. Segment *BC* is parallel to segment *ED*. Find the measure of ∠*ABC*. (Chapter 6)

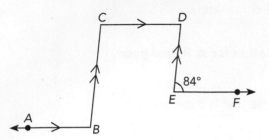

36 The diagram shows a triangular pin. Triangle *ABC* is an isosceles triangle. Line *BD* is parallel to line *EF*. m∠*AEF* = 40° and m∠*DBC* = 27°. Find the measures of ∠*EBD* and ∠*BAC*. (Chapter 6)

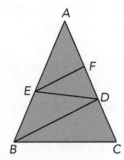

37 *X*, *Y*, and *Z* are the location of three manufacturing factories linked by three straight roads as shown in the diagram. A water pipe will go from Factory *Y*, and will be equidistant from the two roads linking Factory *X* and Factory *Z* to Factory *Y*. (Chapter 7)

a) Construct triangle *XYZ* to represent the locations of the three factories using a scale of 1 centimeter to 100 meters.

b) Using a compass and straightedge only, construct the path of the water pipe.

c) The water department needs to build a temporary construction worksite that must be equidistant from Factory *Y* and Factory *Z* and at a distance of 400 meters from Factory *X*. Label the position of the construction worksite to be set up in your diagram as point *W*.

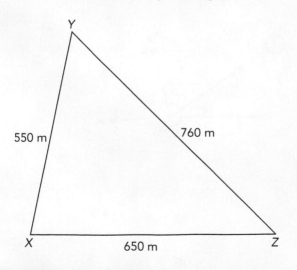

38 A model of a gym uses a scale of 1 : 12. The actual gym will be a rectangular prism. It will be 69.6 feet long, 54 feet wide, and 22.8 feet high. Find, in cubic feet, the volume of the model of the gym. (Chapters 7, 8)

39 Mrs. Sullivan buys a 5-liter bottle of apple juice. She can either use cylindrical glass A or cylindrical glass B to serve the apple juice. Use 3.14 as an approximation for π. (1,000 cm^3 = 1 L) (Chapter 8)

a) What is the volume of glass A?

b) How many glasses of apple juice can she serve if she uses glass A?

c) What is the volume of glass B?

d) How many glasses of apple juice can she serve if she uses glass B?

e) If Mrs. Sullivan sells one glass of apple juice for $1.80, what is the maximum amount of money she can collect?

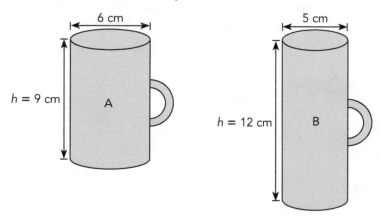

40 Matthew installs a ceiling mirror in his retail bookstore to deter shoplifters. The mirror is a hemisphere. Calculate the exact surface area, in square meters, of the mirror if the diameter of the hemisphere is 600 millimeters. (Chapter 8)

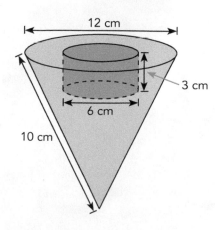

41 Mindy bought a candleholder cup as shown in the diagram. It consists of a cone-shape holder with an iron stand. The cone-shaped holder has a cylindrical hole cut in it to hold the candle, as shown. Mindy wants to paint the whole candleholder, including the hole, with a new layer of varnish. Calculate the surface area of the cone-shaped candleholder she has to paint. Use 3.14 as an approximation for π. Round your answer to the nearest square centimeters. (Chapter 8)

BIG IDEA

▶ Measures of central tendency and measures of variation are used to draw conclusions about populations.

Statistics

Will you ever run a marathon?

Marathons are races that are popular worldwide. A full marathon is just over 26 miles.

Thousands of people participate in marathons all over the world. It takes 4 to 5 hours for most people to finish the race. Some may take an even longer time. Olympic runners usually finish the race in 2 to 3 hours.

What is the difference between the slowest and fastest marathon times? You may take a random sample of the runners to find the average time. You can also find how great the time differences are among runners.

Recall Prior Knowledge

Finding the mean of a set of data

One measure of the center of a data set is the mean. It is the sum of the data values divided by the number of data values.

Find the mean of 12, 34, 56, 78, and 90.

$$\text{Mean} = \frac{12 + 34 + 56 + 78 + 90}{5}$$

$$= \frac{270}{5}$$

$$= 54$$

✓ Quick Check

Find the mean of each set of data. Round your answer to 2 decimal places if it is not exact.

1 9, 11, 6, 29, 5

2 43, 88, 39, 10, 26, 17, 35

3 53.6, 36.7, 88.5, 90.6

4 0.14, 1.05, 3.1, 7.18, 4.3, 8

Solve. Show your work.

5 The heights, in inches, of 10 children are

54, 66, 52, 60.5, 61.25, 55, 58.75, 51.5, 53, 50.

Find the mean height of the children.

Finding the median of a set of data

Another measure of the center of a data set is the median. It is the middle value of the data when the data are arranged from least to greatest.

a)   Find the median of the values 48, 34, 56, 28, and 60.

First order the values from the least to the greatest: 28, 34, 48, 56, 60

The median is the middle value.
So, the median is 48.

Continue on next page

b) Find the median of the values 26, 15, 9, 85, 70, 31, 44, and 6.

First order the values from the least to the greatest: 6, 9, 15, 26, 31, 44, 70, 85.

Since there is an even number of values, the median is the mean of the middle two values.

$$\text{Median} = \frac{26 + 31}{2}$$
$$= \frac{57}{2}$$
$$= 28.5$$

✓ Quick Check

Find the median of each set of numbers.

6 41, 29, 78, 12, 56, 30, 22

7 193, 121.5, 162.3, 125, 103.8, 149.6

8 9, 2, 2, 4, 4, 4, 1, 3, 6, 5, 3, 6

9 1,011, 1,100, 1,001, 1,010, 1,110, 1,000, 1,011, 100

Solve. Show your work.

10 The daily low temperatures for the past 10 days were 30.6°F, 32.1°F, 29.5°F, 30.2°F, 26.4°F, 34.3°F, 31.6°F, 32°F, 25.9°F, and 26.4°F. What was the median daily low temperature?

Drawing frequency tables and dot plots

Frequency tables and dot plots are used to organize and summarize data.

The data show the number of hours spent by 20 students in preparation for a final examination.

5	6	7	4	7	7	12	3	9	6
8	6	7	5	3	7	5	8	7	9

The data can be summarized in a frequency table and a dot plot.

Number of Hours of Study	Number of Students
3	2
4	1
5	3
6	3
7	6
8	2
9	2
10	0
11	0
12	1

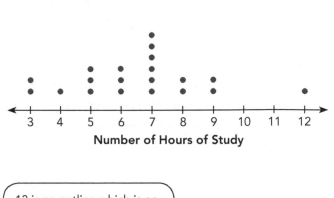

Number of Hours of Study

12 is an outlier, which is an extreme or rare occurrence of a value.

Quick Check

Summarize each of the following data sets in a frequency table and draw a dot plot.

11 The data show the number of misspelled words found in 15 essays.

3	5	0	7	1
0	2	2	1	8
2	1	5	4	2

12 In a game, each child is given 10 balls to hit at moving targets. The data show the number of hits scored by 20 children.

6	0	10	7	4	1	0	8	4	5
0	3	1	3	1	4	10	4	9	4

Interpreting Quartiles and Interquartile Range

Lesson Objectives

- Introduce the concept of measures of variation.
- Understand quartiles and interquartile range.
- Solve problems involving quartiles and interquartile range.

Introduce the Concept of Measures of Variation.

Consider the heights of some of the players in two football teams.

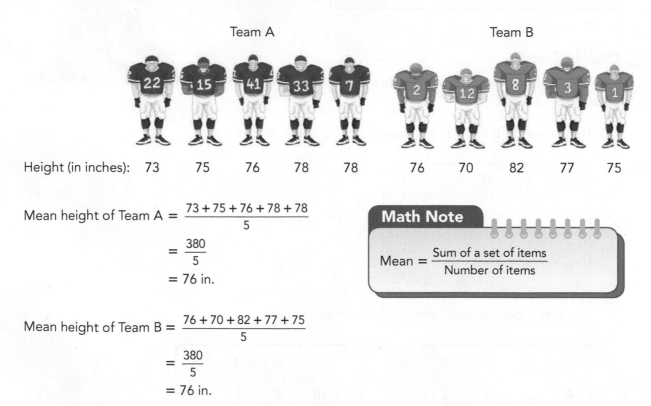

Team A   Team B

Height (in inches):   73   75   76   78   78   76   70   82   77   75

Mean height of Team A = $\dfrac{73 + 75 + 76 + 78 + 78}{5}$

$= \dfrac{380}{5}$

$= 76$ in.

> **Math Note**
>
> Mean = $\dfrac{\text{Sum of a set of items}}{\text{Number of items}}$

Mean height of Team B = $\dfrac{76 + 70 + 82 + 77 + 75}{5}$

$= \dfrac{380}{5}$

$= 76$ in.

The mean height of the two teams is the same. Taking a closer look, you notice that Team A players are roughly the same height but Team B players appear to be more varied in height.

Understand Range.

In statistics, you can measure how data values vary. The simplest way is to measure the difference between two data extremes.

In Team A, the two extreme heights are 73 inches and 78 inches.

Difference: 78 − 73 = 5 in.

The difference is 5 inches.

In other words, the difference between the heights of the tallest and the shortest players is 5 inches.

This difference is called the range.

In Team B, the tallest player is 82 inches and the shortest player is 70 inches.
Range: 82 − 70 = 12 in.

The range is 12 inches.

By comparing the ranges, you can see that there is a greater span of heights among the Team B players.

> The range is a basic way of measuring variation because it takes into account only the two data extremes and disregards all the other data values in between.
>
> Range of a set of data:
>
> Range = The greatest value − The least value

Besides range, there are other statistics that measure variation. They are called measures of variation. They measure how data are spread out from the center of the data.

Example 1 Find the range of a set of data.

The history test scores of 10 students are 68, 73, 64, 70, 86, 54, 66, 89, 82, and 60. Find the range of the test scores.

Solution

Greatest score = 89

Least score = 54

Range = The greatest score − The least score
     = 89 − 54
     = 35

The range is 35 marks.

Guided Practice

Calculate.

1 The table shows the average monthly temperatures in degrees Fahrenheit in New York. Find the range of the these temperatures.

Month	Jan	Feb	Mar	Apr	May	Jun	Jul	Aug	Sep	Oct	Nov	Dec
Temperature (°F)	31.5	33.6	42.4	52.5	62.7	71.6	76.8	75.5	68.2	57.5	47.6	36.6

Understand Quartiles.

Consider the data values 23, 28, 16, 11, 30, 21, 46, 55, 38, 37, 44, and 17.

To find the median, you need to order the 12 data values from the least to the greatest.

11 16 17 21 23 28 30 37 38 44 46 55

$$\frac{28 + 30}{2} = 29$$

The median is 29, halfway between the two middle data items, which are the sixth and the seventh items in the list. It divides the data into two halves, the lower half and the upper half.

Lower half   Upper half

11 16 17 21 23 28 30 37 38 44 46 55

Median

In other words, 50% of the data are less than or equal to the median and 50% of the data are greater than or equal to the median.

Lower half   Upper half

11 16 17 21 23 28 30 37 38 44 46 55

$$\frac{17 + 21}{2} = 19$$ Median $$\frac{38 + 44}{2} = 41$$

Next find the median of the lower half and the median of the upper half. These values are 19 and 41. Together with the median, they divide the data into four equal parts.

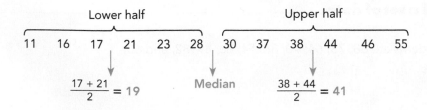

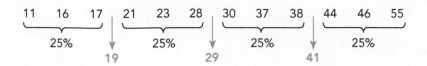

The median of the lower half is called the **first quartile** (or **lower quartile**). It is written as Q_1.

The median of the data is called the **second quartile**. It is written as Q_2.

The median of the upper half is called the **third quartile** (or **upper quartile**). It is written as Q_3.

> You usually read Q_1 as "first quartile," Q_2 as "second quartile," and so on.

How are quartiles read and interpreted? Think about the following scenario:

The math scores of 600 students on a standardized test have been put in order. The quartiles are then identified:

- $Q_1 = 380$
- $Q_2 = 466$
- $Q_3 = 547$

You can draw a diagram to show how the data are related to the quartiles.

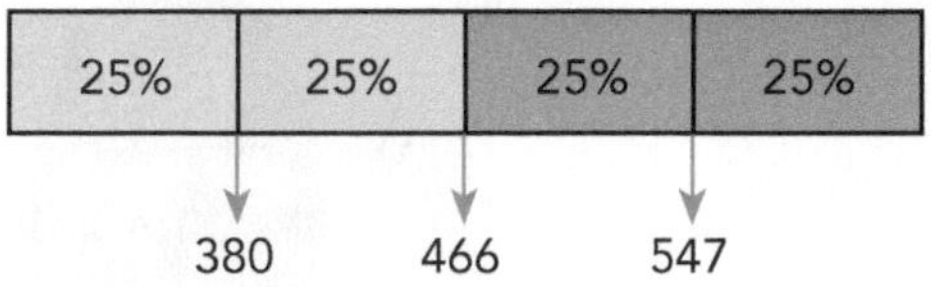

25%	25%	25%	25%

380   466   547

> Each box of the diagram represents 25% of the students taking the test.

Since the quartiles divide the data into 4 equal parts, this is how you read the diagram above.

- 25% of the students scored less than or equal to 380.
- 50% of the students scored less than or equal to 466.
- 75% of the students scored less than or equal to 547.

You may also read the diagram the other way around.

- 75% of the students scored 380 or more.
- 50% of the students scored 466 or more.
- 25% of the students scored 547 or more.

Either way, you add the percents together as you read them from the diagram.

Example 2 **Find the quartiles of a set of data.**

The data below show body weights, in pounds, recorded at a health screening of a group of people. Find the first, second, and third quartiles of the body weights.

100	155	126	98	160	117	160	94	124
95	140	153	142	138	170	125	147	118

Solution

94, 95, 98, 100, 117, 118, 124, 125, 126, | 138, 140, 142, 147, 153, 155, 160, 160, 170

Q_2, halfway between the ninth and tenth data values, is the median of the data.

$Q_2 = \dfrac{126 + 138}{2}$

$= 132$ lb

So, Q_2 is 132 pounds.

First arrange the 18 weights in ascending order. Then you can draw a line to show the point that separates the data into two equal halves.

Q_1 is the median of the lower half of the data:
94, 95, 98, 100, 117, 118, 124, 125, 126.

So, Q_1, the fifth data value in this set, is 117 pounds.

Q_3 is the median of the upper half of the data:
138, 140, 142, 147, 153, 155, 160, 160, 170.

So, Q_3, the fifth data value in this set, is 153 pounds.

Guided Practice

Complete.

2 The heights, in centimeters, of the tomato seedling plants in a greenhouse are listed below. Find the first, second, and third quartiles of the heights of the seedling plants.

9.3	4.3	5.2	3.9	10	7	6
6.4	9.5	7.7	10.6	4.8	8	3.2

First arrange the heights in ascending order: __?__

Q_2 is the median of the data. So, $Q_2 = \dfrac{? + ?}{?}$

$= \underline{\ ?\ }$

Q_1 is the median of the lower half of the data: __?__
$Q_1 = \underline{\ ?\ }$

Q_3 is the median of the upper half of the data: __?__
$Q_3 = \underline{\ ?\ }$

Understand Interquartile Range.

Sometimes people are interested in the middle 50% of a set of data values. Consider the middle 50% of the standardized math scores described earlier.

middle 50%

25%	25%	25%	25%

380   466   547

You can see from the diagram that 50% of the scores are between 380 and 547.
The range between the lower and the upper quartiles is called the interquartile range.

> Interquartile range of a data set:
>
> Interquartile range = Upper quartile − Lower quartile

Example 3   Find and interpret the interquartile range.

Fifteen people were surveyed to find out how many hours they sleep every day.
The findings were as follows:

8	8.4	10	6.5	7.4
9.5	5	7	8	11
6	8	7.2	11.5	7

Find the interquartile range and interpret what it means.

Solution

The median is the eighth of the 15 data values. So, Q_2 is 8 hours.

5, 6, 6.5, ⑦, 7, 7.2, 7.4, |8, 8, 8, 8.4, ⑨.5, 10, 11, 11.5

The lower quartile, Q_1, is 7 hours. The upper quartile, Q_3, is 9.5 hours.

Interquartile range = $Q_3 - Q_1$
$$= 9.5 - 7$$
$$= 2.5 \text{ h}$$

The interquartile range is 2.5 hours.

You can interpret the interquartile range as saying that about 50% of the people in the study sleep from 7 to 9.5 hours each day. The difference in the number of sleeping hours among the middle 50% of the people is at most 2.5 hours.

Arrange the data in ascending order. Drawing a line through the eighth data value helps you understand why the other two 8s are included in the upper half.

Guided Practice

Solve.

3 Out of 50 multiple choice questions, 19 students scored the following numbers of correct answers.

36	49	45	30	27	50	45	44	20	18
14	19	31	50	26	33	10	42	30	

Find the interquartile range and interpret what it means.

Example 4 **Find the quartiles and the interquartile range of a set of data.**

Concert tickets were priced at $100, $70, $60, and $45. Twenty-two tickets were sold in the first hour of sales. The table shows how many of each type of ticket were sold.

Ticket Price	Number of Tickets
$100	2
$70	4
$60	5
$45	11

a) Find the lower quartile, the upper quartile, and the interquartile range.

Solution

List the 22 tickets in ascending order by ticket price.

45, 45, 45, 45, 45, 45, 45, 45, 45, 45, 45, | 60, 60, 60, 60, 60, 70, 70, 70, 70, 100, 100

$$Q_1 \qquad\qquad Q_2 \qquad\qquad Q_3$$

$$Q_1 = \$45 \qquad Q_2 = \frac{\$45 + \$60}{2} \qquad Q_3 = \$70$$

$$= \$52.50$$

Interquartile range = $70 − $45

$$= \$25$$

The interquartile range is $25.

b) Interpret what the interquartile range means.

Solution

The difference in price among the middle 50% of the number of tickets sold is at most $25.

Guided Practice

Calculate.

4 A survey of 50 people asking the number of books they read in a year produced the following results.

Number of Books	0	1	2	3	4	5	6	7	8	9	10
Number of People	5	6	3	6	5	9	7	4	0	2	3

a) Find the lower quartile, the upper quartile, and the interquartile range.

b) Interpret what the interquartile range means.

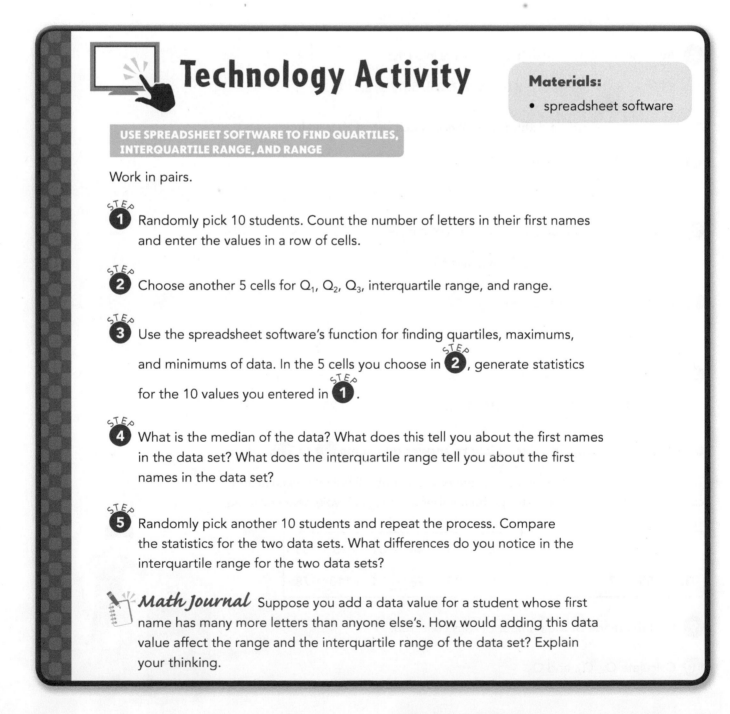

Technology Activity

Materials:
- spreadsheet software

USE SPREADSHEET SOFTWARE TO FIND QUARTILES, INTERQUARTILE RANGE, AND RANGE

Work in pairs.

STEP 1 Randomly pick 10 students. Count the number of letters in their first names and enter the values in a row of cells.

STEP 2 Choose another 5 cells for Q_1, Q_2, Q_3, interquartile range, and range.

STEP 3 Use the spreadsheet software's function for finding quartiles, maximums, and minimums of data. In the 5 cells you choose in **STEP 2**, generate statistics for the 10 values you entered in **STEP 1**.

STEP 4 What is the median of the data? What does this tell you about the first names in the data set? What does the interquartile range tell you about the first names in the data set?

STEP 5 Randomly pick another 10 students and repeat the process. Compare the statistics for the two data sets. What differences do you notice in the interquartile range for the two data sets?

Math Journal Suppose you add a data value for a student whose first name has many more letters than anyone else's. How would adding this data value affect the range and the interquartile range of the data set? Explain your thinking.

Practice 9.1

Find the range of each set of data values.

1 Weights of rabbits in pounds: 15, 9, 10, 22, 14.5, 12.5, 16, 8, and 11.

2 Number of pairs of shoes sold each day for a week at a retail shop:

67, 63, 66, 60, 58, 70, and 75.

3 Time taken in seconds to solve a puzzle by a group of contestants:

20, 25.6, 15.4, 20, 22.8, 18.7, 19, 24, 13.4, and 16.

4 Average monthly rainfall in centimeters in a city:

18.3, 17.8, 17.3, 8.9, 6.1, 2.0, 1.4, 2.2, 2.8, 5, 12.7, and 14.

Find the first, second, and third quartiles of each set of data values.

5 Science test scores of 13 students:

78, 63, 56, 85, 62, 59, 78, 90, 83, 63, 84, 66, and 63.

6 Scores of a basketball team in a series of games:

82, 66, 70, 68, 54, 77, 80, 70, 82, and 65.

7 Ages of 20 children at a party:

6, 9, 5, 12, 7, 8, 9, 10, 7, 7, 7, 6, 9, 9, 12, 10, 8, 10, 11, and 9.

8 Heights of 15 tomato plants in inches:

36, 27, 18, 40, 29, 43, 24, 20, 15, 31, 39, 22, 27, 30, and 20.

Use the information and table below to answer questions 9 to 12.

To create greater public awareness of the environment, 22 volunteers collected cans for recycling. The table shows the number of cans each volunteer collected.

25	105	100	47	61	82	75	44	61	70	53
38	50	73	54	80	36	25	28	24	110	78

9 Find the range of the number of cans collected.

10 Calculate Q_1, Q_2, and Q_3.

11 Find the interquartile range.

12 Interpret Q_3 and the interquartile range.

Use the information and table below to answer questions 13 to 16.

The table shows the results of a survey asking 50 people how many hours they spent using the Internet in a day.

Number of Hours	1	2	3	4	5	6	7	8	9	10
Number of People	3	0	9	5	7	11	5	1	6	3

13 Find the median, the lower quartile, and the upper quartile of the number of hours spent using the Internet.

14 Calculate the interquartile range.

15 Interpret the data values that are greater than the upper quartile.

16 *Math Journal* "A majority of the people surveyed spent 6 hours or less using the Internet." Do you agree with this statement? Justify your argument by using the quartiles.

Use the information and table below to answer questions 17 to 21.

The table shows the lifespans of 29 batteries that were tested.

Battery Life (h)	2	3.5	4.5	5	6	7.5	8	9
Number of Batteries	4	3	5	2	4	2	4	5

17 Find the range of the lifespans.

18 *Math Journal* Explain why the range is not a good statistic to use for evaluating the lifespans of these batteries.

19 Find the median, the lower quartile, and the upper quartile of the lifespans.

20 Calculate the interquartile range.

21 *Math Journal* Compare the lifespans less than the lower quartile to the lifespans greater than the upper quartile. Based on this comparison, do you consider the difference in battery lifespans significant? Explain your reasoning.

22 ✏️ *Math Journal* Another statistic used to analyze data is the midrange.

$$\text{Midrange} = \frac{\text{The greatest data value} + \text{The least data value}}{2}$$

Is the midrange the same as the median of a set of data values? Explain your reasoning by using an example.

Solve.

23 The finishing times of 40 people in a 100-meter freestyle swimming event were collected. The quartiles for the data are shown:

$Q_1 = 62.05$ seconds, $Q_2 = 69.16$ seconds, and $Q_3 = 71.43$ seconds.

List the letters of all the following statements that are correct.

a) 50% of the swimmers managed to complete the 100-meter event in between 69.16 and 71.43 seconds.

b) 75% of the swimmers took longer than 62.05 seconds to complete the event.

c) Swimmers with times greater than the upper quartile are fast swimmers.

d) Swimmers with times between the first and the second quartiles are faster than the first 10 swimmers who finished the swimming event.

e) The interquartile range shows that the time differences of the middle 50% of the swimmers is not more than 9.38 seconds.

f) 50% of the swimmers completed the 100-meter event between 62.05 and 71.43 seconds.

g) 25% of the swimmers took 71.43 or more seconds to complete the event.

h) 10 swimmers completed the event in less than 62.05 seconds.

i) The number of swimmers with times between the first and the second quartiles is more than the number of swimmers with times between the second and the third quartiles.

Stem-and-Leaf Plots

Lesson Objectives

- Represent data in a stem-and-leaf plot.
- Make conclusions and solve word problems involving stem-and-leaf plots.

Vocabulary

stem-and-leaf plot   stem

leaf

Represent Data in a Stem-and-Leaf Plot.

Stem-and-leaf plots are a way to organize data. A stem-and-leaf plot looks similar to a histogram or a bar graph, but retains more information about the data. Like a dot plot, it retains individual items of data, but it can be used with much larger sets of data.

The data are arranged by place value. The larger place values form the **stems**, and the least place values form the **leaves**. Each leaf has only a single digit, but stems can have more than one digit, as in the following example.

The weights, in pounds, of five students are shown in the stem-and-leaf plot.

Weights (in pounds) of Students

Stem	Leaf
6	9
7	8 9
8	
9	4
10	
11	
12	8

> An outlier is a value that is either far less than or far greater than the rest of the values in the data set. It is often preceded by stems that have no leaves.

6 | 9 represents the weight of a student weighing 69 pounds.

7 | 8 9 represents the weights of two students weighing 78 and 79 pounds.

9 | 4 represents the weight of a student weighing 94 pounds.

12 | 8 represents the weight of a student weighing 128 pounds.

A stem-and-leaf plot displays clearly how the data are spread out and whether there are repeated data values or outliers.

Stem-and-leaf plots can be used to organize data values as they are collected. They are commonly used to collect large amounts of data for analyzing. Some examples of data include scores in sports events, temperatures or rainfall over a period of time, classroom test scores, and heights and weights of students.

Example 5 **Display data in a stem-and-leaf plot.**

The data below show the test scores for one student during a semester. Display the data in a stem-and-leaf plot.

| 78 | 23 | 50 | 45 | 43 | 63 | 69 |

Solution

Test Scores in a Semester

Stem	Leaf
2	3
3	
4	3 5
5	0
6	3 9
7	8

2 | 3 represents a score of 23.

STEP 1 Identify the least and greatest data values, and identify the stems that will be used.

The least and greatest values are 23 and 78, so the stems will go from 2 to 7.

STEP 2 Place the leaf for each data value after the correct stem.

STEP 3 Order the leaves from least to greatest if necessary.

STEP 4 Write a key and a title.

Caution ///////

The stems in a stem-and-leaf plot are listed in order without gaps. So, even though there are no data values from 30–39, you need to include 3 as a stem.

Guided Practice

Display data in a stem-and-leaf plot.

1 The data show the math quiz scores for 15 students. Display the data in a stem-and-leaf plot.

| 13 | 8 | 27 | 11 | 15 | 12 | 21 | 10 |
| 31 | 44 | 26 | 11 | 33 | 18 | 20 |

As 8 is the only single digit data value, there will be a zero in the stem.

STEP 1 Identify the least and greatest values, and identify the stems.

STEP 2 Place a leaf on the plot for each item of data.

STEP 3 Arrange the leaves in ascending order for each number on the stem.

STEP 4 Write a title and a key for the stem-and-leaf plot.

Make Conclusions and Solve Problems Involving Stem-and-Leaf Plots.

Besides being a way to display data, a stem-and-leaf plot can also provide the minimum and maximum values of a data set. The mode and median can also be identified from a stem-and-leaf plot.

Example 6 **Find the median, mode, and range, and make inferences from a stem-and-leaf plot.**

The data below show the sizes of classes at a school.

| 25 | 28 | 27 | 29 | 24 | 22 | 30 | 29 | 32 | 25 |
| 26 | 29 | 21 | 31 | 28 | 19 | 23 | 24 | 23 | 29 |

a) Display the data in a stem-and-leaf plot.

Solution

The least and greatest values are 19 and 32. The stems of a stem-and-leaf plot will be 1, 2, and 3. Reorder the data in ascending order:
19, 21, 22, 23, 23, 24, 24, 25, 25, 26, 27, 28, 28, 29, 29, 29, 29, 30, 31, 32

Class Sizes in a School

Stem	Leaf
1	9
2	1 2 3 3 4 4 5 5 6 7 8 8 9 9 9 9
3	0 1 2

1 | 9 represents a class size of 19.

b) How many classes are in the school?

Solution

Since there are 20 leaves in the stem-and-leaf plot, there are 20 classes in the school.

c) What is the range of the class sizes?

Solution

Range = 32 − 19 = 13

d) What is the most common class size? This is the mode of the data.

Solution

A class size of 29 students occurs most often, so 29 is the mode of the data.

Continue on next page

e) What is the median class size?

Solution

Since there are 20 data values, draw a line between the tenth and eleventh data value
to represent the median.

Class Sizes in a School

Stem	Leaf
1	9
2	1 2 3 3 4 4 5 5 6 │ 7 8 8 9 9 9 9
3	0 1 2

1 | 9 represents a class size of 19.

You can count up from the least value on the stem-and-leaf plot to find the tenth and eleventh data values. You can also list the data values in order to find the median.

19, 21, 22, 23, 23, 24, 24, 25, 25, 26, │ 27, 28, 28, 29, 29, 29, 29, 30, 31, 32

Median $= \dfrac{26 + 27}{2} = 26.5$

f) Find the mean class size.

Solution

Total of all the stems: $10 \cdot 1 + 20 \cdot 16 + 30 \cdot 3 = 420$
Total of all the leaves: $9 + 1 + 2 + 3 \cdot 2 + 4 \cdot 2 + 5 \cdot 2 + 6 + 7 + 8 \cdot 2 + 9 \cdot 4 + 0 + 1 + 2$
$= 104$

Sum of the data: $420 + 104 = 524$

Mean $= 524 \div 20 = 26.2$

So, the mean is 26.2.

Guided Practice

Solve.

 The data below show the attendance, in number of days, for some students
during the first month of school.

15	18	19	23	23	22	20	21	22	20	22	20	21
21	20	19	23	23	20	22	23	23	23	23	22	

a) Display the data in a stem-and-leaf plot.

b) How many students are represented by the data?

c) What is the most common attendance, or mode?

d) What is the mean attendance?

e) What is the median attendance?

Example 7 **Find the median and mean and make inferences from a double stem-and-leaf plot.**

The stem-and-leaf plot shows the weights, in pounds, of the players on two football teams.

Weights (in pounds) of Two Football Teams

Team A	Stem	Team B
8 5	17	7
9 8 7 1	18	1 6 8
9 7 2 0	19	1 3 5
0	20	3 5 7 9

Team A: 5 | 17 represents 175 pounds.
Team B: 17 | 7 represents 177 pounds.

a) How many players are there on each team?

Solution

There are 11 players on each team.

b) What is the median weight for each team?

Solution

There are eleven players on each team. So, draw a line through the sixth data value for each team. This represents the median of each team.

Team A

175, 178, 181, 187, 188, 1|89, 190, 192, 197, 199, 200

The median weight of Team A is 189 pounds.

Team B

177, 181, 186, 188, 191, 1|93, 195, 203, 205, 207, 209

The median weight of Team B is 193 pounds.

c) What is the mean weight of each team? Round your answer to the nearest tenth.

Solution

Mean weight of Team A = $\dfrac{175 + 178 + 181 + 187 + 188 + 189 + 190 + 192 + 197 + 199 + 200}{11} \approx 188.7$ lb

Mean weight of Team B = $\dfrac{177 + 181 + 186 + 188 + 191 + 193 + 195 + 203 + 205 + 207 + 209}{11} \approx 194.1$ lb

d) On average, which team has heavier players?

Solution

Team B has a greater mean weight and a greater median weight. So on average, Team B has heavier players.

Guided Practice

Solve. Round your answer to the nearest tenth if necessary.

3 The stem-and-leaf plot shows the heights, in inches, of the players on two football teams.

Heights (in inches) of Two Football Teams

Team A	Stem	Team B
9 8 8 7	6	8 8 8
3 2 1 1 0 0 0	7	0 0 1 1 1 2 2 2

> Team A: 7 | 6 represents 67 inches.
> Team B: 6 | 8 represents 68 inches.

a) How many players are on each team?

b) What is the median height for each team?

c) What is the mean height for each team?

d) On average, which team has taller players?

Example 8 **Compare the median and mean and make inferences from a stem-and-leaf plot with outliers.**

The stem-and-leaf shows the lengths, in centimeters, of some salmon caught during a fishing trip.

Lengths (in centimeters) of Salmon

Stem	Leaf
2	1 1 2 2 2 3 4 4 5
3	
4	
5	1 2
6	1

> 2 | 1 represents a length of 21 centimeters.

a) Find the median length of the salmon.

Solution

21, 21, 22, 22, 22, 23, $\Big|$ 24, 24, 25, 51, 52, 61

$$\text{Median} = \frac{23 + 24}{2} = 23.5$$

The median length of the salmon is 23.5 centimeters.

b) Find the mean length of the salmon.

Solution

$$\text{Mean} = \frac{21 \cdot 2 + 22 \cdot 3 + 23 + 24 \cdot 2 + 25 + 51 + 52 + 61}{12}$$

$$= \frac{368}{12}$$

$$\approx 30.7 \text{ cm}$$

The mean length of the salmon is 30.7 centimeters.

c) Compare the median and mean. What can you infer?

Solution

The median is 23.5 centimeters while the mean is 30.7 centimeters. The value of the mean is much greater due to the presence of outliers with data values of 51, 52, and 61 centimeters.

d) What is the range of the data?

Solution

Range = 61 − 21 = 40 cm

e) Explain how the outliers 51, 52, and 61 centimeters affect the range of the data. How do these outliers affect the mean of the data?

Solution

The range is the difference between the least and greatest values in a data set. So, the range is greater because of the outliers. The mean is also greater because of these outliers.

Guided Practice

Solve.

4 The weights, in pounds, of some newborn babies at a hospital are shown in the stem-and-leaf plot.

a) Find the median weight.

b) Find the mean weight.

c) Compare the median and mean. Explain the differences.

d) What is the range of the data?

e) Explain how the outlier 3.1 pounds affects the range of the data. How does the outlier affect the mean of the data?

Weights (in pounds) of Newborn Babies

Stem	Leaf
3	1
4	
5	
6	0 1 2 5 5 5 6 8
7	1

3 | 1 represents a weight of 3.1 pounds.

Practice 9.2

Display the data using a stem-and-leaf plot. Indicate the range and median of each data set.

1 The masses, in grams, of russet potatoes are 89, 110, 81, 92, 100, 96, 101, 109, 105, and 112.

2 The lengths of salmon, in inches, are 28, 31, 32, 29, 26, 33, 29, 28, 30, and 31.

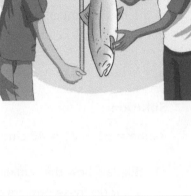

3 The average hourly rate, in dollars, of workers in 8 professions are 26, 13, 10, 17, 12, 15, 14, and 15.

4 The scores of a basketball competition are 70, 56, 93, 92, 72, 74, 76, 72, 78, and 59.

5 The ages of passengers on board a bus are 33, 37, 5, 11, 63, 55, 56, 13, 15, and 19.

Use the data in the table to answer the following.

The table shows the weights, in pounds, of 30 pumpkins.

6 Draw the stem-and-leaf plot of the data.

7 What is the range of the data?

8 What is the mode?

9 What is the median?

10 What is the interquartile range?

8	18	13	11	16
10	16	20	16	10
21	17	9	17	11
19	11	16	12	21
13	17	14	12	9
14	15	16	20	22

Use the data in the table to answer the following.

The table shows the attendance, in working days, of workers in a manufacturing plant over a period of one year.

11 Draw a stem-and-leaf plot.

12 What is the mean number of working days in for this particular year?

13 What is the mode?

14 What is the median?

238	240	235	230	239
240	239	240	237	240
220	233	240	234	232
239	240	231	236	239
240	239	240	232	234
239	239	239	240	239

Solve. Show your work.

15 The weights of 10 pumpkins, in pounds, harvested at a farm is shown in the stem-and-leaf plot.

Compare the median and mean.
Explain the difference in the values.

Weights (in pounds) of Pumpkins

Stem	Leaf
2	1 2 6 7
3	1 3 6 9
4	1
5	
6	
7	
8	1

2 | 1 represents a weight of 2.1 pounds.

16 The speeds, in miles per hour, tracked by a police patrol car along a certain highway, are shown in the stem-and-leaf plot.

Explain how the outliers 40, 43, and 45 miles per hour affect the range of the data. How do these outliers affect the mean of the data?

Speeds (in miles per hour) Along a Highway

Stem	Leaf
4	0 3 5
5	
6	
7	0 1 1 3 4 5
8	1

4 | 0 represents a speed of 40 miles per hour.

17 *Math Journal* The waiting time, in minutes, at a certain bus interchange for two bus routes on a particular day are recorded in the stem-and-leaf plot.

With the data shown, discuss some advantages and disadvantages of the stem-and-leaf plot.

Waiting Time (in minutes) for Two Bus Routes

Bus Route A	Stem	Bus Route B
	1	0 5
4	2	1 6
3	3	2 3 7 8
6 4 1	4	5 8
7 3	5	
5	6	
	7	
5	8	
	9	

Bus Route A: 4 | 2 represents 24 minutes.
Bus Route B: 1 | 0 represents 10 minutes.

18 *Math Journal* Describe a data set that could be represented by a stem-and-leaf plot. Explain how using a stem-and-leaf plot could help you analyze the data set.

Lesson Objectives

- Draw and interpret box plots.
- Understand mean absolute deviation.
- Solve problems involving box plots and mean absolute deviation.

Draw and Interpret Box Plots.

Quartiles and interquartile ranges can be represented by a graphical display called a box plot (also known as **box-and-whisker plot**). This graphical display shows how data are clustered around the median and spread out along a number line.

A box plot uses five values:

- Lower extreme value
- Lower quartile
- Median
- Upper quartile
- Upper extreme value

> **Math Note**
>
> Remember that measures of center estimate how data cluster around the center, while measures of variation estimate how far data are spread from the center.

These five values are collectively known as a **5-point summary** in statistics. A box plot is especially good at showing extreme values and the range of the middle values.

A 5-point summary for one set of data is the following.

Lower extreme value	2
Lower quartile (Q_1)	4
Median (Q_2)	6
Upper quartile (Q_3)	11
Upper extreme value	15

> Unlike a stem-and-leaf plot, a box plot does not show individual data values. Instead, it gives a quick visual summary of data and can be used for large data sets.

The box plot looks like this:

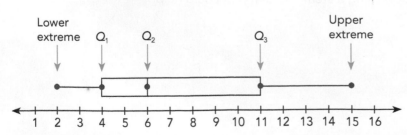

This is how you read a box plot.

- The box captures the middle 50% of the data.
- The red dots at the ends of the box are the lower and the upper quartiles.
- The red dot within the box is the median.
- The vertical line through the median divides the data in the box into two equal halves (25% on each side of the median).
- The red dots on the left and on the right outside the box are the lower and the upper extreme values.
- The two whiskers (the horizontal lines) show the spread of the remaining data from the middle 50% to the two extreme values.
- The length of the box represents the interquartile range.
- The upper and lower extreme values can be used to find the range of the data.

Example 9 Read a box plot.

Solve.

From the box plot, state the lower quartile, the median, the upper quartile, the range, and the interquartile range.

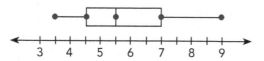

Solution

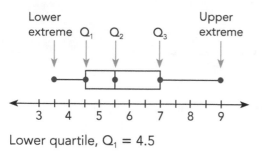

Lower quartile, $Q_1 = 4.5$

Median, $Q_2 = 5.5$

Upper quartile, $Q_3 = 7$

Greatest value $= 9$

Least value $= 3.5$

Range $=$ Greatest value $-$ Least value
$= 9 - 3.5 = 5.5$

Interquartile range $=$ Upper quartile (Q_3) $-$ Lower quartile (Q_1)
$= 7 - 4.5$
$= 2.5$

> **Caution**
>
> $Q_3 - Q_2 = 1.5$ and $Q_2 - Q_1 = 1$ imply that data within the interval Q_2 to Q_3 are more spread out than data within the interval Q_1 to Q_2. Both intervals have the same number of data values.

Guided Practice

Solve.

1 The box plot summarizes the age distribution of people in a play. State the lower quartile, the median, the upper quartile, the range, and the interquartile range.

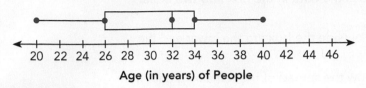

Age (in years) of People

Example 10 **Construct a box plot.**

16 students took a quiz and their scores were 3, 8, 7, 11, 11, 5, 12, 12, 8, 7, 7, 9, 5, 10, 15 and 4. Draw a box plot for the data and label it with the 5-point summary.

Solution

STEP 1 Arrange the data in ascending order.

3, 4, 5, 5, 7, 7, 7, 8, 8, 9, 10, 11, 11, 12, 12, 15

STEP 2 Calculate the 5-point summary.

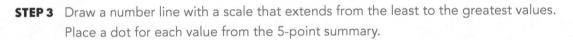

STEP 3 Draw a number line with a scale that extends from the least to the greatest values. Place a dot for each value from the 5-point summary.

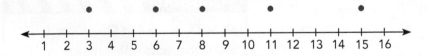

STEP 4 Draw a box above the number line with ends of the box at Q_1 and Q_3. Also, draw a vertical line through the box at Q_2.

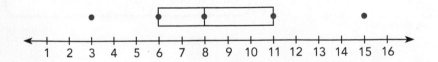

STEP 5 Draw a whisker from the Q_1 end of the box to the least value. Draw a whisker from the Q_3 end to the greatest value.

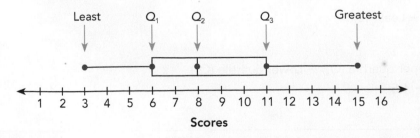

Scores

Guided Practice

Construct a box plot.

2 The table shows the average monthly precipitation of Portland, Oregon, in inches. Draw a box plot of the average monthly rainfall and label it with the 5-point summary.

Month	Jan	Feb	Mar	Apr	May	Jun	Jul	Aug	Sep	Oct	Nov	Dec
Rainfall (in.)	5.1	4.2	3.7	2.6	2.4	1.6	0.7	0.9	1.7	2.9	5.6	5.7

STEP 1 Arrange the data in ascending order.

<u> ? </u>

STEP 2 Calculate the 5-point summary.

$Q_1 = $ <u> ? </u> $Q_2 = $ <u> ? </u> $Q_3 = $ <u> ? </u>

Lower extreme value = <u> ? </u>   Upper extreme value = <u> ? </u>

STEP 3 Draw a number line with a scale that covers both extreme values. Place a dot for each value from the 5-point summary.

STEP 4 Draw a box above the number line.

STEP 5 Draw the whiskers and label the box plot with the 5-point summary.

Understand Mean Absolute Deviation.

Another measure of variation is called the mean absolute deviation.

The mean absolute deviation of a set of data is the average distance of the data values from the mean of the data.

For example, suppose you have this data set: {1, 3, 7, 9}. The mean of the data is 5. On a number line, you can see the distance of each data value from the mean. 1 is 4 units from 5, 3 is 2 units from 5, 7 is 2 units from 5, and 9 is 4 units from 5. The mean of these distances is $\frac{(4+2+2+4)}{4}$, or 3. So, the mean absolute deviation is 3.

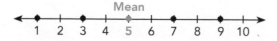

Continue on next page

You can use the same procedure to find the mean absolute deviation for any set of data. For example, suppose you have a set of data {w, x, y, and z} and you plot the data values and the mean on a number line.

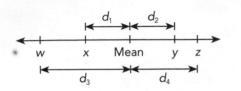

The distance d_1 is the distance of x from the mean. Similarly, the distances d_2, d_3, and d_4 are the distances (or deviations) of the other three data items from the mean, as shown in the diagram.

The mean absolute deviation is the sum of the distances divided by the total number of data values:

$$\frac{d_1 + d_2 + d_3 + d_4}{4}$$

"MAD" is the abbreviation for mean absolute deviation.

Because distances are never negative, the mean absolute deviation is never a negative number.

Now you can draw some conclusions about the mean absolute deviation, or MAD.

Data that are clustered near the mean will have a small mean absolute deviation. Data that are spread over a wide range will have a greater mean absolute deviation.

Examples:

In the data set {1, 2, 2, 2, 2, 3, 4}, the data values are clustered close to the mean. So, the mean absolute deviation is small.

In the data set {1, 1, 1, 50, 50, 50}, the data values are spread over a wide range. So, the mean absolute deviation is large.

Think Math

Suppose you have a set of 20 data values. To find the mean absolute deviation, how many distances will you need to find? When you find the sum of these distances, what number should you divide by?

Example 11 **Calculate and interpret the mean absolute deviation.**

The table shows the scores of 10 people in a dartboard game.

54	40	69	49	73	42	35	60	51	57

a) Find the mean absolute deviation.

Solution

STEP 1 Find the mean score.

$$\text{Mean} = \frac{54 + 40 + 69 + 49 + 73 + 42 + 35 + 60 + 51 + 57}{10}$$

$$= \frac{530}{10}$$

$$= 53$$

STEP 2 Find the distance or deviation of each value from the mean.

Data Item	Mean	Distance of Data from the Mean
54	53	1
40	53	13
69	53	16
49	53	4
73	53	20
42	53	11
35	53	18
60	53	7
51	53	2
57	53	4

Math Note

You can find the distance between each item of data and the mean in two ways:
1. subtract the lesser value from the greater value, or
2. subtract the mean from each data value and find the absolute value of this difference.

The first way may be easier if you are using pencil and paper, but the second way may be easier if you use a calculator.

STEP 3 Find the sum of the distances.

$$\text{Sum} = 1 + 13 + 16 + 4 + 20 + 11 + 18 + 7 + 2 + 4$$

$$= 96$$

STEP 4 Divide the sum by the number of data values to find the MAD.

$$\text{MAD} = \frac{96}{10}$$

$$= 9.6$$

Continue on next page

b) What does the mean absolute deviation tell you about the data?

Solution

On average, the data values are 9.6 units from the mean.

Guided Practice

Solve.

3 The scores on a math quiz are 20, 16, 13, 11, 19, 24, 22, 15, 17, and 13.

a) Find the mean absolute deviation.

STEP 1 Find the mean score.

Mean score = __?__

STEP 2 Find the distance of each value from the mean.

Data Item	Mean	Distance Between Data Item and Mean
20	?	?
16	?	?
13	?	?
11	?	?
19	?	?
24	?	?
22	?	?
15	?	?
17	?	?
13	?	?

STEP 3 Find the sum of the distances.

Sum = __?__

STEP 4 Divide the sum by the number of data values to find the MAD.

MAD = __?__

b) What does the mean absolute deviation tell you about this set of data?

Technology Activity

Materials:
- spreadsheet software
- two sets of 10 data values

USE SPREADSHEET SOFTWARE TO FIND MEAN ABSOLUTE DEVIATION

Work in pairs.

 STEP 1 Enter 10 data values in one row of cells.

STEP 2 Choose a cell in a later row for the mean.

 STEP 3 Use the spreadsheet software's function for finding the mean to find the mean of the 10 data values.

See the screen shot below.

	A	B	C	D	E	F	G	H	I	J
		Sheets	Charts	SmartArt Graphics	WordArt					
1	?	?	?	?	?	?	?	?	?	?
2	Mean =	?								
3	MAD =	?								

 STEP 4 Choose a cell in the next row for the mean absolute deviation.

 STEP 5 Use the spreadsheet software's function for finding the mean absolute deviation to find the MAD of the data values.

 STEP 6 Explain what the MAD tells you about the data.

 STEP 7 Enter a second set of data values and repeat **STEP 1** to **STEP 6**.

Math Journal Compare the two sets of data. Are the data values in each set clustered around the mean, or more spread out? Then compare the mean absolute deviations for the two sets of data. What do you observe?

Practice 9.3

State Q_1, Q_2, Q_3, the lower extreme, and the upper extreme values shown in the box plots. Then calculate the interquartile range.

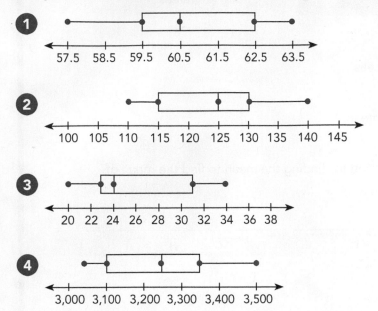

1

57.5 58.5 59.5 60.5 61.5 62.5 63.5

2

100 105 110 115 120 125 130 135 140 145

3

20 22 24 26 28 30 32 34 36 38

4

3,000 3,100 3,200 3,300 3,400 3,500

Draw a box plot for the given 5-point summary. Include a numeric scale for the number line. Label the box plot with the 5-point summary.

5 $Q_1 = 4$, $Q_2 = 7$, $Q_3 = 10$, lower extreme value = 1, upper extreme value = 15

6 $Q_1 = 14$, $Q_2 = 18$, $Q_3 = 23$, lower extreme value = 10, upper extreme value = 28

7 $Q_1 = 6.1$, $Q_2 = 6.6$, $Q_3 = 7.0$, lower extreme value = 5.7, upper extreme value = 7.4

8 $Q_1 = 320$, $Q_2 = 360$, $Q_3 = 380$, lower extreme value = 300, upper extreme value = 400

Calculate the mean absolute deviation. Round your answers to 3 significant digits when you can.

9 2, 2, 5, 3, 9, 6, 10, 4, 7, 5

10 58, 62, 45, 39, 40, 60, 67

11 43.4, 30.5, 20.0, 23.6, 34.5, 36.9, 11.7, 40.2

12 1.15, 1.16, 1.25, 1.22, 1.36, 1.38, 1.49, 1.22, 1.11

Use the data in the table for the following questions.

The table shows the masses, in grams, of a dozen eggs.

| 57 | 53 | 62 | 45 | 56 | 56 | 63 | 61 | 50 | 44 | 43 | 58 |

13 Calculate Q_1, Q_2, and Q_3.

14 Draw a box plot of the masses of the eggs.

15 Calculate the mean absolute deviation of the masses of the eggs. Round to the nearest hundredth.

Use the information to answer the following questions.

The map shows the amounts of snow, in inches, that fell in different parts of Minnesota during one week in winter.

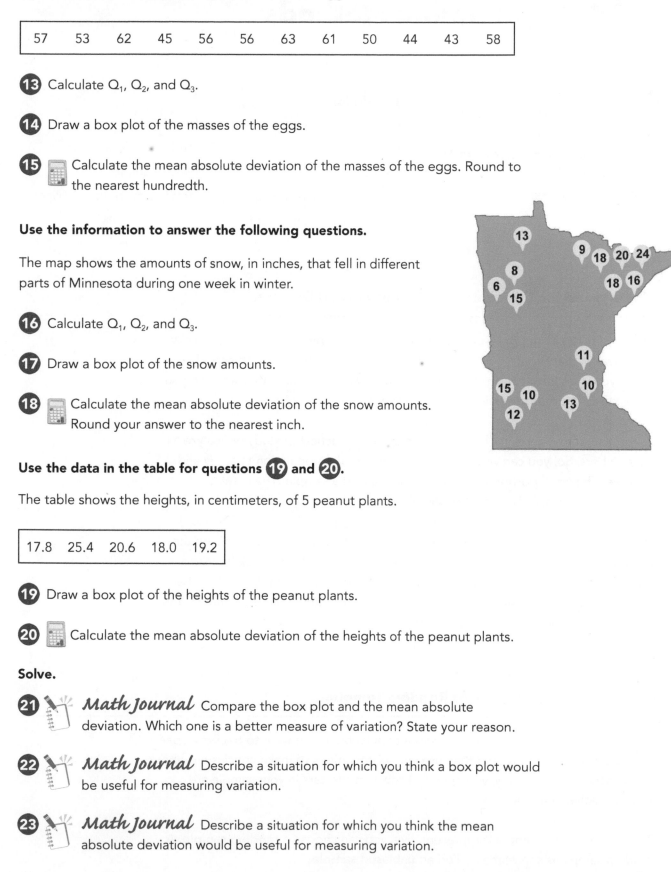

16 Calculate Q_1, Q_2, and Q_3.

17 Draw a box plot of the snow amounts.

18 Calculate the mean absolute deviation of the snow amounts. Round your answer to the nearest inch.

Use the data in the table for questions 19 and 20.

The table shows the heights, in centimeters, of 5 peanut plants.

| 17.8 | 25.4 | 20.6 | 18.0 | 19.2 |

19 Draw a box plot of the heights of the peanut plants.

20 Calculate the mean absolute deviation of the heights of the peanut plants.

Solve.

21 *Math Journal* Compare the box plot and the mean absolute deviation. Which one is a better measure of variation? State your reason.

22 *Math Journal* Describe a situation for which you think a box plot would be useful for measuring variation.

23 *Math Journal* Describe a situation for which you think the mean absolute deviation would be useful for measuring variation.

9.4 Understanding Random Sampling Methods

Lesson Objectives

- Understand the concepts of a population and sample.
- Understand and apply different random sampling methods.
- Simulate a random sampling process.

Vocabulary

population	sample
sample size	random sample
unbiased sample	biased sample
simple random sampling	stratified random sampling
systematic random sampling	

Understand the Concepts of a Population and Sample.

In everyday language, the word "population" refers to people in a country, a city, or a town. In statistics, a population consists of all the members or objects about which you want information. The information may be something that will help you understand the characteristics of the population.

A population may be quite large, and it may be impractical to study or analyze all its members. So, you can choose a small portion of the population to study and observe. The small portion that you choose is called a sample. The number of members in a sample is called the **sample size**.

Consider a busy freeway. You wonder what the average speed of the cars on the freeway during peak hours is. All the cars on the freeway during peak hours make up the population you want to study. The characteristic you want to study is their speed. You cannot possibly track the speeds of all the cars during peak hours. You can, however, track a small sample of 100 cars.

Understand the Purpose of Random Sampling.

A sample needs to be representative of a population. If you want to track the speeds of 100 cars on a freeway, and then use your observations to make conclusions about all the cars on the freeway, you need to know that the cars in your sample are representative of all the cars.

To make sure your sample is representative, you can choose a **random sample**. A random sample is sometimes called an **unbiased sample**.

A random sample has two characteristics:
- Every member of the population has an equal chance of being selected.
- Selection of members is independent of each other.

You cannot predict which members of a population will be chosen for a random sample because members are selected randomly. A sample in which members are not randomly selected is called a **biased sample**.

Random sampling is the process of randomly selecting members from a population to generate a random sample. You will learn three random sampling methods.
- Simple random sampling
- Stratified random sampling
- Systematic random sampling

Understand Simple Random Sampling.

Simple random sampling is a sampling method in which every member of a population has an equal chance of being selected for the sample. In other words, you select members from a population without any pre-planned order.

Examples of simple random sampling

1. **Using a sampling frame**
   In carrying out a household survey using telephone interviews, you may use a telephone directory. You randomly flip to a page of the directory and randomly choose a telephone number. Repeat the process until you have gathered enough members for your sample.

   Think Math

   You want a sample of 50 households. Suppose you randomly flip to a page of telephone directory and pick the first 50 telephone numbers. Is the sample unbiased? Explain.

2. **Lottery method**
   To generate a random sample of 50 students from a school population, you may assign a unique number to each student at the school. Then randomly pick numbers from a box that holds all the numbers, until you have picked 50.

1   2   ③   4   ⑤   ⑥   7   8   9   ⑩   11   12   ⑬   14   15   16   ⑰   18   19   ⑳

Continue on next page

3. Using a random number table

Suppose you want to pick a random sample of 30 people from a town that has only 500 residents. You first assign 3-digit numbers from 001 to 500 to the town residents. You may use a random number table like the one shown below to select the members of the sample.

To use the table, choose any row. Then, from left to right, read off 3-digit numbers. Use only numbers from 001 to 500. If the number is greater than 500, you disregard the number and move on to the next 3-digit number until you have collected 30. The numbers can be matched to the members of the town.

For example, suppose you randomly pick row 20 to start selecting 3-digit numbers. From row 20, you read off numbers 126, 125, 168, 569 (discarded), 231, 039, and so on, until you get 30 numbers.

	1 2 3 4	5 6 7 8	9 10 11 12	13 14 15 16	17 18 19 20
1	8 0 9 4	2 5 2 5	6 2 4 7	1 3 4 7	7 4 3 3
2	3 5 6 3	2 1 9 8	8 2 1 1	9 0 4 5	2 6 1 8
3	1 3 3 0	6 3 3 1	3 7 5 3	9 6 9 3	8 7 3 8
4	3 5 6 5	0 0 1 6	2 2 4 3	6 4 3 2	4 7 9 6
5	7 8 5 0	5 9 2 6	5 5 8 8	7 3 1 1	2 1 9 2
6	4 4 9 0	5 4 1 7	9 7 2 7	6 1 5 3	5 9 8 1
7	6 5 4 5	9 1 0 4	9 3 1 8	8 8 1 9	7 5 3 7
8	3 6 2 6	5 9 9 5	1 2 1 5	9 7 5 3	9 2 2 3
9	4 6 6 5	4 8 2 0	7 5 5 4	0 6 1 2	9 6 6 3
10	6 4 9 8	7 5 1 9	0 4 7 4	7 8 1 8	6 8 3 2
11	6 7 2 2	9 8 6 9	9 3 6 1	7 8 7 5	4 8 8 3
12	9 7 4 8	5 9 3 2	5 1 1 5	2 7 2 1	0 0 3 3
13	5 6 4 1	1 4 1 7	1 4 1 9	7 4 3 4	8 1 6 5
14	7 4 4 4	9 2 0 0	8 8 4 0	5 8 8 2	4 3 9 8
15	8 2 7 9	3 0 1 9	4 6 7 2	3 7 4 3	3 9 7 9
16	0 1 6 1	7 6 1 7	1 0 2 4	2 3 6 7	2 8 9 1
17	7 3 8 8	9 7 5 9	7 5 5 5	6 6 2 4	9 9 7 7
18	7 8 3 0	4 7 1 4	3 6 9 5	2 9 1 9	1 8 0 4
19	9 8 8 7	4 2 1 6	6 5 2 6	4 5 3 5	8 4 3 0
20	1 2 6 1	2 5 1 6	8 5 6 9	2 3 1 0	3 9 3 9

4. Using a computer

Instead of using a random number table, you may also use a random number generator on a calculator or a computer to generate random numbers.

Hands-On Activity

Materials:
- list of names of 40 students
- a random number table

EXPLORE HOW A RANDOM SAMPLING PROCESS AFFECTS DATA COLLECTION

Work in groups of four or five.

STEP 1 Choose 40 students to participate in this activity. They will be asked how long it took them to get to school today.

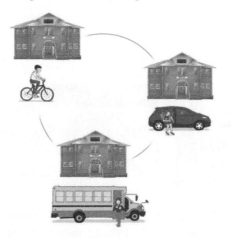

STEP 2 Assign each of the 40 students a 2-digit number from 01 to 40.

STEP 3 Use the random number table to pick five 2-digit numbers. Discard any 2-digit numbers greater than 40.

6545   91<u>04</u>   93<u>18</u>   88<u>19</u>   75<u>37</u>   <u>27</u>35

STEP 4 Ask the 5 students whose numbers match those you picked in **STEP 3** the following question and record the results.

About how many minutes did it take you to commute to school today?

STEP 5 Find the mean and the mean absolute deviation of the data you collected in **STEP 4**.

STEP 6 Repeat **STEP 3** to **STEP 5** to generate new random samples, and to collect and analyze the data from each sample.

✏️ *Math Journal* Does the mean number of minutes vary greatly from sample to sample? Does the mean absolute deviation vary greatly from sample to sample? What are some problems you encountered in the random sampling process? Describe.

In a stratified random sampling method, you first divide the population into nonoverlapping groups. Then you randomly select members from each group.

Examples of stratified random sampling

1. **By schools**

   Suppose you want to know the mean height of middle school students in a district with three middle schools. You first divide the students by their schools. Then you randomly select students from each school. The number of students selected from each school is not necessarily the same.

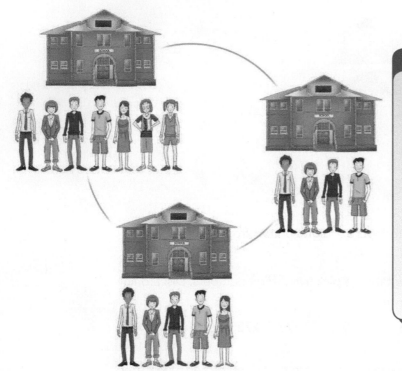

Math Note

Before you carry out stratified random sampling, you need to address 3 basic questions. Your sampling will be guided by your answers to these questions.

1. What characteristics will you use to divide the population into nonoverlapping goups?
2. How many groups will you use?
3. How much data will you collect from each group?

2. **By genders**

   Suppose you want to conduct a survey on whether people prefer to eat organic food. To make sure that you have an equal number of men and women in your survey, you may want to divide people by genders.

Men	Women
30	30

   You then sample randomly 30 men and 30 women to interview.

3. By chapters

Suppose you want to find the mean word length of the words in a book. You may randomly select a few words from each chapter, as shown in the table below.

Chapter 1	Chapter 2	Chapter 3	Chapter 4	Chapter 5
10 words	15 words	18 words	12 words	20 words

Then you calculate the mean word length of all the selected words.

Understand Systematic Random Sampling.

To carry out a systematic random sampling, you select the first member randomly and then select subsequent members at regular intervals.

Examples of systematic random sampling

1. Every twelfth household

There are 300 households in a district. Suppose you want to obtain a 25-member sample. Label all the households in some numeric sequence.

Divide the number of households by the sample size: $\frac{300}{25} = 12$.

Pick the first household at random among the first 12 households according to the numeric sequence. Then select every twelfth household from there for subsequent members of the sample. For example, if the first household is number 5, then the numbers for subsequent members are 17, 29, 41, 53, 65, and so on.

2. Every eighth minute

To conduct an opinion poll among tourists at a historical site, you intend to spend 4 hours polling 30 tourists at random.

Time taken: $\frac{4 \cdot 60}{30} = 8$ min per tourist.

After you poll the first tourist at random, you will poll subsequent tourists at 8-minute intervals.

3. Every 200th item

A canned food manufacturing site produces about 5,000 cans every day. The quality inspector intends to pick a random sample of 25 cans for examination.

Interval: $\frac{5,000}{25} = 200$.

After he picks the first item, he will then pick every 200th item from the production line.

Example 12 **Find a random sample using a suitable sampling method.**

For each of the following scenarios, describe which sampling method you will choose and how you apply it. Justify your choice.

Scenario 1

A journalist would like to find out what attendees think of the large computer fair they are attending. He decides to interview 50 people.

Scenario 2

A poultry farm keeps 3,000 birds. An agricultural safety and health officer needs to check whether any of the birds might be infected with a virus and would like to take a random sample of 20 birds for inspection.

Scenario 3

A local authority plans to conduct an opinion poll of people in McCree county as to whether they are in favor of putting more restaurants in a historical landmark site. The county consists of six districts. The authority intends to generate a random sample of 300 to 400 people.

Solution

Scenario 1

A simple random sampling can be used because the journalist simply wants to get a general sense of what attendees feel about the computer fair. Randomly pick any person in the computer fair to interview until 50 people have been interviewed.

Scenario 2

A systematic random sampling is a better sampling method.

Interval: $\dfrac{3,000}{20} = 150$.

The officer can count off every 150 birds and randomly select one bird. The process is repeated until he gets 20 birds.

Systematic sampling enables the officer to evenly space out his random selection of birds over the entire population.

Scenario 3

A stratified random sampling is an appropriate method for this opinion poll. The authority may take each district as a group and do a simple random sampling within each group as follows:

District 1	District 2	District 3	District 4	District 5	District 6
60	60	60	60	60	60

Guided Practice

Determine which sampling method is best suited for each situation.

1 Describe how you would carry out the sampling process. You may use a combination of methods, if you see fit. Justify your process.

Scenario 1

A truck load of 3,000 oranges were delivered to a wholesale market. You are allowed to check 1% of the oranges as a random sample before deciding whether to accept the shipment.

Scenario 2

A grocer would like to find what items the store should carry to attract more customers. The grocer wants to survey 100 people in the neighborhood.

Hands-On Activity

Materials:
- computer
- relevant books

COMPARE THE STRENGTHS AND WEAKNESSES OF RANDOM SAMPLING METHODS

Work in pairs.

Background

Every sampling method has its own strengths and weaknesses. Each method is designed for specific purposes. Sometimes you may find more than one method can be used in a particular situation. At another time, you may find it necessary to combine two methods to obtain the best possible random sample.
Be creative when you apply a random sampling method!

STEP 1 Research the strengths and weaknesses of the three random sampling methods.

STEP 2 Compile the information in a table shown below.

Sampling Method	Strengths	Weaknesses
Simple random sampling	?	?
Stratified random sampling	?	?
Systemtic random sampling	?	?

 Math Journal Do you find that a weakness of one method can be addressed by another method? Explain.

Answer the following.

1 Explain what a random sampling process is.

2 Give an example of how a random sampling process is used in a real-world situation.

3 Why do people want to use random samples to collect information about a population?

4 Explain why a biased sample is not an appropriate sample.

State which sampling method is being described.

5 A frozen yogurt store sells 5 flavors: vanilla, chocolate, strawberry, macadamia nut, and peppermint. To check the quality of the frozen yogurt, 5 tubs of each flavor were sampled.

6 A group of students conducted an online poll of Internet users by randomly selecting 500 Internet users.

7 To check the freshness of the bagels at a bakery, the baker randomly picked 5 bagels at an interval of every hour.

8 Unique numbers were assigned to the members of a country club. The club manager used a random number generator to choose 150 numbers that were matched to members of the club.

9 Out of 100 students, the teachers randomly choose the first student and every sixth student thereafter.

10 To assess pollution levels in a region, water samples are taken from 5 rivers and 2 lakes for analysis.

Refer to the situation to answer the following.

11 *Math Journal* A corn field is divided into five areas. To determine whether the corn plants are healthy, you are asked to collect a random sample of 100 ears of corn for analysis.

a) If you use a stratified random sampling method, describe how you will go about collecting the random sample.

b) Explain why the stratified random sampling method is preferred.

12 *Math Journal* Explain why the simple sampling method may not give you a representative sample.

Refer to the situation below to answer the following.

2,000 runners participated in a marathon. You want to randomly choose 60 of the runners to find out how long it took each one to run the race.

 Describe how you would select the 60 runners if you use a simple random sampling method.

 Describe how you would select the 60 runners if you use a systematic random sampling method.

15 Describe how you would select the 60 runners if you use stratified random sampling method.

Refer to the situation below to answer the following.

There are 1,650 trees growing in 5 areas within a park. The trees are numbered from 1 to 1,650. A systematic random sample of 40 trees is needed to check whether there are fungi causing root rot among the trees.

16 Describe how you would carry out a systematic random sampling.

17 Describe how you would carry out a stratified random sampling.

Refer to the situation below to answer the following.

18 A poll is taken in a small town to find out which candidate voters will choose in an election. A stratified sampling method is used to generate a random sample of 500 residents. The table shows the town population and the sample size within each group.

	Men	Women
Number of Residents	5,000	8,000
Sample Size	250	250

a) The stratified random sample has been criticized for not being representative of the population. What could possibly be the problem with the random sample?

b) How would you improve the above stratified random sampling?

9.5 Making Inferences About Populations

Lesson Objectives

- Make inferences about a population using statistics from a sample.
- Use an inference to estimate a population mean.
- Make comparative inferences about two populations using two sets of sample statistics.

Vocabulary
inference

Make Inferences About a Population Using Statistics from a Sample.

A sample inherits certain characteristics from the population. If you know the sample characteristics, hopefully the sample reflects similar characteristics of the population. This happens when the sample is random. This is the reason why you need random samples.

When you make an inference about a population, you draw a conclusion about a population based on a sample. Inference is needed because characteristics of the population are usually unknown and often impossible to obtain. For example, it would be difficult to collect data about the number of eggs laid and eaglets hatched in every eagle's nest in a state. Instead, you could use a random sample to make inferences about the population.

To infer means to conclude something from evidence or facts.

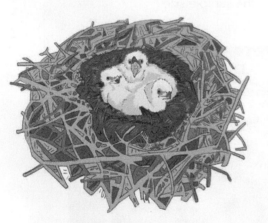

When you infer characteristics of a population based on a random sample, you are making an approximation. Suppose you collect numerical data about a sample and calculate that the mean of the data is 50. You then infer that the mean for the population is also 50. In reality, the mean for the population may not be exactly 50, because the population's characteristics are probably not exactly the same as the sample's.

Use an Inference to Estimate a Population Mean.

Suppose that a population consists of 10 test scores:

67, 80, 54, 76, 90, 48, 65, 60, 73, and 80.

Since the population is small, the population mean can be easily calculated.

$$\text{Population mean} = \frac{67 + 80 + 54 + 76 + 90 + 48 + 65 + 60 + 73 + 80}{10}$$

$$= 69.3$$

Suppose you take a random sample of four of the test scores: $S_1 = \{80, 48, 73, 80\}$.

$$\text{Sample mean of } S_1 = \frac{80 + 48 + 73 + 80}{4}$$

$$= 70.25$$

Suppose you take another random sample of four of the test scores:
$S_2 = \{67, 54, 90, 60\}$.

$$\text{Sample mean of } S_2 = \frac{67 + 54 + 90 + 60}{4}$$

$$= 67.75$$

Suppose you take yet another random sample of four of the test scores:
$S_3 = \{80, 54, 76, 90\}$.

$$\text{Sample mean of } S_3 = \frac{80 + 54 + 76 + 90}{4}$$

$$= 75$$

You can then find the average of all of the sample means:

$$\text{Average of sample means} = \frac{70.25 + 67.75 + 75}{3}$$

$$= 71$$

When you average the three sample means, you get 71. This value is also an approximation of the population mean. In general, the population mean is usually unknown.

> The sample means show that none of them is equal to the population mean. All three sample means are only approximations of the population mean.

Different samples of the same sample size produce different approximations of the population mean. The mean of the sample means is also an estimate the population mean.

Example 13 — Use an inference to estimate a population mean.

A population consists of test scores of 60 students. A random sample {18, 10, 6, 9, 10, 14, 17, 10, 9, 11} of 10 scores has been collected from the population.

a) Calculate the sample mean and use it to approximate the population mean.

Solution

$$\text{Sample mean} = \frac{18 + 10 + 6 + 9 + 10 + 14 + 17 + 10 + 9 + 11}{10}$$

$$= 11.4$$

The population mean is estimated to be 11.4.

b) Calculate the mean absolute deviation (MAD) of the sample.

Solution

Calculate the distance of each value from the mean.

Data Item	Mean	Distance of Data from the Mean
18	11.4	6.6
10	11.4	1.4
6	11.4	5.4
9	11.4	2.4
10	11.4	1.4
14	11.4	2.6
17	11.4	5.6
10	11.4	1.4
9	11.4	2.4
11	11.4	0.4

Sum of the distances = 6.6 + 1.4 + 5.4 + 2.4 + 1.4 + 2.6 + 5.6 + 1.4 + 2.4 + 0.4

$$= 29.6$$

$$\text{MAD} = \frac{29.6}{10}$$

$$= 2.96$$

c) Draw a dot plot for the scores and the mean.

Solution

Mean

6   7   8   9   10   11   12   13   14   15   16   17   18

11.4

Scores

d) Using MAD to mean ratio and the dot plot, describe informally how varied the scores are.

Solution

The dot plot shows that many of the scores are close together, but there are also obvious outliers. The ratio of the mean absolute deviation to the mean confirms this observation:

MAD to mean ratio = 2.96 ÷ 11.4
$$\approx 0.26$$
$$= 26\%$$

By comparing the MAD to the mean in a ratio, you see that the MAD is about 26% of the value of the mean. So, the data are fairly well spread out.

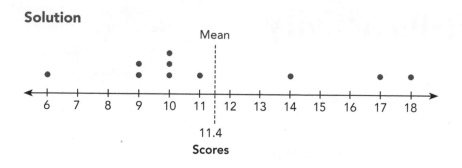

Guided Practice

Solve.

1 A random sample of ages {15, 5, 8, 7, 18, 6, 15, 17, 6, 15} of 10 children was collected from a population of 100 children.

   a) Calculate the sample mean age of the children and use it to estimate the population mean age.

   b) Calculate the MAD of the sample.

   c) Calculate the MAD to mean ratio.

   d) Draw a dot plot for the ages and the mean age.

   e) Using the MAD to mean ratio and the dot plot, describe informally how varied the population ages are.

Hands-On Activity

USE STATISTICS FROM A SAMPLE TO DESCRIBE THE VARIABILITY OF A POPULATION

Work in pairs.

The activity can be a collaborative effort for the whole class.

Background

The population is made up of all the words in a book. The length of a word is defined by the number of letters in it. The population characteristic is the mean word length.

STEP 1 Determine which sampling method you intend to use.

STEP 2 Generate five random samples. Each sample consists of 20 words.

STEP 3 For the 20 words in each sample, record each word and its length in a table like the one shown. Then calculate the mean and the mean absolute deviation for each sample.

	Word	Word Length (x)	Distance from Mean
1	?	?	?
2	?	?	?
.	?	?	?
20	?	?	?
Total =		?	?
Sample mean =		?	
MAD =		?	

STEP 4 When you have completed **STEP 1** to **STEP 3** for all 20 samples, calculate the mean of the sample means.

Math Journal What is the estimate of the population mean word length? By observing the mean absolute deviations of the five samples, describe informally whether the words in the book vary greatly in length.

Make Comparative Inferences About Two Populations.

When you compare the means or medians of two populations, you need to take into account their measures of variation.

Example 14 | Compare the medians of two populations with the same measure of variation.

The weights of the players on two football teams are summarized in the box plots.

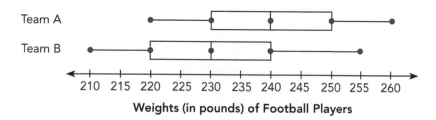

Weights (in pounds) of Football Players

a) Show that the two teams have the same measure of variation (that is, the difference between the three quartiles) and the same interquartile range.

Solution

Team A

$Q_2 - Q_1 = 240 - 230$
$= 10$ lb

$Q_3 - Q_2 = 250 - 240$
$= 10$ lb

Interquartile range $= 250 - 230$
$= 20$ lb

Team B

$Q_2 - Q_1 = 230 - 220$
$= 10$ lb

$Q_3 - Q_2 = 240 - 230$
$= 10$ lb

Interquartile range $= 240 - 220$
$= 20$ lb

So, the difference between the quartiles and the interquartile range are the same for the two teams.

b) Express the difference in median weight in terms of the interquartile range.

Solution

The difference in median weight between the two teams is half the interquartile range.

c) What inference can you draw about the weight distributions of the players of the two teams?

Solution

50% of the Team A players are heavier than the upper quartile of Team B. Only 25% of the Team B players are heavier than the median of Team A. Team A players are heavier in general.

Guided Practice

Solve.

2 The ages of two groups of children are summarized in the box plots.

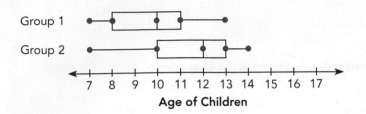

a) Show that the two groups have the same measure of variation (that is, the difference between quartiles) and the same interquartile range.

b) Express the difference in median age in terms of the interquartile range.

c) What inference can you draw about the age distributions of the children in the two groups?

Example 15 **Use box plots to compare two populations.**

A class of students completed two science tests. The scores are presented in the box plots.

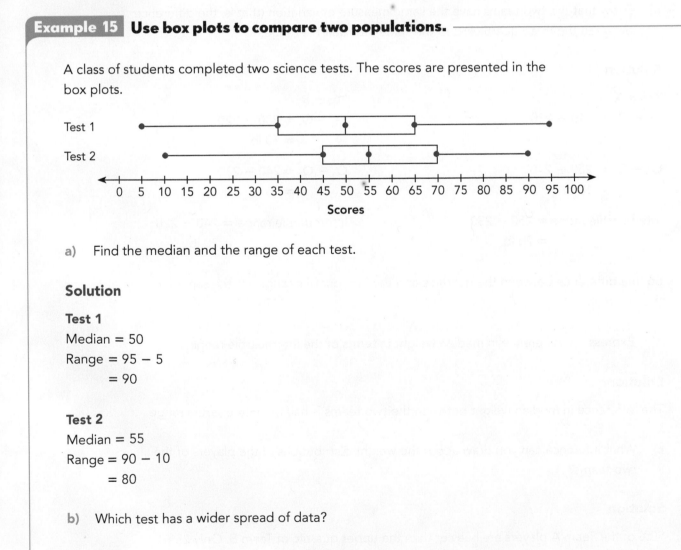

a) Find the median and the range of each test.

Solution

Test 1
Median = 50
Range = 95 − 5
   = 90

Test 2
Median = 55
Range = 90 − 10
   = 80

b) Which test has a wider spread of data?

Solution

Test 1 has a greater range than Test 2. So, Test 1 has a wider spread of data.

c) On which test did the class perform better?

Solution

Test 1: 50% of the scores are between 35 and 65.

Test 2: 50% of the scores are between 45 and 70.

So, the class performed better on Test 2.

> The box plot visually shows that students did better on Test 2. On 4 of the 5 statistics of the 5-point summary the results were better on Test 2 than on Test 1.

Guided Practice

Solve.

3 Two classes took a math test. The results are summarized in the box plots.

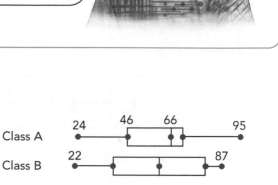

a) For which class are the data more spread out? Explain.

b) Comment on the performance of the two classes.

Example 16 **Compare two populations with the same mean but different mean absolute deviations.**

The table shows the game scores of Mark and Jason.

Mark's Scores	2	3	8	5	3	4	4	6	5	4
Jason's Scores	9	5	1	1	2	8	9	2	1	6

a) Find the mean scores for Mark and Jason.

Solution

Mark's mean score

$$= \frac{2+3+8+5+3+4+4+6+5+4}{10}$$

$$= \frac{44}{10}$$

$$= 4.4$$

Jason's mean score

$$= \frac{9+5+1+1+2+8+9+2+1+6}{10}$$

$$= \frac{44}{10}$$

$$= 4.4$$

Continue on next page

b) Calculate the mean absolute deviation of Mark's and Jason's scores.

Solution

Mark's Scores	Mark's Mean	Distance of Data from the Mean	Jason's Scores	Jason's Mean	Distance of Data from the Mean
2	4.4	2.4	9	4.4	4.6
3	4.4	1.4	5	4.4	0.6
8	4.4	3.6	1	4.4	3.4
5	4.4	0.6	1	4.4	3.4
3	4.4	1.4	2	4.4	2.4
4	4.4	0.4	8	4.4	3.6
4	4.4	0.4	9	4.4	4.6
6	4.4	1.6	2	4.4	2.4
5	4.4	0.6	1	4.4	3.4
4	4.4	0.4	6	4.4	1.6

Sum of the distances for Mark
= 2.4 + 1.4 + 3.6 + 0.6 + 1.4 + 0.4 + 0.4 + 1.6 + 0.6 + 0.4
= 12.8

MAD for Mark = $\dfrac{12.8}{10}$

   = 1.28

Sum of the distances for Jason
= 4.6 + 0.6 + 3.4 + 3.4 + 2.4 + 3.6 + 4.6 + 2.4 + 3.4 + 1.6
= 30

MAD for Jason = $\dfrac{30}{10}$

   = 3

c) Draw separate dot plots for Mark's scores and for Jason's scores.

Solution

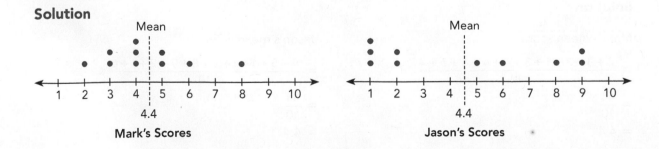

d) Compare Mark's and Jason's statistics. Then compare their dot plots.

Solution

Both Mark and Jason have the same mean score. Jason's mean absolute deviation is more than twice Mark's mean absolute deviation. The dots in Mark's dot plot tend to cluster around the mean score while the dots in Jason's dot plot tend to be spread out from the mean score. This confirms that Mark's mean absolute deviation is less than Jason's mean absolute deviation.

e) What conclusion can you make about the two players' performance in the game?

Solution

Mark's performance is more consistent since most of his scores are close to the mean. Jason's performance is more inconsistent since his scores vary widely between very low and very high scores.

Guided Practice

Solve.

4 The numbers of questions that two groups of students answered correctly in a recent mathematics test are shown in the table.

Group A	Group B
5	11
15	13
20	10
14	14
6	18
19	15
10	10
10	11
7	6
14	12

a) Find the mean number of correct questions for each of the two groups.

b) Calculate the mean absolute deviation of each of the two groups.

c) Draw separate dot plots for the two groups.

d) Interpret the above statistics and the dot plots.

e) What conclusion can you make about the performance of the two groups of students on the test?

Practice 9.5

Solve. Show your work.

1 A random sample of a certain type of ball bearing produces a mean weight of 28 grams and a mean absolute deviation of 2.1 grams. What can be inferred from the sample about the population mean weight of this type of ball bearing?

2 You interviewed a random sample of 25 marathon runners and compiled the following statistics.
Mean time to complete the race = 220 minutes and MAD = 50 minutes
What can you infer about the time to complete the race among the population of runners represented by your sample?

Refer to the random sample below to answer the following. Round your answers to the nearest tenth.

The table shows a random sample of the volume, in milliliters, of 15 servings of orange juice from a vending machine.

251	254	254	249	250
248	250	252	251	253
247	245	255	254	251

3 Use the sample mean volume to estimate the population mean volume of a serving of orange juice.

4 Calculate the MAD and the MAD to mean ratio.

5 Use the MAD to informally infer whether the volume of orange juice in a serving varies greatly.

Refer to the box plots at the right to answer the following.

Two large random samples of car speeds on two highways from 4 P.M. to 6 P.M. were collected. The data were summarized in two box plots.

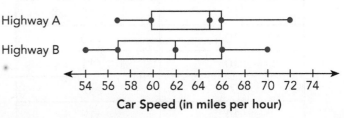

6 By comparing the interquartile ranges of the two box plots, what can you infer about car speeds on the two highways for the middle 50% of the cars?

7 By comparing the medians of the two plots, what inference can you make?

8 Suppose the speed limit on the two highways is 65 miles per hour. What percent of the cars drove faster than the speed limit on the two highways?

9 What can you infer about the overall car speeds on the two highways?

Refer to the scenario below to answer the following.

Henry and Carl go jogging every morning for several weeks. The following are the mean and the MAD of the distances they jog.

Henry   Carl

	Henry	Carl
Mean	5.25 km	4.20 km
MAD	2 km	0.75 km

10 What would you infer about the distances they jog if you only compare their mean distances?

11 What can you conclude if you take into account both the mean and the MAD for your comparison?

Refer to the random samples below to answer the following. Round your answers to the nearest tenth.

3 random samples of time taken, in seconds, to solve a crossword puzzle during a competition were collected.

$S_1 = \{100, 87, 95, 103, 110, 90, 84, 88\}$
$S_2 = \{75, 98, 120, 106, 70, 79, 100, 90\}$
$S_3 = \{60, 68, 110, 88, 78, 90, 104, 73\}$

12 Calculate the mean time of each of the 3 samples.

13 Estimate the population mean time of the competition using the mean of the 3 sample means.

14 Combine S_1, S_2, and S_3 into one sample and use the mean in question **13** to calculate the MAD of the combined sample.

15 If you use the MAD found in question **14** to gauge the time variation among competitors, what can you infer?

Refer to the random samples below to answer the following. Round your answers to the nearest hundredth when you can.

Below are the history test scores of two classes of 20 students each.

Class A				
84	63	90	68	42
43	31	60	88	70
25	40	32	37	79
66	55	65	35	42

Class B				
63	66	62	66	80
55	72	77	66	58
66	68	44	60	70
66	76	75	71	74

16 Find the range of scores for each class.

17 Calculate the mean scores for each class.

18 Calculate the MAD for each class.

19 By comparing the mean scores and the MADs of the two classes, what can you infer about the performance of the two classes?

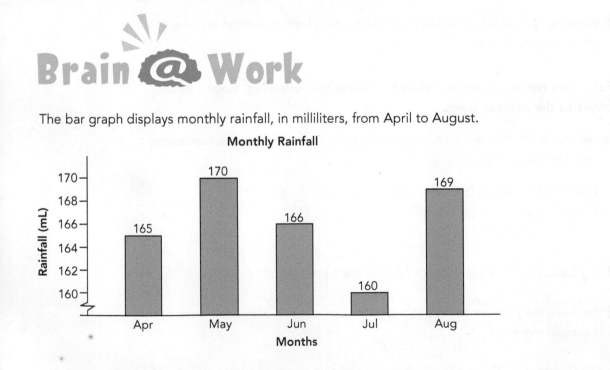

Brain @ Work

The bar graph displays monthly rainfall, in milliliters, from April to August.

Monthly Rainfall

Alex draws the conclusion that rainfall varies greatly from April to August.

a) Find the mean rainfall.

b) Calculate the mean absolute deviation.

c) Based on your mean absolute deviation, do you agree with Alex's conclusion? Explain why you agree or disagree.

Chapter Wrap Up

Concept Map

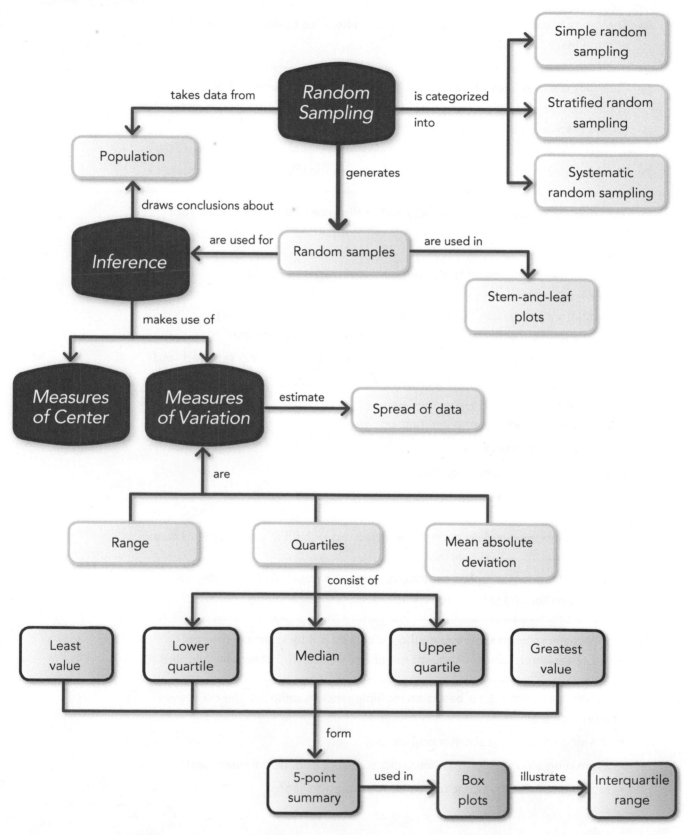

Key Concepts

▶ Measures of variation are statistics that measure the spread of data.

▶ The range is a measure of variation. It is the difference between the greatest and the least data values.

▶ Quartiles are measures of variation that divide data into four equal parts. There are three quartiles: first quartile (or the lower quartile), second quartile (or the median), and third quartile (or the upper quartile).

▶ The interquartile range is the difference between the third and the first quartiles.

▶ The mean absolute deviation is the average distance of the data values from the mean.

▶ Data sets can be represented by stem-and-leaf diagrams.

▶ A sample is a set of data taken from a population. Random sampling is a process of collecting data from a population in such a way that

- every member of the population has an equal chance of being selected, and
- the selection of members is independent of each other.

▶ Three types of random sampling methods are

- simple random sampling,
- stratified random sampling, and
- systematic random sampling.

▶ A simple random sampling method is carried out without any pre-planned order.

▶ A stratified random sampling method requires the population to be divided into nonoverlapping groups from which members are randomly selected.

▶ A systematic random sampling method is carried out by selecting the first member randomly, and subsequent members are selected at regular intervals.

▶ An inference in statistics is based on multiple random samples. The objectives of inference are

- drawing conclusions about a population,
- estimating a population characteristic, such as a population mean, and
- drawing comparative conclusions about two populations.

Chapter Review/Test

Concepts and Skills

Find the range, the three quartiles, and the interquartile range.

1 2, 4, 1, 7, 3, 3, 9, 10, 1, 0, 6, 8, 5, 5, 9

2 34, 66, 90, 25, 46, 81, 40, 67, 95, 104, 36, 49

3 1.23, 1.45, 1.09, 1.78, 1.55, 1.67, 1.37, 1.05, 1.23, 1.11

4 162.5, 248.6, 130.7, 344.9, 322.0, 234.2, 150.8, 304.7, 326.4

Use the information below to answer the following.

Tara tossed two number dice 24 times. She found the sum of the values for each throw and displayed the sums in a dot plot.

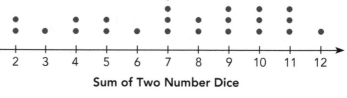

5 Find the range of the data.

6 Find the 3 quartiles of the data.

Sum of Two Number Dice

7 Find the interquartile range.

Solve. Show your work.

8 The map shows the maximum temperature, in degrees Fahrenheit, recorded in 20 cities across the United States in a certain year. Display the data in a stem-and-leaf plot.

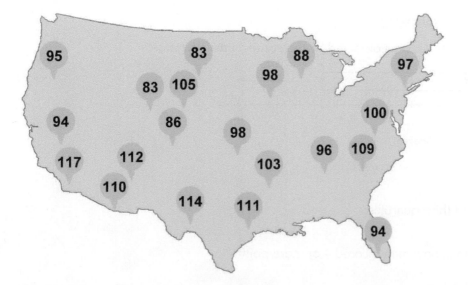

9 The table shows the weights of Labrador dogs, in pounds.

72	73	79	68	101
88	78	71	85	94
93	77	98	95	75
81	56	51	62	70

a) Draw a stem-and-leaf plot for the data.

b) How many Labrador dogs are there?

c) What is the range?

d) What is the mode of the data?

e) What is the median weight?

Find the mean absolute deviation.

10  57, 60, 31, 30, 26, 46, 52, 40, 35, 60

11 1.46, 2.03, 3.12, 2.55, 4.25, 1.80, 4.08, 2.87

Refer to the box plot to answer the following.

The box plot summarizes the heights of bean sprouts, in centimeters.

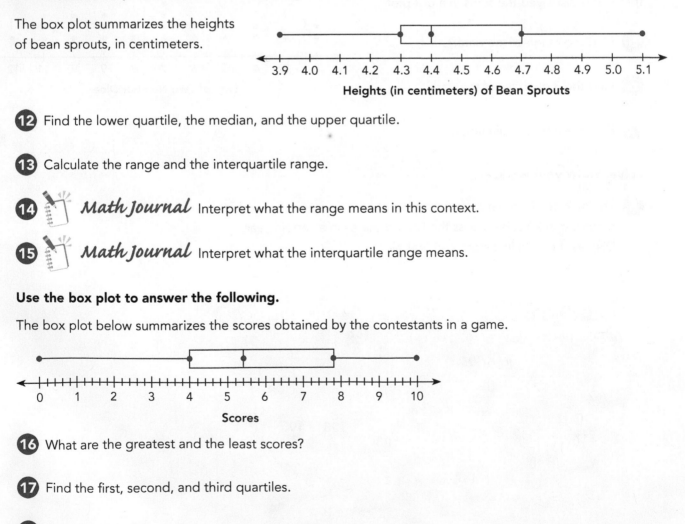

Heights (in centimeters) of Bean Sprouts

12 Find the lower quartile, the median, and the upper quartile.

13 Calculate the range and the interquartile range.

14 *Math Journal* Interpret what the range means in this context.

15 *Math Journal* Interpret what the interquartile range means.

Use the box plot to answer the following.

The box plot below summarizes the scores obtained by the contestants in a game.

Scores

16 What are the greatest and the least scores?

17 Find the first, second, and third quartiles.

18 If there are 160 contestants, how many scored 4 or more points?

Problem Solving

Use the statistics given in the table to answer questions 19 to 21.

In a population of 200 students taking a science test, the following statistics for the test scores were compiled.

Mean	Median	Mode	Lower Quartile	Upper Quartile	Highest Score	Lowest Score	MAD
68.5	67.4	67	38	76	96	26	25

 19 **Math Journal** By comparing the mean, the median, and the mode, what can you infer about the distribution of the test scores?

 20 **Math Journal** By analyzing the statistics in the table, what can you infer about the variation of the scores?

21 Estimate the number of students who scored 76 or less.

Use the data in the table to answer questions 22 to 27.

The table summarizes the monthly sales figures, in thousands of dollars, for the women's and men's clothing departments at a store. For instance, sales in the women's department in January were $10,000.

	Jan	Feb	Mar	Apr	May	Jun	Jul	Aug	Sep	Oct	Nov	Dec
Women ($1,000)	10	15	8	12	28	34	36	18	14	16	27	40
Men ($1,000)	8	10	11	15	20	30	24	14	10	9	17	28

22 Calculate the 5-point summary for each of the two departments.

23 Using the same scale, draw 2 box plots, one for each departments.

 24 **Math Journal** By comparing the two box plots, describe the sales performance of the two departments.

 25 Calculate the mean sales figure for each of the two departments. Give your answers to the nearest dollar when you can.

 26 Calculate the mean absolute deviation for each of the two departments. Give your answers to the nearest dollar.

 27 **Math Journal** By comparing the means and the mean absolute deviations of the two clothing departments, what can you infer about their variability in sales?

Probability

Will it snow tomorrow?

The weather forecast predicts that snow is likely tomorrow. Will school be canceled? Based on existing conditions and past weather history, weather forecasters try to predict the likelihood of a snowstorm. Of course, weather conditions change all the time. So what was a likely chance of snow the day before might become possible or certain today.

In this chapter, you will use probability to predict how likely something is to occur.

BIG IDEA

▶ Events happen around you every day, some more likely than others. You can use probability to describe how likely an event is to occur.

Recall Prior Knowledge

Expressing a part of a whole as a fraction and a percent

Suppose you have 12 liters of water. Express 3 liters out of 12 liters as a fraction and as a percent.

Draw a model to represent the fraction as follows:

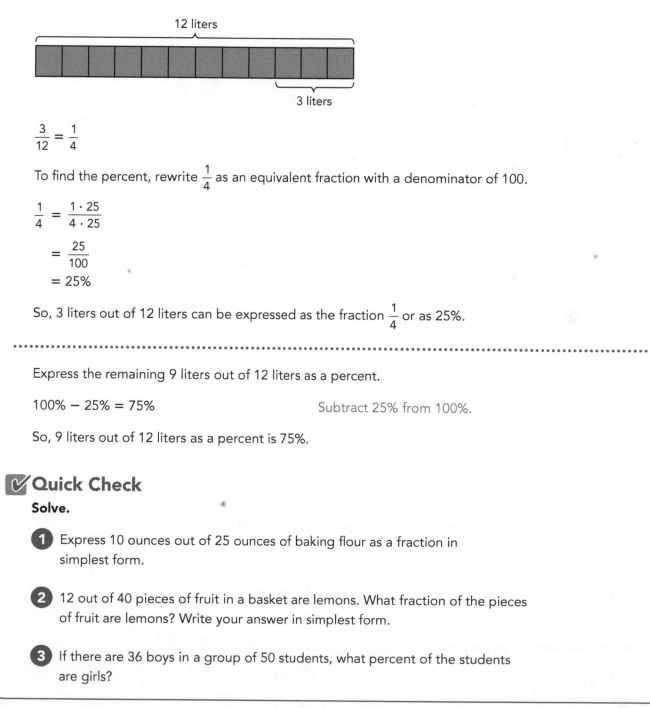

12 liters

3 liters

$$\frac{3}{12} = \frac{1}{4}$$

To find the percent, rewrite $\frac{1}{4}$ as an equivalent fraction with a denominator of 100.

$$\frac{1}{4} = \frac{1 \cdot 25}{4 \cdot 25}$$
$$= \frac{25}{100}$$
$$= 25\%$$

So, 3 liters out of 12 liters can be expressed as the fraction $\frac{1}{4}$ or as 25%.

· ·

Express the remaining 9 liters out of 12 liters as a percent.

100% − 25% = 75%   Subtract 25% from 100%.

So, 9 liters out of 12 liters as a percent is 75%.

✓ Quick Check

Solve.

1. Express 10 ounces out of 25 ounces of baking flour as a fraction in simplest form.

2. 12 out of 40 pieces of fruit in a basket are lemons. What fraction of the pieces of fruit are lemons? Write your answer in simplest form.

3. If there are 36 boys in a group of 50 students, what percent of the students are girls?

Expressing a fraction as a percent

Express $\frac{7}{9}$ as a percent. Round your answer to 2 decimal places.

$$\frac{7}{9} = \frac{7}{9} \cdot 100\%$$ Multiply the fraction by 100%.

$$= \frac{700}{9}\%$$ Write the improper fraction as a mixed number.

$$= 77.78\%$$ Round.

✓ Quick Check

Write each fraction as a percent. Round your answer to 2 decimal places when you can.

4 $\frac{5}{8}$ **5** $\frac{2}{5}$ **6** $\frac{24}{9}$

Expressing a percent as a fraction or decimal

Express 55% as a fraction in simplest form.

$$55\% = \frac{55}{100}$$ Express the percent as a fraction.

$$= \frac{55 \div 5}{100 \div 5}$$ Divide both the numerator and denominator by the greatest common factor 5.

$$= \frac{11}{20}$$

Express 126% as a decimal.

$$126\% = \frac{126}{100}$$ Express the percent as a fraction.

$$= 1.26$$ Express the fraction as a decimal.

✓ Quick Check

Write each percent as a fraction or a mixed number in simplest form.

7 54%   **8** 19.5%

9 1.4%   **10** 115%

Write each percent as a decimal.

11 28%   **12** 9%

13 34.5%   **14** 256%

Expressing a ratio as a fraction or percent

A ratio that compares a part to a whole can also be expressed as a fraction and as a percent.

The trees in an orchard are pear trees and apple trees. The ratio of pear trees to apple trees is 7 to 13.

a) What fraction of the trees are pear trees?

b) What percent of the trees are pear trees?

....

a) Use bar models.

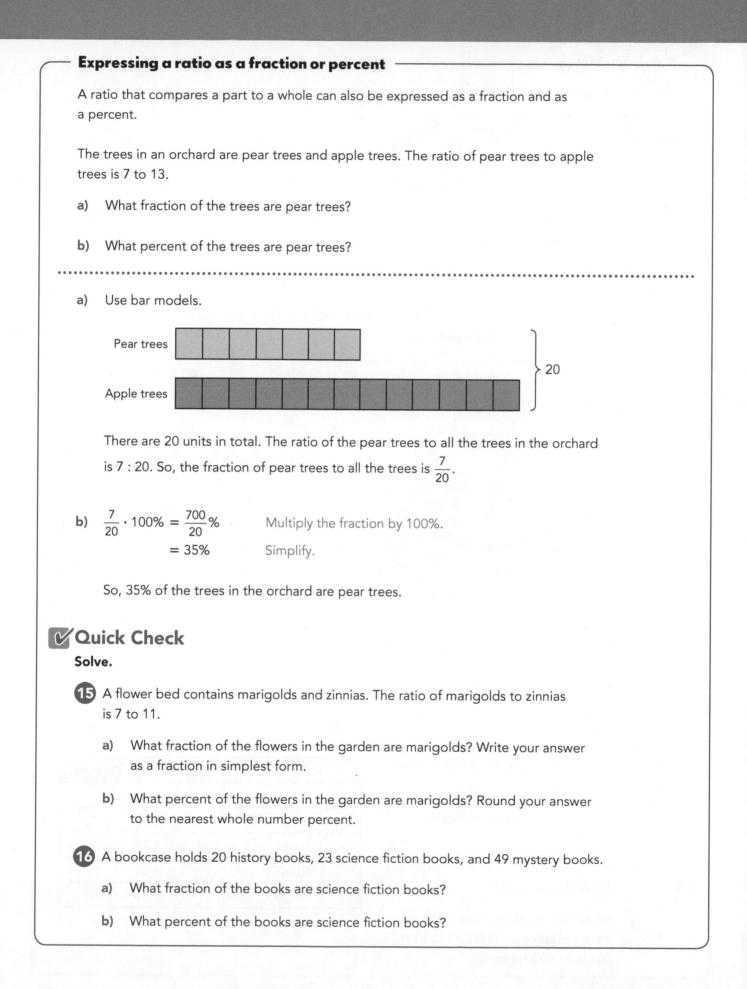

There are 20 units in total. The ratio of the pear trees to all the trees in the orchard is 7 : 20. So, the fraction of pear trees to all the trees is $\frac{7}{20}$.

b) $\frac{7}{20} \cdot 100\% = \frac{700}{20}\%$ Multiply the fraction by 100%.

           $= 35\%$ Simplify.

So, 35% of the trees in the orchard are pear trees.

☑ Quick Check

Solve.

15 A flower bed contains marigolds and zinnias. The ratio of marigolds to zinnias is 7 to 11.

    a) What fraction of the flowers in the garden are marigolds? Write your answer as a fraction in simplest form.

    b) What percent of the flowers in the garden are marigolds? Round your answer to the nearest whole number percent.

16 A bookcase holds 20 history books, 23 science fiction books, and 49 mystery books.

    a) What fraction of the books are science fiction books?

    b) What percent of the books are science fiction books?

Solving a histogram problem

The table shows the heights of 78 trees in a park rounded to the nearest foot.

Height (ft)	Number of Trees
60–69	11
70–79	20
80–89	22
90–99	15
100–109	6
110–119	4

The histogram displays the information about the tree heights.

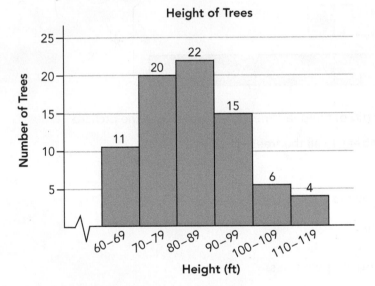

The heights of 25 trees are at least 90 feet.
42 of 78 trees have heights of 70 to 89 feet.
So, 54% of the trees are from 70 to 89 feet tall.

✔ Quick Check

Solve.

17 The table shows the mass of 100 steel bars rounded to the nearest kilogram.

Mass (kg)	Number of Steel Bars
10–19	15
20–29	33
30–39	18
40–49	24
50–59	10

a) Draw a histogram to display this information.

b) How many steel bars have a mass from 10 to 39 kilograms?

c) What percent of the steel bars have a mass of at least 20 kilograms, but less than 50 kilograms?

Defining Outcomes, Events, and Sample Space

Lesson Objective

- Understand the concepts of outcomes, events, and sample space and apply them to everyday life.

Vocabulary

outcome   sample space

event

List Outcomes and Sample Space for an Activity.

When you play chess with your friend, the game may end in three possible ways: You win, you lose or there is a draw. All the possible results of an activity are called outcomes. In the case of chess, there are three possible outcomes from your perspective: Win, lose, draw. The collection of all possible outcomes from an activity is known as a sample space.

Flipping a coin

When you flip a coin, it will land on either heads or tails. This activity has 2 possible outcomes: Heads or Tails.

Rolling a number die

A number die has six face values. When you roll a number die, one of these six values will appear on the top face. So, the sample space consists of six possible outcomes: 1, 2, 3, 4, 5, and 6.

> **Math Note**
>
> An activity such as flipping a coin or rolling a number die is often called an *experiment*.

Weather forecast

The weather forecast on television uses different symbols to indicate the weather conditions. The weather conditions can be classified into six possible outcomes:

| Sunny | Partly Cloudy | Cloudy | Rain | Snow | Thunderstorm |

Hands-On Activity

Materials:
- paper
- scissors

Work in pairs.

STEP 1 Make a set of four small cards with the following digits written on them.

| 1 | 2 | 3 | 4 |

STEP 2 Pick three cards and form a 3-digit number. Record the number.

STEP 3 Find all the possible 3-digit numbers that you can form. The list of numbers represents all the possible outcomes for the activity.

STEP 4 Tell how many outcomes are in the sample space for this activity.

Example 1 **List outcomes in an event.**

List all the types of outcomes in each event. State the number of the outcomes.

a) You spin the spinner shown and record the number where the spinner lands.

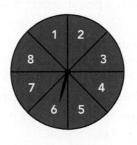

Solution

The outcomes are 1, 2, 3, 4, 5, 6, 7, and 8. There are 8 equally possible outcomes.

b) You place the cards shown face down. Then you draw one and record the color.

> **Math Note**
>
> There are two green cards. Because you count the repeated cases when counting the possible outcomes, there are 6 equally possible outcomes but 5 types of outcomes.

Solution

The types of outcomes are blue, green, purple, brown, and white. There are 6 equally possible outcomes.

Guided Practice

Solve.

1 Select a letter from the list of letters: A, D, E, G, K.

   a) List all the possible outcomes.

   b) State the number of outcomes in the sample space.

2 Use the letter cards below to form all possible 3-letter English words.

   a) List all the possible outcomes.

   b) State the number of outcomes in the sample space.

List Outcomes Favorable to an Event.

An event is a collection of outcomes from an activity.

For example, if you roll a number die, the sample space is {1, 2, 3, 4, 5, 6}. The event of rolling an even number consists of the outcomes 2, 4, and 6.

Events are usually named with capital letters. If E stands for the event of getting an even number, then you can write $E = \{2, 4, 6\}$ to show the outcomes favorable to event E.

> **Math Note**
>
> "Favorable outcomes" are outcomes that make an event happen.

Picking a letter

There are 26 tiles placed face down on the table, each printed with a letter from the alphabet. You pick one letter.

Let D be the event that the letter you picked is a vowel,
    E be the event that the letter you picked comes after
    the letter v in the alphabet, and
    F be the event that the letter you picked is a consonant
    and comes before the letter p in the alphabet.

The outcomes favorable to each event are shown below:
- $D = \{a, e, i, o, u\}$
- $E = \{w, x, y, z\}$
- $F = \{b, c, d, f, g, h, j, k, l, m, n\}$

Use braces { } to show the set of outcomes in a sample space, or to show the outcomes favorable to an event.

Example 2 **List favorable outcomes for an event and describe the sample space.**

List the outcomes that are favorable to each event. State the number of outcomes in the sample space.

a) For breakfast, you can choose one item from the following list: Toast, hash browns, bagels, oatmeal, cornflakes, or scrambled eggs. B is the event of choosing oatmeal, cornflakes, or scrambled eggs for breakfast.

Solution

B = {oatmeal, cornflakes, scrambled eggs}.
You choose from 6 choices, so there are 6 outcomes in the sample space.

b) X is the event of choosing a word with exactly two Es in it from the following word list.

mathematics	theme	eerie	share	employer	these
employee	here	there	maritime	those	

Solution

X = {theme, employer, here, there, these}. You choose from the 11 words in the list, so there are 11 outcomes in the sample space.

Guided Practice

Solve.

3 Y is the event of choosing a prime number from a list of whole numbers from 1 to 20.

a) List the outcomes favorable to event Y.

The prime numbers up to 20 are __?__, __?__, __?__, __?__, __?__, __?__, __?__, __?__.
Y = {__?__, __?__, __?__, __?__, __?__, __?__, __?__, __?__}

b) State the number of outcomes in the sample space.

You choose from __?__ outcomes. There are __?__ outcomes in the sample space.

4 You choose a shape from a bag containing these cardboard geometric shapes.

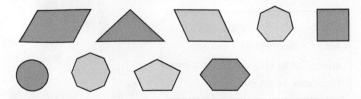

a) List all the favorable outcomes for the event of choosing a shape with at most 6 sides.

b) List all the favorable outcomes for the event of choosing a shape with more than 4 angles.

Practice 10.1

Solve.

1 A bag contains 2 red balls and 1 green ball. A ball is taken out from the bag. What are the types of outcomes?

2 A number die with faces numbered 1 to 6 is rolled once. What are the favorable outcomes for the event of getting a value that is evenly divisible by 3?

3 A spinner has 5 values, as shown in the diagram. You spin the spinner and record where the spinner lands.

a) List all the outcomes in the sample space.

b) If event *A* is the event of landing on an even number, what are the outcomes favorable to event *A*?

4 A basketball coach has 5 forwards, 2 centers, and 5 guards. *E* is the event of the coach picking a forward to be the team captain. How many outcomes are favorable to event *E*?

5 A letter is selected from the letters in the name TYRANNOSAURUS REX. What is the number of possible outcomes?

6 A colored disk is drawn from a bag which contains the following disks.

a) If you record only the color of the disk, what are the types of outcomes?

b) If you record only the letter on the disk, what are the types of outcomes?

c) If you record both the color and the letter of the disk, what are the types of outcomes?

7 There are 10 multiple-choice questions in a test. A student gets 1 point for every correct answer and 0 points for every wrong answer. No point is awarded for a question that the student does not try to answer.

a) What is the highest score a student could receive on the test?

b) What is the lowest possible score a student could receive?

c) What are the possible outcomes for a score on the multiple choice test?

8 A student is to be selected to play a supporting role in a drama from the list of names below.

Name	Age	Height (m)
Bob	14	1.69
John	15	1.58
Denise	14	1.80
Michael	16	1.55
Josephine	16	1.70
Margaret	15	1.50

Name	Age	Height (m)
Timothy	16	1.82
Brenda	14	1.66
Henry	13	1.47
Gary	16	1.74
Chloe	16	1.60
Benjamin	14	1.52

a) X is the event that the selected student is 14 years old. List the outcomes favorable to event X.

b) Y is the event that the selected student is at least 1.56 meters tall. List all the outcomes favorable to event Y.

c) Z is the event that the selected student is at least 1.7 meters tall and at least 15 years old. How many outcomes are favorable to this event?

d) W is the event that the name of the selected student has at most 5 letters. What outcomes are favorable to event W?

9 From the list of digits, 0, 5, 7, 8, you form a 3-digit number without any repeating digits. You do not include any numbers that start with 0.

a) List all the outcomes of the sample space.

b) List all the favorable outcomes for the event that the 3-digit number is an even number.

c) List all the favorable outcomes for the event that the 3-digit number is an odd number.

10 You pick a whole number between 1 and 100. If A is the event that the number you picked is divisible by 3 and 7, what are the outcomes favorable to event A?

11 The 5 numeric tiles 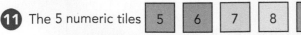 are placed face down. You pick 4 tiles to form a 4-digit number. How many outcomes are favorable to the event of forming a number greater than 8,755?

10.2 Finding Probability of Events

Lesson Objectives

- Calculate the probability of events.
- Use Venn diagrams to illustrate events and their relationships.
- Solve real-world problems involving probability.

Vocabulary

probability	fair
biased	Venn diagram
mutually exclusive	complementary events
complement	

Use Probability to Describe the Likelihood of an Event.

Jar A and Jar B each contain a collection of black and white marbles. You know that Jar A has more black marbles than white marbles, and that Jar B has more white marbles than black marbles.

Jar A   Jar B

Now suppose that without looking, you pick a marble from one of the jars. If you want to increase your chance of getting a black marble, you would probably choose from Jar A.

The word "chance" implies likelihood. Probability is a way to describe how good the chances are that an event will occur. A number from 0 to 1 is used to express the probability of an event.

The number line below shows what different values mean in probability.

A probability closer to 1 means the chances of an event happening are more likely. A probability closer to 0 means the chances of an event happening are less likely.

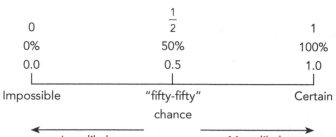

A probability can be expressed as a percent, a decimal, or a fraction between 0 and 1.

Example 3   **Find the probability of an event when flipping a fair coin.**

You flip a fair coin. It is impossible for the coin to land on its edge.

a)   What is the probability that it will land on heads?

Solution

The word "fair" means that the chances of landing on heads or tails are equal — the coin does not favor either outcome. A coin that favors a particular outcome is called **biased**.

Since the coin is equally likely to land on heads or tails, the probability of the coin landing on heads is $\frac{1}{2}$ or 50%.

b)   What is the probability that the coin will land on both heads and tails?

Solution

The coin cannot land on heads and on tails. Such an event is impossible. So, the probability of the coin landing on both heads and tails is 0.

>
> **Think Math**
>
> Suppose a coin is biased so that it is more likely to land on heads than tails. Will the probabiity of getting heads be greater than or less than $\frac{1}{2}$?

Guided Practice

Copy and complete. Solve.

1 You roll a fair number die.

a)   Find the probability of getting a four.

There are __?__ outcomes when you roll a number die. All the outcomes are equally likely.

So, the probability of getting a four is __?__.

b)   Find the probability of getting a seven.

It is impossible to get a seven when you roll a standard number die.

So, the probability of getting a seven is __?__.

Solve.

2 When you spin the spinner, what is the probability that the arrow will point to a number?

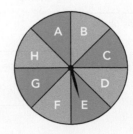

Find the Probability of an Event.

An event may have one or more favorable outcomes. Suppose an activity generates n equally likely possible outcomes. Let A be an event with m favorable outcomes. The probability of event A occurring, P(A), is given by:

$$P(A) = \frac{\text{Number of outcomes favorable to event } A}{\text{Total number of equally likely outcomes}}$$

$$= \frac{m}{n}$$

Example 4   Find the probability of an event.

A pebble is picked at random from a bag containing 6 gray pebbles, 9 white pebbles, and 5 tan pebbles. Let B be the event of picking a white pebble.

a)   Find the probability that event B will occur.

Solution

$6 + 9 + 5 = 20$ First find the total number of outcomes.

The total number of possible outcomes is 20.

Event B has 9 favorable outcomes because there are 9 white pebbles.

$$P(B) = \frac{\text{Number of outcomes favorable to event } B}{\text{Total number of equally likely outcomes}}$$ Use the formula.

$$= \frac{9}{20}$$ There are 9 white pebbles out of 20 pebbles.

b)   Express your answer in **a)** as a percent.

Solution

$$P(B) = \frac{9}{20} \cdot 100\%$$ Multiply the fraction by 100%.

$$= 45\%$$

There is a 45% chance that event B will occur.

The probability can be expressed as a percent and also as a fraction in simplest form, $\frac{9}{20}$.

Guided Practice

Complete.

3 Max has 4 short-sleeved shirts and 5 long-sleeved shirts in his closet. *X* is the event of Max randomly choosing a long-sleeved shirt. Find P(*X*). Express the probability as a fraction.

Event *X* has __?__ favorable outcomes.

$$P(X) = \frac{\text{Number of outcomes favorable to event } X}{\text{Total number of equally likely outcomes}}$$

Use the formula.

$$= \underline{}$$

There are __?__ long-sleeved shirts out of 9 shirts.

Solve.

4 A box contains 28 pink ribbons and 12 green ribbons. You randomly take a ribbon from the box without looking. Find the probability of picking a pink ribbon. Express the probability as a percent.

Use Venn Diagrams to Show Relationships for Events.

In certain situations, one event may not occur at the same time another event occurs.

Flipping a coin

You flip a coin. Let *H* be the event that the coin lands on heads. Let *T* be the event that the coin lands on tails. It is obvious that a coin cannot land on heads and on tails at the same time.

When two events cannot happen at the same time, they are said to be **mutually exclusive** events.

You can use a Venn diagram to represent mutually exclusive events. The Venn diagram below represents the mutually exclusive events of getting heads and getting tails when you flip a coin.

Each circle in the Venn diagram represents an event. Because the circles for event *H* and event *T* do not overlap, the events are mutually exclusive.

Rolling a number die

You roll a number die. Let A_1, A_2, A_3, A_4, A_5, and A_6 be the events that you get 1, 2, 3, 4, 5, and 6. It is obvious that any two of these events cannot happen at the same time. In a Venn diagram, these events are represented by nonoverlapping circles. The Venn diagram shows that these events are mutually exclusive.

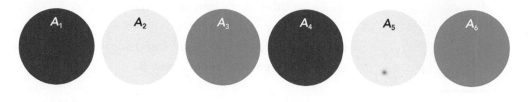

Now think about these two events.
E is the event of rolling an even number, and
F is the event of rolling a number greater than 3.

The outcomes favorable for these events are $E = \{2, 4, 6\}$ and $F = \{4, 5, 6\}$. The sample space S for rolling the number die is $\{1, 2, 3, 4, 5, 6\}$.

In the Venn diagram below, the sample space S is shown by a rectangle. The circles for events E and F overlap because the outcomes 4 and 6 are common to both events. Events E and F are not mutually exclusive.

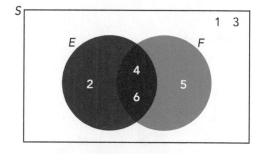

If a 4 or a 6 is rolled, both events occur at the same time. So, events E and F are not mutually exclusive.

Example 5　**Represent mutually exclusive events with a Venn diagram.**

Ten cards, each printed with a different whole number from 16 to 25, are shuffled and placed face down. A card is drawn at random from the ten cards. Let A be the event of getting a number that is a multiple of 3. Let B be the event of getting a number that is a multiple of 5.

a)　List all the outcomes favorable to events A and B.

Solution

$A = \{18, 21, 24\}$　　List multiples of 3 from 16 to 25.
$B = \{20, 25\}$　　　List multiples of 5 from 16 to 25.

Continue on next page

b) Draw a Venn diagram for the sample space and the two events. Place all possible outcomes in the Venn diagram.

Solution

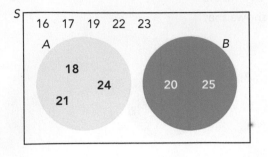

The rectangle that represents the sample space includes all the whole numbers from 16 to 25. Some of these numbers are outcomes favorable to event A and some are outcomes favorable to event B.

c) Are events A and B mutually exclusive? Explain.

Solution

Events A and B are mutually exclusive. In the Venn diagram, the circles for the two events do not overlap because there are no favorable outcomes common to both events.

d) Find P(A) and P(B).

Solution

The sample space, S, has 10 possible outcomes. Event A has 3 favorable outcomes. Event B has 2 favorable outcomes.

$P(A) = \dfrac{3}{10}$ or 0.3

$P(B) = \dfrac{2}{10}$ or 0.2

Remember that you can write a probability as a fraction, a decimal, or a percent.

Guided Practice

Solve.

5 Ten cards have the following numbers printed on them: 3, 6, 9, 11, 19, 27, 35, 39, 40, and 45. A card is randomly drawn from the ten cards. Let W be the event of getting a number that is an odd number greater than 20. Let V be the event of getting a prime number.

a) List all the outcomes favourable to events W and V.

b) Draw a Venn diagram for the sample space and the two events. Place all possible outcomes in the Venn diagram.

c) Are events W and V mutually exclusive? Explain.

d) Find P(W) and P(V).

Example 6 **Represent nonmutually exclusive events using a Venn diagram.**

A name is randomly chosen from a list of names: Bill, Jesse, Eva, Chloe, Mary, Ruth, Kim, Henry, Elsa, and Sean. Let X be the event of choosing a name with two vowels. Let Y be the event of choosing a name made up of three letters.

a)   Draw a Venn diagram for the sample space and the two events. Place all possible outcomes in the Venn diagram.

Solution

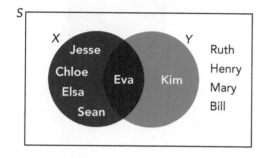

The Venn diagram includes all the outcomes from the sample space. Some outcomes are favorable to event X, some are favorable to event Y, and one outcome is favorable to events X and Y. Four outcomes are not favorable to events X or Y.

b)   Are events X and Y mutually exclusive? Explain.

Solution

Events X and Y are not mutually exclusive. The circles for events X and Y overlap because the events have one favorable outcome in common.

c)   Find $P(X)$ and $P(Y)$.

Solution

The sample space, S, has 10 possible outcomes. Event X has 5 favorable outcomes. Event Y has 2 favorable outcomes.

$P(X) = \dfrac{5}{10}$ or 0.5

$P(Y) = \dfrac{2}{10}$ or 0.2

Guided Practice

Solve.

6 A letter is selected at random from the state name RHODE ISLAND. Let C be the event of getting a consonant. Let H be the event of getting a letter that comes after H in the alphabet.

a)   Draw a Venn diagram for the sample space and the two events. Place all possible outcomes in the Venn diagram.

b)   Are events C and H mutually exclusive? Explain.

c)   Find $P(C)$ and $P(H)$.

Define Complementary Events.

Given an event E, the **complement** of event E is the event that E does not occur. The complement of event E is written as E'.

The Venn diagram shows event E and its complement, E', in the sample space. Event E is represented by the circle in the sample space S. The complementary event, E', is the region outside the circle. So, events E and E' have no common outcomes.

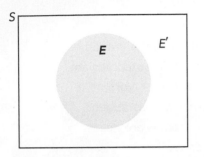

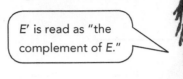

E' is read as "the complement of E."

The Venn diagram illustrates two properties of complementary events:
- events E and E' are mutually exclusive.
- $P(E) + P(E') = 1$.

Example 7   **Find the probability of a complementary event.**

A basket contains 18 red flower petals and 12 white flower petals. A flower petal is randomly picked from the basket. Let W be the event of picking a white flower petal.

a)   Draw a Venn diagram to represent events W and W'. Give the meaning of event W', the complement of event W.

Solution

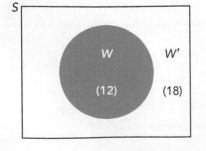

Write "(12)" in the circle for event W to represent the 12 white flower petals.

Write "(18)" outside the circle for event W' to represent the 18 red flower petals.

W' is the event of picking a flower petal which is not white. It is the event of picking a red flower petal.

b) Find P(W) and P(W').

Solution

12 + 18 = 30   Add the number of choices.

The total number of outcomes is 30.

The event W has 12 possible outcomes.

$P(W) = \dfrac{12}{30}$ 12 of the 30 petals are white.

$= \dfrac{2}{5}$ Simplify.

There is more than one way to find P(W').

Method 1

30 − 12 = 18   Find the number of petals that are not white.

There are 18 nonwhite petals.

So, $P(W') = \dfrac{18}{30}$ 18 of the 30 petals are not white.

$= \dfrac{3}{5}$ Simplify.

Method 2

$P(W) + P(W') = 1$ Use the formula.

$P(W') = 1 - P(W)$ Rewrite the formula.

$P(W') = 1 - \dfrac{2}{5}$ Substitute the value of P(W).

$P(W') = \dfrac{3}{5}$

Guided Practice

Solve.

7 You randomly choose a month from the twelve months in a year. Let A be the event of randomly choosing a month that has the letter a in its name.

a) Draw a Venn diagram to represent events A and A'. Give the meaning of event A', the complement of event A.

b) What outcomes are favorable to event A'?

c) Find P(A) and P(A').

Example 8   **Solve a probability problem involving percents.**

25% of the students in the school band play brass instruments. Among the brass players, 20% play the trombone. The band director randomly chooses a band member to play a solo.

a)   Draw a Venn diagram to represent the information.

Solution

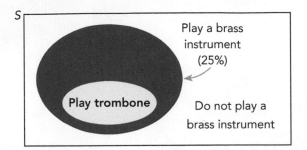

> You know that 25% of the band members play brass instruments. Of these brass players, 20% play the trombone. So, 20% of 25% of the band members play the trombone.

b)   What is the probability that a band member who does not play a brass instrument is selected?

Solution

Since 25% of the band members play brass instruments, this means 75% of the band members do not play a brass instrument. The probability of choosing a band member who does not play a brass instrument is 75%, or 0.75.

c)   What is the probability that a trombone player is selected?

Solution

Percent of band members who play the trombone:

$$20\% \text{ of } 25\% = 0.20 \cdot 0.25 \qquad \text{Write percents as decimals and multiply.}$$
$$= 0.05 \qquad\qquad\qquad \text{Simplify.}$$
$$= 5\% \qquad\qquad\qquad\; \text{Write as a percent.}$$

> "20% of 25%" is the same as saying "20% · 25%," or "0.20 · 0.25."

The probability that a trombone player is selected is 5%, or 0.05.

Guided Practice

Complete.

8 40% of the apples in an orchard are green and the rest of the apples are red. 5% of the red apples are rotten.

a) Copy the Venn diagram to represent the information.

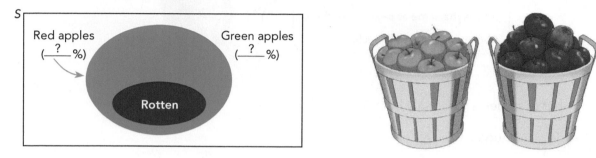

b) If you pick an apple at random in the orchard, what is the probability the apple you pick is red that is not rotten? Give your answer as a decimal and as a percent.

Of all the red apples, ___?___ % of them are not rotten.

$$\underline{\quad?\quad} \text{ of } 60\% = \underline{\quad?\quad} \cdot 0.60 \qquad \text{Write percents as decimals and multiply.}$$

$$= \underline{\quad?\quad} \qquad \text{Simplify.}$$

$$= \underline{\quad?\quad} \% \qquad \text{Write as a percent.}$$

The probability of picking a red apple that is not rotten is ___?___.

Example 9 **Solve a probability problem involving a ratio.**

Out of 500 students, 156 students study Spanish as a foreign language. Of those studying Spanish, 1 out of 6 students also study French.

a) Draw a Venn diagram to represent the information.

Solution

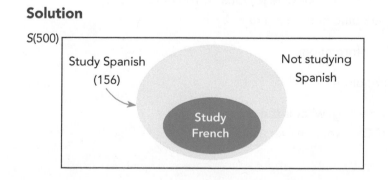

Continue on next page

b) What fraction of the students study both Spanish and French?

Solution

1 out of 6 of the 156 students studying Spanish also study French. This is the same as saying $\frac{1}{6}$ of these 156 students study French.

Number of students who study both Spanish and French:

$$\frac{1}{6} \cdot 156 = 26 \text{ students}$$

Fraction of students who study both Spanish and French:

$$\frac{26}{500} = \frac{13}{250}$$

$\frac{13}{250}$ of the students study both Spanish and French.

c) If a student is selected at random from the 500 students, what is the probability that a student who studies both Spanish and French is selected? Give your answer as a decimal.

Solution

$$\frac{13}{250} = 0.052 \qquad \text{Rewrite the fraction as a decimal.}$$

The probability that a student who studies both Spanish and French is selected is 0.052.

Guided Practice

Solve.

9 Among the 200 jellybeans in a bag, 3 out of every 5 are blue jellybeans. The blue jellybeans consist of light blue ones and dark blue ones in the ratio 2 : 1.

a) Draw a Venn diagram to represent the information.

b) What fraction of the jellybeans are light blue?

c) If you pick a jellybean randomly from the bag, what is the probability that a jellybean that is light blue is selected? Give your answer as a decimal.

Solve.

1 You roll a fair number die with faces labeled 1 to 6.

a) What is the probability of rolling an odd number?

b) What is the probability of rolling a number less than 3?

c) What is the probability of rolling a prime number?

d) What is the probability of rolling a number greater than 1?

2 Abigail randomly chooses a disk from 6 green, 4 black, 2 red, and 2 white disks of the same size and shape.

a) What is probability of getting a red disk?

b) What is probability of *not* getting a green or white disk?

c) What is the probability of getting a black disk?

3 A letter is randomly chosen from the word MATHEMATICS. What is the probability of choosing letter M?

4 There are 6 red marbles and 10 white marbles in a bag. What is probability of randomly choosing a white marble from the bag?

5 Numbers made up of two digits are formed using the digits 2, 3, and 4 with no repeating digits.

a) List all possible outcomes.

b) Find the probability of randomly forming a number greater than 32.

c) Find the probability of randomly forming a number divisible by 4.

6 Jack picks a letter randomly from the following list:
h, i, m, o, p, q, r, t, u, and x.
The event *V* occurs when Jack picks a vowel.

a) Draw a Venn diagram to represent the information. Explain the meaning of the complement of event *V*.

b) Find P(*V*) and P(*V*').

7 A number is randomly selected from 1 to 20. *X* is the event of selecting a number divisible by 4. *Y* is the event of getting a prime number.

a) Draw a Venn diagram to represent the information.

b) Are events *X* and *Y* mutually exclusive? Explain.

c) Find P(*X*) and P(*Y*).

8 A dodecahedron number die has 12 faces. Each face is printed with one of the numbers from 1 to 12. Suppose you roll a fair dodecahedron number die and record the value on the top face. Let *A* be the event of rolling a number that is a multiple of 3. Let *B* be the event of rolling a number that is a multiple of 4.

a) Draw a Venn diagram to represent the information.

b) From the Venn diagram, tell whether events *A* and *B* are mutually exclusive. Explain your answer.

c) Find P(*A*) and P(*B*).

9 This year, some students in the Drama Club have the same first names. Name tags for the students are shown below.

One of the name tags is selected at random. Event *E* occurs when the name has the letter e. Event *J* occurs when the name tag is | John |.

a) Draw a Venn diagram to represent the information.

b) List all the types of outcomes of event *E'*, the complement of event *E*.

c) Are events *E* and *J* mutually exclusive? Explain your answer.

d) Find P(*E*), P(*E'*), and P(*J*).

10 *Math Journal* Explain why mutually exclusive events are not necessarily complementary.

11 At a middle school, 39% of the students jog and 35% of the students do aerobic exercise. One out of every five students who do aerobic exercise also jogs.

    a) Draw a Venn diagram to represent the information.

    b) What percent of the students do both activities?

    c) What fraction of the students only jog?

    d) What is the probability that a randomly selected student at the middle school does neither activity? Give your answer as a decimal.

12 A teacher chooses a student at random from a class with 20 boys and 36 girls. 25% of the students wear glasses. 15 boys in the class do not wear glasses.

    a) Draw a Venn diagram to represent the information.

    b) What fraction of the students in the class are girls who do not wear glasses?

    c) What is the probability that a randomly selected student is a boy who wears glasses?

13 Alex has a pair of red socks, a pair of white socks, and a pair of black socks in his drawer. Unfortunately, the socks are not matched up with each other. Alex reaches into the drawer in the dark and pulls out two socks.

    a) What is the probability that the two socks are the same color?

    b) What is the probability that the two socks are different colors?

    c) Are the two events described in **a)** and **b)** complementary? Explain.

14 A small town has a population of 3,200. 30% of the townspeople speak Italian, 20% speak French, and the rest do not speak either of these languages. 360 people speak both Italian and French.

    a) Draw a Venn diagram to represent the information.

    b) What percent of the townspeople speak only Italian?

    c) If you randomly pick a person in the town and speak to the person in Italian, what is the probability that the person does not understand you?

15 The 6,000 oranges harvested at an orange grove are a combination of Valencia and Navel oranges. The ratio of Valencia oranges to Navel oranges is 7 : 5. The owner of the orange grove finds that 1 in every 20 Valencia oranges and 1 in every 25 Navel oranges are rotten.

    a) What fraction of the oranges is not rotten?

    b) What is the probability that a randomly selected orange is a good orange?

    c) What is the probability that a randomly selected orange is a rotten Valencia?

Lesson Objectives

- Find relative frequencies for data in a chance process.
- Interpret relative frequencies as probabilities and use them to make predictions.
- Compare long-run relative frequencies to related theoretical probabilities.

Vocabulary

relative frequency	observed frequency
experimental probability	theoretical probability

Find the **Relative Frequency** in a Chance Process.

In a chance process, you keep repeating an action and keep track of the outcomes. Although you know all the possible types of outcomes beforehand, you do not know what the next outcome is. The outcomes you have collected are data or observations.

Hands-On Activity

Materials:
- a coin

FIND RELATIVE FREQUENCIES OF FLIPPING A COIN

Work in pairs.

 STEP 1 Flip a coin 20 times. Record whether it lands heads or tails after each flip. The table below shows that the number of times the coin landed heads and the number of times it landed tails.

Data Value	Observed Frequency
Heads	?
Tails	?
Total	?

The **observed frequency** is the number of observations of a data value. It refers to how many times a data value appears in the chance process.

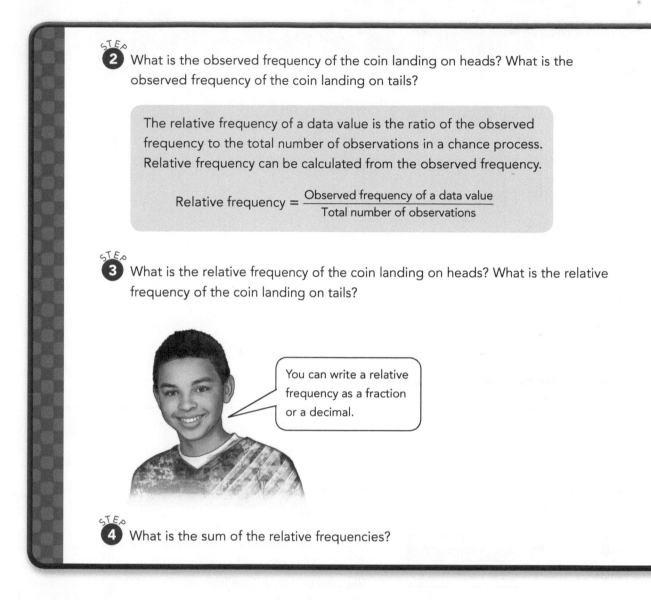

STEP 2 What is the observed frequency of the coin landing on heads? What is the observed frequency of the coin landing on tails?

> The relative frequency of a data value is the ratio of the observed frequency to the total number of observations in a chance process. Relative frequency can be calculated from the observed frequency.
>
> $$\text{Relative frequency} = \frac{\text{Observed frequency of a data value}}{\text{Total number of observations}}$$

STEP 3 What is the relative frequency of the coin landing on heads? What is the relative frequency of the coin landing on tails?

> You can write a relative frequency as a fraction or a decimal.

STEP 4 What is the sum of the relative frequencies?

Example 10 **Use relative frequency as a fraction.**

The table shows the relative frequencies of men, women, and children at a park on a particular day. On that day, 600 people were in the park.

People	Relative Frequency
Men	0.54
Women	0.37
Children	0.09

> Because each relative frequency represents a fraction of the total number of people, the sum of the relative frequencies is 1.
> $0.54 + 0.37 + 0.09 = 1$

Continue on next page

a) How many children were at the park?

Solution

The relative frequency 0.09 means that $\frac{9}{100}$ of the 600 people at the park were children.

$0.09 \cdot 600 = 54$ Multiply the relative frequency for children by the total number of people.

There were 54 children at the park.

b) How many more men than women were at the park?

Solution

$0.54 \cdot 600 = 324$	Find the number of men.
$0.37 \cdot 600 = 222$	Find the number of women.
$324 - 222 = 102$	Subtract the number of women from the number of men.

There were 102 more men than women at the park.

Guided Practice

Complete.

1 The table shows the relative frequencies for three sizes of monitors sold during a sale at a computer store. 640 monitors were sold during the sale.

Monitor	Relative Frequency
14-inch	0.15
15-inch	0.55
17-inch	0.30

Each relative frequency represents a fraction of the total number of monitors sold.
The sum of the relative frequencies is 1.
$0.15 + 0.55 + 0.30 = 1$

a) How many 17-inch monitors were sold during the sale?

The relative frequency 0.30 means that $\frac{30}{100}$ of the 640 monitors sold were 17-inch monitors.

$\underline{\;?\;} \cdot 640 = \underline{\;?\;}$ Multiply the relative frequency for 17-inch monitors by the total number of monitors sold.

$\underline{\;?\;}$ 17-inch monitors were sold during the sale.

b) How many fewer 14-inch monitors were sold than 15-inch monitors?

$\underline{\;?\;} \cdot 640 = \underline{\;?\;}$ Find the number of 14-inch monitors.

$\underline{\;?\;} \cdot 640 = \underline{\;?\;}$ Find the number of 15-inch monitors.

$\underline{\;?\;} - \underline{\;?\;} = \underline{\;?\;}$ Subtract the number of 14-inch monitors from the number of 15-inch monitors.

There were $\underline{\;?\;}$ fewer 14-inch monitors sold than 15-inch monitors.

Find the Relative Frequency from a Frequency Histogram.

A histogram shows frequencies for data grouped in intervals. You can also use a relative frequency histogram to display the data.

Example 11 **Use a frequency histogram to solve problems.**

At some schools, a grade point average (GPA) is used to describe academic progress. The histogram shows data about the GPAs of 400 students at a school.

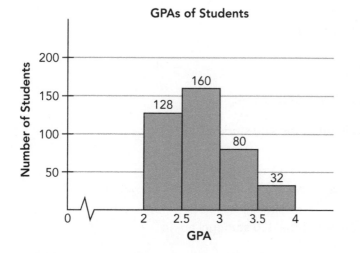

Math Note

The break $\wedge$ in the horizontal axis means that there is a break in the scale from 0 to 2 on the horizontal axis.

A histogram is a vertical bar graph with no spaces between the bars. Each bar represents an interval of the same size.

The lower value of each interval on the histogram shows the least possible value for the interval. The upper value shows the least possible value for the next interval. For example, the bar for the interval 2–2.5 shows the frequency for GPAs in the range: $2 \le$ GPA < 2.5.

a) What is the relative frequency of students whose GPA is at least 3? Give your answer as a fraction.

Solution

Relative frequency of students whose GPA is at least 3:

$80 + 32 = 112$ Find the number of students whose GPA is greater than or equal to 3.

$\dfrac{112}{400} = \dfrac{7}{25}$ Write 112 out of 400 students as a fraction. Simplify.

The relative frequency of students whose GPA is at least 3 is $\dfrac{7}{25}$.

Continue on next page

b) Find the relative frequency of students whose GPA is greater than or equal to 3, but less than 3.5. Give your answer as a percent.

Solution

The bar for the interval 3–3.5 shows that there are 80 out of 400 students whose GPA is greater than or equal to 3 but less than 3.5.

Relative frequency for this GPA range:

$$\frac{80}{400} \cdot 100\% = 20\%$$

The relative frequency of the number of students whose GPA is greater than or equal to 3 but less than 3.5 is 20%.

c) Draw a relative frequency histogram using percent.

Solution

Relative frequency of GPA for the intervals 2–2.5, 2.5–3, 3.5–4:

The bar for the interval 2–2.5 shows that 128 out of the 400 students are in this interval.

$$\frac{128}{400} \cdot 100\% = 32\%$$ Find the relative frequency of GPA for the interval 2–2.5.

The bar for the interval 2.5–3 shows that 160 out of the 400 students are in this interval.

$$\frac{160}{400} \cdot 100\% = 40\%$$ Find the relative frequency of GPA for the interval 2.5–3.

The bar for the interval 3.5–4 shows that 32 out of the 400 students are in this interval.

$$\frac{32}{400} \cdot 100\% = 8\%$$ Find the relative frequency of GPA for the interval 3.5–4.

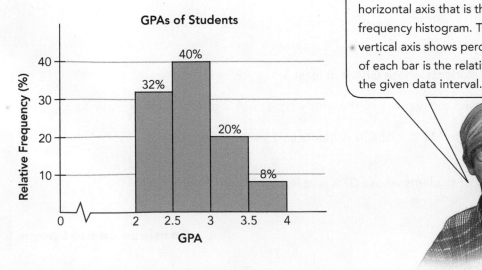

The relative frequency histogram has a horizontal axis that is the same as the frequency histogram. The scale on the vertical axis shows percents. The height of each bar is the relative frequency for the given data interval.

Guided Practice

Copy and complete. Solve.

2 Alexis and Joe caught 40 fish over the weekend. The histogram shows the masses of the fish they caught. On the histogram, the interval 14–16 includes data for fish that have a mass of at least 14 kilograms, but less than 16 kilograms.

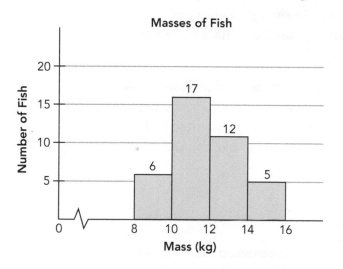

Masses of Fish

a) Find the relative frequency for fish that have a mass of at least 8 kilograms but less than 10 kilograms. Give your answer as a percent.

There are __?__ fish that have a mass of at least 8 kilograms but less than 10 kilograms.

$$\frac{?}{?} = \underline{\ ?\ }$$ Write __?__ out of 40 fish as a fraction and simplify.

$$\underline{\ ?\ } \cdot 100\% = \underline{\ ?\ }$$ Multiply by 100%.

The relative frequency for fish that have a mass of at least 8 kilograms but less than 10 kilograms is __?__%.

b) Draw a relative frequency histogram using percent.

$$\underline{\ ?\ } \cdot 100\% = \underline{\ ?\ }$$ Find the relative frequency of fish that have a mass of at least 10 kilograms but less than 12 kilograms.

$$\underline{\ ?\ } \cdot 100\% = \underline{\ ?\ }$$ Find the relative frequency of fish that have a mass of at least 12 kilograms but less than 14 kilograms.

$$\underline{\ ?\ } \cdot 100\% = \underline{\ ?\ }$$ Find the relative frequency of fish that have a mass of at least 14 kilograms but less than 16 kilograms.

The horizontal axis of the relative frequency histogram is the same as the horizontal axis of the original histogram. The vertical axis shows percents.

Use a Relative Frequency as a Probability.

Relative frequency is based on observations of what has happened in a chance process. It is also used as a probability measure to predict the likelihood of a future outcome.

For instance, suppose you toss a number die 100 times. You find that the relative frequency of rolling a 5 is 0.18. You say that the **experimental probability** of rolling a 5 is 0.18. An experimental probability is a probability based on data collected or observations made in an experiment.

The type of probability you learned about earlier is called **theoretical probability**. A theoretical probability is the ratio of the number of favorable outcomes to the total number of possible outcomes. You do not have to perform an experiment to find a theoretical probability. For instance, suppose you roll a number die. You know that the theoretical probability of rolling a 5 on a number die is $\frac{1}{6}$, or $0.1\overline{6}$.

Observing the types of vehicles passing an intersection

The types of vehicles passing through an intersection were observed one morning. The observed frequencies and relative frequencies are summarized below.

Type of Vehicles	Observed Frequency	Relative Frequency
Car	108	$\frac{108}{160} = \frac{27}{40}$
Motorcycle	12	$\frac{12}{160} = \frac{3}{40}$
Van	16	$\frac{16}{160} = \frac{1}{10}$
Truck	24	$\frac{24}{160} = \frac{3}{20}$
Total	160	1

In this experiment, 160 vehicles were observed. Among the five types of vehicles observed, cars had the greatest relative frequency, $\frac{27}{40}$. You may also write this relative frequency as a decimal or as a percent:

$\frac{27}{40} = 0.675$ or 67.5%

You may use the relative frequencies in the table as the experimental probabilities to predict what is likely to occur. For example, you can predict that there is a 67.5% chance that the next vehicle passing through the intersection will be a car.

Example 12 **Use a relative frequency as an experimental probability to make a prediction.**

You spin the spinner shown 200 times and record the letter that the pointer lands on. The data are summarized below.

Letter	Observed Frequency
A	36
B	44
C	28
D	52
E	40

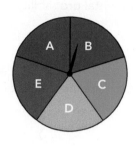

a) Find the relative frequency for each of the letters. Write each relative frequency as a decimal.

Solution

Relative frequency for each letter on the spinner:

$\dfrac{36}{200} = \dfrac{9}{50}$ Find the relative frequency of getting letter A.

$= 0.18$ Write the fraction as a decimal.

$\dfrac{44}{200} = \dfrac{11}{50}$ Find the relative frequency of getting letter B.

$= 0.22$ Write the fraction as a decimal.

$\dfrac{28}{200} = \dfrac{7}{50}$ Find the relative frequency of getting a letter C.

$= 0.14$ Write the fraction as a decimal.

$\dfrac{52}{200} = \dfrac{13}{50}$ Find the relative frequency of getting a letter D.

$= 0.26$ Write the fraction as a decimal.

$\dfrac{40}{200} = \dfrac{1}{5}$ Find the relative frequency of getting a letter E.

$= 0.20$ Write the fraction as a decimal.

The relative frequency for letter A is 0.18, B is 0.22, C is 0.14, D is 0.26, and E is 0.20.

> Letter E has a relative frequency of 0.20, which means that the spinner landed on letter E about $\frac{1}{5}$ of the time.

b) If you spin the spinner again, which letter would you predict is the spinner most likely to land on? Explain your answer.

Solution

The spinner is mostly likely to land on letter D because letter D has the greatest relative frequency, 0.26. This means that the experimental probability the spinner will land on letter D is 0.26, or 26%.

Continue on next page

c) What is the experimental probability that the spinner will not land on letter D on the next spin?

Solution

The event of landing on letter D and the event of not landing on letter D are complementary events.The experimental probability that the spinner will land on letter D is 0.26.

$1 - 0.26 = 0.74$

The experimental probability that the spinner will not land on letter D is 0.74.

Guided Practice

Copy and complete. Solve.

3 Lucas made a dartboard as shown in the diagram. He threw a dart at the dartboard 100 times. He recorded the number of times the dart landed on each color. The number of times he missed hitting the dartboard was also recorded.

Outcome	Observed Frequency
Red	10
Yellow	35
Blue	48
Misses	7

a) Find the relative frequency, expressed as a decimal, for each event.

$\underline{\quad?\quad} = \underline{\quad?\quad}$ Find the relative frequency of landing on red.

$\quad\quad = \underline{\quad?\quad}$ Write the fraction as a decimal.

$\underline{\quad?\quad} = \underline{\quad?\quad}$ Find the relative frequency of landing on yellow.

$\quad\quad = \underline{\quad?\quad}$ Write the fraction as a decimal.

$\underline{\quad?\quad} = \underline{\quad?\quad}$ Find the relative frequency of landing on blue.

$\quad\quad = \underline{\quad?\quad}$ Write the fraction as a decimal.

$\underline{\quad?\quad} = \underline{\quad?\quad}$ Find the relative frequency of misses.

$\quad\quad = \underline{\quad?\quad}$ Write the fraction as a decimal.

b) Explain what the relative frequency of the dart landing in the red region means.

The event of landing in the red region has a relative frequency of __?__, which means that the dart landed in the red region about __?__ of the time.

c) If Lucas throws the dart again, predict in which region the dart is most likely to land.

The dart is most likely to land in the __?__ region, because it has the greatest relative frequency of __?__.

Compare Long-Run Relative Frequency and Theoretical Probability.

Most of the time, the experimental probability of an event differs somewhat from the theoretical probability. Even the same chance process carried out at different times will generate different experimental probabilities. In a long-run chance process, however, experimental probability resembles the theoretical probability more closely.

Hands-On Activity

Materials:
- 10 counters (5 red, 3 blue, and 2 green)
- a paper bag

COMPARE EXPERIMENTAL AND THEORETICAL PROBABILITIES

Work in pairs.

STEP 1 Place the 10 counters into the bag. Shake the bag to mix the counters. Without looking into the bag, select a counter randomly. Record its color in a tally chart, and then put the counter back in the bag. Repeat this procedure 20 times.

STEP 2 Combine your group's data from **STEP 1** with data from other groups. Use the class data to make a relative frequency table like the one shown below.

Color	Observed Frequency	Relative Frequency (as a decimal)
Red	?	?
Blue	?	?
Green	?	?

STEP 3 Find the theoretical probabilities for the colors. Copy and complete the table below.

Color	Experimental Probability	Theoretical Probability
Red	?	?
Blue	?	?
Green	?	?

STEP 4 Compare the experimental and the theoretical probabilities for each color. What do you observe?

Practice 10.3

Solve.

1 A library conducted a survey on 2,000 library users about the types of books they usually borrow. The table shows the relative frequencies of the types of books borrowed.

Type of Books	Relative Frequency
Romance	0.28
Science fiction	0.40
Mystery	0.11
Biography	0.15
Philosophy	0.06

a) How many library users borrowed biography titles?

b) What percent of the library users borrowed mystery titles?

c) What percent of the library users borrowed romance or science fiction titles?

2 A coin is tossed 66 times and lands on heads 36 times.

a) Find the relative frequency of the coin landing on heads.

b) Find the relative frequency of the coin landing on tails.

3 A number die is rolled 50 times. After each roll, the result is recorded. The table gives the observed frequency for each number on the die.

Value	1	2	3	4	5	6
Observed Frequency	11	4	6	14	8	7
Relative Frequency	?	?	?	?	?	?

a) Copy and complete the table. Write each relative frequency as a fraction.

b) Find the relative frequency for rolling a number greater than 4. Give your answer as a fraction.

c) Find the relative frequency of rolling an odd number. Give your answer as a fraction.

4 The ice hockey team Blue Thunder played 25 times during the winter season. The team had 14 wins, 8 losses, and 3 ties.

a) Find the relative frequency for each of the following: wins, losses, ties. Give your answers as percents.

b) Draw a relative frequency bar graph that uses percents.

c) What percent of the total number of games ended in a loss or a tie?

5 You are given a deck of 52 cards showing scenes of the four seasons of the year. There are 13 cards for each season. You randomly select a card from the deck 100 times. After each selection, you record the season shown on the card and replace it in the deck for the next selection. The results are given in the table below.

Season	Spring	Summer	Fall	Winter
Observed Frequency	23	34	19	24

a) Find the relative frequency of the appearance of each season.

b) What is the experimental probability of selecting a card with a summer scene?

c) What is the theoretical probability of selecting a card with a summer scene?

d) *Math Journal* The experimental and the theoretical probabilities of selecting a card with a summer scene are not equal. Describe some factors that cause the two probabilities to be different.

e) Suppose that the spring and summer cards have a red background and the fall and winter cards have a black background. What is the experimental probability of selecting a card with a black background?

f) What is the theoretical probability of selecting a card with a red background?

6 A group of researchers catch and measure the length of fish before releasing them back to a river. The lengths of the 50 fish are categorized in the table below.

Length of Fish (L inches)	$L < 7$	$7 \leq L < 14$	$14 \leq L < 21$
Number of Fish	16	23	11

a) Find the relative frequency of each category of fish.

b) If the researchers catch and measure one more fish, what is the probability of catching a fish that is less than 7 inches long?

c) What is the probability that the next fish caught will be at least 7 inches long?

d) Draw a relative frequency histogram using percent.

7 A car dealership has sold 75 new cars this year. The histogram below shows frequencies for cars sold in different price ranges.

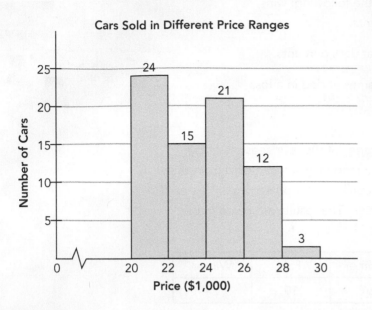

Cars Sold in Different Price Ranges

The bar for the interval 24–26 shows that 21 out of 75 cars were sold for prices that were greater than or equal to $24,000 but less than $26,000.

a) Find the relative frequency of the cars sold in the price range of $26,000 to $28,000. Give your answer as a percent.

b) Find the relative frequency of the cars sold in the price range of $20,000 to $24,000. Give your answer as a percent.

c) What is the probability that the next car will be sold in the price range of $28,000 to $30,000?

8 A light bulb manufacturer estimates that 10% of a shipment of 600 bulbs will have a lifespan greater than or equal to 1,000 hours, but less than 2,000 hours. The manufacturer also estimates that 240 of the bulbs will have a lifespan greater than or equal to 2,000 hours, but less than 3,000 hours, and that the remaining light bulbs will have a lifespan greater than or equal to 3,000 hours, but less than 4,000 hours.

a) Copy and complete the table below.

Lifespan (x hours)	$1,000 \leq x < 2,000$	$2,000 \leq x < 3,000$	$3,000 \leq x < 4,000$
Number of Bulbs	?	?	?

b) Draw a frequency histogram for the three lifespans shown in the table.

c) Find the relative frequency for the bulbs with each of the lifespans. Then draw a relative frequency histogram using percents.

d) If you buy a light bulb from this shipment, what do you predict is the most likely lifespan of your light bulb? Explain your answer using experimental probability.

10.4 Developing Probability Models

Lesson Objectives

- Understand and apply uniform and nonuniform probability models.
- Compare experimental probability with theoretical probability.
- Use a probability model to predict outcomes of events.

Vocabulary

probability model

probability distribution

uniform probability model

nonuniform probability model

Understand a Probability Model.

Randomness is central to the concept of probability. All random phenomena have one common characteristic: they yield outcomes that are unpredictable.

A probability model consists of a sample space of outcomes, events, and the probabilities of these outcomes and events. All the outcomes of a sample space and their probabilities can be presented in a table or a graph. Such a presentation is known as a **probability distribution**. A probability model is used to estimate and predict the occurrence of events.

Develop a Uniform Probability Model.

A probability model in which all the outcomes have an equal probability is called a uniform probability model. So, each outcome is equally likely to occur.

Tossing a fair coin is an example of a uniform probability model, because the probability of each outcome is the same.

Example 13 **Graph the probability distribution of a uniform probability model.**

Ben randomly selects a counter from the group of counters below. He then records the color of the selected counter.

a) Define the sample space.

Solution

The sample space consists of 5 outcomes.
Sample space = {yellow, red, blue, green, black}

b) What is the probability of selecting a counter with a particular color?

Solution

Since every counter has an equal chance of being selected, the probability of a counter with a particular color being selected is $\frac{1}{5}$.

c) Construct a probability model for selecting a counter with a particular color. Then use a bar graph to show the probability distribution.

Solution

Color	Yellow	Red	Blue	Green	Black
Probability	$\frac{1}{5}$	$\frac{1}{5}$	$\frac{1}{5}$	$\frac{1}{5}$	$\frac{1}{5}$

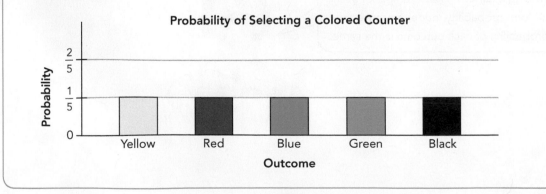

Probability of Selecting a Colored Counter

Guided Practice

Complete. Solve.

1 There are eight letter tiles in a bag. The tiles are labeled with the letters from S to Z. June randomly selects a tile from the bag.

a) Define the sample space.

The sample space consists of 8 outcomes.

Sample space = { _?_ , _?_ , _?_ , _?_ , _?_ , _?_ , _?_ , _?_ }

b) What is the probability of selecting a tile with a particular letter?

Every tile has an equal chance of being selected. The probability of selecting a particular tile with a particular letter is _?_ .

c) Construct the probability model.

d) Present the probability distribution in a bar graph.

Write the Probability of Outcomes in a Uniform Probability Model.

If the sample space of a uniform probability model consists of n possible outcomes, then the probability of each outcome is $\frac{1}{n}$.

Example 14 **Write the probability of outcomes of events in a uniform probability model.**

Jane, Mark, Jason, Ruth, Albert, Kenny, and Chloe are students. A teacher randomly chooses one of them to answer a question.

a) Explain why a uniform probability model describes this situation.

Solution

Since the selection is random, each student has an equal chance of being chosen. So, the model is a uniform model.

b) What is the probability that Ruth is chosen to answer the question?

Solution

The probability that any student is chosen is $\frac{1}{7}$.

In particular, the probability that Ruth is chosen is $\frac{1}{7}$.

Continue on next page

c) If A is the event that a girl is selected, find P(A).

Solution

Three outcomes are favorable to event A: Jane, Ruth, and Chloe.

$P(A) = \frac{1}{7} + \frac{1}{7} + \frac{1}{7}$ The probability of each girl being selected is $\frac{1}{7}$.

$= \frac{3}{7}$

So, P(A) is $\frac{3}{7}$.

Guided Practice

Solve.

2 A number is chosen at random from the list: 1, 4, 7, 12, 21, 25, 38, 40, 45, and 48.

a) Explain why a uniform probability model describes this situation.

b) What is the probability of choosing 25?

c) T is the event of choosing a number that is a multiple of 3. List all the outcomes that are favorable to event T.

d) Find P(T).

Develop a Nonuniform Probability Model.

A probability model in which outcomes do not necessarily have equal probabilities is called a nonuniform probability model. So, at least two outcomes have different probabilities.

Example 15 **Graph the probability distribution of a nonuniform probability model.**

An art teacher has a bunch of colored pencils: 3 yellow, 6 orange, 2 green, and 4 brown. She randomly chooses a color to give to a student.

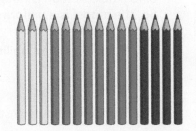

a) Define the sample space.

Solution

There are 4 different color outcomes: yellow, orange, green, and brown.

3 + 6 + 2 + 4 = 15   Find the total number of colored pencils.

The sample space has 15 outcomes.

b)   What is the probability of choosing a brown pencil?

Solution

Let B be the event of choosing a brown pencil.

$P(B) = \dfrac{\text{Number of outcomes favourable to event } B}{\text{Total number of equally likely outcomes}}$ Use the formula.

$ = \dfrac{4}{15}$ There are 4 brown pencils out of 15 colored pencils.

The probability of choosing a brown pencil is $\dfrac{4}{15}$.

c)   Construct a probability model for choosing a colored pencil and a bar graph for the probability distribution.

Solution

First calculate and record the probability of choosing a pencil of each color:

The probability of picking a yellow pencil is $\dfrac{3}{15}$.

The probability of picking an orange pencil is $\dfrac{6}{15}$.

The probability of picking a green pencil is $\dfrac{2}{15}$.

The probability model is as follows:

Color	Yellow	Orange	Green	Brown
Probability	$\dfrac{3}{15}$	$\dfrac{6}{15}$	$\dfrac{2}{15}$	$\dfrac{4}{15}$

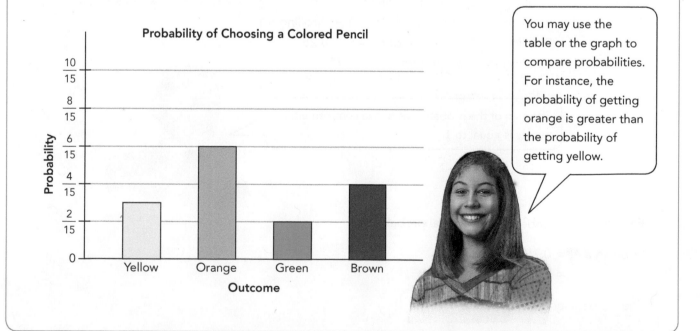

You may use the table or the graph to compare probabilities. For instance, the probability of getting orange is greater than the probability of getting yellow.

Guided Practice

Solve.

3 There are 10 herbal tea bags of assorted flavors in a jar: 4 peppermint, 2 raspberry, 3 camomile, and 1 blackberry. Suppose you randomly pick a tea bag from the jar and note the flavor.

  a) Define the sample space.

  b) What is the probability of picking a raspberry tea bag?

  c) Construct the probability model of picking a tea bag.
      Then use a bar graph to represent the probability distribution.

Example 16 **Find the probability of events in a nonuniform model.**

A number die was made incorrectly at the factory. The probability of rolling the number 1 with this die is $\frac{1}{4}$. Each of the five other numbers has an equal probability of being rolled.

  a) Find the probability of rolling a 4.

Solution

$$P(\text{rolling a 1}) = \frac{1}{4}$$
$$= 0.25$$

There are 5 other numbers, and each of these numbers has an equal probability of occurring.

P(rolling a 1) + P(rolling the 5 other numbers) = 1
  So, P(rolling the 5 other numbers) = 1 − P(rolling a 1)
      P(rolling the 5 other numbers) = 1 − 0.25
      P(rolling the 5 other numbers) = 0.75

> The sum of the probabilities of two complementary events is equal to 1.

Each of the 5 numbers has an equal probability.

P(rolling a 4) = 0.75 ÷ 5
           = 0.15

The probability of rolling a 4 is 0.15.

b) Construct the probability model.

Solution

Value	1	2	3	4	5	6
Probability	0.25	0.15	0.15	0.15	0.15	0.15

Caution

Check to make sure that the probabilities in the table add up to 1.

c) If B is the event of rolling an odd number, find $P(B)$.

Solution

For event B to occur, there are three possible outcomes: 1, 3, and 5.

$P(B) = 0.25 + 0.15 + 0.15$
$\quad\ = 0.55$

Guided Practice

Solve.

4 Nine cards are made from each of the letters from the word "BEGINNING". You select a card at random.

a) Find the probability of getting a letter N.

b) Construct the probability model.

c) What is the probability of selecting a card with a consonant?

Example 17 **Develop an experimental model.**

The data below show the heights, in inches, of 20 players of a junior baseball team.

$63\frac{1}{4}$	70	68	59	$60\frac{1}{4}$	62	$58\frac{1}{2}$	$67\frac{5}{8}$	64	71
55	$66\frac{1}{8}$	66	57	$68\frac{1}{2}$	61	$64\frac{3}{8}$	$70\frac{1}{4}$	$55\frac{5}{8}$	60

a) Group the heights into 4 intervals: 55–60, 60–65, 65–70, and 70–75.

Solution

Interval	55–60	60–65	65–70	70–75
Frequency	5	7	5	3

The interval 55–60 includes heights that are greater than or equal to 55 inches, and less than 60 inches.

Continue on next page

b) Find the relative frequencies of the 4 intervals. Construct a probability model.

Solution

Interval	55–60	60–65	65–70	70–75
Relative Frequency	$\frac{5}{20} = 0.25$	$\frac{7}{20} = 0.35$	$\frac{5}{20} = 0.25$	$\frac{3}{20} = 0.15$

> Remember that
> Relative frequency
> $= \dfrac{\text{Observed frequency}}{\text{Total number of observations}}$

The probability model is shown below.

Interval	55–60	60–65	65–70	70–75
Probability	0.25	0.35	0.25	0.15

c) Represent the probability distribution in a histogram. State which type of probability model you have drawn.

Solution

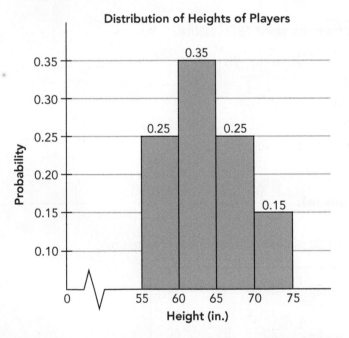

Distribution of Heights of Players

> **Think Math**
>
> Why is a histogram used to model this probability distribution instead of a bar graph?

The distribution shows a nonuniform probability model.

d) If a player is selected at random, what is the probability of selecting a player who is at least 65 inches tall?

Solution

A player who is at least 65 inches tall could be in one of two intervals: 65–70 or 70–75.

Probability of selecting a player who is at least 65 inches tall:

0.25 + 0.15 = 0.40   Add the probabilities for 65–70 or 70–75

The probability of selecting a player who is at least 65 inches tall is 0.40.

Guided Practice

Solve.

5 The data below show the heights, in centimeters, of 25 tomato plants in a greenhouse.

100	124	86	110	90
96	82	117	104	132
102	120	104	90	125
121	130	111	103	84
89	106	123	94	100

a) Group the heights into 6 intervals: 80–89, 90–99, 100–109, 110–119, 120–129, and 130–139.

b) Find the relative frequencies of the 6 intervals. Construct the probability model.

c) Represent the probability distribution in a histogram. State which type of probability distribution you have drawn.

d) A plant is selected at random. What is the probability of selecting a plant whose height is greater than or equal to 100, but less than 120 centimeters tall?

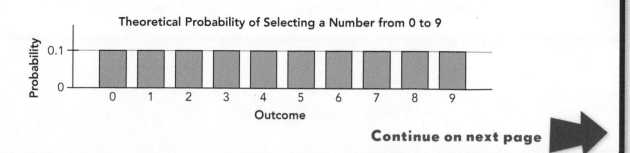

Hands-On Activity

COMPARE AN EXPERIMENTAL PROBABILITY MODEL TO A THEORETICAL PROBABILITY MODEL

Materials:
- random number table

Work in pairs.

Suppose one of the digits from 0 to 9 is randomly selected. This is a theoretical uniform probability model. The probability distribution table and bar graph are given below.

Digit	0	1	2	3	4	5	6	7	8	9
Probability	0.1	0.1	0.1	0.1	0.1	0.1	0.1	0.1	0.1	0.1

Continue on next page

STEP 1 Choose any row or column of a random number table. Circle every other digit until you have circled 50 digits. Two rows of the random number table with sample digits are shown below:

⑧ 0 ④ 1 ⑧

0 ⑥ 4 ④ 9

STEP 2 Use the digits you circled. Find the relative frequency for each digit from 0 to 9. Each digit's relative frequency is the experimental probability of randomly choosing that digit. Record your results in a probability model like the one shown below.

Digit	0	1	2	3	4	5	6	7	8	9
Probability	?	?	?	?	?	?	?	?	?	?

STEP 3 Present the probability distribution from **STEP 2** in a bar graph.

STEP 4 Use a different row or column of the random number table and repeat **STEP 1** so that you circle an additional 50 digits.

STEP 5 You have now circled 100 digits. Find the relative frequency for each digit when the total number of circled digits is 100. The experimental probability of each randomly chosen digit (the relative frequency of the digit) is based on 100 observations. Record your results in a probability model like the one shown in **STEP 2**.

STEP 6 Present the probability distribution from **STEP 5** in a bar graph.

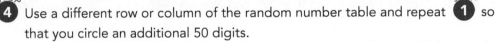 *Math Journal* Compare each of the experimental probability models you made with the theoretical probability model at the beginning of this activity. What effect does increasing the number of digits chosen have on the experimental probabilities? Which experimental probability model resembles the theoretical probability model more closely? Explain.

Practice 10.4

Solve.

1 You toss a fair coin and record whether it lands on heads or tails.

   a) Define the sample space.

   b) What is the probability of the coin landing on heads?

   c) Construct the probability model.

   d) Present the probability distribution in a bar graph.

2 A fair icosahedron number die is a 20-faced number die which has values from 1 to 20 on its faces. You roll a fair icosahedron number die and record the number on the face the number die rests on when it lands.

   a) Define the sample space.

   b) What is the probability of rolling a 14?

   c) Construct a probability model of all possible values.

   d) If A is the event of rolling a prime number, find $P(A)$.

   e) If B is the event of rolling a number divisible by 4, find $P(B)$.

3 The spinner shown is used in a game. Before spinning the wheel, a player is given 50 points. The player then spins the wheel and adds the points indicated by the red arrow to the 50 points he or she was given. The spinner has an equal chance of landing on any one of the sections.

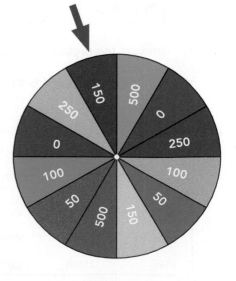

   a) List all the possible outcomes of the game.

   b) What is the probability of getting a total of 100 points?

   c) Construct a probability model for all possible outcomes.

   d) Is the probability distribution uniform? State your reason.

   e) If G is the event of getting a total of 300 points, find $P(G)$.

4 ✎ *Math Journal* Tell whether you agree or disagree with the statement below. Explain your reasoning.

All events having the same number of outcomes have equal probability in a uniform probability distribution.

5 A rectangular wooden block is painted gold on one large face and white on the other large face. The other four faces are painted green. After tossing the block many times, Sue finds that the block lands on the gold face one-third of the time. She also finds that the block has a 4% chance of landing on a green face.

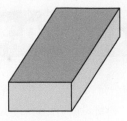

a) Describe all the types of outcomes of tossing the block.

b) Construct a probability model for all the outcomes. Write the probabilities as fractions. Is the model a uniform probability model?

c) What is the probability that the block lands on the white face?

6 The data show the ages of 25 people in a group. A person is selected at random from the group.

23	27	44	34	22
30	16	48	14	31
15	33	30	43	28
40	29	21	22	15
36	19	17	27	45

a) Copy and complete the following frequency table.

Age	10–20	20–30	30–40	40–50
Number of People	?	?	?	?

In the table, the interval 20–30 includes all people at least 20 years old but less than 30 years old.

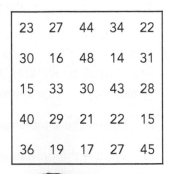

b) Copy and complete the following probability model.

Age	10–20	20–30	30–40	40–50
Probability	?	?	?	?

c) Present the probability distribution in a histogram.

d) What is the probability that the selected person's age is 30 or above?

7 The table below shows 20 words taken from a novel. You randomly select a word from the 20 words.

aye	bite	cycles	don	ending
absent	band	calm	done	elm
around	bye	can	donuts	emu
ate	base	canes	drown	enough

a) Complete the following frequency table.

Word Length	3-letter words	4-letter words	5-letter words	6-letter words
Number of Words	?	?	?	?

b) Complete the following probability distribution table.

Word Length	3-letter words	4-letter words	5-letter words	6-letter words
Probability	?	?	?	?

c) Present the probability distribution in a bar graph.

d) What is the probability of selecting a word with at most 5 letters?

8 A quiz has three True-False questions. The correct answers, in order, are True-True-False (TTF). A student does not know any of the answers and decide to guess.

a) Give the sample space of all the possible outcomes for the student guessing the three answers.

b) Is this situation an example of a uniform probability model? Explain.

c) Construct a probability distribution table for the model.

d) What is the probability that the student gets all three answers correct?

e) Let X be the event that the student gets only two correct answers. List all the possible outcomes of event X.

f) Find $P(X)$.

g) *Math Journal* Suppose you don't know that the correct answers, in order, are True-True-False. Would you be able to answer **e)** and **f)**? Explain.

Brain @ Work

In a game, you and your friend are asked to choose a number. The number is randomly selected from a set of ten numbers from 1 to 10. Your friend chooses a card from the pack. Then you choose a card from the ones remaining in the pack. You do not know your friend's number. You win if the difference between your number and your friend's number is at least 3.

a) For which of your friend's numbers do you have the greatest chance of winning?

b) For which of your friend's numbers do you have the least chance of winning?

c) What is the probability that you will win?

Chapter Wrap Up

Concept Map

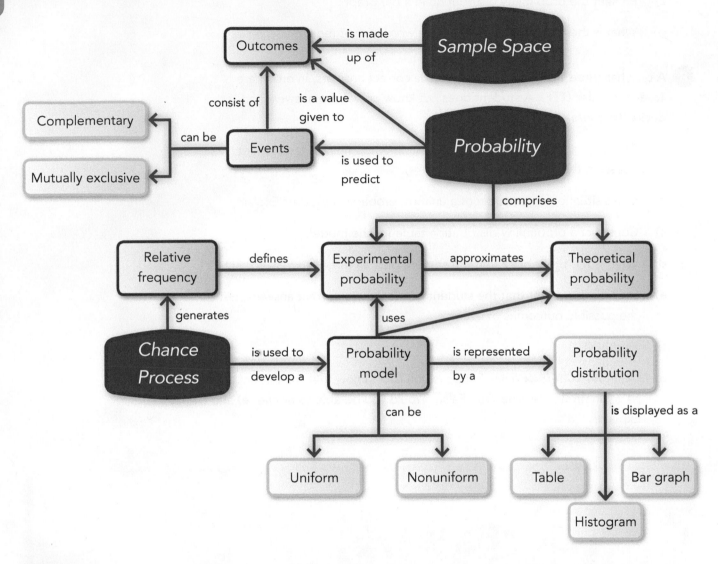

Key Concepts

▶ A sample space is a collection of all possible outcomes from an activity.

▶ An event is a collection of outcomes. Two events are mutually exclusive if they cannot happen at the same time.

▶ Given an event E, the complement of event E is the event that E does not occur. The complement of event E is written as E'.

▶ Venn diagrams can be used to illustrate mutually exclusive events, nonmutually exclusive events, complementary events, and sample spaces.

▶ Probability is a measure of how likely an event is to occur. It has a numeric value from 0 to 1. The number line shows what the different values mean in probability.

	$\frac{1}{2}$	
0		1
0%	50%	100%
0.0	0.5	1.0
Impossible	"fifty-fifty" chance	Certain

← Less likely   More likely →

▶ You can use theoretical probability to predict how likely an event is to occur.

▶ The probability of event A, P(A), is given by:

$$P(A) = \frac{\text{Number of outcomes favorable to event } A}{\text{Total number of equally likely outcomes}}$$

▶ The theoretical probability of an event is the ratio of the number of ways the event can occur to the total number of all outcomes in the sample space.

▶ The experimental probability of an event is the ratio of the number of times the event has occurred to the total number of trials performed. The experimental probability approximates the theoretical probability of the event as the number of trials increases.

▶ A chance process is one in which data are collected as they occur by chance. You do not know the outcome before it occurs.

▶ Relative frequency is the ratio of the observed frequency of a data value to the total number of observations in a chance process. Relative frequency is used to compute the experimental probability.

▶ A probability model can be constructed using theoretical probability or experimental probability. The model is either uniform or nonuniform. A uniform probability model is one where all outcomes have equal probabilities. A nonuniform probability model is one where the outcomes do not necessarily have equal probabilities.

▶ A probability model can be represented by its probability distribution, which is displayed as a table, a bar graph, or a histogram.

Chapter Review/Test

Concepts and Skills

Solve.

1. You select a card at random from 50 cards numbered from 1 to 50. What are the possible outcomes for the event of choosing a number that is a multiple of 6?

2. Three fair coins are tossed together once. List the outcomes that are favorable for the event of only two of the coins landing on heads.

3. Daniel wants to write all the 2-digit numbers with no repeating digits that can be formed using the digits 5, 6, and 7.

   a) List all the possible outcomes.

   b) X is the event that the 2-digit number is divisible by 5. How many of the outcomes are favorable to event X?

4. Amy writes a computer program that will choose two letters from her own name to make a two-letter "string." The order of the letters matters. For example, AM and MA are different strings.

   a) List all the possible outcomes for forming a two-letter string.

   b) What is the probability that Amy forms a two-letter string with the letter M in it?

5. Two-digit numbers are formed using digits 2, 3, and 4, with no repeating digits.

   a) List all the possible outcomes.

   b) What is the probability of forming a number greater than 32?

6. Tim has three DVDs. One is a science fiction movie, one is an action movie, and the other is a documentary. If he stacks the DVDs randomly, what is the probability that the science fiction movie is on top, the action movie is in the middle, and the documentary is on the bottom?

7. A ribbon is selected at random out of a total of 4 orange ribbons, 5 yellow ribbons, and 3 red ribbons. What is the probability of selecting an orange ribbon?

8 Use the spinner shown.

a) What is the probability of landing on an even number?

b) What is the probability of landing on a number less than 4?

Problem Solving

Solve.

9 Olivia and Jackie played a game with the spinner shown.

Olivia spun a 2 on 12 spins out of 50, while Jackie spun a 2 on 19 spins out of 100.

a) Find each person's experimental probability of spinning a 2. Express your answers as decimals.

b) Suppose the spinner is fair, meaning that it is equally likely to land on any of the numbers. What is the theoretical probability of spinning a 2?

c) Assuming the spinner is fair, what do you predict will happen to the experimental probability of getting a 2 if the spinner is spun 500 times?

10 A red number die and a green number die each have faces labeled 1 to 6. Suppose you roll the number dice and record the values for each die as an ordered pair of numbers: (red value, green value). The event *E* is the event of getting a pair of values in which the number on the green die is greater than the number on the red die.

a) Find all the outcomes favorable to event *E*.

b) Find P(*E*).

11 Two fair counters are tossed together. One of the counters is white on one side and black on the other side, the other counter is white on one side, and red on the other side. They are tossed together and the face up colors of the two counters are noted. Let E be the event that red and black appear, and F be the event that at least one is white.

a) Define the sample space of the experiment.

b) Calculate the probability of each outcome.

c) Construct the probability distribution table. Is it a uniform probability model?

d) Draw a Venn diagram for events E and F. Are they mutually exclusive?

e) Calculate $P(E)$ and $P(F)$.

12 Joan keeps track of the number of emails she receives each day for 100 days. She then makes a table showing how many days she received 0 emails, 1 email, 2 emails, and so on, as shown in the table.

Number of Emails Per Day	0	1	2	3	4	5 or more
Number of Days	5	20	15	31	27	2
Relative Frequency	?	?	?	?	?	?

a) Copy and complete the table above by finding each relative frequency.

b) Present the relative frequencies in a bar graph.

13 At a music school, 400 students were given a survey on the number of hours they practice each week. The results of this survey are shown in the relative frequency histogram.

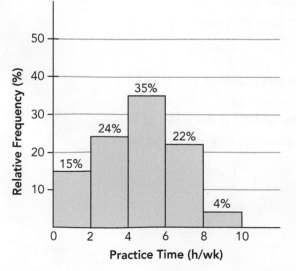

Survey Results on Students' Practice Time

a) How many students practiced at least 2 hours but less than 4 hours per week?

b) One of the students is selected at random. What is the probability that this student has practiced 6 or more hours per week?

14 Fifty students at a school kept track of how many books they read last semester. Each student wrote the number of books he or she read in a table provided by the school librarian.

5	1	8	1	2	15	20	28	20	5
12	9	12	6	0	10	13	6	0	26
8	10	7	12	1	6	25	16	4	10
4	27	14	0	20	24	0	8	9	18
17	9	11	22	0	8	3	6	15	4

a) Copy and complete the frequency table .

Number of Books Read	0–5	6–10	11–15	16–20	21–25	26–30
Number of Students	?	?	?	?	?	?

b) Copy and complete the probability distribution table below.

Number of Books Read	0–5	6–10	11–15	16–20	21–25	26–30
Probability	?	?	?	?	?	?

c) Suppose the librarian selects one of the students at random. What is the probability that the student has read at least 6 books but not more than 15 books?

d) What percent of the students had read 10 or fewer books?

e) Present the probability distribution in a bar graph.

Cumulative Review Chapters 9—10

Concepts and Skills

Find the range, the three quartiles, and the interquartile range. (Lesson 9.1)

1 32, 65, 90, 25, 46, 81, 30, 57, 85, 104, 33, 48

2 12.6, 13.0, 15.5, 18.6, 14.4, 12.0, 11.0, 11.0, 15.6, 15.9

Find the mean absolute deviation. Round to the nearest hundredth. (Lesson 9.3)

3  103, 111, 150, 165, 192, 144, 144, 163, 121

4 2.0, 3.2, 4.5, 5.6, 7.0, 7.9, 8.6, 9.1, 10.2, 12.3

Use the information below to answer questions 5 to 10. (Lessons 9.1, 9.2)

The heights of plants, in centimeters, are shown in a stem-and-leaf plot.

Heights (in centimeters) of Plants

Stem	Leaf
10	5 7 7
11	0 3 4 5 8
12	0 0 6 6 7 9
13	
14	3 3 3 8
15	0 0 1 7 7 8 9

10 | 5 represents a height of 10.5 centimeters.

5 Find the range of the data.

6 Find the mode of the data.

7 Find the median height.

8 Find the mean height.

9 Calculate Q_1 and Q_3.

10 Find the interquartile range.

Use the following information to answer questions ⑪ **to** ⑭. (Lessons 9.1, 9.3)

The history test scores of twenty students are tabulated below.

75	92	56	60	50	60	67	87	88	74
60	78	90	61	64	92	50	75	58	70

⑪ Find the range of the scores.

⑫ Find the 3 quartiles of the scores.

⑬ Find the interquartile range of the scores.

⑭ 🖩 Find the mean absolute deviation of the scores. Round to the nearest hundredth.

Use the data in the table to answer questions ⑮ **to** ⑰. (Lesson 9.3)

The table shows the speeds, in miles per hour, of twelve vehicles.

80	65	72	58	60	70	75	68	48	51	88	90

⑮ Calculate Q_1, Q_2, and Q_3.

⑯ Draw a box plot of the speeds of the vehicles.

⑰ 🖩 Calculate the mean absolute deviation of the speeds of vehicles. Round to the nearest hundredth.

Use the box plot to answer questions ⑱ **to** ⑳. (Lesson 9.3)

The box plot below summarizes the reaction times, in seconds, of 300 drivers in an experiment.

Reaction Times (in seconds) of Drivers

⑱ State the 5-point summary.

⑲ How many drivers have reaction time more than 2 seconds?

⑳ If a driver with reaction time less than 2 seconds is considered fast, how many drivers are fast?

Solve. Show your work. (Lesson 9.5)

 21 Six random samples of inner diameters, in millimeters, of metal pipes were collected. The sample means are 112, 103.5, 98.4, 106.2, 110, and 99.7. Use the 6 sample means to generate a mean length to estimate the population mean diameter of the pipes. Round your answer to the nearest tenth.

22 A bag contains 5 red cards, 4 yellow cards, and 7 blue cards. A card is randomly drawn from the bag. (Lessons 10.1, 10.2)

a) How many outcomes are in the sample space?

b) If X is the event of drawing a card which is not yellow, what are the outcomes favorable to X?

c) Find P(X).

d) If Y is the event of drawing a blue card, what does the complement of Y mean?

23 The numbers in the Venn diagram indicate the number of outcomes favorable to the events. For example, there are 12 outcomes favorable to event A. (Lesson 10.2)

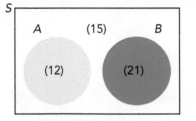

a) What is the total number of possible outcomes?

b) Find P(A), P(B), and P(B').

c) Copy and complete the table.

Relationship Between	Mutually Exclusive	Nonmutually Exclusive
A and B	✓	?
A and B'	?	?
A' and A	?	?
B and B'	?	?
A' and B'	?	?

24 A coin is flipped repeatedly and the outcomes are HTTHHHTHTHTHTHHTHHTH. What is the experimental probability that the coin lands on heads when you flip the coin again? (Lesson 10.3)

25 A spinner with outcomes A, E, O, and B is spun and the letter at which the arrow is pointing is recorded. After spinning the spinner several times, it generates the following outcomes: OABBBEAOOBAA. What is the experimental probability that the arrow points at a vowel if you spin the spinner again? (Lesson 10.3)

Problem Solving

Solve. Show your work.

26 The table shows 100 responses on the level of satisfaction of a service. Customers evaluate their experiences, as 1 very dissatisfied, 2 somewhat dissatisfied, 3 neutral, 4 somewhat satisfied or 5 very satisfied. (Chapters 9, 10)

Level of Satisfaction	1	2	3	4	5
Frequency	7	18	27	23	25

a) Find the lower quartile, median, and upper quartile.

b) Draw a box plot of the level of satisfaction.

c) If a customer's response is randomly selected, what is the probability that the level of satisfaction is at least 4?

d) Construct a relative frequency table. Write each relative frequency as a percent.

e) Present the relative frequency in a bar graph.

27 A survey was conducted on 100 randomly selected people about the types of books they usually read. The survey results show that 58 people read novels, 40 people read science fiction, and 10 people read neither. (Chapter 10)

a) Find the number of people surveyed who read both novels and science fiction.

b) Draw a Venn diagram to represent the different types of books read.

c) Copy and complete the following relative frequency table. Write each
    relative frequency as a decimal.

Types of Books Read	Novel only	Science fiction only	Both novel and science fiction	Neither
Relative Frequency	?	?	?	?

d) Draw a relative frequency bar graph using decimals.

e) If a person is randomly selected from this population to do the survey, what
    is the probability that the selected person reads novels?

28 The table shows the number of children surveyed for each age group. (Chapter 10)

Age (a years)	$10 \leq a < 12$	$12 \leq a < 14$	$14 \leq a < 16$	$16 \leq a < 18$
Frequency	14	28	20	18

a) Construct a probability model. Express each probability of the age groups
    as a percent.

b) If a child is randomly selected, what is the probability that the selected child
    is at least 10 years old but not yet 14 years old?

c) Display the probability distribution in a histogram using percent.

29 The data show the masses, in kilograms, of 14 grass carps. (Chapters 9, 10)

7	12	18	20	6	16	9
15	23	8	10	10	16	24

a) Construct a stem-and-leaf plot of the masses of the grass carps.

b) Make a frequency table. Group the data into 4 intervals: 5−10, 10−15, 15−20,
    and 20−25. Note: The interval 5−10 includes masses greater than or equal
    to 5 kilograms, but less than 10 kilograms.

c) Draw a probability model. Give probabilities in fractions.

d) Present the probability distribution, in fractions, in a histogram.

e) Is the model a uniform probability model? Explain your answer.

30 In a game, the scores given to each student are in multiples of 5 up to a maximum of 25. The bar graph and dot plot show the scores of Groups A and B, respectively. (Chapters 9, 10)

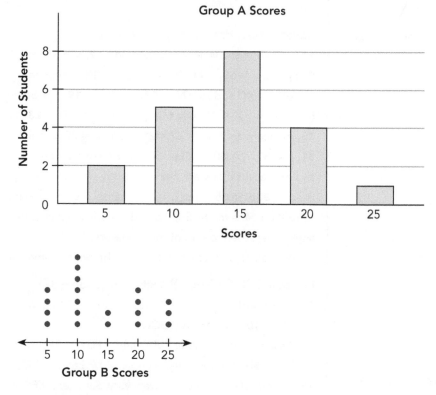

a) Calculate the mean score of each group.

b) Calculate the mean absolute deviation of the scores of each group.

c) Which group's scores deviate more about its mean score?

d) A randomly selected student from one of these groups has a score of 10 or 15. Which group is the student likely to be selected from? Explain your answer using probability.

31 The table shows the place of origin of incoming freshman students at a university. (Chapter 9)

Place of Origin (in U.S.A.)	Northern	Southern	Eastern	Western	Midwest	Other
Students (%)	30	10	12	16	24	8

Describe how you would conduct a stratified random sampling of 500 of the 6,000 incoming freshman, considering the student distribution within their place of origins.

Selected Answers

CHAPTER 6

Lesson 6.1, Guided Practice (pp. 7–16)

1. ∠ABC and ∠PQR; ∠DEF and ∠MNO; ∠GIH and ∠JKL

2.

m∠A	m∠B
28°	90° − 28° = 62°
73°	90° − 73° = 17°
36°	90° − 36° = 54°
15°	90° − 15° = 75°

3a. No **3b.** No **3c.** Yes **3d.** Yes

4.

m∠A	m∠B
82°	180° − 82° = 98°
26°	180° − 26° = 154°
136°	180° − 136° = 44°
105°	180° − 105° = 75°

5. 90°; 90°; 23°; 90°; 23°; 23°; 67 **6.** 180°; 180°; 37°; 180°; 37°; 37°; 143 **7.** 180°; 180°; 5; 180°; 5; 70°; 180°; 70°; 70°; 5; 110; $\frac{5}{5}$; $\frac{110}{5}$; 5; 22 **8.** 18; 18; 72; 4; $4x$; $4x$; 5; $\frac{5}{5}$; 5; 5; 18; 18; 72

Lesson 6.1, Practice (pp. 17–19)

1. Yes **3.** No **5.** Yes **7.** Yes **9.** 71° **11.** 83°
13. 102° **15.** 27° **17.** 25 **19.** 151 **21.** 83°
23a. Complement of ∠W = 88°; Supplement of ∠W = 178°; Complement of ∠X = 50°; Supplement of ∠X = 140°; Complement of ∠Y = 58°; Supplement of ∠Y = 148°; There is no complement of ∠Z. Supplement of ∠Z = 65° **23b.** ∠Z **23c.** The measure of an angle must be less than 90° for it to have both a complement and a supplement. **25.** 18 **27.** 12 **29.** 74
31. $a = 36$; $b = 54$ **33.** ∠EBD = 60°; ∠CBD = 150°

Lesson 6.2, Guided Practice (pp. 22–27)

1. $7p°$; 75°; 145°; 360°; $7p°$; 220°; 360°; $7p°$; 220°; 220°; 360°; 220°; 220°; 7p; 140; $\frac{7p}{7}$; $\frac{140}{7}$; 7; p; 20
2. 152°; $r°$; 180°; 152°; $r°$; 152°; 180°; 152°; r; 28; $q°$; 68°; $3q°$; 180°; $4q°$; 68°; 180°; $4q°$; 68°; 68°; 180°; 68°; 4q; 112; $\frac{4q}{4}$; $\frac{112}{4}$; 4; q; 28 **3.** $m = 31$; $n = 17$
4. a; 3a; 5a; 360; 9a; 360; $\frac{9a}{9}$; $\frac{360}{9}$; 9; a; 40; 3; 40; 40; 120; 5; 40; 40; 200 **5.** $3y°$; 120°; $\frac{3y}{3}$; $\frac{120}{3}$; y; 40

6. 114°; $r°$; 180°; 114°; $r°$; 114°; 180°; 114°; 114°; r; 66; q; 114; $p°$; $r°$; p; 66

Lesson 6.2, Practice (pp. 28–31)

1. $x = 307$ **3.** $x = 100$ **5.** $p = 34$ **7.** $a = 35$; $b = 106$
9. $x = 58$; $y = 61$ **11.** 40 **13.** 23 **15.** ∠HKF and ∠GKN; ∠HKG and ∠FKN **17.** $e = 91$ **19.** $a = 36$; $b = 72$; $c = 72$ **21.** $p = 60$; $q = 120$; $r = 180$ **23.** 176
25. Adjacent angles **27.** 42° **29.** $b = 30$; $c = 60$
31. $p = 50$; $q = 80$ **33a.** ∠4 and ∠6 are not vertical angles, because they are not formed by two intersecting lines. **33b.** m∠5 + m∠6 = 180° (supp. ∠s); m∠5 + m∠4 = 180° (m∠4 = m∠6); So, ∠5 and ∠4 are supplementary angles, because the sum of their measures is 180°. Supplementary angles do not have to be on the same line.

Lesson 6.3, Guided Practice (pp. 36–37)

1a. ∠ABF and ∠ACG; ∠XBC and ∠WCD; ∠FBC and ∠GCD **1b.** ∠FBC and ∠BCW **2.** $\overleftrightarrow{EH}$
3a. Answers vary. Sample: ∠EFY and ∠FGZ; ∠BFG and ∠CGH **3b.** Answers vary. Sample: ∠YFG and ∠FGC; ∠BFG and ∠FGZ **3c.** Answers vary. Sample: ∠EFB and ∠HGZ; ∠EFY and ∠CGH **4.** 81°; 81°; m∠2; 81°; 81°; 81°; 81°; 81°; 81°; 99°

Lesson 6.3, Practice (pp. 38–42)

1. Alternate interior angles **3.** None of the above
5. Corresponding angles **7.** Alternate interior angles
9. Any two of these angles: ∠4, ∠6, ∠7 **11.** 134°
13. m∠1 = 78°; m∠2 = 78°; m∠3 = 78° **15.** m∠1 = 87°; m∠2 = 52° **17.** m∠1 = 126°; m∠2 = 126°
19. $a = 142$; $b = 19$ **21.** $\overleftrightarrow{AB}$ is not parallel to $\overleftrightarrow{CD}$ because m∠BMN = 66° and m∠DNS = 65° by vertical angles. So, m∠BMN ≠ m∠DNS. **23.** $\overleftrightarrow{AB}$ is parallel to $\overleftrightarrow{CD}$ because m∠NMB = 72° = m∠SND (Supp. ∠s); ∠NMB and ∠SND are congruent corresponding angles.
25. m∠1 = 25°; m∠2 = 65° **27.** m∠1 = 58°
29. m∠1 = 77°; m∠2 = 61° **31.** 96 **33.** 78
35. If a line is perpendicular to one of two parallel lines, it is also perpendicular to the other. This is because the line is a transversal to the parallel lines, and it forms congruent corresponding angles with the pair of parallel lines.
37. $3x° = (60 − x)°$; $x = 15$; m∠4 = 45°

Lesson 6.4, Guided Practice (pp. 45−50)

1. 35°; *p*°; 57°; 180°; *p*°; 92°; 180°; *p*°; 92°; 92°; 180°; 92°; 92°; *p*; 88   **2.** 55°; 55°; *x*°; 180°; 110°; *x*°; 180°; *x*°; 110°; 110°; 180°; 110°; 110°; *x*; 70   **3.** *x*°; 62°; 132°; *x*°; 62°; 62°; 132°; 62°; 62°; *x*; 70   **4.** *x*°; 35°; 70°; 41°; *x*°; 35°; 111°; *x*°; 35°; 35°; 111°; 35°; 35 *x*; 76   **5.** 75°; 75°; 75°; 150°; 75°; 105°   **6.** 30°; 30°; *x*°; 30°; 30°; 180°; *x*°; 60°; 180°; *x*°; 60°; 60°; 180°; 60°; 60°; *x*; 120

Lesson 6.4, Practice (pp. 51−54)

1. 61   **3.** 28   **5.** 58   **7.** m∠1 = 28°; m∠2 = 118°   **9.** m∠1 = 60°; m∠2 = 120°   **11.** 40   **13.** *x* = 60; Equilateral triangle   **15.** *x* = 28; Right triangle   **17.** m∠1 = 40°; m∠2 = 125°   **19.** m∠1 = 60°; m∠2 = 127°   **21a.** A triangle cannot have two right angles because the sum of the measures of the three interior angles of a triangle is 180°. Two right angles have angle measures that total 180°, so the measure of the third angle would need to be 0°. This is impossible, because you would no longer have a triangle.   **21b.** The interior angles of a triangle cannot be 96°, 43°, and 43° because 96° + 43° + 43° = 182°, which is more than 180°.   **23.** 56   **25.** 50

Lesson 6.4, Brain@Work (p. 54)

15°

Chapter Review/Test (pp. 58−61)

1. Supplementary   **3.** Neither   **5.** Neither   **7.** Answers vary. Sample: ∠B and ∠G; ∠P and ∠S   **9.** Complementary: ∠ABR and ∠RBS; ∠CBT and ∠TBS; Supplementary: Answers vary. Sample: ∠ABT and ∠TBC; ∠ABR and ∠RBC   **11.** m∠2 = 120°   **13.** m∠4 = 73°   **15.** *w* = 28   **17.** *v* = 37; *u* = 53   **19.** *x* = 36   **21.** m∠1 = 52°; m∠2 = 52°; m∠3 = 66°   **23.** m∠1 = 70°; m∠2 = 55°   **25.** Complementary angles: ∠PNS and ∠SNR; ∠MNQ and ∠QNR; Supplementary angles: Answers vary. Sample: ∠PNS and ∠SNM; ∠PNR and ∠RNM; ∠PNQ and ∠QNM   **27.** m∠1 = 55°; m∠2 = 55°; Because m∠1 = m∠2 and they are corresponding angles, $\overleftrightarrow{PQ}$ is parallel to $\overleftrightarrow{RS}$.

CHAPTER 7

Lesson 7.1, Guided Practice (pp. 74−75)

1.   **2a.**

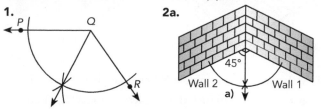

2b. 45°; Because the two walls intersect at a right angle and the position where the players are to line up is on the angle bisector of this angle, the required angle has a measure of 45°.

3.

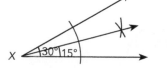

Lesson 7.1, Practice (pp. 76−77)

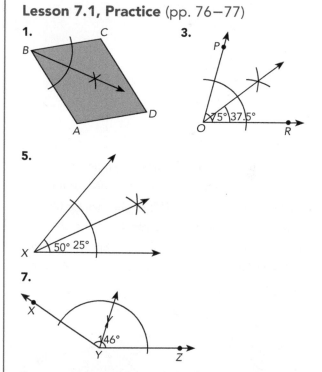

Steps to construct the angle bisector of ∠XYZ are as follows: Step 1: Draw an arc, centered at *Y*, of any radius, to intersect $\overrightarrow{YX}$ and $\overrightarrow{YZ}$; Step 2: With the same radius, set the compass at the intersections of the arcs with $\overrightarrow{YX}$ and $\overrightarrow{YZ}$ to draw two arcs that intersect at a point inside ∠XYZ; Step 3: Use a straightedge and draw a line joining the intersection of the arcs in Step 2 and point *Y*. This line is the angle bisector.

9.

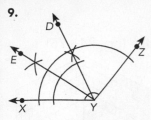

First, bisect ∠XYZ to obtain $\overrightarrow{YD}$ as its angle bisector. The bisected angles are such that m∠XYD = m∠ZYD; Then, bisect ∠XYD to obtain $\overrightarrow{YE}$ as its angle bisector. The bisected angles are such that m∠XYE = m∠DYE; Each of the angles, ∠XYE and ∠EYD, is one-fourth the measure of ∠XYZ.

11.

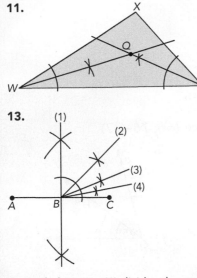

13.

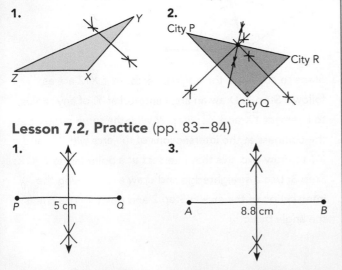

4; Angle bisector (1) divides the straight angle into 180° ÷ 2 = 90°; Angle bisector (2) further divides the resulting angle into 90° ÷ 2 = 45°; Angle bisector (3) further divides the resulting angle into 45° ÷ 2 = 22.5°; Angle bisector (4) further divides the resulting angle into 22.5° ÷ 2 = 11.25°; So, Kimberly needs to bisect 4 times.

Lesson 7.2, Guided Practice (pp. 81−82)

1.   **2.**

Lesson 7.2, Practice (pp. 83−84)

1.   **3.**

5. No. There is only one perpendicular bisector of a line segment.

7.

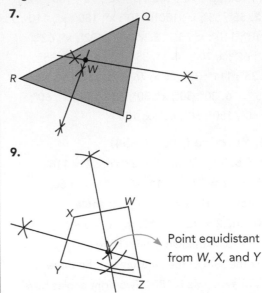

9.

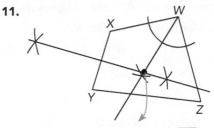

Point equidistant from W, X, and Y

Construct two perpendicular bisectors of any two segments: $\overline{WX}$, $\overline{XY}$, or $\overline{WY}$. The intersection of any two perpendicular bisectors gives the required point.

11.

Point equidistant from $\overline{WX}$ and $\overline{WZ}$, and from points X and Y

Construct the angle bisector of ∠XWZ and the perpendicular bisector of $\overline{XY}$. The intersection of both bisectors gives the required point.

13.

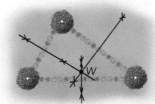

15. 4 arcs and 2 lines. To construct the perpendicular bisector of one short side, you can construct two arcs that intersect at two points. But each of these arcs can also be used to construct the perpendicular bisector of a

longer side of the rectangle. So, you only need four arcs altogether. A line that bisects one short side also bisects the other short side. A line that bisects one long side also bisects the opposite side. So, you need only two lines.

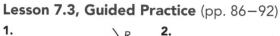

Lesson 7.3, Guided Practice (pp. 86–92)

1.
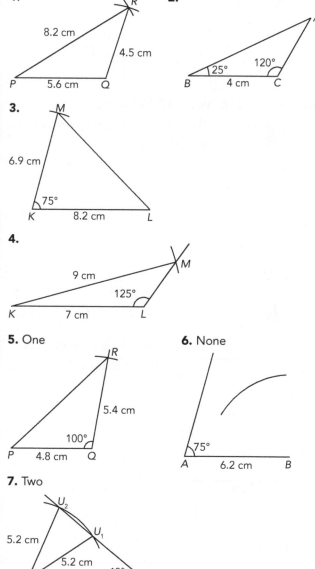

8.2 cm
4.5 cm
P 5.6 cm *Q*
R

2.
A
120°
25°
B 4 cm *C*

3.
M
6.9 cm
75°
K 8.2 cm *L*

4.
9 cm
125°
M
K 7 cm *L*

5. One
R
5.4 cm
100°
P 4.8 cm *Q*

6. None
75°
A 6.2 cm *B*

7. Two
U₂
U₁
5.2 cm
5.2 cm
40°
S 7.7 cm *T*

Lesson 7.3, Practice (p. 93)

1.
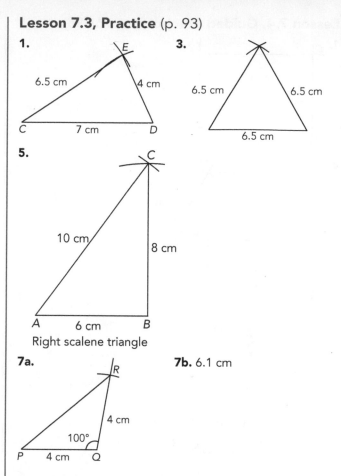

E
6.5 cm
4 cm
C 7 cm *D*

3.
6.5 cm 6.5 cm
6.5 cm

5.
C
10 cm
8 cm
A 6 cm *B*
Right scalene triangle

7a.
R
4 cm
100°
P 4 cm *Q*

7b. 6.1 cm

7c. 40° and 40°; The triangle is isosceles, so the angles opposite the sides with the same length have the same measure.

9a.
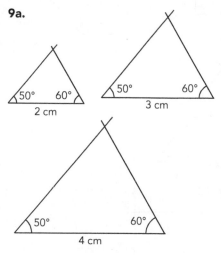

50° 60°
2 cm

50° 60°
3 cm

50° 60°
4 cm

9b. 70°   **9c.** Infinite number of triangles can be constructed.

Lesson 7.4, Guided Practice (pp. 96–98)

1.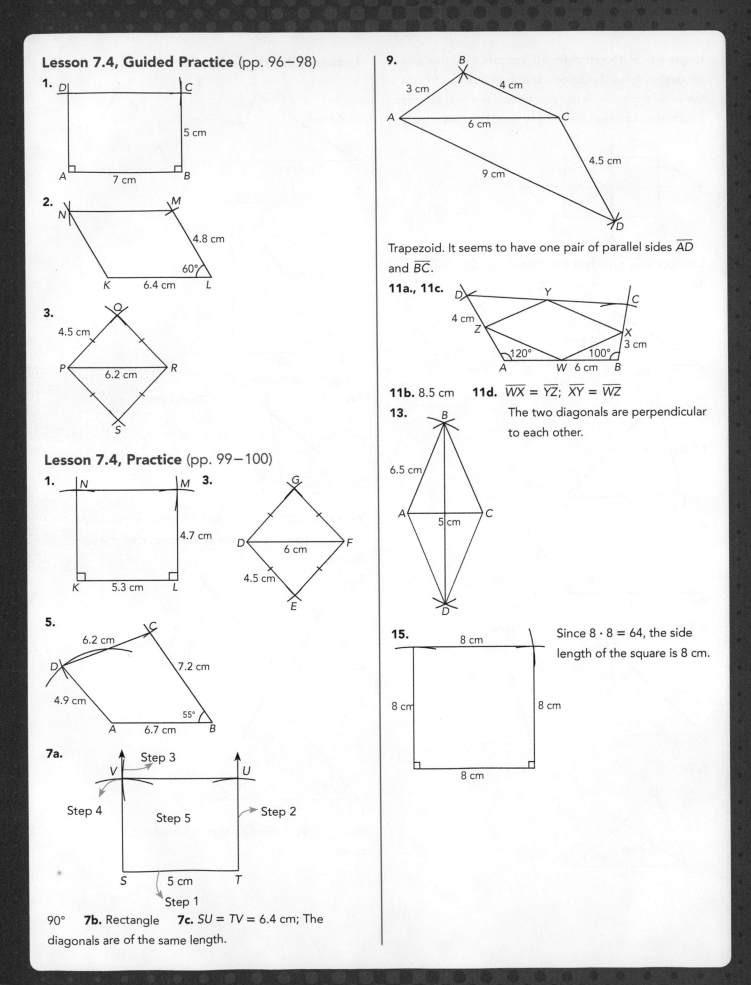

2.

3.

Lesson 7.4, Practice (pp. 99–100)

1.

3.

5.

7a.

Step 3

Step 4

Step 2

Step 5

Step 1

90°   **7b.** Rectangle   **7c.** $SU = TV = 6.4$ cm; The diagonals are of the same length.

9.

Trapezoid. It seems to have one pair of parallel sides $\overline{AD}$ and $\overline{BC}$.

11a., 11c.

11b. 8.5 cm   **11d.** $\overline{WX} = \overline{YZ}$; $\overline{XY} = \overline{WZ}$

13.

The two diagonals are perpendicular to each other.

15.

Since $8 \cdot 8 = 64$, the side length of the square is 8 cm.

Lesson 7.5, Guided Practice (pp. 103–110)

1. 7.8; 2.6; $\frac{7.8}{2.6}$; 3   **2.** 1 inch: 15 miles; 1 inch on the map represents 15 miles on the ground; 15; 0.6; 9; 9

3. 25; 220; $\frac{25}{25}$; $\frac{220}{25}$; 25; 8.8; 8.8 inches   **4.** 18 ft

5. 1 in. : 8 ft; 1 in² : 8² ft²; $\frac{12}{y}$; $\frac{1}{64}$; 12; 64; 768; 768

6. 1 in. : 7 ft; 1 in² : 7² ft²; $\frac{1}{49}$; $\frac{y}{196}$; $\frac{1}{49}$; 49y; 196; $\frac{49y}{49}$; $\frac{196}{49}$; 49; y; 4; 4

Lesson 7.5, Practice (pp. 111–113)

1. $\frac{1}{1,100}$ **3.** $\frac{2}{3}$ **5.** $\frac{1}{20}$ **7.** 42 mi   **9a.** 1,190 mi

9b. 9 in.   **11.** 1,980 mi   **13.** 1.92 in²

15a. Road A = 2.4 cm; Road B = 3.3 cm

15b. Road A = 1.2 km; Road B = 1.65 km

17a. Length = 4.5 m; Width = 3.5 m

17b. 0.32 cm

17c. About 142 m² to 144 m²

19a. 637.5 m

19b. 612.5 m   **19c.** 662.5 m

Lesson 7.5, Brain@Work (p. 114)

1. Step 1: Construct the vertices A, P, and Q of an equilateral triangle. Draw $\overrightarrow{AQ}$ and $\overrightarrow{AP}$.

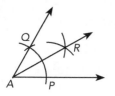

Step 2: Bisect the 60° angle with $\overrightarrow{AR}$ to form two adjacent 30° angles.

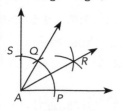

Step 3: Then construct $\overrightarrow{AS}$ perpendicular to $\overrightarrow{AP}$ at A. This line forms one side of the third 30° angle, and is also a side of the right angle, ∠PAS.

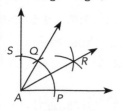

2. About 11.6 cm

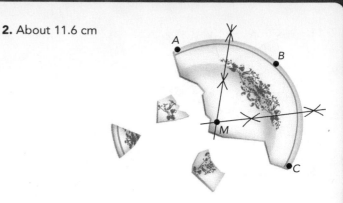

Chapter Review/Test (pp. 117–119)

1.

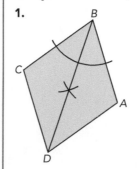

3.

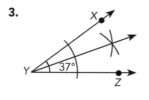

5.

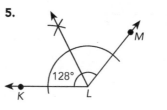

7.

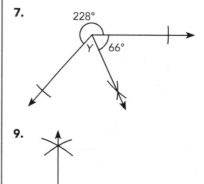

9.

11.

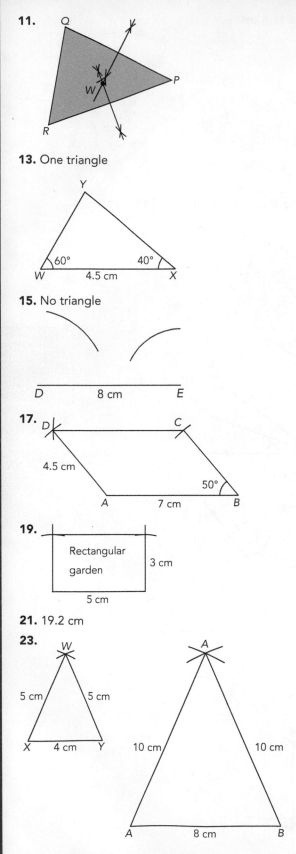

13. One triangle

15. No triangle

17.

19.

Rectangular garden

3 cm

5 cm

21. 19.2 cm

23.

Triangle *ABC* is an enlargement of triangle *WXY*, with every side of triangle *WXY* increased to twice its original length; Scale factor = 2

25.

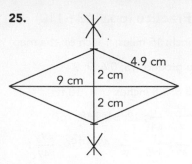

Length of skirting = 39.2 m

27. 3.8 in²   **29.** 5.5 acres

CHAPTER 8

Lesson 8.1, Guided Practice (p. 129)

1. Rectangle   **2.** Rectangle   **3.** Rectangle

4. Triangle

Lesson 8.1, Practice (pp. 130−132)

1. f)   **3.** d)   **5.** b)   **7.** Cylinder   **9.** Square pyramid

11a. Triangle   **11b.** Square   **13.** $\overline{AB}$ and $\overline{CD}$

15. 3 in. by 6 in. by 4 in.

Lesson 8.2, Guided Practice (pp. 134−137)

1. 588.8 cm³   **2.** 192.3 in³   **3.** $\pi r^2 h$; 1,808.64; 3.14; 12;

12; h; 1,808.64; 452.16; h; $\dfrac{1,808.64}{452.16}$; $\dfrac{452.16h}{452.16}$; 452.16;

4; 4   **4.** 276.3 in²   **5.** 162π; 9; 162π; 9; 9; 162π; 18πr;

$\dfrac{162\pi}{18\pi}$; $\dfrac{18\pi r}{18\pi}$; 18π; 9; 18

Lesson 8.2, Practice (pp. 138−139)

1. 263.0 cm³   **3.** 3,165.1 cm³   **5a.** 50.2 cm²

5b. 351.7 cm²   **5c.** 401.9 cm²   **7.** 2.5 in.   **9a.** 5.5 in.

9b. 104.5π in²   **11a.** 15 cm   **11b.** 4.5 cm

13. 115.9 pt   **15.** Yes; $S = 2\pi r^2 + 2\pi rh$

Lesson 8.3, Guided Practice (pp. 143−152)

1. $\dfrac{1}{2}$; 3; 5; 6; 15; 15   **2.** 121 m³   **3.** 400; 10; 10; 400 · 3;

$\dfrac{100 \cdot 3}{3}$; 3; $\dfrac{400 \cdot 3}{100}$; $\dfrac{\frac{100 \cdot 3}{3}(h)}{100}$; 100; 12; 12   **4.** 11.6 m

5. π; 6; 6; 14; 168π; 527.5; 168π; 527.5

6. 94.5π cm³; 296.7 cm³   **7.** 2,923.34; 3.14; 57; 2,923.34;

59.66; $\dfrac{2,923.34}{59.66}$; $\dfrac{59.66(r^2)}{59.66}$; 59.66; 49; $\sqrt{49}$; 7; 7   **8.** 5 in.

9. 1,674.7 cm³   **10a.** π; 7; 14; 98π; 98π **10b.** 98π;

98π; π; 7; 7; 98π; 7; 49π; 98π; 147π; 462; $\dfrac{22}{7}$; 147π; 462

11a. 36π in²   **11b.** 45π in²; 141.3 in²

12. 251.2; 3.14; 8; 251.2; 25.12; $\dfrac{251.2}{25.12}$; $\dfrac{25.12\ell}{25.12}$; 25.12; 10; 10

13. 3,925 in²

Lesson 8.3, Practice (pp. 153–155)

1. 360 cm³   **3.** 210 in³   **5.** $\frac{16\pi}{3}$ cm³; 16.7 cm³

7. $\frac{200\pi}{3}$ cm³; 209.3 cm³   **9.** 20.25π cm²; 64 cm²

11. 279π m²; 876 m²   **13.** 10 cm   **15a.** 106.8 cm²

15b. 125.6 cm²   **17.** The volume of a cone that has the

same height and radius as a cylinder is $\frac{1}{3}$ · Volume of

cylinder; $\frac{1}{3}$ · 393 = 131 cm³   **19.** 6.5 cm

Lesson 8.4, Guided Practice (pp. 157–160)

1. 2; 4.4; 3.14; 4.4; 4.4; 4.4; 356.637; 356.64; 356.64

2. 1,450; 3.14; 1,450; $\frac{12.56}{3}$·r³; 1,450; $\frac{12.56}{3}$·r³; 4,350;

12.56r³; $\frac{4,350}{12.56}$; $\frac{12.56·r³}{12.56}$; 12.56; 346.34; $\sqrt[3]{346.34}$; 7; 7

3. About 452.16 cm²   **4.** 3,215.36; 3.14; 3,215.36; 12.56;

$\frac{3,215.36}{12.56}$; $\frac{12.56·r²}{12.56}$; 12.56; 256; $\sqrt{256}$; 16; 16

Lesson 8.4, Practice (pp. 161–162)

1. 523.3 cm³   **3a.** 1,256 in²   **3b.** 4,186.7 in²   **5.** 2.6 cm

7a. Radius   **7b.** Volume increases by the factor of 8 while

surface area increases by the factor of 4 when the radius is

doubled. So, volume increases by a greater amount.

9. 125 balls   **11a.** 9 m   **11b.** 1,017.4 m²

Lesson 8.5, Guided Practice (pp. 164–166)

1a. π; 12; 12; 15; 2,160π; 37; 15; 22; π; 12; 12; 22; 1,056π;

2,160π; 1,056π; 3,216π; 10,098; 10,098   **1b.** 12; 25; 12;

15; 12; 12; 300π; 360π; 144π; 804π; 2,525; 2,525

2. About 747.44 in²   **3.** 5,186 cm³

Lesson 8.5, Practice (pp. 167–168)

1. 199.0 cm³   **3a.** 107,178.7 mm³   **3b.** 40,192 mm³

5. 314.8 cm³   **7.** 1129$\frac{1}{5}$ in³   **9a.** 8,393.2 cm³

9b. 2,373.8 cm³

Lesson 8.5, Brain@Work (p. 168)

a. Choose any vertex A. Mark 2 points say B and C on any
two edges such that AB = AC. Mark a
third point D such that AD ≠ AB or AC.
When a cube is sliced with plane BCD,
a cross section of an isosceles triangle
is formed.

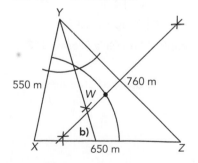

b. A cross section of a hexagon can
be obtained by slicing a cube with
a plane that cuts through all 6 faces
of the cube.   **c.** A square, an
equilateral triangle, a rectangle,
a triangle of any shape, a pentagon
and a parallelogram.

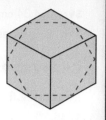

Chapter Review/Test (pp. 170–171)

1a. 775 in³   **1b.** 1,846 cm³   **3a.** 48 cm³   **3b.** 46.2 in³

5a. 54π ft²   **5b.** 784π m²   **5c.** 96π in²   **7.** 17.2 cm

9a. 4.5 in.   **9b.** 127.2 in³   **11.** 76.8 cm²

13. 919.8 cm³   **15.** 1 in.

Cumulative Review Chapters 6–8 (pp. 172–177)

1. Neither   **3.** Supplementary   **5.** m∠1 = 54°

7. m∠3 = 94°   **9.** m∠1 = 81°; m∠2 = 81°; m∠3 = 81°

11. m∠1 = 74°; m∠2 = 106°   **13a.** m∠A = 79°;

m∠B = 42°; m∠C = 59°

13b., 13c., 13d.

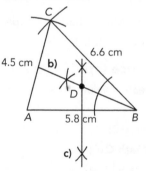

13e. BD = 3.2 cm; CD = 3.8 cm   **15.** $\frac{1}{50}$ **17.** c)

19. Square of length 6 cm   **21.** Right triangle

23. 187.05π m²   **25.** 277.3 cm³   **27.** 619.1 cm³

29. 3,704.1 ft³   **31.** x = 37   **33.** a = 16; b = 33

35. 96°   **37a. to 37c.**

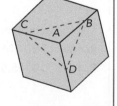

39a. 254.34 cm^3 **39b.** 19 glasses   **39c.** 235.5 cm^3
39d. 21 glasses   **39e.** $37.80   **41.** 358 cm^2

CHAPTER 9

Lesson 9.1, Guided Practice (p. 184)

1. 45.3°F   **2.** 3.2, 3.9, 4.3, 4.8, 5.2, 6, 6.4, 7, 7.7, 8, 9.3,
9.5, 10, 10.6; $\frac{6.4 + 7}{2}$; 6.7 cm; 3.2, 3.9, 4.3, 4.8, 5.2, 6, 6.4;
4.8 cm; 7, 7.7, 8, 9.3, 9.5, 10, 10.6; 9.3 cm   **3.** 25 points.
The differences in scores represented by the middle 50%
of the students is not more than 25 points.   **4a.** $Q_1 = 2$;
$Q_3 = 6$; Interquartile range = 4   **4b.** The differences
among the number of books read by the middle 50% of
the people is not more than 4.

Lesson 9.1, Practice (pp. 190–192)

1. 14 lb   **3.** 12.2 s   **5.** $Q_1 = 62.5$; $Q_2 = 66$; $Q_3 = 83.5$
7. $Q_1 = 7$ yr; $Q_2 = 9$ yr; $Q_3 = 10$ yr   **9.** 86 cans
11. 40 cans   **13.** Median = 6 h; $Q_1 = 4$ h; $Q_3 = 7$ h
15. 25% of the people spent at least 7 hours on Internet.
17. 7 h   **19.** Median = 6 h; $Q_1 = 4$ h; $Q_3 = 8$ h   **21.** The
difference is significant. The battery lifespans above the
upper quartile are more than double the battery lifespans
below the lower quartile.   **23.** b; e; f; g; h

Lesson 9.2, Guided Practice (pp. 194–199)

1. Step 1: Least value = 8; Greatest value = 44; The stems
go from 0 to 4.

Step 2:

Math Quiz Scores

Stem	Leaf
0	8
1	3 1 5 2 0 1 8
2	7 1 6 0
3	1 3
4	4

0 | 8 represents 8.

Step 3:

Math Quiz Scores

Stem	Leaf
0	8
1	0 1 1 2 3 5 8
2	0 1 6 7
3	1 3
4	4

0 | 8 represents 8.

Step 4: Answers vary. Sample: Math Quiz Scores; 0 | 8
represents a score of 8.

2a. **Attendance (in number of days) of Students**

Stem	Leaf
0	5 8 9 9
2	0 0 0 0 0 1 1 1
	2 2 2 2 2 3 3 3
	3 3 3 3 3

1 | 5 represents 15 days.

2b. 25   **2c.** 23 days   **2d.** 21.12 days   **2e.** 22 days
3a. 11   **3b.** Team A: 70 in.; Team B: 71 in.
3c. Team A: 69.9 in.; Team B: 70.3 in.   **3d.** On average,
Team B has taller players because both its mean and
median are greater. But the means and medians for both
teams are very close, so the players on Team B are not
much taller on average.   **4a.** 6.5 lb   **4b.** 6.14 lb
4c. The median is 6.5 lb while the mean is 6.14 lb. The
value of the median is much greater due to the presence
of an outlier with a value of 3.1 lb.   **4d.** 4 lb
4e. The range is the difference between the least and
the greatest values in a data set. So, the range is greater
because of the outlier. The mean is also smaller because of
the outlier.

Lesson 9.2, Practice (pp. 200–201)

1. **Masses (in grams) of Russet Potatoes**

Stem	Leaf
8	1 9
9	2 6
10	0 1 5 9
11	0 2

8 | 1 represents 81 grams.

Range = 31 g; Median = 100.5 g

3. **Average Hourly Rate (in dollars) of Workers**

Stem	Leaf
1	0 2 3 4 5 5 7
2	6

1 | 0 represents $10.
Range = $16; Median = $14.50

5. **Ages of Passengers on Board a Bus**

Stem	Leaf
0	5
1	1 3 5 9
2	
3	3 7
4	
5	5 6
6	3

0 | 5 represents 5 years.

Range = 58 yr; Median = 26 yr

7. 14 lb   **9.** 15.5 lb

11. Student Attendance (in number of days)

Stem	Leaf
2 2	0
2 3	0 1 2 2 3
	4 4 5 6 7
	8 9 9 9 9
	9 9 9 9 9
2 4	0 0 0 0 0
	0 0 0 0

22 | 0 represents 220 days.

13. 239 days and 240 days   **15.** Median = 3.2 lb; Mean = 3.57 lb; The median is 3.2 pounds while the mean is 3.57 pounds; The value of the mean is greater due to the presence of the outlier with a value of 8.1 pounds.   **17.** Advantages: It is easy to identify the minimum and maximum values from the data set. The range, median, and mode can be identified easily from a stem-and-leaf plot. The individual data values are preserved, unlike in a histogram. Disadvantages: When the range is too narrow, there would be too many leaves. When the range is wide, there would be some stems that have no leaf, especially when outliers cause the range to widen. Bus Route B has a relatively small range, with data concentrated within a few stems. Bus Route A has range that is much wider. So, when both bus routes are plotted in a double stem-and-leaf plot, Bus Route A has many stems without any leaf and the stem is much longer.

Lesson 9.3, Guided Practice (pp. 204–208)

1. Q_1 = 26 yr; Q_2 = 32 yr; Q_3 = 34 yr; Range = 20 yr; Interquartile range = 8 yr   **2.** Step 1: 0.7, 0.9, 1.6, 1.7, 2.4, 2.6, 2.9, 3.7, 4.2, 5.1, 5.6, 5.7; Step 2: Q_1 = 1.65 in.; Q_2 = 2.75 in.; Q_3 = 4.65 in.; Lower Extreme Value = 0.7 in.; Upper Extreme Value = 5.7 in.

Step 3:

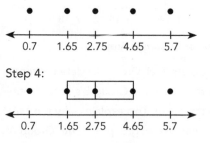

Step 4:

0.7   1.65 2.75   4.65   5.7

Step 5:

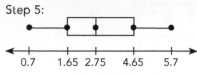

Average Monthly Rainfall

3a. Step 1: 17;

Step 2:

Data Item	Mean	Distance Between Data Item and Mean
20	17	3
16	17	1
13	17	4
11	17	6
19	17	2
24	17	7
22	17	5
15	17	2
17	17	0
13	17	4

Step 3: Sum = 34; Step 4: MAD = 3.4

3b. On average, the data values are 3.4 units from the mean.

Lesson 9.3, Practice (pp. 210–211)

1. Q_1 = 59.5; Q_2 = 60.5; Q_3 = 62.5; Lower = 57.5; Upper = 63.5; Interquartile range = 3   **3.** Q_1 = 23; Q_2 = 24; Q_3 = 31; Lower = 20; Upper = 34; Interquartile range = 8

5.

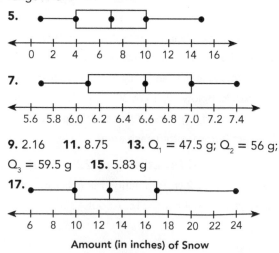

7.

9. 2.16   **11.** 8.75   **13.** Q_1 = 47.5 g; Q_2 = 56 g; Q_3 = 59.5 g   **15.** 5.83 g

17.

Amount (in inches) of Snow

19.

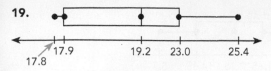

Heights (in inches) of Peanut Plants

21. Mean absolute deviation is a better measure of variation. A box plot is not meaningful with only 5 data values.   **23.** The mean absolute deviation is most useful when you are interested in how data are spread from the mean.

Lesson 9.4, Guided Practice (p. 219)

1. Scenario 1: Systematic random sampling; Scenario 1 uses systematic random sampling because you want the sample to cover a wide range of oranges in the shipment.
Scenario 2: Simple random sampling; Scenario 2 uses simple random sampling because it is just an opinion poll of people in the neighborhood.

Lesson 9.4, Practice (pp. 220−221)

1. A random sampling process is a procedure during which a sample is taken from a population in such a way that every member of the population has an equal chance of being selected and that selection of members does not affect other members.   **3.** They want to collect information to understand the characteristics of the population.   **5.** Stratified random sampling
7. Systematic random sampling   **9.** Systematic random sampling   **11a.** The 5 areas of the cornfield constitute 5 groups of corn plants. 20 ears of corn are randomly selected from each group.   **11b.** It gives a fair representation from each of the five areas.
13. Pick runners randomly in the marathon to interview until 60 runners have been interviewed.   **15.** Use age bands. For example, select randomly 15 runners from each of the 4 age bands: Below 20, 20 to 30, 30 to 40, Above 40.
17. Use the 5 areas as 5 groups of trees in the park. Randomly select 8 trees within each area.

Lesson 9.5, Guided Practice (pp. 225−231)

1a. Sample mean = 11.2 yr; Population mean is estimated to be 11.2 years.   **1b.** 4.8 yr   **1c.** About 43%

1d.

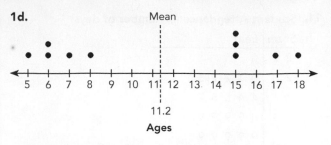

Ages

1e. Since MAD to mean ratio is about 43%, the data vary from the mean significantly. The dot plot confirms that the data are spread far away from the mean.

2a. Group 1: $Q_2 - Q_1 = 2$ yr; $Q_3 - Q_2 = 1$ yr; Interquartile range = 3 yr; Group 2: $Q_2 - Q_1 = 2$ yr; $Q_3 - Q_2 = 1$ yr; Interquartile range = 3 yr   **2b.** $\frac{2}{3}$ yr   **2c.** Since Q_1 of Group 2 is the same as Q_2 of Group 1, it means that 75% of the children in Group 2 are older than 50% of the children in Group 1. Also the median of Group 2 is greater than the median of Group 1. So, the children in Group 2 are generally older than children in Group 1.   **3a.** Class B; Interquartile range: Class A = 24; Class B = 40; Class B data are more spread out than Class A because the interquartile range of Class B is larger.   **3b.** Class A performed moderately better than Class B because the median of Class A is slightly higher at 66 and that of Class B is 60.   **4a.** Group A: 12; Group B: 12
4b. Group A: 4.4; Group B: 2.4
4c.

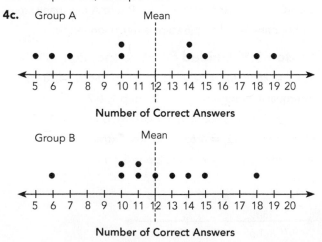

Number of Correct Answers

Number of Correct Answers

4d. From the two dot plots in c), Group A's data are more scattered away from the mean and Group B's data cluster more closely around the mean. This explains why the MAD of Group A is greater than that of group B.   **4e.** Group A's performance is more varied whereas Group B's performance is more uniform.

Lesson 9.5, Practice (pp. 232–234)

1. The estimated population mean weight is 28 grams with MAD to mean ratio of 7.5%. **3.** 250.9 mL
5. As the average deviation from the mean is less than 1%, the volume of orange juice per serving does not vary significantly. **7.** The median car speeds on Highway A is higher than that on Highway B. **9.** 50% of the cars on Highway A go faster than the speed limit but less than 50% of the cars on Highway B go faster than the speed limit. **11.** Henry's jogging distance is more varied than Carl's jogging distance. **13.** 90.3 s **15.** On the average, time variation from the mean is about 13.3% of the value of the mean time. **17.** Class A: 55.75; Class B's 66.75 **19.** The mean score of Class B is greater than the mean score of Class A. In other words, Class B's performance on average is better than Class A's performance. In addition, the MAD shows that Class B's scores are less varied than Class A's scores.

Lesson 9.5, Brain@Work (p. 234)

a. 166 mL **b.** 2.8 mL **c.** No, I disagree with Alex's conclusion. The MAD to mean ratio is 1.69%. It means that the average deviation from the mean is very insignificant. The vertical axis of the bar graph is not drawn to scale. As such, it creates visual distortion of the differences in heights of the vertical bars.

Chapter Review/Test (pp. 237–239)

1. Range = 10; $Q_1 = 2$; $Q_2 = 5$; $Q_3 = 8$; Interquartile range = 6 **3.** Range = 0.73; $Q_1 = 1.11$; $Q_2 = 1.3$; $Q_3 = 1.55$; Interquartile range = 0.44 **5.** 10 **7.** 5

9a. Weights (in pounds) of Labrador Dogs

Stem	Leaf
5	1 6
6	2 8
7	0 1 2 3 5 7 8 9
8	1 5 8
9	3 4 5 8
10	1

5 | 1 represents 51 pounds.

9b. 20 **9c.** 50 lb **9d.** There is no modal weight.
9e. 77.5 lb **11.** 0.81 **13.** Range = 1.2 cm; Interquartile range = 0.4 cm **15.** The spread of the middle 50% of the heights of bean sprouts is 0.4 centimeter. **17.** $Q_1 = 4$; $Q_2 = 5.4$; $Q_3 = 7.8$

19. The middle 50% of the science scores are moderately spread out from 38 to 76 and the mean is quite close to the median, making the distribution fairly symmetrical about the mean.

21. 150 students

23. Sales in women's department / Sales in men's department

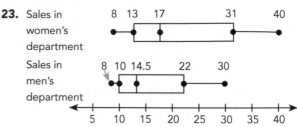

25. Women: $21,500; Men: $16,333 **27.** The MAD to mean ratio for the women's department is 44.6% and that of the men's department is 38.1%. These two ratios show that the sales in the women's department are slightly more varied than the sales in the men's department.

CHAPTER 10

Lesson 10.1, Guided Practice (pp. 247–248)

1a. A; D; E; G; K **1b.** 5 **2a.** add, bad, cab, cad, dab, dad **2b.** 6 **3a.** The prime numbers up to 20 are 2, 3, 5, 7, 11, 13, 17, 19; Y = {2, 3, 5, 7, 11, 13, 17, 19}
3b. 20; 20 **4a.** Brown parallelogram, triangle, green parallelogram, square, pentagon, and hexagon
4b. Heptagon, octagon, pentagon, hexagon

Lesson 10.1, Practice (pp. 249–250)

1. Red, green **3a.** 0, 1, 2, 3, and 4 **3b.** A = {0, 2, 4}
5. 16 **7a.** 10 **7b.** 0 **7c.** 0, 1, 2, 3, 4, 5, 6, 7, 8, 9, 10
9a. 507, 508, 570, 578, 580, 587, 705, 708, 750, 758, 780, 785, 805, 807, 850, 857, 870, and 875 **9b.** 508, 570, 578, 580, 708, 750, 758, 780, 850, and 870 **9c.** 507, 587, 705, 785, 805, 807, 857, and 875 **11.** 36

Lesson 10.2, Guided Practice (pp. 252–262)

1a. 6; $\frac{1}{6}$ **1b.** 0 **2.** 0 **3.** 5; $\frac{5}{9}$ **4.** 70%
5a. W = {27, 35, 39, 45}; V = {3, 11, 19}
5b. S

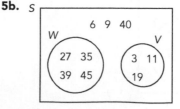

5c. Yes; The circles representing events W and V in the Venn diagram do not overlap because there are no outcomes common to both events.   **5d.** $\frac{2}{5}$; $\frac{3}{10}$

6a.

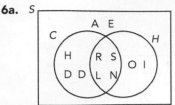

6b. No. C and H are not mutually exclusive events because the circles for the events overlap.   **6c.** $\frac{7}{11}$; $\frac{6}{11}$

7a.

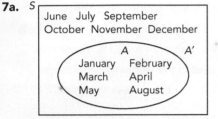

A' is the event of selecting a month without the letter a in its name.   **7b.** A' = {June, July, September, October, November, December}   **7c.** $\frac{1}{2}$ or 0.5; $\frac{1}{2}$ or 0.5

8a. 60; 40   **8b.** 95; 95%; 0.95; 0.57; 57; 0.57 or 57%

9a.

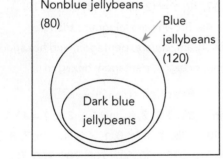

9b. $\frac{2}{5}$ **9c.** 0.4

Lesson 10.2, Practice (pp. 263–265)

1a. $\frac{1}{2}$ **1b.** $\frac{1}{3}$ **1c.** $\frac{1}{2}$ **1d.** $\frac{5}{6}$ **3.** $\frac{2}{11}$

5a. 23, 24, 32, 34, 42, 43   **5b.** $\frac{1}{2}$ **5c.** $\frac{1}{3}$

7a.

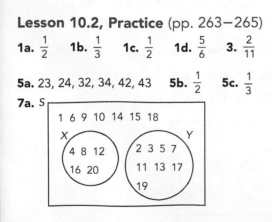

7b. In the Venn diagram, the circles for the two events do not overlap because a number cannot be both divisible by 4 and prime. So, events X and Y are mutually exclusive.

7c. $\frac{1}{4}$; $\frac{2}{5}$

9a.

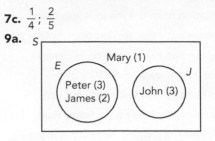

9b. John, Mary   **9c.** Yes; The two circles for the events do not overlap because there is no outcome common to both events. Events E and J are mutually exclusive.

9d. $\frac{5}{9}$; $\frac{4}{9}$; $\frac{1}{5}$

11a.

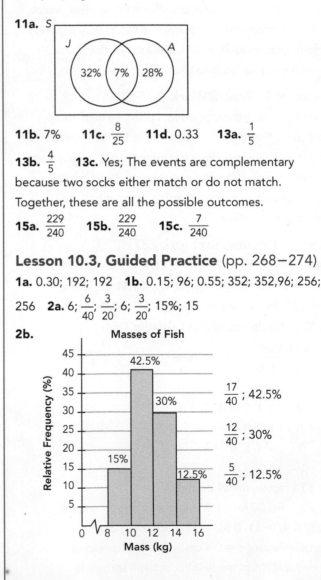

11b. 7%   **11c.** $\frac{8}{25}$ **11d.** 0.33   **13a.** $\frac{1}{5}$

13b. $\frac{4}{5}$ **13c.** Yes; The events are complementary because two socks either match or do not match. Together, these are all the possible outcomes.

15a. $\frac{229}{240}$ **15b.** $\frac{229}{240}$ **15c.** $\frac{7}{240}$

Lesson 10.3, Guided Practice (pp. 268–274)

1a. 0.30; 192; 192   **1b.** 0.15; 96; 0.55; 352; 352,96; 256; 256   **2a.** 6; $\frac{6}{40}$; $\frac{3}{20}$; 6; $\frac{3}{20}$; 15%; 15

2b.

Masses of Fish

$\frac{17}{40}$; 42.5%

$\frac{12}{40}$; 30%

$\frac{5}{40}$; 12.5%

3a. $\frac{10}{100}$; $\frac{1}{10}$; 0.1; $\frac{35}{100}$; $\frac{7}{20}$; 0.35; $\frac{48}{100}$; $\frac{12}{25}$; 0.48; $\frac{7}{100}$; $\frac{7}{100}$; 0.07

3b. 0.1; 10%   **3c.** blue; 0.48

Lesson 10.3, Practice (pp. 276–278)

1a. 300   **1b.** 11%   **1c.** 68%

3a.

Value	1	2	3	4	5	6
Observed Frequency	11	4	6	14	8	7
Relative Frequency	$\frac{11}{50}$	$\frac{2}{25}$	$\frac{3}{25}$	$\frac{7}{25}$	$\frac{4}{25}$	$\frac{7}{50}$

3b. $\frac{3}{10}$ **3c.** $\frac{1}{2}$ **5a.** $\frac{23}{100}$; $\frac{17}{50}$; $\frac{19}{100}$; $\frac{6}{25}$ **5b.** $\frac{17}{50}$

5c. $\frac{1}{4}$ **5d.** Some possible factors are as follows: The cards may not be well shuffled; Different people choose a card in different ways; How the cards are placed may make a difference; The theoretical probability may have assumptions that cannot be achieved from experiments.   **5e.** $\frac{43}{100}$ **5f.** $\frac{1}{2}$ **7a.** 16%

7b. 52%   **7c.** 4%

Lesson 10.4, Guided Practice (pp. 281–287)

1a. Sample space = {S, T, U, V, W, X, Y, Z}   **1b.** $\frac{1}{8}$

1c.

Letter	S	T	U	V	W	X	Y	Z
Probability	$\frac{1}{8}$	$\frac{1}{8}$	$\frac{1}{8}$	$\frac{1}{8}$	$\frac{1}{8}$	$\frac{1}{8}$	$\frac{1}{8}$	$\frac{1}{8}$

1d.

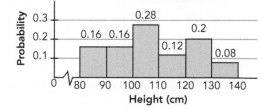

2a. Since the choice is random, each number has an equal chance of being chosen. So, the probability of each outcome is the same.   **2b.** $\frac{1}{10}$ **2c.** 12, 21, 45, 48

2d. $\frac{2}{5}$ or 0.4   **3a.** There are 4 different flavor outcomes: peppermint, raspberry, camomile, and blackberry. The sample space has 4 peppermint + 2 raspberry + 3 camomile + 1 blackberry = 10 possible outcomes.

3b. $\frac{1}{5}$ or 0.2

3c.

Tea Bag	Peppermint	Raspberry	Camomile	Blackberry
Probability	0.4	0.2	0.3	0.1

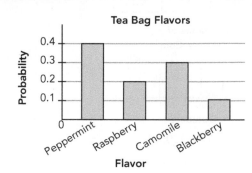

4a. $\frac{1}{3}$

4b.

Letter	B	E	G	I	N
Probability	$\frac{1}{9}$	$\frac{1}{9}$	$\frac{2}{9}$	$\frac{2}{9}$	$\frac{3}{9}$

4c. $\frac{2}{3}$

5a.

Interval	80–90	90–100	100–110	110–120	120–130	130–140
Frequency	4	4	7	3	5	2

5b. $\frac{4}{25}$; $\frac{4}{25}$; $\frac{7}{25}$; $\frac{3}{25}$; $\frac{1}{5}$; $\frac{2}{25}$

Interval	80–90	90–100	100–110	110–120	120–130	130–140
Probability	0.16	0.16	0.28	0.12	0.2	0.08

5c.

Greenhouse Tomato Plants

A nonuniform probability distribution

5d. $\frac{2}{5}$ or 0.4

Lesson 10.4, Practice (pp. 289–291)

1a. Sample space = {heads, tails} **1b.** $\frac{1}{2}$

1c.

Outcome	Heads	Tails
Probability	0.5	0.5

1d.

Outcomes of Tossing a Coin

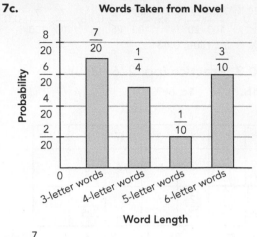

3a. 50, 100, 150, 200, 300, 550 **3b.** $\frac{1}{6}$

3c.

Outcome	50	100	150	200	300	550
Probability	$\frac{1}{6}$	$\frac{1}{6}$	$\frac{1}{6}$	$\frac{1}{6}$	$\frac{1}{6}$	$\frac{1}{6}$

3d. Yes; All the outcomes have an equal probability of occuring. **3e.** $\frac{1}{6}$ **5a.** Gold, white, green

5b.

Color	Gold	White	Green
Probability	$\frac{1}{3}$	$\frac{47}{75}$	$\frac{1}{25}$

No.

5c. $\frac{47}{75}$

7a.

Word Length	3-letter words	4-letter words	5-letter words	6-letter words
Number of Words	7	5	2	6

7b.

Word Length	3-letter words	4-letter words	5-letter words	6-letter words
Probability	$\frac{7}{20}$	$\frac{1}{4}$	$\frac{1}{10}$	$\frac{3}{10}$

7c.

Words Taken from Novel

7d. $\frac{7}{10}$

Lesson 10.4, Brain@Work (p. 291)

a. Friend picks 1 or 10 **b.** Friend picks 3, 4, 5, 6, 7, or 8

c. $\frac{56}{90}$

Chapter Review/Test (pp. 294–297)

1. 6, 12, 18, 24, 30, 36, 42, 48 **3a.** 56, 57, 65, 67, 75, 76

3b. 2 **5a.** 23, 24, 32, 34, 42, 43 **5b.** $\frac{1}{2}$ or 0.5 **7.** $\frac{1}{3}$

9a. 0.24, 0.19 **9b.** $\frac{1}{6}$ or $0.1\overline{6}$ **9c.** It will be closer to the theoretical probability. **11a.** Let W, B, and R represent White, Black, and Red respectively. The sample space is {WW, WR, BW, BR}. **11b.** $\frac{1}{4}$

11c.

Outcome	WW	WR	WB	RB
Probability	$\frac{1}{4}$	$\frac{1}{4}$	$\frac{1}{4}$	$\frac{1}{4}$

Yes. All the outcomes have an equal probability of occuring.

11d. S

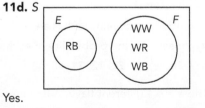

Yes.

11e. $\frac{1}{4}$; $\frac{3}{4}$ **13a.** 96 **13b.** $\frac{13}{50}$ or 0.26

Cumulative Review Chapters 9–10
(pp. 298–303)

1. Range = 79; Q_1 = 32.5; Q_2 = 52.5; Q_3 = 83;
Interquartile range = 50.5 **3.** 21.33 **5.** 5.4 cm
7. 12.7 cm **9.** Q_1 = 11.45 cm; Q_3 = 15.0 cm **11.** 42
13. 22.5 **15.** Q_1 = 59 mi/h; Q_2 = 69 mi/h;
Q_3 = 77.5 mi/h **17.** 10.42 mi/h **19.** 225 drivers
21. 105.0 mm **23a.** 48 **23b.** $\frac{1}{4}$; $\frac{7}{16}$; $\frac{9}{16}$

23c.

Relationship Between	Mutually Exclusive	Nonmutually Exclusive
A and B	✓	
A and B'		✓
A' and A	✓	
B and B'	✓	
A' and B'		✓

25. $\frac{2}{3}$ **27a.** 8

27b. S (100)

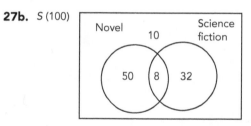

27c.

Types of Books Read	Novel only	Science fiction only	Both novel and science fiction	Neither
Relative Frequency	0.5	0.32	0.08	0.1

27d.

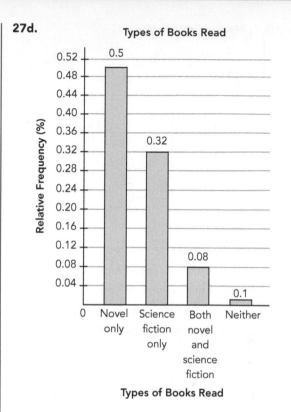

Types of Books Read

27e. 0.58

29a. Mass (in kilograms) of Grass Carps

Stem	Leaf
0	6 7 8 9
1	0 0 2 5 6 6 8
2	0 3 4

0 | 6 represents a mass of 6 kilograms.

29b.

Mass (kg)	5–10	10–15	15–20	20–25
Frequency	4	3	4	3

29c.

Mass (kg)	5–10	10–15	15–20	20–25
Probability	$\frac{2}{7}$	$\frac{3}{14}$	$\frac{2}{7}$	$\frac{3}{14}$

29d.

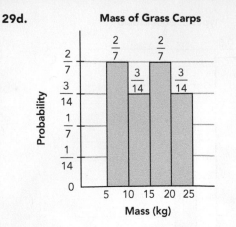

Mass of Grass Carps

29e. No; All possible outcomes do not have the same relative frequency.　**31.** Use the percent to determine how many of the 500-student sample will be selected from each region. Then conduct a simple random sampling within each region. The total number of students sampled will be 500.

Glossary

A

adjacent angles

Two angles that share a common vertex and side, but have no common interior points.

Example:

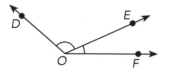

∠DOE and ∠EOF are adjacent angles.

alternate exterior angles

The pairs of angles on opposite sides of the transveral for two lines, but outside the two lines.

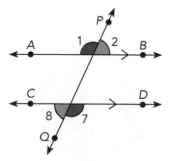

∠1 and ∠7 are alternate exterior angles; ∠2 and ∠8 are alternate exterior angles.

alternate interior angles

The pairs of angles on opposite sides of the transveral for two lines, but inside the two lines.

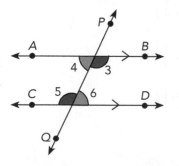

∠3 and ∠5 are alternate interior angles; ∠4 and ∠6 are alternate interior angles.

B

biased

A sample space in which one or more outcomes are favored.

biased sample

A sample in which members are not randomly selected.

bisect

To divide into two equal parts.

bisector

A ray that divides an angle into two angles with equal measures.

Example:

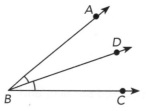

$\overrightarrow{BD}$ bisects ∠ABC. $\overrightarrow{BD}$ is the angle bisector of ∠ABC.

box plot

A graphical display of the 5-point summary.

Example:

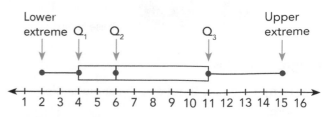

box-and-whisker plot

Also known as the box plot.

C

circumference

The distance around a circle.

complementary angles

Two angles whose angle measures total 90°.

Example:

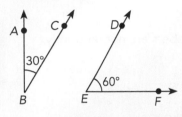

$\angle ABC$ and $\angle DEF$ are complementary angles.

complementary event

The complement of an event E consists of all the outcomes in the sample space that are not in event E.

Example: When trying to roll a 6 on a die (event E), rolling a 1, 2, 3, 4, or 5 is the complement of event E.

cone

A solid with a circular base, a curved surface, and one vertex.

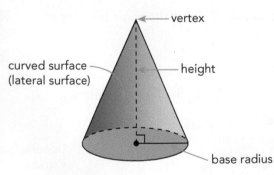

congruent angles

Two or more angles that have the same angle measure.

corresponding angles

The pairs of angles on the same side of the transversal for two lines and on the same side of the given lines.

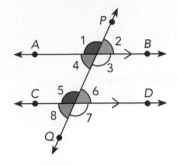

$\angle 1$ and $\angle 5$ are corresponding angles; $\angle 4$ and $\angle 8$ are corresponding angles.

cross section

A figure formed by the intersection of a solid figure and a plane.

Example: Two possible cross sections of a cube are a square and a triangle.

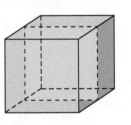
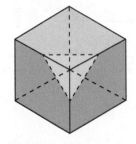

cylinder

A solid with a curved surface and two parallel bases that are congruent circles.

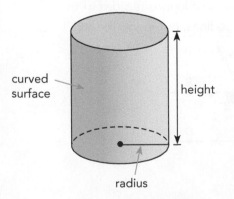

D

dot plot

A data display similar to a line plot. It shows frequency of data on a number line using a • to represent each occurrence.

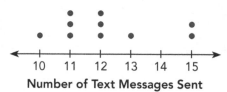

Number of Text Messages Sent

E

equidistant

At the same distance.

Example:

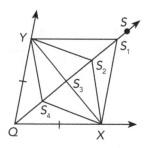

Points *X* and *Y* are equidistant from point *Q*.

event

A collection of outcomes from an activity.

experimental probability

Probability based on data collected or observations made in an experiment.

exterior angles

The angle formed by one side of a polygon and the extension of an adjacent side.

Example:

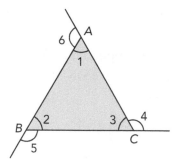

∠4, ∠5, and ∠6 are exterior angles.

F

fair

An experiment in which the probability of each outcome is the same.

first quartile

Also known as the lower quartile. It is the median of the lower half of a data set.

5-point summary

Consists of five data values: the lower extreme value, the first quartile, the median, the third quartile, and the upper extreme value.

Example:

Lower extreme value	2
Lower quartile (Q_1)	4
Median (Q_2)	6
Upper quartile (Q_3)	11
Upper extreme value	15

H

hemisphere

Half of a sphere.

histogram

A data display that divides the range of data into equal intervals and shows how often each interval occurs in a data set.

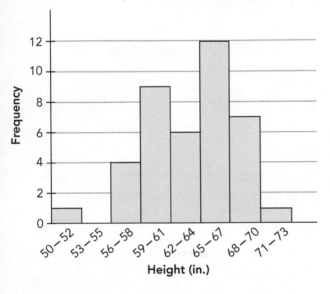

Height of Students in a Class

I

included angle

The angle in a triangle formed by two given sides.

included side

The side in a triangle that is common to two given angles in the triangle.

inference

A conclusion about a population, made by projecting the results of a representative sample onto the whole population.

interior angles

Angles formed by two adjacent sides of a polygon.

Example:

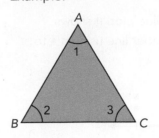

In triangle *ABC*, $\angle 1$, $\angle 2$, and $\angle 3$ are its interior angles.

interquartile range

The difference between the first and the third quartiles.

Example:

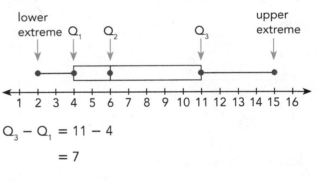

$$Q_3 - Q_1 = 11 - 4$$
$$= 7$$

L

lateral surface

The curved surface of a cone or cylinder or the nonbase surfaces of a pyramid or prism.

leaf

The least digit in each item of a data set when displayed in a stem-and-leaf plot.

lower quartile

The median of the lower half of a data set. 25% of the data fall on or below this value.

M

mean absolute deviation

The average distance of each item of data from the mean.

measure of variation

A measure of the spread of data from a measure of center.

midpoint

The point on a line segment that is equidistant from both endpoints.

mutually exclusive events

Two events that cannot happen at the same time.

N

nonuniform probability model

A probability model in which the outcomes do not necessarily have equal probabilities.

O

observed frequency

The number of observations of a data value in an experiment.

outcomes

All the possible results of an activity or experiment.

P

parallelogram

A quadrilateral in which both pairs of opposite sides are congruent and parallel.

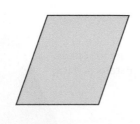

perpendicular bisector

A line that bisects a line segment and is perpendicular to it.

Example:

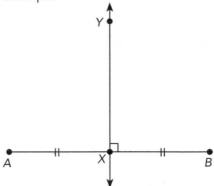

$\overleftrightarrow{XY}$ is the perpendicular bisector of line segment AB.

plane

A flat surface that extends infinitely in two dimensions.

population

All the members or objects about which you want information.

prism

A solid with two parallel congruent polygons for bases, which are joined by faces that are parallelograms. It is named by the shape of its base.

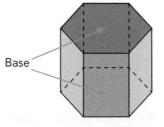
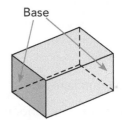

Base

Hexagonal prism   Rectangular prism

probability

A description of how likely an event is to occur.

probability distribution

A table or a graphical display presenting all the outcomes of the sample space and their probabilities.

probability model

A model that represents a sample space of outcomes, events, and the probabilities of these outcomes and events.

Example:

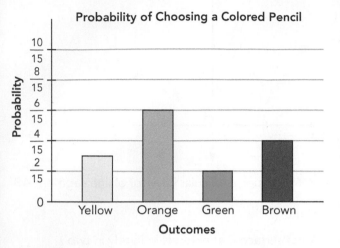

Probability of Choosing a Colored Pencil

pyramid

A solid whose base is a polygon and whose other faces are triangles that share a common vertex.

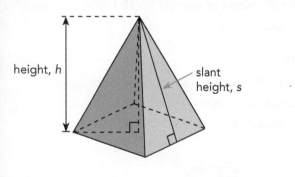

R

random sample

A set of data randomly selected from a population so that every member of the population has an equal chance of being selected.

range

The difference between the greatest and least data values in a data set.

Example: In the data set 2, 4, 7, 10, the range of the data is 10 − 2 = 8.

relative frequency

The ratio of the observed frequency of a data value to the total number of observations in a chance process.

S

sample

A set of data taken from a population.

sample size

The number of members in a sample.

sample space

The collection of all possible outcomes from an activity or experiment.

Example: If you roll a number die, the sample space is {1, 2, 3, 4, 5, 6}.

scale

A comparison of a length in a scale drawing to the corresponding length in the actual object.

Example: 1 foot = 12 inches

scale factor

The ratio of a length in a scale drawing to the corresponding length in the actual figure.

second quartile

The median of a data set. 50% of the data fall on or below this value.

slant height

On a cone, it is the distance from the vertex to any point on the circumference of the base. On a regular pyramid, it is the distance from the vertex to the midpoint of any edge of the base.

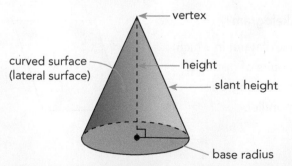

simple random sampling

A sampling method in which every member of a population has an equal chance of being selected.

sphere

A solid figure whose every point is the same distance from its center.

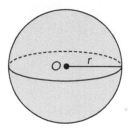

stem

All digits except the one of least place value in a item of data displayed in a stem-and-leaf plot.

stem-and-leaf plot

A two-column graphical display in which the least digit of each item of data is displayed in the right column and the other digits in the left column.

Example:

Weights (in pounds) of Students

Stem	Leaf
6	9
7	8 9
8	
9	4
10	
11	
12	8

6 | 9 represents 69 pounds.

straightedge

A geometric tool that is used to draw a line segment between two points or to extend an existing line segment.

stratified random sampling

A sampling method in which the population is divided into nonoverlapping groups from which members are randomly selected.

supplementary angles

Two angles whose angle measures total 180°.

Example:

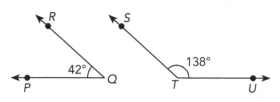

∠PQR and ∠STU are supplementary angles.

surface area

The sum of the areas of the faces and curved surfaces of a solid figure.

systematic random sampling

A sampling method in which the first member is randomly selected, and subsequent members are selected at regular intervals.

T

theoretical probability

The ratio of the number of favorable outcomes to the total number of possible outcomes in an experiment.

third quartile

The median of the upper half of a set of data, also known as the upper quartile. 75% of the data fall on or below this value.

transversal

A line that intersects two or more (usually parallel) lines.

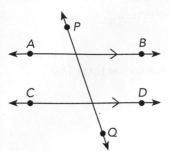

$\overrightarrow{PQ}$ is a transveral.

trapezoid

A quadrilateral with exactly one pair of parallel sides.

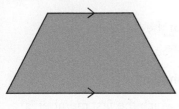

U

unbiased sample

Also known as random sample.

uniform probability model

A probability model in which all the outcomes have an equal probability of occurring.

upper quartile

The value in the data set such that 75% of the data fall on or below this value.

V

vertical angles

When two lines intersect at a point, they form four angles. The nonadjacent angles are vertical angles.

Example:

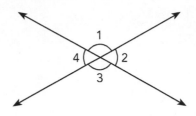

∠1 and ∠3 are vertical angles;

∠2 and ∠4 are also vertical angles.

Venn diagram

A diagram that uses circles to represent relationships for simple events.

Example:

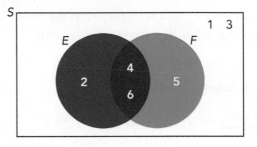

volume

A measure of the space enclosed within a solid figure.

Table of Measures, Formulas, and Symbols

METRIC | CUSTOMARY

Length

METRIC	CUSTOMARY
1 kilometer (km) = 1,000 meters (m)	1 mile (mi) = 1,760 yards (yd)
1 meter = 10 decimeters (dm)	1 mile = 5,280 feet (ft)
1 meter = 100 centimeters (cm)	1 yard = 3 feet
1 meter = 1,000 millimeters (mm)	1 yard = 36 inches (in.)
1 centimeter = 10 millimeters	1 foot = 12 inches

Capacity

METRIC	CUSTOMARY
1 liter (L) = 1,000 milliliters (mL)	1 gallon (gal) = 4 quarts (qt)
	1 gallon = 16 cups (c)
	1 gallon = 128 fluid ounces (fl oz)
	1 quart = 2 pints (pt)
	1 quart = 4 cups
	1 pint = 2 cups
	1 cup = 8 fluid ounces

Mass and Weight

METRIC	CUSTOMARY
1 kilogram (kg) = 1,000 grams (g)	1 ton (T) = 2,000 pounds (lb)
1 gram = 1,000 milligrams (mg)	1 pound = 16 ounces (oz)

TIME

1 year (yr) = 365 days	1 week = 7 days
1 year = 12 months (mo)	1 day = 24 hours (h)
1 year = 52 weeks (wk)	1 hour = 60 minutes (min)
leap year = 366 days	1 minute = 60 seconds (s)

You can use the information below to convert measurements from one unit to another.

To convert from a smaller unit to a larger unit, divide.	To convert from a larger unit to a smaller unit, multiply.
Example: 48 in. = ___?___ ft	Example: 0.3 m = ___?___ cm

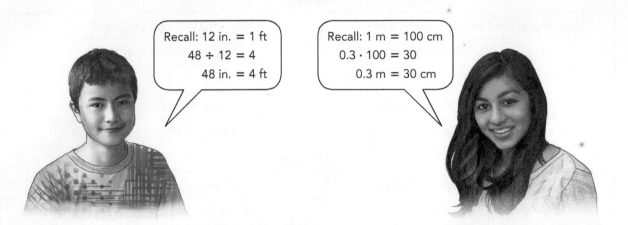

Recall: 12 in. = 1 ft
$48 \div 12 = 4$
48 in. = 4 ft

Recall: 1 m = 100 cm
$0.3 \cdot 100 = 30$
0.3 m = 30 cm

PERIMETER, CIRCUMFERENCE, AND AREA

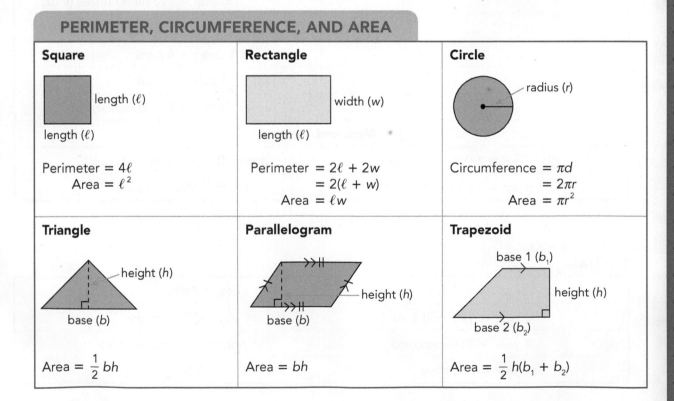

Square

length (ℓ)

length (ℓ)

Perimeter = 4ℓ
Area = ℓ^2

Rectangle

width (w)

length (ℓ)

Perimeter = $2\ell + 2w$
= $2(\ell + w)$
Area = ℓw

Circle

radius (r)

Circumference = πd
= $2\pi r$
Area = πr^2

Triangle

height (h)

base (b)

Area = $\frac{1}{2} bh$

Parallelogram

height (h)

base (b)

Area = bh

Trapezoid

base 1 (b_1)

height (h)

base 2 (b_2)

Area = $\frac{1}{2} h(b_1 + b_2)$

SURFACE AREA AND VOLUME

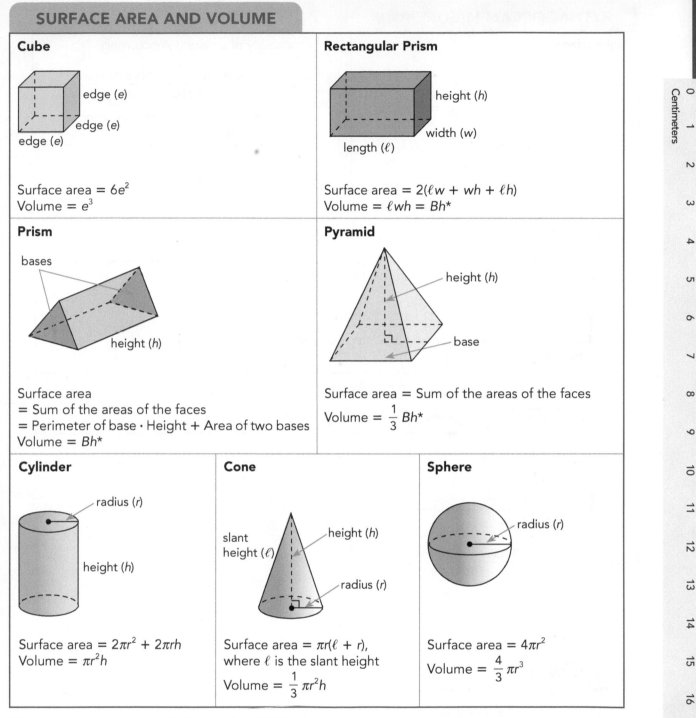

Cube

edge (e)
edge (e)
edge (e)

Surface area = $6e^2$
Volume = e^3

Rectangular Prism

height (h)
width (w)
length (ℓ)

Surface area = $2(\ell w + wh + \ell h)$
Volume = $\ell wh = Bh$*

Prism

bases

height (h)

Surface area
= Sum of the areas of the faces
= Perimeter of base · Height + Area of two bases
Volume = Bh*

Pyramid

height (h)

base

Surface area = Sum of the areas of the faces
Volume = $\frac{1}{3} Bh$*

Cylinder

radius (r)

height (h)

Surface area = $2\pi r^2 + 2\pi rh$
Volume = $\pi r^2 h$

Cone

slant
height (ℓ)
height (h)

radius (r)

Surface area = $\pi r(\ell + r)$,
where ℓ is the slant height
Volume = $\frac{1}{3} \pi r^2 h$

Sphere

radius (r)

Surface area = $4\pi r^2$
Volume = $\frac{4}{3} \pi r^3$

*B represents the area of the base of a solid figure.

PYTHAGOREAN THEOREM

Right Triangle

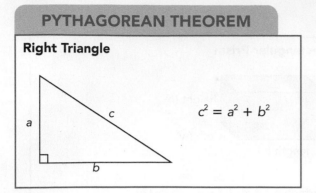

$$c^2 = a^2 + b^2$$

PROBABILITY

Probability of an event A occurring:

$$P(A) = \frac{\text{Number of favorable outcomes}}{\text{Total number of equally likely outcomes}}$$

Probability of an event A not occurring:
$$P(A') = 1 - P(A)$$

LINEAR GRAPHS

The slope, m, of a line segment joining points $P\,(x_1, y_1)$ and $Q\,(x_2, y_2)$ is given by

$$m = \frac{y_2 - y_1}{x_2 - x_1} \text{ or } m = \frac{y_1 - y_2}{x_1 - x_2}.$$

Given the slope, m, the equation of a line intersecting the y-axis at $(0, b)$ is given by $y = mx + b$.

The distance, d, between two points $P\,(x_1, y_1)$ and $Q\,(x_2, y_2)$ is given by

$$d = \sqrt{(x_2 - x_1)^2 + (y_2 - y_1)^2} \text{ or } d = \sqrt{(x_1 - x_2)^2 + (y_1 - y_2)^2}.$$

RATE

Distance = Speed · Time

$$\text{Average speed} = \frac{\text{Total distance traveled}}{\text{Total time}}$$

Interest = Principal · Rate · Time

TEMPERATURE

Celsius (°C) $C = \frac{5}{9} \cdot (F - 32)$

Fahrenheit (°F) $F = \left(\frac{5}{9} \cdot C\right) + 32$

SYMBOLS

$<$	is less than	$\|a\|$	absolute value of the number a
$>$	is greater than	(x, y)	ordered pair
$\leq$	is less than or equal to	$1 : 2$	ratio of 1 to 2
$\geq$	is greater than or equal to	$/$	per
$\neq$	is not equal to	$\%$	percent
$\approx$	is approximately equal to	$\perp$	is perpendicular to
$\cong$	is congruent to	$\|\|$	is parallel to
$\sim$	is similar to	$\overleftrightarrow{AB}$	line AB
10^2	ten squared	$\overrightarrow{AB}$	ray AB
10^3	ten cubed	$\overline{AB}$	line segment AB
2^6	two to the sixth power	$\angle ABC$	angle ABC
$2.\overline{6}$	repeating decimal 2.66666...	$m\angle A$	measure of angle A
7	positive 7	$\triangle ABC$	triangle ABC
-7	negative 7	$°$	degree
$\sqrt{a}$	positive square root of the number a	π	pi; $\pi \approx 3.14$ or $\pi \approx \frac{22}{7}$
$\sqrt[3]{a}$	cube root of the number a	$P(A)$	the probability of the event A happening

Graphing Calculator Guide

A graphing calculator has function keys you can use for mathematical calculations and graphing. The screen supports both text and graphic displays.

Four Operations

Enter expressions into the Home Screen. Then press **ENTER** to evaluate.

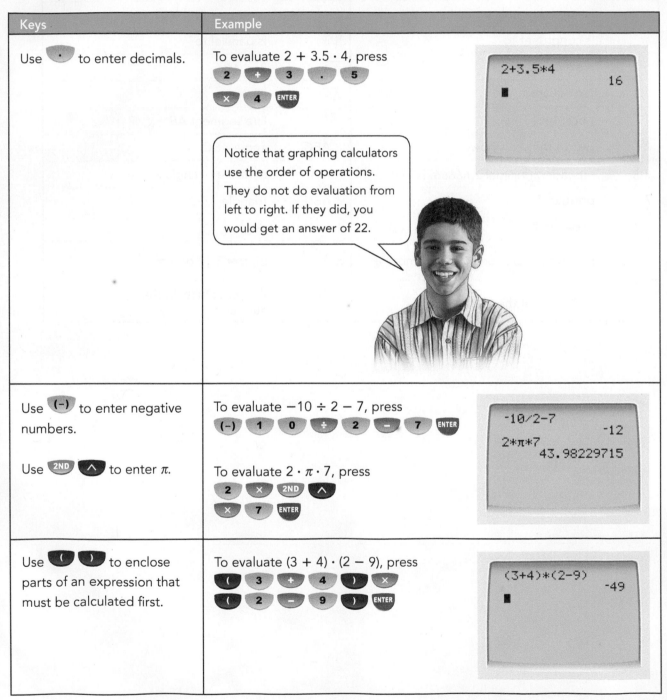

Keys	Example
Use **.** to enter decimals.	To evaluate 2 + 3.5 · 4, press **2** **+** **3** **.** **5** **×** **4** **ENTER** Notice that graphing calculators use the order of operations. They do not do evaluation from left to right. If they did, you would get an answer of 22. Screen: 2+3.5*4 16
Use **(-)** to enter negative numbers. Use **2ND** **^** to enter π.	To evaluate −10 ÷ 2 − 7, press **(-)** **1** **0** **÷** **2** **−** **7** **ENTER** To evaluate 2 · π · 7, press **2** **×** **2ND** **^** **×** **7** **ENTER** Screen: -10/2-7 -12 2*π*7 43.98229715
Use **(** **)** to enclose parts of an expression that must be calculated first.	To evaluate (3 + 4) · (2 − 9), press **(** **3** **+** **4** **)** **×** **(** **2** **−** **9** **)** **ENTER** Screen: (3+4)*(2-9) -49

Fractions

Use **MATH** to enter and convert fractions.

Keys	Example	
Use **MATH** to access Frac to enter fractions.	To enter $\frac{2}{5}$, press **2** **÷** **5** **MATH** then select 1: Frac and press **ENTER** To enter $\frac{5}{2}$, press **5** **÷** **2** **MATH** then select 1: Frac and press **ENTER**	2/5▸Frac $\frac{2}{5}$ 5/2▸Frac $\frac{5}{2}$ ■
Use **MATH** to access Frac and Dec to swap between fractions and decimals.	To convert 0.25 to a fraction, press **.** **2** **5** **MATH** then select 1: Frac and press **ENTER** To convert the fraction back to a decimal, press **MATH** then select 2: Dec and press **ENTER**	.25▸Frac $\frac{1}{4}$ Ans▸Dec .25 ■

Squares and Cubes of Numbers

Use **∧** to enter squares and cubes.

Keys	Example	
Use **x^2** to find the square of numbers. Use **∧** to find the cube of numbers.	To evaluate 3^2, press **3** **x^2** **ENTER** To evaluate 5^3, press **5** **∧** **3** **ENTER**	3^2 9 5^3 125
Use **2ND** **x^2** to find the square root of numbers. Use **MATH** to find the cube root of numbers.	To evaluate $\sqrt{25}$, press **2ND** **x^2** **2** **5** **ENTER** To evaluate $\sqrt[3]{27}$, press **MATH** then select 4: $\sqrt[3]{(}$ and press **2** **7** **ENTER**	$\sqrt{25}$ 5 $\sqrt[3]{27}$ 3 ■

Exponents

Use $\boxed{\wedge}$ to enter numbers in exponential notation.

Keys	Example	
Use $\boxed{\wedge}$ to enter positive exponents.	To evaluate $2^2 \cdot 5^0$, press $\boxed{2}$ $\boxed{\wedge}$ $\boxed{2}$ $\boxed{)}$ $\boxed{\times}$ $\boxed{5}$ $\boxed{\wedge}$ $\boxed{0}$ $\boxed{\text{ENTER}}$ To evaluate $(4^2)^3$, press $\boxed{(}$ $\boxed{4}$ $\boxed{\wedge}$ $\boxed{2}$ $\boxed{)}$ $\boxed{)}$ $\boxed{\wedge}$ $\boxed{3}$ $\boxed{\text{ENTER}}$	 2^2*5^0 $\qquad\qquad 4$ $(4^2)^3$ $\qquad\qquad 4096$
Use $\boxed{\wedge}$ and $\boxed{(-)}$ to enter negative exponents.	To evaluate $2^{-2} \cdot 10$, press $\boxed{2}$ $\boxed{\wedge}$ $\boxed{(-)}$ $\boxed{2}$ $\boxed{)}$ $\boxed{\times}$ $\boxed{1}$ $\boxed{0}$ $\boxed{\text{ENTER}}$	 $2^{-2}*10$ $\qquad\qquad 2.5$

Scientific Notation

Use $\boxed{\text{2ND}}$ $\boxed{,}$ to enter numbers in scientific notation.

Keys	Example	
Use $\boxed{\text{2ND}}$ $\boxed{,}$ to enter powers of 10.	To evaluate $3.4 \cdot 10^2 + 1.5 \cdot 10^3$, press $\boxed{3}$ $\boxed{.}$ $\boxed{4}$ $\boxed{\text{2ND}}$ $\boxed{,}$ $\boxed{2}$ $\boxed{+}$ $\boxed{1}$ $\boxed{.}$ $\boxed{5}$ $\boxed{\text{2ND}}$ $\boxed{,}$ $\boxed{3}$ $\boxed{\text{ENTER}}$ To evaluate $1.4 \cdot 10^3 \div 2.4 \cdot 10^{-6}$, press $\boxed{1}$ $\boxed{.}$ $\boxed{4}$ $\boxed{\text{2ND}}$ $\boxed{,}$ $\boxed{3}$ $\boxed{\div}$ $\boxed{2}$ $\boxed{.}$ $\boxed{4}$ $\boxed{\text{2ND}}$ $\boxed{,}$ $\boxed{(-)}$ $\boxed{6}$ $\boxed{\text{ENTER}}$	 $3.4\text{E}2+1.5\text{E}3$ $\qquad\qquad 1840$ $1.4\text{E}3/2.4\text{E}^-6$ $\qquad 583333333.3$ $\blacksquare$

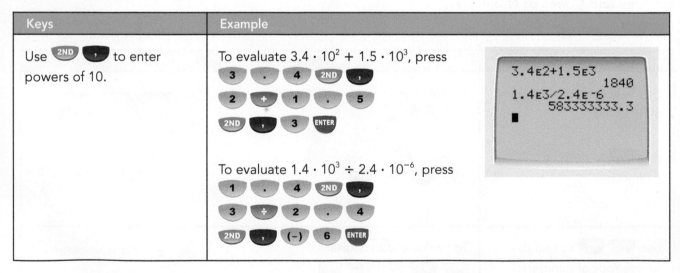

Probability

Use 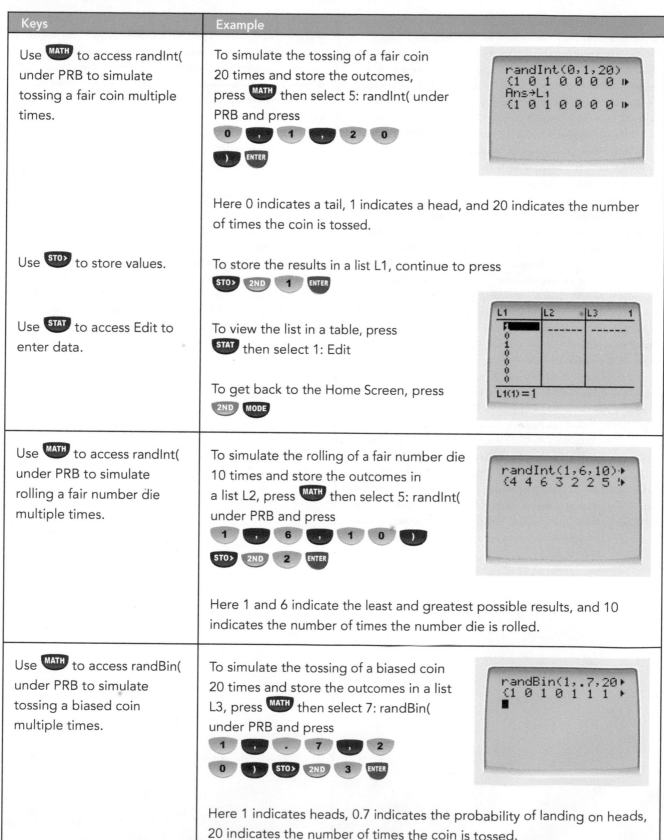 **MATH** to generate random numbers.

Keys	Example

Use **MATH** to access randInt(under PRB to simulate tossing a fair coin multiple times.	To simulate the tossing of a fair coin 20 times and store the outcomes, press **MATH** then select 5: randInt(under PRB and press **0** **,** **1** **,** **2** **0** **)** **ENTER**
	
	`randInt(0,1,20)`
	`{1 0 1 0 0 0 0 ▶`
	`Ans→L1`
	`{1 0 1 0 0 0 0 ▶`
	
	Here 0 indicates a tail, 1 indicates a head, and 20 indicates the number of times the coin is tossed.

Use **STO›** to store values.	To store the results in a list L1, continue to press **STO›** **2ND** **1** **ENTER**

Use **STAT** to access Edit to enter data.	To view the list in a table, press **STAT** then select 1: Edit
	
	To get back to the Home Screen, press **2ND** **MODE**
	
	`L1   L2   ·L3   1`
	`1`
	`0`
	`1`
	`0`
	`0`
	`0`
	`L1(1)=1`

Use **MATH** to access randInt(under PRB to simulate rolling a fair number die multiple times.	To simulate the rolling of a fair number die 10 times and store the outcomes in a list L2, press **MATH** then select 5: randInt(under PRB and press **1** **,** **6** **,** **1** **0** **)** **STO›** **2ND** **2** **ENTER**
	
	`randInt(1,6,10)▶`
	`{4 4 6 3 2 2 5 ▶`
	
	Here 1 and 6 indicate the least and greatest possible results, and 10 indicates the number of times the number die is rolled.

Use **MATH** to access randBin(under PRB to simulate tossing a biased coin multiple times.	To simulate the tossing of a biased coin 20 times and store the outcomes in a list L3, press **MATH** then select 7: randBin(under PRB and press **1** **,** **.** **7** **,** **2** **0** **)** **STO›** **2ND** **3** **ENTER**
	
	`randBin(1,.7,20▶`
	`{1 0 1 0 1 1 1 ▶`
	
	Here 1 indicates heads, 0.7 indicates the probability of landing on heads, 20 indicates the number of times the coin is tossed.

Credits

Cover: © Tim Laman/Getty Images   Chapter 6: 5, © Fuse/Getty Images; 8, © Jupiter Images/Getty Images; 10, © Image Source/Getty Images; 12, © David De Lossy/Getty Images; 13, © Dennis Wise/Getty Images, 14, © Glow Asia RF/Alamy; 15, © Jose Luis Pelaez, Inc/Getty Images; 20, © Ronnie Kaufman/Getty Images; 21, © Flying Colours Ltd/Getty Images; 24, © Jose Luis Pelaez, Inc/Getty Images; 26, © Jupiter Images/Getty Images; 32, © Dennis Wise/Getty Images; 35 (c), © Glow Asia RF/Alamy; 35 (b), © Dennis Wise/Getty Images; 37, © Image Source/Getty Images; 44, © Fuse/Getty Images; 45, © Jose Luis Pelaez, Inc/Getty Images; 47 (t), © Image Source/Getty Images; 47 (b), © Jupiter Images/Getty Images; 49, © Image Source/Getty Images Chapter 7: 63, © Image Source/Getty Images; 69, © Photodisc/Getty Images; 70, © Fuse/Getty Images; 71, © Jupiter Images/Getty Images; 72 (t), © Jose Luis Pelaez, Inc/Getty Images; 72 (c), © Image Source/Getty Images; 73, © Fuse/Getty Images; 75, © Jupiter Images/Getty Images; 78 (t), © Flying Colours Ltd/Getty Images; 78 (b), © Dennis Wise/Getty Images; 79, © Jose Luis Pelaez, Inc/Getty Images; 80, © Image Source/Getty Images; 85, © Jose Luis Pelaez, Inc/Getty Images; 86 (t), © Glow Asia RF/Alamy; 86 (b), © Dennis Wise/Getty Images; 87, © Flying Colours Ltd/Getty Images; 89, © Image Source/Getty Images; 90 (c), © Kevin Peterson/Getty Images; 90 (b), © Ronnie Kaufman/Getty Images; 92 (t), © Fuse/Getty Images; 92 (c), © Image Source/Getty Images; 95, © Ronnie Kaufman/Getty Images; 102 (c), © MCE; 102 (b), © Jose Luis Pelaez, Inc/Getty Images; 104, © Ronnie Kaufman/Getty Images; 106, © Fuse/Getty Images; 108, © Photodisc/Getty Images; 109, © Jupiter Images/Getty Images Chapter 8: 124 (c), © David De Lossy/Getty Images; 124 (b), © Jose Luis Pelaez, Inc/Getty Images; 125 (c), © Fuse/Getty Images; 125 (b), © Dennis Wise/Getty Images; 126 (t), © Flying Colours Ltd/Getty Images; 126 (b), © Jupiter Images/Getty Images; 133, © Photodisc/Getty Images; 137, © Fuse/Getty Images; 144, © Kevin Peterson/Getty Images; 147, © Dennis Wise/Getty Images; 149, © Flying Colours Ltd/Getty Images; 152, © Thorsten/Dreamstime.com; 154, © Eneri LLC/iStockphoto; 156, © Jupiter Images/Getty Images; 157, © Image Source/Getty Images; 164, © Jose Luis Pelaez, Inc/Getty Images; 165, © Glow Asia RF/Alamy; 166, © Ronnie Kaufman/Getty Images; 168 (c), © MCE; Chapter 9: 181, © Jupiter Images/Getty Images; 185 (t), © Image Source/Getty Images; 185 (c), © David De Lossy/Getty Images; 186, © Jupiter Images/Getty Images; 187, © Image Source/Getty Images; 193, © Photodisc/Getty Images; 194, © Image Source/Getty Images; 196, © Jose Luis Pelaez, Inc/Getty Images; 202, © Kevin Peterson/Getty Images; 206, © Jose Luis Pelaez, Inc/Getty Images; 214, © Photodisc/Getty Images; 218, © Image Source/Getty Images; 222, © Fuse/Getty Images; 223, © Jupiter Images/Getty Images; 225, © Image Source/Getty Images; 229, © Glow Asia RF/Alamy Chapter 10: 247, © Jose Luis Pelaez, Inc/Getty Images; 251, © Ronnie Kaufman/Getty Images; 253, © Glow Asia RF/Alamy; 256, © Jupiter Images/Getty Images; 258, © Kevin Peterson/Getty Images; 260 (t), © Image Source/Getty Images; 260 (b), © Glow Asia RF/Alamy; 262, © Jose Luis Pelaez, Inc/Getty Images; 267 (c), © Photodisc/Getty Images; 267 (b), © Dennis Wise/Getty Images; 270, © David De Lossy/Getty Images; 271, © Ronnie Kaufman/Getty Images; 273, © Photodisc/Getty Images; 278, © Image Source/Getty Images; 279, © Fuse/Getty Images; 283, © Jupiter Images/Getty Images; 284, © Image Source/Getty Images; 286, © Jose Luis Pelaez, Inc/Getty Images; 290, © Image Source/Getty Images; 330 (l), © Glow Asia RF/Alamy; 330 (r),© Ronnie Kaufman/Getty Images; 334, © Fuse/Getty Images

Index

Pages listed in black type refer to Book A.
Pages listed in blue type refer to Book B.
Pages in **boldface** type show where a term is introduced.

D

Data
- box plots, **202**–204
- clusters, **202**
- collecting, 193, 215
- dot plots, **180**–181, 225
- 5-point summary, **202**
- frequency tables, **180**–181, 244, 275
- generating, 189, 209, 246, 266–267, 275
- graphing on the number line, 205–206
- interquartile ranges, **187**–189
- mean absolute deviation, **205**–209
- mean of, **179**
- measure of center, **179**
- measure of variation, 202, 205
- median of, **179**–180, 184–185
- organizing, 193
- outliers, **193**
- quartiles, 184–186, 188–189
- and random sampling process, 213
- range, **183**, 199
- simulating, 215–219
- spreadsheets, 189, 209
- stem-and-leaf plots, **193**–199
- summarizing, 180–181
- tables 184, 207, 218, 224, 229–230

Decimal coefficients
- adding, 133–134, 145–146
- equations with, 204
- subtracting, 140–141

Decimals, **3**
- absolute value of, 8
- adding, 112–115
- algebraic expressions involving, 155
- comparing, 3, 21–24
- dividing, 56, 117
- irrational numbers as, 34
- in $\frac{m}{n}$ form, 11
- multiplying, 56, 115–116
- order of operations with, 118
- rational numbers, 16–21
- percent as a, 118, 167
- percent as a, 242
- probability as, 251, 256
- rational numbers, 16–21
- relative frequency as, 267
- repeating, 18–20
- rounding, 4, 43–44
- subtracting, 112–115
- terminating, 16–17

Degrees (as angle measure), **3**

Determining triangles, 86–92

Denominator(s), **55**
- unlike, 55
- of zero, 9

Deviation. *See* Mean absolute deviation

Diagrams
- identifying the constant of proportionality in, 102–103
- map scales, 104
- modeling quartiles, 186–187
- using ratios to find angle measures in, 15–16, 24
- Venn, showing relationships for events, 254–258
- tree diagram, 246
- writing algebraic expressions using, 170, 211

Difference of rational numbers
- with different denominators, 102–105
- with same denominator, 102

Direct proportion, **248**–253
- checking
  - cross products, 266
  - unitary method, 267
- constant of proportionality, 249, 251, 253–256, 259–260, 262
- equations, 249, 251–256, 259–260, 262, 266–268
- from graph, 259–262
- real-world problem solving, 266–268
- representing
  - in experiment, 250
  - using table, 248, 250–251
  - using verbal description, 255
- solving
  - using percent, 271
  - using table, 270
- from table, 251

Direct variation, **249**

Direction, positive or negative, **59**–60

Discount, **271**

Distance
- absolute value as measure of, 6–9, 34, 60
- calculating on map, 105
- between integers on number line, 81–82
- between points, 70, 78
- positive or negative direction, 59–60
- from zero, on number line, 6, 58–59, 61, 63–64

Distance formula, 251

Distributive property, 94, 130, 153–158, 161, 192, 205–208

Division
- decimals, 56, 117
- fractions, 55–56

I

Identify angles
  alternate exterior and interior, 35–36
  complementary, 7
  corresponding, 35–36
  formed by parallel lines and a transversal, 32–33
  interior and exterior, of a triangle, 43, 46
  supplementary angles, 10

Identify a constant of proportionality
  from an equation, 250, 252–254, 278–280
  from a graph, 259–262, 280–281
  from inverse proportion equation, 278–279
  from scale drawings, 102–103
  from table, 254, 270, 276–277

Identify direct proportion
  from an equation, 252–253
  equation from table, 250–251, 254
  from an experiment, 250
  from a graph, 260–261

Identify cross sections, **126**–129

Identify equivalent expressions, 131, 192

Identify inverse proportion, 275
  from equation, 278–279
  from a graph, 280–281
  from table, 275, 277

Improper fractions, **10**
  as mixed numbers, **54**
  and multiplying rational numbers, 106

Included angle of a triangle, **85**

Included side of a triangle, **85**, 87

Inequalities, **3**, 220
  algebraic. *See* Algebraic inequalities
  checking possible solutions for, 222–225
  equivalent, **221**
  of the form $px + q > r$ or $px + q < r$, 229–231
  graph the solution set of algebraic, 221–222, 228–232
  representing on number line, 190
  solution set, **220**
  translating phrases into, 235
  writing, 191

Inequality symbols, **3**, 220–221, 226–227
  equivalent verbal phrases, 235

Inferences, **222**
  estimating population mean using, 223–225

Inferences, making
  about populations, 222–225, 227
  based on a random sample, 222–225

from stem-and-leaf plots, 195–199

Integers, **7**
  adding, 58–61, 63–72
    with different signs, 63–72
    more than two, 69–70
    opposites, 63–64
    order of operations, 94–96
    real-world situations, 71–72
    with same signs, 58–61
  dividing, 91–92
    order of operations, 94–96
  finding distance between, on number line, 81–82
  in $\frac{m}{n}$ form, 9–10
  multiplying, 88–90
    order of operations, 94–96
    as repeated addition, 86–88
  negative, **7**
  as opposites of whole numbers, 7
  order of operations, 94–96
  positive, **7**
  as real numbers, 35
  rounding, 42–43
  set of, **7**
  subtracting, 74–78, 80
    by adding opposites, 76–77
    negative integers, 80
    order of operations, 94–96
    positive integers, 78
    using counters, 74–76
  zero as, 7

Interior angles, **32**, 43
  alternate, **32**, 33, 35, 37
  finding angle measures using, 48–49
  of quadrilaterals, 64
  of triangle, 43–46

Interpret
  data, 187
  graphs
    box plots, 202–203
    of direct proportions, 259–262
    of inverse proportions, 280–281
  interquartile range, 187
  proportional relationships, 259–262
  relative frequency as probability, 272–274

Interquartile ranges, **187**–189

Intersecting lines, 4
  finding measures of angles formed by, 27

Inverse operations, 76, 189, 198, 206–207, 221
  solving equations with, 189

Inverse proportion, **275**–285
  equations, 283–284

Pages listed in black type refer to Book A.
Pages listed in blue type refer to Book B.
Pages in **boldface** type show where a term is introduced.

base, 125, 142
height, 143
nets of, 123
pentagonal, 148
square, 121–122, 128, 148
triangular, 148
volume, 140–143

Q

Quadrilaterals, **64–65**
constructing, 94–98
properties of, 94

Quantities
combined to make zero, 63–64, 66
comparing unequal, 191
comparing with ratios, 245
deciding whether two are in proportional
relationship, 245
percent of, 247, 271

Quartiles, **184**–186, 188–189
finding and modeling, 186–189, 202
in the five-point summary, 202–204

Quotient
of rational numbers, 107–109

R

Radius
of circle, 122
of cone, 145
of cylinder, 124, 134, 137
of sphere, 126, 157, 160

Random number table, 214–215, 287–288

Random sampling, **212**–219
choosing sampling method for, 218
lottery method, 213
purpose of, 212–213
simple, 213–214
sampling frame, 213
stratified, **216**–217
systematic, **217**
using computer, 214
using random number table, 214–215, 287–288
using sampling frame, 213

Randomness, 279

Range, **183**, 195–196, 199, 203
interquartile ranges, **187**–189, 203

Rate(s), **246**
as constant of proportionality, 254
finding, 246

speed, 251
unit, **246,** 254

Rational approximations, 30–32

Rational numbers, **9**, 28
adding, 98–100, 112–114
with different denominators, 98
with same denominator, 98
approximating irrational numbers using, 31–32
classifying, 20–21
comparing, 21–24
as decimals, 18–19
dividing, 107–109, 117, 200
in $\frac{m}{n}$ form, 9
locating irrational numbers using, 26–32
multiplying, 106, 115–116, 200
on number line, 7–8, 12, 21–24
order of operations with, 118–119
as real numbers, 35
as repeating decimals, 18–19
subtracting, 102–105
with different denominators, 102
with same denominator, 102
as terminating decimals, 16–17
writing, using long division, 16–19

Ratios
algebraic expressions for, 179
areas and lengths in scale drawings, 102, 109–110
comparing parts to whole, 243
comparing quantities using, 245
equivalent, 245
expressing as fractions or percents, 243
finding angle measures using, 15–16, 24
of lengths, 250
map scales, 104–106
modeling
using a bar diagram, 243
using Venn diagrams, 261
probability problems involving, 261
real-world problems, 179
simplest form of, **245**
writing, 245

Ray, **66**

Real number line, 35
irrational numbers on, 48
real numbers on, 35–36

Real number system, **34**–35

Real numbers, **35**
on real number line, 35–36

Real-world problems
alebraic equations for, 211, 214–215
algebraic expressions in, 174–175